Measuring and monitoring immigrant integration in Europe

Measuring and monitoring immigrant integration in Europe

Integration policies and monitoring efforts in 17 European countries

Rob Bijl and Arjen Verweij (eds.)

The Netherlands Institute for Social Research | scp
The Hague, March 2012

The Netherlands Institute for Social Research | scp was established by Royal Decree of March 30, 1973 with the following terms of reference:

a. to carry out research designed to produce a coherent picture of the state of social and cultural welfare in the Netherlands and likely developments in this area;
b. to contribute to the appropriate selection of policy objectives and to provide an assessment of the advantages and disadvantages of the various means of achieving those ends;
c. to seek information on the way in which interdepartmental policy on social and cultural welfare is implemented with a view to assessing its implementation.

The work of the Netherlands Institute for Social Research focuses especially on problems coming under the responsibility of more than one Ministry. As Coordinating Minister for social and cultural welfare, the Minister for Health, Welfare and Sport is responsible for the policies pursued by the Netherlands Institute for Social Research. With regard to the main lines of such policies the Minister consults the Ministers of General Affairs; Security and Justice; the Interior and Kingdom Relations; Education, Culture and Science; Finance; Infrastructure and the Environment; Economic Affairs, Agriculture and Innovation; and Social Affairs and Employment.

© The Netherlands Institute for Social Research | scp, The Hague 2012
scp publication 2012-8
Editing: Julian Ross, Carlisle, uk
dtp: Textcetera, The Hague
Figures: Mantext, Moerkapelle
Cover illustration: Shutterstock images
Cover design: Bureau Stijlzorg, Utrecht
isbn 978 90 377 0569 0
nur 740

Distribution outside the Netherlands and Belgium: Transaction Publishers, New Brunswick (usa)

The Netherlands Institute for Social Research | scp
Parnassusplein 5
2511 vx Den Haag
The Netherlands
Tel. +31 70 340 70 00
Fax +31 70 340 70 44
Website: www.scp.nl
E-mail: info@scp.nl

The authors of scp publications can be contacted by e-mail via the scp website.

Content

1	Measuring and monitoring immigrant integration in Europe: facts and views	11
1.1	European efforts on integration and monitoring	12
1.2	Migrants in Europe: the figures	18
1.3	Why monitor integration?	31
1.4	Monitoring integration. But what is integration?	34
1.5	Measuring and monitoring: the empirical approach	38
	References	42
2	Monitoring integration in Austria	43
2.1	Introduction	43
2.2	Austria – a diverse country with a diverse population	43
2.3	National integration policy	48
2.4	Integration reporting and related research in Austria	52
2.5	Data on the integration of immigrants – practices, possibilities and limitations of national statistical data	53
2.6	Integration monitoring in Austria	55
2.7	Conclusions	61
	Notes	65
	References	66
3	Monitoring integration in Belgium	69
3.1	A history of immigration and integration policies in Belgium	69
3.2	Migrants in Belgium: facts and figures	71
3.3	Belgian integration policies: regional competencies in a federal context	71
3.4	What does the 'integration package' offered to foreigners contain?	72
3.5	Which categories of foreigners can benefit from the integration measures?	73
3.6	Belgian monitoring instruments: unity in diversity	74
3.7	Putting monitoring into practice: organising the collection of data on origin	75
3.8	Making monitoring systems work: what are the first results and what is the added value?	76
3.9	Monitoring integration policies: back to the future	78
	Notes	79
4	Monitoring integration in the Czech Republic	81
4.1	Introduction and integration policy changes in the Czech Republic	81
4.2	Different target groups for specific integration policies	85
4.3	Data monitoring system	90

4.4   Interpretation issues and recommendations   94
       Notes   97
       References   98

5   Monitoring the integration process in Denmark   100
5.1   Introduction   100
5.2   Danish integration policy since 1999   100
5.3   Danish integration policy in the year 2010   101
5.4   Definition of integration   105
5.5   Definition of immigrants and descendants   106
5.6   Statistical basis for monitoring   108
5.7   Monitoring through analysis, assessment and effectiveness
       measurement   109
5.8   Monitoring through performance management   113
5.9   Discussion   123
       Notes   126

6   Monitoring integration in Estonia[1]   127
6.1   Introduction   127
6.2   Background: history of immigration and integration   128
6.3   The birth of Estonian integration policy under EU conditionality
       pressures   130
6.4   Successes and failures of the first integration programme 132
6.5   National integration programme 2008-2013   134
6.6   Conclusions   138
       Notes   139
       References   141

7   Germany: Monitoring integration in a federal state[1]   144
7.1   Becoming a country of immigration   144
7.2   Integration as participation   146
7.3   Goals of monitoring   146
7.4   Data sources   147
7.5   Monitoring integration at federal level   153
7.6   Monitoring at the local level   157
7.7   Monitoring experiences and perceptions   157
7.8   Summary   159
       Notes   160
       References   161

8   Monitoring integration in Ireland   165
8.1   Introduction   165
8.2   Migration in figures   165
8.3   Integration policy   168

8.4	Data sources in Ireland	173
8.5	Integration research	175
8.6	Conclusion	181
	References	182
9	Measuring integration in a reluctant immigration country: the case of Italy	183
9.1	A short overview of foreign immigration in Italy	183
9.2	Migration policies of a reluctant immigration country	185
9.3	Integration policies	187
9.4	Measuring integration in Italy	190
9.5	Conclusions	197
	References	197
10	Monitoring Integration in Latvia	200
10.1	Introduction	200
10.2	Historical background to integration: the legacy of the Soviet period	202
10.3	After independence: stumbling towards an integration policy	206
10.4	Official understanding of integration, 2001-2010	209
10.5	Evolution of Integration Policy	211
10.6	City integration programmes	213
10.7	Measurement of integration	214
10.8	Conclusion: recent policy developments	216
	Notes	217
11	Monitoring systems for the integration of ethnic minorities and immigrants in Lithuania	221
11.1	Introduction	221
11.2	Integration policy	223
11.3	National policy documents and measures as an instrument for the development of an integration infrastructure	225
11.4	Institutional infrastructure for establishing integration policy and monitoring tools	229
11.5	Evaluation of integration policy	230
11.6	Public attitudes towards immigration and the media response	231
11.7	Examples of monitoring	233
11.8	Conclusions	234
	Notes	235
	References	236
12	Monitoring integration in the Netherlands	239
12.1	Introduction	239
12.2	Overview of Dutch policy	240
12.3	Monitoring integration in the Netherlands	245

12.4	Concluding remarks	250
	Notes	252
	References	252
13	Monitoring integration in Norway	253
13.1	Introduction	253
13.2	Indicators and monitoring systems – current use and future development	258
13.3	Goals for social inclusion of the immigrant population	264
13.4	Summary	269
	Notes	270
	References	270
14	From (many) datasets to (one) integration monitoring system in Poland?	272
14.1	Introduction	272
14.2	Integration policy in Poland – legislation, practice and assessment of results	274
14.3	Sources of information on immigrants – in search of monitoring basis	278
14.4	Conclusions	284
	Notes	286
	References	287
15	Monitoring immigrant integration in Portugal: Managing the gap between available data and implemented policy	291
15.1	Introduction	291
15.2	Immigration flows to Portugal	292
15.3	Integration policies during three decades of a 'new' immigration country	293
15.4	Monitoring integration in Portugal: challenges and opportunities ensuing from official data on immigration	302
15.5	Conclusion	310
	Notes	311
	References	311
16	Monitoring integration in Sweden	313
16.1	Immigration and integration in Sweden	313
16.2	Swedish integration policy	315
16.3	Current system for monitoring integration policy	316
	Notes	325

17	Monitoring immigrant integration in Switzerland	326
17.1	Introduction	326
17.2	Swiss integration policy	327
17.3	Concepts of integration	330
17.4	Monitoring systems, indicators and data on immigrant integration on the national level	331
17.5	Local monitoring systems	336
17.6	Concluding remarks	339
	Notes	341
	References	341
18	Monitoring Integration in the UK	344
18.1	Integration in the UK	344
18.2	Changing immigration patterns in the UK	346
18.3	UK integration policy since 2000	347
18.4	Measurement and monitoring in UK policy	350
18.5	A framework for monitoring integration in the UK	351
18.6	The practice of monitoring integration in the UK	354
18.7	Gaps in knowledge	357
18.8	Conclusion	358
	Notes	359
About the authors		361
Publications of the Netherlands Institute for Social Research | SCP in English		365

1   Measuring and monitoring immigrant integration in Europe: facts and views

Rob Bijl and Arjen Verweij

Europe is a favoured destination for many migrants. The region's economic prosperity, relatively high level of political stability and democratic principles are appealing to many migrants, whether they be asylum-seekers or regular migrants in search of work or looking to study. Most EU Member States have experienced increasing migration in recent decades. Migrants from *third countries* represent around 20 million people, four per cent of the total EU population. The composition of the EU's population is thus changing, and European societies are faced with increasing diversity. This in turn is creating new conditions for social cohesion and the government response to public concerns.

Europe is also heavily influenced by demographic changes, including population ageing, longer life expectancies and a declining working-age population. Migration can help to address these issues, in addition to maximising the use of the labour force and the skills already available and improving the productivity of the EU economy. Demographic trends vary from region to region and need to be addressed through tailor-made solutions. If the full benefits from migration are to be realised, Europe needs to find a way to cope better with its diverse and multicultural societies through more effective integration of migrants. Integration is thus not only important as a means of safeguarding social cohesion, but also has economic significance; if migrants are not integrated into the host society, and especially the labour market, Europe is in danger of losing economic power.

In this book we examine views on integration in seventeen European countries, both EU Member States and others, and explore how these are translated into national policy and what efforts are being made in the various countries to map out the integration processes of migrants and track them over time. We describe the degree to which migrants participate in their 'new' country and look at precisely what is meant by 'participation'. Because although the aim is to streamline European integration policy and base it more on common principles, ultimately integration is primarily a responsibility of the individual European countries themselves. The EU has no competence for harmonising legislation on integration. While the EU does apply official definitions and descriptions of key issues, for example what constitutes a migrant and what the important domains of integration are, this does not mean that countries always feel bound to apply those definitions (fully) within their national policy. Political reality and social sensitivities often lead countries to make their own choices and apply their own definitions of concepts. European countries have a diverse history in relation to migration; for some countries it is a new phenomenon, while for others – for example those with a colonial past – it has been a familiar phenomenon for many years. The inward and outward flows of migrants vary considerably from one country to another, as do the motives for migration and the population profile. These are just a few of the factors which mean that integration policy and the way it is evaluated and monitored currently present a very diverse picture across Europe.

1.1 European efforts on integration and monitoring

Europe has spent more than ten years trying to achieve greater uniformity in integration policy across the Member States. European Union cooperation on the integration of non-EU nationals has developed since the Tampere Programme was adopted in 1999. This programme stated that the separate but closely related issues of asylum and migration call for the development of a common EU policy to include the following elements: partnership with countries of origin, a Common European Asylum System, fair treatment of third-country nationals, and management of migration flows. The Common Basic Principles for Immigrant Integration Policy, agreed in 2004 on the initiative of the Dutch presidency, provide a strong framework for policymaking in this area (see box 1.1). Since the adoption of the Hague Programme, the importance of evaluating integration policies has been stressed. They underline the importance of a holistic approach to integration and are aimed inter alia at assisting EU Member States in formulating integration policies. They also serve as a basis for EU Member States to explore how EU, national, regional and local authorities can interact in the development and implementation of integration policies. Finally, they assist in evaluating EU-level mechanisms and policies with a view to supporting future integration policy developments.

The Commission's 2005 Common Agenda for Integration has helped to implement these Common Basic Principles. EU policy here has been further framed by the 2009 Stockholm Programme and the Europe 2020 Strategy, where one of the headline targets is to raise the employment rate of 20-64 year-olds in the EU to 75%. One of the means of achieving this is by improving the integration of legal migrants.

Box 1.1   EU Common Basic Principles for immigrant integration policy
           (Council of the European Union, 14615/04, 2004)

– Integration is a dynamic, two-way process of mutual accommodation by all immigrants and
  residents of Member States.
– Integration implies respect for the basic values of the European Union.
– Employment is a key part of the integration process and is central to the participation of
  immigrants, to the contributions immigrants make to the host society, and to making such
  contributions visible.
– Basic knowledge of the host society's language, history and institutions is indispensable to
  integration; enabling immigrants to acquire this basic knowledge is essential to successful
  integration.
– Efforts in education are critical to preparing immigrants, and particularly their descendants,
  to be more successful and more active participants in society.
– Access for immigrants to institutions, as well as to public and private goods and services, on
  a basis equal to national citizens and in a non-discriminatory way is a critical foundation for
  better integration.
– Frequent interaction between immigrants and Member State citizens is a fundamental
  mechanism for integration. Shared forums, inter-cultural dialogue, education about
  immigrants and immigrant cultures, and stimulating living conditions in urban
  environments enhance the interactions between immigrants and Member State citizens.
– The practice of diverse cultures and religions is guaranteed under the Charter of
  Fundamental Rights and must be safeguarded, unless practices conflict with other
  inviolable European rights or with national law.
– The participation of immigrants in the democratic process and in the formulation of
  integration policies and measures, especially at the local level, supports their integration.
– Mainstreaming integration policies and measures in all relevant policy portfolios and levels
  of government and public services is an important consideration in public-policy formation
  and implementation.
– Developing clear goals, indicators and evaluation mechanisms are necessary to adjust
  policy, evaluate progress on integration and to make the exchange of information more
  effective.

The Stockholm Programme called for the 'development of core indicators in a limited
number of relevant policy areas for monitoring the results of integration policies in
order to increase the comparability of national experiences and reinforce the European
learning process'. Consequently, the conclusions of the expert meeting organised by
the Swedish Presidency in Malmö on 14 to 16 December 2009 presented the results of
a process to identify European core indicators. In 2010 the Zaragoza Declaration was
adopted by EU ministers responsible for immigrant issues, and approved at the Justice
and Home Affairs Council on 3-4 June 2010. It called upon the Commission to undertake
a pilot study to examine proposals for common integration indicators and to report on
the availability and quality of the data from agreed harmonised sources necessary for
the calculation of these indicators. Eurostat published the results of a pilot study in 2011
(EU/Eurostat, Indicators of Immigrant Integration. A pilot study, 2011). The agreed policy
areas monitored were employment, education, social inclusion and active citizenship

(see table 1.1). The report includes calculations for each Member State of the proposed common indicators of migrant integration based on data currently available from the European Union Labour Force Survey (EU-LFS), the European Union Statistics on Income and Living Conditions (EU-SILC), Eurostat's migration statistics as well as the OECD's Programme for International Student Assessment (PISA). This pilot is a first step towards finding agreement about the most relevant and available indicators in Europe. The results of the pilot study show, however, that there still is a very long way to go in many countries in building a firm statistical infrastructure.

Moreover, opinions on whether the domain of active citizenship is well represented by the core indicators as shown in table 1.1 are not yet unified. European countries differ in terms of the views, goals and regulatory frameworks of integration policies. Active citizenship is however an important area of development, considering that the participation of immigrants in the democratic process as active citizens supports their integration and enhances their sense of belonging.

Table 1.1

Indicators of migrant integration

policy area	indicators
employment	core indicators: – employment rate – unemployment rate – activity rate
education	core indicators: – highest educational attainment (share of population with tertiary, secondary and primary or less than primary education) – share of low-achieving 15 year-olds in reading, mathematics and science – share of 30-34 year-olds with tertiary educational attainment – share of early leavers from education and training
social inclusion	core indicators: – median net income – the median net income of the immigrant population as a proportion of the median net income of the total population – at risk of poverty rate – share of population with net disposable income of less than 60 per cent of national median – share of population perceiving their health status as good or poor – ratio of property owners to non-property owners among immigrants and the total population
active citizenship	core indicators: – the share of immigrants that have acquired citizenship – the share of immigrants holding permanent or long-term residence permits – the share of immigrants among elected representatives

Source: Zaragoza Declaration (2010)

A renewed European agenda for the integration of non-EU nationals

In July 2011, the European Commission proposed a European Agenda For The Integration Of Non-EU Migrants (European Commission COM (2011) 455), focusing on action to increase economic, social, cultural and political participation by migrants and putting the emphasis on local action. This new agenda highlights challenges that need to be resolved if the EU is to benefit fully from the potential offered by migration and the value of diversity. It also explores the role of countries of origin in the integration process.

Member States have confirmed their commitment to further developing the core idea of integration as a driver for economic development and social cohesion, in order to enhance migrants' contribution to economic growth and cultural richness . There is already a framework for EU cooperation on integration through the Common Basic Principles for Immigrant Integration Policy in the European Union, which were agreed by the Council in 2004. The Principles underline that integration is a dynamic, two-way process of mutual accommodation by migrants and by the societies that receive them. All EU actions presented by the Commission in the 2005 Common Agenda for Integration have been completed. However, the social, economic and political context has changed and not all integration measures have been successful in meeting their objectives. Integration policies also require the will and commitment of migrants to be part of the society that receives them.

Figures confirm that the most pressing challenges include:

- the prevailing low employment levels of migrants, especially migrant women;
- rising unemployment and high levels of 'overqualification';
- increasing risks of social exclusion;
- gaps in educational achievement;
- public concerns about the lack of integration of migrants.

The renewed European Agenda for the Integration of Third-Country Nationals is a contribution to the debate on how to understand and better support integration. A diversity of approaches is called for, depending on the different integration challenges faced by various types of migrants, both low and high- skilled, as well as beneficiaries of international protection. Europe needs to adopt a positive attitude towards diversity and strong guarantees of fundamental rights and equal treatment, building on the mutual respect of different cultures and traditions. Actions specifically targeting vulnerable groups of migrants are also needed.

As part of this agenda, the Commission is putting together a flexible 'tool-box', from which national authorities will be able to pick the measures most likely to prove effective in their specific context, and most suited to their particular integration objectives. There are plans to develop modules offering an established but flexible point of reference to support integration policies in EU Member States. Common indicators have also been identified for monitoring the results of integration policies.

Immigration and integration are closely intertwined. The causal relationship between them is twofold. On the one hand we see that immigrants, after entry to a country

and having secured a permit to stay, are expected to acquire economic independence as quickly as possible. On the other hand, it is plain that migrants who have made a place for themselves in a new country not infrequently serve as an example for their compatriots to try to gain access to that same country, hoping to emulate the success of the 'pioneers'. In the first place, these are often family members, but others also see having a social network with the same cultural background in the new country as a useful tool to increase their chances of a successful future. This 'chain migration' explains why some European countries have relatively large numbers of migrants from countries with which there are no historical ties, for example Somalis in the UK and Romanians in Spain.
In reaction to this, several European countries have imposed ever stricter legislation and regulations in recent years in order to combat the influx of migrants. Mandatory civic integration courses for immigrants to enable them to become proficient in the language and culture of the host country have become a natural part of the integration policy in several countries in Europe (see e.g. the chapters on Austria, the Netherlands and Denmark).

Some countries have defined the influx of migrants as a public order problem. In Italy, for example, the basic idea is that foreigners on national territory are first and foremost a national security issue, in the 'true' sense of the protection and defence of public order. Consequently, a series of instruments was devised to provide continuous control of the immigrant population on two fronts. First, there was the need to control the entry flows and the irregular immigrant population more effectively, with stricter policing of regular entry channels and an increase in the number of expulsions. Second, control of regular immigrants already present in Italy was to be increased by creating a new kind of permit to stay, linked to an employment contract, and by tightening up the procedures for the renewal of permits in order to make immigration more temporary in nature and also to discourage stabilisation. In short, the measures contained in this law seemed to constitute a migration regime that reflected what might be termed a 'reluctant' approach.

In other countries, such as the Netherlands, marriage migration has for example been made more difficult by placing demands on the partner in the receiving country and setting more stringent requirements in terms of age and language proficiency and other civic integration requirements for the potential partner in the country of origin. A trend is also under way in which specified minimum qualifications have to be acquired in the country of origin before migration actually takes place, whereas in the past it was more usual for migrants to have to acquire these (integration) qualifications in the host country, after they had migrated. Labour migration has also been made more difficult in many countries for migrants from outside the EU. Following the system that has been in force for many years in countries such as Canada and the United States, European countries are increasingly selecting the migrant workers that they really need at any given moment.
The declaration cited earlier from the European Agenda for Integration 2011 that 'Europe needs a positive attitude towards diversity and strong guaranties for fundamental rights and equal treatment, building on the mutual respect of different cultures and traditions' appears to be at odds with present policy practice in many EU Member States. Europe is struggling to strike a balance between accessibility and hospitality on the one hand and

protecting the interests of its own citizens and economy on the other. Partly under the influence of global political developments, such as the terrorist attacks in New York on 9/11 and later attacks in Madrid and London, many European countries have tightened up their policy on migration. It has become more difficult to enter Europe, while expecting migrants who have obtained a permit to stay in the host country to make greater efforts for their own integration, assimilation and adaptation to the host country are more often and more openly used as guidelines in formulating policy. Coercion and repression are words that are appearing more frequently in policy documents. More duties are imposed on migrants to adapt, and their efforts to do so are monitored more strictly. If a migrant fails to meet their obligations, for example successfully completing a language course, sanctions are more often imposed; these sanctions are frequently financial, but in the most extreme cases may lead to the rescission of their permit to stay. The twofold nature of the integration process, in which the host society also has a duty to offer migrants the opportunity to acquire a place in that society, with all the associated rights, appears to have shifted more to the background. In one case (Switzerland), it is even stated that immigrants must dissociate themselves from their former community. In Italy, too, the authors conclude in their chapter that there has been a shift away from seeing integration as a basis for positive social inclusion to a juridical and policy mechanism of control. Since 2009 immigrants are obliged to sign an Integration Agreement in order to obtain a permit to stay. According to this rule, the immigrant must commit to learn the Italian language and the fundamentals of the Italian Constitution, to respect the principles of the Charter of the values of citizenship and integration). The permit to stay gives a number of credits that can be reduced in the event of criminal convictions or fines for administrative or tax offences. On expiry of the Agreement, a certification test is administered to assess whether the immigrant has fulfilled his/her obligations. If the score exceeds 30 credits, the contract is fulfilled, a score from 1 to 29 leads to an extension, less than 1 implies immediate expulsion.

Many measures aimed at integration have the formal objective of ensuring that migrants are prepared for their arrival in Europe sufficiently well that they will be able to lead a full and independent life in the host society. Seen from this perspective, language courses and language proficiency examinations in the country of origin, as required by the Netherlands, for example, are a logical idea: without a good command of the language it is very difficult to participate in a society and there is an immediate threat of unemployment and dependence on the social security system, or worse. At the same time, however, these measures not infrequently have the effect of discouraging and curbing immigration, as the figures demonstrate. Doubts are therefore sometimes expressed about the underlying motivation for this kind of policy. After all, it is argued, the fastest way to integrate in a new country is surely to participate through work or school and by mastering the language through contacts in the host country and learning the host country customs?
The policy on integration in several countries (including Sweden and the Netherlands) has undergone a radical change to what can be characterised as 'mainstreaming'. The recent situation in the Netherlands is that the coalition of liberals, Christian Democrats

and populist parties which took office in 2010 pushes it to its extremes: the policy objective is to eliminate autonomous integration policy as such within the next five years. The integration goals should from that point on be achieved through the general policy instruments: unemployment among minorities will be part of the general labour market policy, reducing drop-out rates in secondary education will be a responsibility of the Minister of Education, and so on. It is still too early to say with any certainty what the consequences of such a paradigm shift are.

1.2 Migrants in Europe: the figures

It is not easy to determine how many migrants there are in Europe, how many enter the continent and how many leave it again. This is partly because of a lack of consensus about what constitutes a migrant. Traditionally, nationality was used as the distinguishing criterion; a migrant is then a non-national, a person with a different nationality from that of the country in which he or she lives. Many European statistics (still) apply this definition. To make things even more complicated, the EU refers to third-country nationals, i.e. persons with the nationality of a country outside the EU. EU enlargement has meant that people who were initially defined as migrants from the EU perspective are no longer migrants since their country's accession to the EU. The number of migrants in the EU fell suddenly, for example, following the accession of the Central and Eastern European countries. This example shows that a formal definition based on nationality is not very stable. Changes in national legislation or – as the history of Europe has shown – changing national borders or countries becoming independent can lead to changes in the ability to obtain a passport in the host country. Migrants are then defined 'out of existence', as it were, without their actual situation having changed at all. In some cases, people who were born on the territory of a Member State's former colony, and who later migrated to that Member State, are recorded as foreign-born, although they have held the citizenship of the reporting country since birth. In other cases they are administered as indigenous and statistically not recognised as a specific ethnic group. In other cases, the recorded country of birth no longer exists under the same name or borders, as, for example, the former Yugoslavia, or the former Soviet Union, and those people would be included in the foreign-born population even though they may never have migrated to another country. Furthermore the magnitude of the immigrant population fluctuates depending on the number of naturalisations. The core issue is that nationality says little about the size of ethnic groupings within a population, nor about how and to what extent someone is integrated in a society. Based on the idea that a person's cultural background helps determine whether or not they will succeed in a new country, be able to build a life for themselves and be able to participate in civil society, country of birth is a better criterion. This is an unchanging given and is not subject to changing political views about nationality; it also provides a more usable indication of the size of migrant groups within a society. The country of birth criterion has now been adopted by most European countries as the usual distinguishing criterion.

In many European countries, immigration is a phenomenon that has existed for decades. A following question is therefore whether, and if so how the second generation

– i.e. the children of migrants – who were born in the host country should be defined. Strictly speaking, they are not migrants, since they have not immigrated into the host country. There is now a consensus in Europe that children born to parents who were themselves born in another country should also be regarded as part of the minority population. The idea behind this is that their roots lie partly in the country of origin of their parents and that this will influence their chances of building a life for themselves in the host country. This idea is not without controversy; young members of the second generation sometimes feel that being classified as migrants has a stigmatising effect on them. They were born and raised in the country where they live, they sometimes do not speak the language of their parents – for example, recent research in the Netherlands suggests that one fifth of second-generation Chinese do not speak a Chinese language (Gijsberts et al. 2011) – and have often never been to their parents' country of origin. In their view, therefore, there is no reason why they should not simply be regarded as German, Dutch or any other nationality. There is a tension here between the individual perspective of a young member of the second generation and the macro-perspective of policymakers who observe that second-generation migrants/minorities function differently, and often less well, in society than the indigenous population.

There are also several variants of the country of birth criterion, especially for the second generation, so that comparability between countries is still difficult. In the Netherlands, for example, a migrant is defined as a person at least one of whose parents was born in another country. Someone who was themselves born abroad belongs to the first generation, while someone born in the Netherlands is part of the second generation. In Denmark and Austria, by contrast, a definition of the second generation is preferred in which both parents were born abroad.

The recent Eurostat pilot study mentioned earlier to examine proposals for common integration indicators draws a distinction between foreign-borns (to be subdivided into EU-born and non-EU born) and foreigners (to be subdivided into EU citizens and third-country nationals). The criterion for foreigners is their nationality, while for foreign-borns it is their country of birth. A foreign-born is a person whose place of birth (or place of usual residence of the mother at the time of the birth) is outside his/her usual country of residence. This definition by Eurostat leaves the second generation out of consideration altogether.

The conclusion cannot be other than that there is wide divergence in the views and definitions of migrants in Europe. The definitions used are not uniform, but are also not neutral; they have political/policy implications. For example, the decision on whether or not to include second-generation migrants in a definition is not simply a statistical choice, but has significance for a country's migration and integration policy. Opting for the nationality criterion makes the social and cultural background of groups in society 'invisible'. This can be a positive thing, because it can help avoid discrimination and stereotyping. But it can also have a negative impact, because relevant social and cultural explanations for social problems in specific population groups become impossible to trace.

Whilst heeding these words of warning, we present important data here on the number of migrants in Europe. The figures are based chiefly on data from Eurostat and give an impression of how big a phenomenon immigration is in Europe. First we present the flows of immigrants in the countries of Europe. These figures show the number of migrants entering the various countries each year. They show the dynamic of migration in Europe. In section 1.2.2, we describe the number of migrants present (the 'stock') at any given moment. these figures allow us to determine what proportion of the total population of a country is made up of migrants.

1.2.1   Migration flows

Migration is the main driver for population growth in the majority of the EU-27 Member States (EC – Demography Report 2010 2011). During 2008 about 3.8 million persons immigrated into one of the EU Member States and at least 2.3 million emigrants are reported to have left one of the EU Member States. Compared with 2007, immigration to EU Member States is estimated to have decreased by 6% and emigration to have increased by 13%. It should be noted that these figures do not represent the migration flows to/from the EU as a whole, since they also include international flows within the EU, i.e. between different Member States. Just over half the total immigrants to EU Member States, in other words 1.9 million people, were previously residing outside the EU. In absolute numbers, citizens from Romania, Poland and Morocco were the largest groups of immigrants in the EU.

Table 1.2

Top ten countries of citizenship of immigrants to EU-27 member states, 2008 (in numbers x 1000)

EU citizens[a] – country of citizenship		non-EU citizens – country of citizenship	
Romania	384	Morocco	157
Poland	266	China	97
Bulgaria	91	India	93
Germany	88	Albania	81
Italy	67	Ukraine	80
France	62	Brazil	62
United Kingdom	61	United States	61
Hungary	44	Turkey	51
Netherlands	40	Russian Federation	50
Portugal	38	Colombia	49

a   Excluding returning nationals.

Source: Eurostat – Statistics in focus 1/2011 (A. Oblak Flander – Population and social conditions)

Table 1.2 shows that most immigrants in Europe do not come from the traditional refugee countries; most immigrants have a different reason for migrating. Nonetheless, Europe is still an important receiver of refugees. Worldwide, more than 845,800 people submitted individual applications for asylum or refugee status in 2010 (UNHCR, Global Trends 2010, 2011). With more than 180,600 asylum claims – one fifth of applications globally – South Africa was the world's largest recipient of individual applications, followed by the United States of America (54,300) and France (48,100).

By continent, in the first six months of 2011 Europe registered the highest number of claims, with 73% of all asylum applications in industrialised countries. By country, the United States had more claims (36,400) than any other industrialised nation, followed by France (26,100), Germany (20,100), Sweden (12,600) and the United Kingdom (12,200). The report *Asylum Levels and Trends in Industrialized Countries, First Half 2011* complements UNHCR's annual Global Trends Report, which is published in June each year, and which in 2011 found that 80% of refugees were being hosted in developing countries.

In absolute numbers, asylum-seekers form a small group. Work, study and family reunification are all-important motives for leaving the country of origin.

Within Europe, the country that reported the largest number of *immigrants* in 2008 was Spain (726,000), followed by Germany (682,000), the United Kingdom (590,000) and Italy (535,000). Two-thirds of the total number of immigrants into the EU-27 were recorded as immigrating into one of these four Member States.

Germany reported the highest number of *emigrants* in 2008 (738,000, resulting in negative net migration), followed by the United Kingdom with 427,000 and Spain with 266,000. There was also a significant level of emigration from Romania and Poland. Most EU Member States reported more immigration than emigration in 2008, but in Germany, Poland, Romania, Bulgaria and the three Baltic states, emigrants outnumbered immigrants.

Relative to the size of the resident population, the country that recorded the highest number of immigrants in 2008 was Luxembourg, with 36 immigrants per 1,000 inhabitants, followed by Malta with 22 and Cyprus with 18 immigrants per 1,000 inhabitants. Immigration was also high in the EFTA countries (Iceland, Liechtenstein, Norway and Switzerland), far exceeding the EU Member States' average of 7.6 immigrants per 1,000 inhabitants. Overall, the highest rate of emigration among the countries reporting in 2008 was in Iceland, where almost 29 residents per 1,000 inhabitants left the country. Not only foreigners immigrate to a particular Member State, but also nationals – both those returning 'home' and citizens born abroad who are immigrating for the first time. Some 600,000 immigrants, or 16% of all immigrants into the EU Member States in 2008, were nationals. In 2008 the share of nationals among immigrants varied from one Member State to another. The EU Member States reporting the highest shares in 2008 were Poland (75%), Lithuania (68%) and Estonia (48%). By contrast, the Czech Republic, Spain, Hungary, Luxembourg, Italy, Slovakia, Cyprus and Slovenia reported very low shares, with nationals making up under 10% of immigrants.

As regards the gender distribution of immigrants, there was a slight prevalence of men over women for the EU as a whole (51% versus 49%). Only a few Member States, namely Cyprus, Italy, Spain, France and Ireland, reported more women than men among immigrants.

Immigrants to EU Member States in 2008 were on average much younger than the population of their country of destination. On 1 January 2009 the median age of the EU population was 40.6 years, while the median age of immigrants in 2008 ranged from 24.8 years (in Portugal) to 37.5 years (in Greece).

1.2.2   Migration stocks

Foreigners

The total number of foreigners or non-nationals (i.e. persons who are not citizens of their country of residence) living on the territory of the EU Member States on 1 January 2010 was 32.5 million, representing 6.5% of the total EU population of 501 million persons (Eurostat, Statistics in focus, 34/2011). The majority of them, 20.2 million, were third-country nationals (i.e. citizens of non-EU countries), while the remaining 12.3 million were citizens of another Member State.

Citizens of Turkey and Romania were the most numerous among foreigners in the EU, exceeding two million people in each country. Among the other EU nationals living outside their country of citizenship, Poles and Italians ranked second and third, respectively, each with more than one million citizens living in another Member State. Among the non-EU foreigners, citizens of Morocco and Albania followed those of Turkey (each more than one million citizens living in another Member State).

In most Member States the majority of foreigners – 20.2 million out of 32.5 million in 2010 – are citizens of a non-EU member country (i.e. third-country nationals) (see table 1.3). In the case of Latvia and Estonia, the proportion of citizens from non-Member States is particularly high due to the large number of 'recognised non-citizens'. These are persons who are not citizens of the reporting country nor of any other country, but who have established links to that country which include some, but not all, rights and obligations of full citizenship. Recognised non-citizens are mainly former Soviet Union citizens, who are permanently resident in these countries but have not acquired Latvian/Estonian citizenship or any other citizenship.

Analysis of the age profile of the resident population shows that, for the EU-27 as a whole, the non-national population is overall younger than the national population. In 2009 the median age of the EU-27 population was 40.6 years, while the median age of non-nationals living in the EU was 34.3 years (36.9 for citizens of other EU Member States and 33.0 for nationals from non-Member States).

Foreign-born

Thanks to better data availability, information on citizenship has often been used to study populations with a foreign background. However, since citizenship can change over time, as stated earlier, more and more users prefer information on country of birth. There were 47.3 million foreign-born residents in the EU in 2010, corresponding to 9.4% of the total population. Of these, 31.4 million were born outside the EU and 16.0 million were born in another EU Member State (table 1.3).

Table 1.3

Foreign and foreign-born population by group of citizenship and country of birth, 2010 (in numbers x 1000 and in percentages)

	total population		foreigners total		foreigners citizens of other EU member states		foreigners citizens of non-EU member countries		foreign-born total		foreign-born born in (other) EU member states		foreign-born born in a non-EU country	
	x 1000		x 1000	%	x 1000	%	x 1000	%	x 1000	%	x 1000	%	x 1000	%
EU-27	501,098		32,493	6.5	12,336	2.5	20,157	4.0	47,348	9.4	15,980	3.2	31,368	6.3
Belgium	10,840		1,053	9.7	715	6.6	338	3.1	..	..	..	..	..	..
Bulgaria (2009)	7,564		24	0.3	4	0.0	20	0.3	..	..	..	..	..	..
Czech Republic	10,507		424	4.0	137	1.3	287	2.7	399	3.8	126	1.2	272	2.6
Denmark	5,535		330	6.0	116	2.1	214	3.9	501	9.0	152	2.8	349	6.3
Germany	81,802		7,131	8.7	2,546	3.1	4,585	5.6	9,812	12.0	3,397	4.2	6,416	7.8
Estonia	1,340		213	15.9	11	0.8	202	15.1	218	16.3	17	1.2	201	15.0
Ireland	4,468		384	8.6	309	6.9	75	1.7	566	12.7	437	9.8	128	2.9
Greece	11,305		955	8.4	163	1.4	792	7.0	1,256	11.1	316	2.8	940	8.3
Spain	45,989		5,664	12.3	2,328	5.1	3,336	7.3	6,423	14.0	2,329	5.1	4,094	8.9
France	64,716		3,769	5.8	1,318	2.0	2,451	3.8	7,197	11.1	2,118	3.3	5,078	7.8
Italy	60,340		4,235	7.0	1,241	2.1	2,994	5.0	4,799	8.0	1,593	2.6	3,206	5.3
Cyprus	803		127	15.9	84	10.4	44	5.5	151	18.8	42	5.3	109	13.5
Latvia	2,248		392	17.4	10	0.4	382	17.0	343	15.3	37	1.6	306	13.6
Lithuania	3,329		37	1.1	2	0.1	35	1.0	215	6.5	32	0.9	184	5.5
Luxembourg	502		216	43.0	186	37.1	30	5.9	163	32.5	135	26.9	28.1	5.6
Hungary	10,014		200	2.0	119	1.2	81	0.8	437	4.4	292	2.9	144	1.4
Malta	413		17	4.0	5	1.3	11	2.7	27	6.4	11	2.6	16	3.8
Netherlands	16,575		652	3.9	311	1.9	341	2.1	1,833	11.1	428	2.6	1,404	8.5
Austria	8,368		876	10.5	328	3.9	548	6.5	1,276	15.2	512	6.1	764	9.1
Poland	38,167		46	0.1	15	0.0	31	0.1	456	1.2	171	0.4	285	0.7
Portugal	10,638		457	4.3	94	0.9	363	3.4	793	7.5	191	1.8	602	5.7
Romania (2009)	21,462		31	0.1	6	0.0	25	0.1	..	..	..	..	..	..

Table 1.3   (continued)

	total population		foreigners total		foreigners citizens of other EU member states		citizens of non-EU member countries		foreign-born total		foreign-born born in (other) EU member states		born in a non-EU country	
	x 1000	%	x 1000	%	x 1000	%	x 1000	%	x 1000	%	x 1000	%	x 1000	%
Slovenia	2,047	4.0	82	4.0	5	0.2	78	3.8	254	12.4	2	1.4	226	11.0
Slovakia	5,425	1.2	63	1.2	39	0.7	24	0.4	:	:	:	:	:	:
Finland	5,351	2.9	155	2.9	56	1.0	99	1.8	229	4.3	81	1.5	147	2.8
Sweden	9,341	6.3	591	6.3	266	2.8	325	3.5	1,337	14.3	478	5.1	860	9.2
United Kingdom	62,008	7.0	4,368	7.0	1,923	3.1	2,445	3.9	7,012	11.3	2,245	3.6	4,767	7.7
Iceland	318	6.8	22	6.8	17	5.4	5	1.4	35	11.0	23	7.3	12	3.7
Norway	4,855	6.8	332	6.8	186	3.8	146	3.0	525	10.8	211	4.3	314	6.5
Switzerland	7,786	22.0	1,714	22.0	1,074	13.8	640	8.2	:	:	:	:	:	:

: Data not available.

Source: Vasileva (2011), Eurostat Statistics in focus 34

In absolute terms, the largest numbers of foreign-born residents living in the EU on 1 January 2010 were in Germany (9.8 million persons), Spain (6.4 million), France (7.2 million), the United Kingdom (7.0 million) and Italy (4.8 million). Four more countries had more than one million foreign-born persons: the Netherlands (1.8 million), Sweden (1.3 million), Austria (1.3 million) and Greece (1.3 million). The highest shares of foreign-borns were in Luxembourg (32.5%), Cyprus (18.8%), Estonia (16.3%), Latvia (15.3%), Austria 15.2%), Sweden (14.3%) and Spain 14.0%). By contrast, the share of foreign-borns was less than 1.5% in Poland, and probably at an equally low level in Romania and Bulgaria.

The share of the foreign-born population exceeded that of foreigners by more than 5 percentage points in Slovenia (12.4%-4.0%), Sweden (14.3%-6.3%), the Netherlands (11.1%-3.9%), Lithuania (6.5%-1,1%) and France (11.1%-5.8%). This may be due to a high rate of acquisition of citizenship (Sweden and the Netherlands), migrants born in the territory of a former colony (France and the Netherlands), or persons with a country of birth that previously constituted part of a former state (Slovenia and Lithuania).

European countries differ considerably in terms of the origin of the foreign population. Common factors influencing the choice of the country of residence are employment opportunities, language, geographical proximity, historical links, established networks or simply opportunities for intra-EU mobility. Table 1.4 presents a summary of the five main citizenships and countries of birth for the EU and EFTA Member States for which detailed data are available (source: Eurostat – Statistics in focus 34/2011, Vasileva, 2011). In some countries, the population with foreign background (citizenship and/or country of birth) is quite diverse, i.e. the five main countries of origin represent only a small share of the total foreigners/foreign-born. By contrast, in a few cases like Latvia, Slovenia and the Czech Republic, more than 70% of the foreign/foreign-born population come from just a few countries.

Table 1.4

Main countries of citizenship and birth of the foreign/foreign-born population, 2010
(in absolute numbers and as percentage of the total foreign/foreign-born population)

Belgium

citizens of	(1000)	(%)	born in	(1000)	(%)
Italy	165	15.7	:	:	
France	140	13.3	:	:	
Netherlands	134	12.7	:	:	
Morocco	82	7.8	:	:	
Spain	45	4.3	:	:	
other	487	46.2	:	:	

Czech Republic

citizens of	(1000)	(%)	born in	(1000)	(%)
Ukraine	131	30.8	Ukraine	124	31.2
Slovakia	73	17.3	Slovakia	70	17.5
Vietnam	61	14.3	Vietnam	53	13.2
Russia	28	6.7	Russia	29	7.1
Poland	19	4.5	Poland	18	4.6
other	112	26.3	other	105	26.4

Germany

citizens of	(1000)	(%)	born in	(1000)	(%)
Turkey	1,763	24.7	:	:	
Italy	556	7.8	:	:	
Poland	426	6.0	:	:	
Greece	298	4.2	:	:	
Croatia	234	3.3	:	:	
other	3,854	54.1	:	:	

Ireland

citizens of	(1000)	(%)	born in	(1000)	(%)
Poland	90	23.5	United Kingdom	212	37.4
United Kingdom	84	21.9	Poland	78	13.8
Lithuania	36	9.5	Lithuania	32	5.6
Latvia	20	5.2	Un States	19	3.4
Romania	12	3.1	Latvia	18	3.2
other	142	36.9	other	207	36.6

Italy

citizens of	(1000)	(%)	born in	(1000)	(%)
Romania	888	21.0	Romania	848	17.7
Albania	467	11.0	Albania	482	10.1
Morocco	432	10.2	Morocco	356	7.4
China	188	4.4	Germany	209	4.4
Ukraine	174	4.1	Ukraine	150	3.1
other	2,087	49.3	other	2,754	57.4

Latvia

citizens of	(1000)	(%)	born in	(1000)	(%)
Recognised non-citizen	343	87.5	Russia	178	51.8
Russia	31	7.9	Belarus	60	17.4
Lithuania	4	0.9	Ukraine	43	12.6
Ukraine	3	0.8	Lithuania	22	6.4
Belarus	2	0.5	Kazakhstan	8	2.2
other	9	2.3	other	33	9.5

Netherlands

citizens of	(1000)	(%)	born in	(1000)	(%)
Turkey	91	13.9	Turkey	197	10.7
Germany	68	10.5	Surinam	187	10.2
Morocco	67	10.2	Morocco	167	9.1
Poland	43	6.6	Indonesia	141	7.7
United Kingdom	41	6.4	Germany	121	6.6
other	342	52.4	other	1,021	55.7

Poland

citizens of	(1000)	(%)	born in	(1000)	(%)
Ukraine	10	22.5	Ukraine	125	27.4
Germany	4	9.8	Former SovietUnion	68	15.0
Russia	4	9.2			
Belarus	3	7.1	Germany	63	13.8
Vietnam	3	6.3	Belarus	40	8.7
other	21	45.1	France	24	5.3
			other	136	29.9

Denmark citizens of	(1000)	(%)	born in	(1000)	(%)
Turkey	29	8.8	Germany	34	6.7
Poland	21	6.4	Turkey	32	6.4
Germany	21	6.4	Poland	26	5.2
Iraq	17	5.1	Iraq	21	4.2
Norway	15	4.5	Sweden	21	4.1
other	227	68.8	other	367	73.3

Slovenia citizens of	(1000)	(%)	born in	(1000)	(%)
Bosnia and Herzegevina	39	47.5	Bosnia and Herzegovina	103	40.6
FYR Macedonia	9	11,1	Croatia	56	22.1
Croatia	8	9.5	Serbia	21	8.2
Serbia	7	8.7	FYR Macedonia	14	5.6
Ukraine	1	1.4	Serbia and		
other	18	22.0	Montenegro	13	5.0
			other	47	18.6

Spain citizens of	(1000)	(%)	born in	(1000)	(%)
Romania	823	14.5	Romania	767	11.9
Morocco	741	13.1	Morocco	738	11.5
Ecuador	392	6.9	Ecuador	470	7.3
United Kingdom	384	6.8	United Kingdom	381	5.9
Colombia	287	5.1	Colombia	360	5.6
other	3,037	53.6	other	3,708	57.7

Sweden citizens of	(1000)	(%)	born in	(1000)	(%)
Finland	74	12.5	Finland	172	12.9
Iraq	55	9.3	Iraq	118	8.8
Denmark	40	6.8	Former		
Poland	39	6.5	Yugoslavia	72	5.4
Norway	35	6.0	Poland	68	5.0
other	347	58.8	Iran	60	4.5
			other	848	63.4

Hungary citizens of	(1000)	(%)	born in	(1000)	(%)
Romania	73	36.4		:	:
Germany	19	9.4		:	:
Ukraine	17	8.6		:	:
China	11	5.6		:	:
Serbia	10	5.1		:	:
other	70	35.0		:	:

Switzerland citizens of	(1000)	(%)	born in	(1000)	(%)
Italy	291	17.0		:	:
Germany	252	14.7		:	:
Portugal	206	12.0		:	:
Serbia and Montenegro	181	10,6		:	:
France	93	5.4		::	::
other	692	40,4		:	:

Portugal citizens of	(1000)	(%)	born in	(1000)	(%)
Brazil	117	25.5		:	:
Ukraine	52	11.5		:	:
Cape Verde	49	10.8		:	:
Romania	33	7.1		:	:
Angola	27	5.9		:	:
other	180	39.3		:	:

Slovakia citizens of	(1000)	(%)	born in	(1000)	(%)
Czech Republic	8	13.3		:	:
Ukraine	6	9.4		:	:
Romania	5	8.6		:	:
Poland	5	8.5		:	:
Hungary	5	7.3		:	:
other	33	52.9		:	:

Table 1.4   (continued)

Iceland citizens of	(1000)	(%)	born in	(1000)	(%)		Norway citizens of	(1000)	(%)	born in	(1000)	(%)
Poland	10	44.2	Poland	10	28.8		Poland	46	14.0	Poland	49	9.4
Lithuania	2	7.1	Denmark	3	8.3		Sweden	36	10.8	Sweden	42	8.0
Germany	1	4.8	United States	2	5.3		Germany	21	6.3	Germany	25	4.7
Denmark	1	4.1	Sweden	2	5.3		Denmark	21	6.2	Denmark	23	4.3
Latvia	1	2.9	Germany	2	4.8		United			Iraq	21	3.9
other	8	37.1	other	17	47.6		Kingdom	13	4.0	other	366	69.7
							other	195	58.8			

Finland citizens of	(1000)	(%)	born in	(1000)	(%)
Russia	28	18.2	Former		
Estonia	26	16.5	SovietUnion	47	20.7
Sweden	9	5.5	Sweden	31	13.6
Somalia	6	3.6	Estonia	22	9.5
China	5	3.4	Russia	7	3.2
other	82	52.8	Somalia	7	3,1
			other	114	49.9

Eurostat has recently started collecting data which show the distribution of EU residents by the level of development of their country of birth (Eurostat- Statistics in focus 34/2011). The Human Development Index (HDI) is used for this purpose. The HDI is calculated by the United Nations under the UN Development Programme as a composite index that measures progress in three basic dimensions – health, education and living standards. Countries are classified as High, Medium and Less Developed countries. The group of High HDI countries consists mainly of Europe, North America, Australia, New Zealand, Japan, large parts of South America and some countries in Western Asia. Medium and Less Developed countries are mainly situated in the rest of Asia and Africa. At EU level, 63.4% of the foreign-born population were born in High HDI countries, 31.5% in Medium HDI countries and 5.1% in Less Developed countries. In Slovenia the percentage of people born in other Highly Developed countries was the highest (98.5%), while in France it was the lowest (40.9%).

In four of the five Member States with the largest foreign-born populations – France, the United Kingdom, Spain and Italy – the share of those born in High HDI countries was below the EU average. This has the effect of lowering the EU-27 average, as a result of which the share of most Member States exceeds the average.

1.2.3   How migrants shape the structure of EU-27 populations

The migration flows of recent decades have left their mark on the population size and structure in many Member States. In the Demography Report 2010, Eurostat (2011) presented some simulations comparing the population in 2007 with what it would have been if no migration had taken place since 1960. These simulations take account of the fact that immigrants settle down and have partners, children and grandchildren in the host country.

Table 1.5 shows the impact of migration on the population size of different Member States. The population of Germany and France has increased by 16% and 17%, respectively, as a result of migration. An increase of more than 10% can also be noted in Belgium, Spain, Austria and Sweden, whereas in the United Kingdom migration has only resulted in a 5% increase in the total population. Portugal (–21%) and Bulgaria (–14%), on the other hand, would have had a larger population without migration. In the case of Italy, recent immigration has compensated for the effects of emigration losses at the beginning of the period under review.

Table 1.5

Differences between actual 2007 population and 2007 population based on projections that exclude migration from 1960, age 0-79 years (in numbers x 1000 and in percentages of actual population)

	x 1000	%
BE – Belgium	1,204	12
BG – Bulgaria	–1,010	–14
CZ – Czech Republic	–19	0
DK – Denmark	346	7
DE – Germany	12,352	16
EE – Estonia	106	8
ES – Spain	5,555	13
FR – France	10,047	17
IE – Ireland	158	4
IT – Italy	1,867	3
LT – Lithonia	–42	–1
HU – Hungary	46	0
NL – The Netherlands	1,412	9
AT – Austria	1,139	14
PL – Poland	–1,731	–5
PT – Portugal	–2,144	–21
SK – Slovakia	–182	–3
FI – Finland	–243	–5
SE – Sweden	1,226	14
UK – Ukraine	2,671	5

Source: Eurostat, Demography Report 2010 (2011)

France has been receiving migrants for a long time, and their impact is particularly visible in the younger age groups, which if there had been no immigration would be about 25% smaller. In 2007, the actual population was about 60.5 million; had there been no migration, it would have been only 50.5 million. Of the 10 million difference caused by migration since 1960, non-nationals accounted for 3.5 million in 2007; the remaining 6.5 million had a wider demographic impact, taking into account the immigrants' children and grandchildren. Moreover, the difference is larger in the younger age groups. The vast majority of these additional young people are French nationals, whereas in the older age groups immigrants are much less likely to have acquired French citizenship.

Spain presents a very different picture, due to the fact that it has only recently experienced large-scale immigration. As a result, the population increase resulting from immigration is concentrated in the working-age population. Most of the additional population resulting from migration since 1960 (some 5.6 million) is made up of foreign nationals, although there are also a few additional people of very young age, representing the children of recent immigrants.

Ireland has traditionally been an emigration country, but in recent years – before the recession – it experienced a significant inflow of migrants, including Irish nationals returning to their country. As a result, the working-age population is significantly larger than it would have been in the absence of migration. In the youngest age groups, however, past emigration has left a small deficit. The 2008 recession has dampened the effect of immigration to Ireland, as many foreigners have left the country.

Portugal's population today is significantly smaller than it would have been in the absence of migration. In 2007, the total population was slightly over 10 million; if there had been no migration, it would have been well over 12 million. Portuguese nationals represent the largest group of foreigners in Luxembourg and France. The effect of emigration is visible across almost the entire age range of the population, with the exception of the very elderly age group.

Some Central and Eastern European Member States have recently become emigration countries on a significant scale. Lithuania is a case in point. Emigration has resulted in a population deficit among the prime working-age groups, which has also led to fewer children being born in the country.
Like Lithuania, Bulgaria, Latvia and Romania have experienced a decade of large population losses due to the emigration of young adults.

This brief description of the migration flows in a number of countries illustrates that receiving societies are changed to a greater or lesser extent by those migratory flows. In some countries, migration has a direct influence on the size of the population, while in others it changes the age profile of the population. These changes have an impact on the education system or labour market in these countries. Countries that are in transition, such as those of Central and Eastern Europe, which have been transformed within a short space of time into countries with high levels of emigration and additional return-immigration, face specific problems as a result. Conversely, too, however, countries which have long had an emigration surplus and have changed into countries of immigration (e.g. the Netherlands, Ireland) face not just demographic changes, but often also culture shocks as a result of an influx of migrants with a significantly different cultural and religious background. Migration also influences the lives of citizens in the receiving countries. There are several ways in which this can happen: for example, the individual migrant comes into contact with inhabitants of the 'new' country as a neighbour or work colleague, but on a collective level too, as migrant communities, migrants help change the host society, for example by developing their own media, newspapers, radio and television stations, websites and interest groups. It is a myth to assume that societies are unchangeable; every migrant leaves their mark on the society in which they live.

Global migration flows will only increase and become more volatile in the future. Mobility throughout the world has increased sharply within the space of a few decades. Travel has become easier and cheaper, and migrant flows will ebb and flow with the ups and downs of the global economy. We are already seeing how quickly migration flows can switch direction when economic and political circumstances change. For example, many migrants from Central and Eastern Europe who had found employment elsewhere in Europe have returned to their countries of origin in the wake of the financial and economic crisis which began in 2008, as their labour became surplus to needs. The recent political upheavals in the Arabic countries may also be expected to lead to migration. These examples show that migration flows can change direction within a very short space of time and can have far-reaching consequences for both the sending and receiving countries.

1.3   Why monitor integration?

There are many reasons why governments want information on how and to what extent migrants participate in society. In many countries, immigration and integration are loaded issues. The public debate and policy formation in relation to these issues often arouse strong emotions. There are few policy domains where views and ideological standpoints clash so fiercely as in the field of migration and integration. The frequent black and white portrayal of these debates often stems from a simplification of reality. Dichotomy of thought and stereotyping are frequent phenomena in the public and political debate about migration and integration. People are very ready to generalise about migrants, not only in the public debate but also in the political arena, ignoring the substantial differences in backgrounds, starting positions, needs and wishes of migrants with diverse migration motives, such as refugees, labour migrants, family reunifiers and students. Images of an unstoppable tide of mass immigration – some even describe it as a 'tsunami' – in Europe and of failed integration are commonplace in many countries. The stereotypically negative perceptions are widespread and deep-rooted: migrants almost by definition end up in disadvantaged neighbourhoods where they exacerbate the existing problems, have virtually no chance of finding work and place disproportionate demands on unemployment and other social security benefits or displace the original inhabitants on the labour market, and often choose a path of crime. The positive accounts mostly form a minority, but once again there are stereotypes: society is culturally enriched by the co-existence of different cultures: different music and exciting food are things from which we can learn and which lead to greater mutual understanding. These views are not only highly politically charged, but often also not based on any research. Fact and fiction are not infrequently confused.

Facts are needed in order to separate reality from perception. This demands an objectifiable measurement of migration and integration processes, and this is one of the biggest contributions that monitoring can make: supplying facts for policymakers on which groups in which social domains are successfully building a life in a new country and which groups are finding it difficult or impossible to do so. This information opens the way to an evidence-based search for the background to both successes and failures and makes it possible to determine whether policy goals are being achieved (on time) and which instruments are more effective than others. Monitoring – periodically tracking developments over an extended period in a standardised way – enables these questions to be answered and patterns to be discovered. Policymakers then have the option of tailoring their actions accordingly.

Great diversity of migration processes – and therefore integration processes

If we analyse the chapters in this book, we realise that migration and processes of integration and participation in Europe can take extremely diverse forms. There are differences in all countries between migrant groups as regards their migration motives, their cultural backgrounds, existing (colonial) ties with the host country, the degree to which the migration was voluntary, and how permanent or temporary their migration will be. There is no such thing as 'the' migrant. The history of immigration and emigration also varies widely across Europe. There are countries which have only recently begun experiencing the phenomenon of immigration, and there are countries which have seen migrants arriving for more than a century. Attention for integration processes and specific policy formulation in this area is a recent development in many European countries.

Different types of migration processes are distinguished in the literature. They are often presented as dichotomies, although the reality is generally more complex (King, 2010). A first distinction is that between internal and international migration. The former refers to migrant flows within a state, the latter to flows between countries. In the European reality, the emphasis is less on nation-states and much more on migration flows from outside the EU, by third-country nationals, to EU Member States. International migration is then migration to the territory of the EU. The rights and obligations of internal and international migrants may vary, as may their integration options.

A second distinction is that between voluntary and forced migration. Many refugees will be subject to forced migration, for example because they are persecuted in their country of origin because of their ethnic background or religious conviction. Voluntary migrants include groups such as pensioners from the UK, Germany and the Netherlands who choose to go and live on the Spanish Costas. However, this twofold division is also not entirely unambiguous: is a refugee from a country without an economic future and characterised by extreme poverty and political instability a voluntary migrant, or are they forced to migrate because of the situation in order to seek a future for themselves or their children?

The third relevant distinction is that between temporary and permanent migration. Highly educated knowledge workers who are sent to Europe by their employers for a fixed period are obviously temporary migrants, and many of this group make little effort to integrate. The picture becomes less clear for the many seasonal workers who come to Western Europe from Eastern Europe; a sizeable number stay behind in the country where they have worked – not always with the intention of staying permanently, but in anticipation of an improvement in the economic situation and labour market opportunities in their country of origin. History shows that large groups of migrants have moved to the various European countries in recent decades as labour migrants. Initially they had the firm intention of returning to their country of origin after a few years, once they had earned enough money. Consequently, the necessity and desire to make an effort to integrate in their host country were not great. Governments in these countries made the same assumption that this migration would be temporary and therefore did not pursue an active integration policy. Looking back today, it transpires that for many migrants, their envisaged temporary migration turned into permanent migration. Their process of integration is consequently more problematic than that of migrants who planned from the start to settle permanently in the host country and who therefore adjusted mentally to this.

After the Second World War, major migration flows began within Europe, especially from Southern Europe to the north. There was a great need for labour in the developing industries of the north, and many Italian, Spanish, Greek and Portuguese 'guest workers' headed to Northern and Western Europe. Italy, Spain, Greece and Portugal continued to be countries with an emigration surplus for a very long time. As we have seen, Portugal would have had 2 million more inhabitants today if it had not been for the years of net emigration.

Many European countries only began focusing specific attention on integration policy around the turn of the last century. Policy in this domain is often reactive: thoughts in many European countries only seriously turned to the design of an integration policy in reaction to social problems, when social unrest, high unemployment and other forms of marginalisation among migrant groups demanded attention. Many governments only became aware late in the day that many migrants were not present on a temporary basis at all, but had settled permanently. It also became apparent that the social problems associated with the relationship between migrants and the host society were not resolving themselves.

Until ten years ago, Germany did not regard itself as an immigration country, despite the fact that it had been receiving a steady influx of (mainly) labour migrants for many years. After the United States, Germany has in fact long been the country with the highest influx of immigrants in absolute numbers. In other European countries, too, such as the Netherlands and Belgium, the myth that migrants would return to their country of origin was kept alive for a very long time. Guest workers, as labour migrants were called at the time, were after all in the country only temporarily, and would return home after a few years. The reality proved otherwise, but politicians were unable or unwilling to accept this. In fact the same applied for many migrant groups themselves, who also long cherished the idea that their stay in the host country was merely temporary and that in time they would return to their country of origin.

Switzerland has been an immigration country since the start of the 20th century. In that country too, however, it is only recently that an immigrant integration policy has been developed. Like other countries, Switzerland for a long time worked on the premise that the immigration was temporary.

Austria is a case apart because of its geographical location, and has for many decades been used as a safe haven by refugees. In countries such as Portugal and Spain, the colonial ties with the countries of origin of many migrants have long played a role. A very high proportion of the migrants in Spain originate from Southern and Central America, while those in Portugal come mainly from the former colonies in Africa. The Netherlands also has a colonial past which is reflected in its migrant population. Scandinavian countries, for their part, number a relatively high proportion of refugees among their migrant populations; in Sweden, immigration has been dominated by this category of migrants since the 1980s, and subsequently by the immigration of close relatives, particularly from the former Yugoslavia, the Middle East and Somalia.

Ireland, Poland and Latvia have a different history. Ireland was for a very long time an emigration country, and Poland and Latvia still are. The political interest in developing specific integration policy is therefore not great in these countries.

As the relevant chapters of this book show, the population in the Eastern European countries have a difficult relationship with those population groups that were members of the occupying nationality in earlier times. An example are citizens of the former Soviet Union who live permanently in Estonia and Latvia but are unable to obtain citizenship and who do not regard themselves as migrants.

1.4 Monitoring integration. But what is integration?

There is a very extensive body of literature on the question of what could or should be understood by the term 'integration'. Does it refer to assimilation, based around the requirement that migrants abandon their cultural identity and assume the identity of the host country in its place? Or does integration mean multiculturalism, in which both migrant and host society retain their own identities and only limited adaptation is required? The EU definition of integration is close to this second approach: integration is a two-way process in which neither group need give up their cultural identity but in which both add a shared dimension to that identity.

The ambitions with regard to integration are sometimes set high, especially in Northern Europe. The authors from Norway report in this book that:

The aim of Norwegian integration policy is to foster the development of an inclusive and diverse society. In accordance with the principles of the Norwegian welfare state, all persons living in Norway have the same rights, obligations and opportunities, regardless of their ethnic background, gender, religion, sexual orientation or functional ability. Equal rights, equal opportunities, solidarity, fairness and an equitable wealth distribution are fundamental values which underpin the government's integration policy.

Sweden adopts a similar approach. The overall goal of the Swedish integration policy is 'equal rights, obligations and opportunities for all, regardless of ethnic or cultural background'. The integration policy is based on a vision of a society where individuals with different cultural and ethnic backgrounds can co-exist. However, it is also important that an individual's freedom does not encroach on the fundamental values of society. Swedish integration policy seeks to ensure that 'respect for fundamental values such as human rights, democratic governance and equality between women and men are maintained and strengthened'

A substantial number of European countries adopt an approach that is in stark contrast to this vision. These countries (currently) have no explicit integration policy at all, either because there are few migrants or because there is a lack of political will to be concerned with immigrants. In the case of Poland, for example, the authors observe that the Polish approach to immigrant integration may still be called a policy of non-policy or a policy of 'assimilation via abandonment'. Poland does not have an integration policy understood as a comprehensive, cohesive strategy. It would be difficult to find some definition of 'immigrant integration' in Polish legal acts or political documents.

Integration policy in Estonia, too, is virtually non-existent. A complex and sensitive situation has reigned in this country since it achieved independence in 1991 in relation to the position of Russian citizens who migrated to Estonia during the era of the Soviet Union. In official government policies, settlers from the Soviet era are classified as immigrants from an occupying regime, and in this way their legal status in the re-established Estonian republic became that of foreigners. However, the significant difference is that most of these Russians do not see themselves as immigrants. Although they migrated from one geographical location to another, this move took place within the borders of one state. It was the border which eventually moved in 1991.

In a 'young' immigration country such as Ireland, yet other considerations play a role. It is only in the last fifteen years that the number of immigrants entering Ireland has outstripped the number of emigrants leaving. Another difference between many European countries and Ireland is that the vast majority of Ireland's immigrants are EU citizens and that a large number are well educated. Ireland has applied its migration legislation to safeguarding the high educational standard of its migrants, by limiting non-EU immigration to those who are well educated and those working in professions where Ireland has a shortage of staff. The recentness and rapidity of immigration to Ireland has meant that the state has generally responded to increasing numbers in an ad hoc manner. In its policy documents, the Irish state has allowed a great deal of cultural diversity, but in practice this diversity is not always accommodated and infrastructure and services for social and structural integration are not provided by the government. For example, language classes are not provided by the state, even though it is very aware that language proficiency lies at the core of integration opportunities.

It emerges from the overview presented in this book that many countries apply a pragmatic interpretation to the notion of 'integration'. While it is true that EU Member States endorse the definition as set out in the EU Common Basic Principles on Integration (see box 1.1), only a few countries have actually worked up those principles into policy documents. A contributory factor is that there is often not one single coordinating ministry with responsibility for integration issues, but rather that several players and stakeholders are involved. In some countries the distribution of responsibilities is made even more complex by the fact that regional authorities also have a say in addition to national government and are able to apply their own interpretation to migration and integration issues (Belgium, Switzerland).

Generally speaking, pragmatic working definitions are used, which talk about participation by migrants in key domains of society. A clear example of this approach is Germany. Despite considering integration to be 'one of the most important domestic tasks', the government has not issued one standardised definition of integration. However, while definitions vary and are quite vague at times, official accounts generally pick up on the Independent Commission of Migration's recommendations. The Federal Office for Migration and Refugees (Bundesamt für Migration und Flüchtlinge – BAMF) refers to integration as a long-term process, its aim being to

> include everyone in society who lives in Germany on a permanent and legal basis [...]. Immigrants should have the opportunity to participate fully in all areas of society on an equal footing. Their responsibility is to learn German and to respect and abide by the Constitution and its laws.

The Ministry of the Interior (Bundesministerium des Innern – BMI) also stipulates among other things that 'integration should allow for equal opportunities and actual participation in all areas, especially in social, economic and cultural life'. Like the BAMF, the Ministry also points to a two-way-process that is necessary to accomplish successful integration, including efforts on the part of the immigrant population to learn the language and to gain a basic civic education, and on the part of the majority population a willingness to live in a tolerant and intercultural society.

Portugal applies a definition of integration which places heavy emphasis on the acceptance of norms and values that apply in Portugal. In the chapter on Portugal we read that in 2002 the principle set out in the law was that 'integration' was considered to have been achieved if immigrants 'accept the language, laws and moral and cultural rights of the Portuguese nation'. A further principle is that all citizens legally residing in Portugal have equal dignity and opportunities.

Several countries wrestle with the two-way nature of the integration process. This reciprocity is not always unequivocally supported. Latvia is an example; the authors of the chapter on Latvia make the following observation about the conceptual basis of the Framework Document and Integration Programme in Latvia.

According to the Framework Document, 'social integration means mutual understanding and cooperation between individuals and groups within a common state' (p. 4). This initial emphasis on contact and interdependence is supplemented by a strong focus on the normative dimension: 'the goal of integration is to create a democratic, cohesive civil society based on common values' (p. 4). In many ways, the document tries to square a circle: it posits the two-way nature of integration, then proceeds to stress the primacy of the Latvian language, culture and values and the adaptation required by minorities and non-citizens (new immigrants or refugees are mentioned in one sentence).

Socio-economic participation (being in work or education/training) is often seen as the area of life which provides the most important indicator of whether migrant integration is successful. Acquiring the host-country language is also regarded as a key element of integration in most countries. The approach to integration is predominantly a segmented one, in which differing levels of 'success' can be achieved in different areas of life. Migrants can for example be successful in terms of their participation in the labour market but still be at a disadvantage on the housing market. Even then, opinions differ on what 'successful' means; many countries implicitly assume that integration is successful if migrants achieve equal scores on what are considered to be relevant domains of society (the criterion of proportionality). For example, if the same percentage of migrants have a job as the indigenous population, this is seen as an indicator of successful integration. Similarly, if the pass rates in higher education are equally high for both groups, this too is seen as evidence of successful integration.

It is however debatable whether such a criterion – equal pass rates – is appropriate. After all, many migrants come from a very different background from the indigenous population. They often start from a much lower education level, have a very different cultural background, and are faced with discrimination. The question then is whether it is reasonable given this disadvantaged position to expect migrants to attain the same level as indigenous citizens. The demographic composition of many migrant groups is also different from that of the native population. Most migrant groups contain a relatively high proportion of young people or a skewed distribution of men and women, or are in a vulnerable socioeconomic position. Caution is therefore called for when comparing the social participation of migrants with that of the indigenous population if no allowance is made for proportionality which takes into account relevant background characteristics or circumstances of the migrant groups.

When measuring and monitoring the progress of integration, many countries focus mainly on the 'hard' sectors of society such as the labour market and education system, and devote less attention to socio-cultural integration, for example in the form of social participation, contacts between migrants and the host population, personal perceptions of migrants as to whether they feel at home and accepted, or mutual trust between different population groups, as well as in the form of experiences of discrimination. The reciprocal nature of integration, in which both migrants and the host society have to accommodate and adapt to each other in order to be able to live together, is not something that is made explicit and monitored in many countries.

Full and equal participation in key areas of life is especially problematic for first-generation migrants, and as a group they often fail to achieve this level of integration. The situation is different for their descendants, as evidenced by several chapters in this book. Second-generation migrants, who were born in the host country and who are therefore in reality not migrants at all, generally tend to be more successful than their parents. They tend to be more strongly focused on the country where they live and less on the country where their parents were born. They speak the host-country language, are familiar with its culture and often know about their parents' country of birth only from having heard about it. The distinction between first and second-generation migrants is therefore essential in understanding and explaining integration processes. Unfortunately, many countries do not apply this distinction, or else data which would make this distinction possible are not available.

The UK is a case apart in this respect. Because of the strong links to the Empire and Commonwealth, and Britain's traditional pattern of conferring citizenship by birth in the UK (jus soli), the country's large population of migrant origin has for many decades been understood by policymakers and the public at large as being of 'ethnic minority' status rather than 'migrant' status. The concept of 'second-generation migrant' is not used in the UK, and migrants and especially their descendents often identify themselves as 'black British', 'British Asian' and so on. Consequently, there is no straightforward correlation between ethnicity and migration status in the UK.

Many European countries appear to apply the norm of equal achievements by migrants and the indigenous population in different areas of society as an implicit element of their integration policy. There are only a few cases where the government has put forward targets or formulated different kinds of norms. And there is no case where different norms or targets are applied for different groups of origin. The diversity in social and cultural background, migration background, available social capital – in short, the starting position of migrant groups with a different origin – is very considerable. There is no such thing as 'the' migrant. The degree to which or the speed with which groups of migrants (are able to) integrate differs widely. However, few countries mention this explicitly in their policy. Many quantitative summaries and monitors also make little or no distinction by country of birth.

1.5   Measuring and monitoring: the empirical approach

In the following chapters, experts from seventeen European countries describe the current status with regard to measuring and monitoring the integration of migrants in their country. For each country, a description is first given of the political context and policy efforts made in respect of migration and migrant integration. This produces an interesting overview of the differing views that prevail about migrants, the sense of urgency – often associated with the absolute number of migrants present in a country – and the degree of willingness in the different countries to invest energy and resources in accommodating and supporting migrants. For some countries, the authors also describe the difficulties with the concept of 'migrant'. Minority groups who have sometimes lived for decades in a country are sometimes seen as a target group for integration policy, sometimes not. In the countries which formed part of the former Soviet Union, this affects the position of the Russian population, who are unable to obtain citizenship in their country of residence. Elsewhere, a similar situation applies to Roma, for example, who are regarded as migrants (Latvia) and for whom the problematic aspects of their presence in the country are emphasised. The approach taken in this country can be more accurately described as an emigration policy than an integration policy.

Earlier in this chapter, we discussed the size of the migrant population in the various European countries. The attention devoted by politicians and policy to integration bears a direct relationship to the percentage of migrants in the country. In the countries on the eastern borders of Europe, immigration is sometimes a negligible phenomenon, and such immigration as does take place consists largely of returning expatriates who have been working temporarily elsewhere. In the north and west of Europe, by contrast, there are clear and constant immigration flows involving considerable numbers of migrants. As stated, the realisation that this immigration is permanent only dawned at a late stage in many countries, but without exception the countries of North-western Europe and Scandinavia have formulated an explicit integration policy. The picture in Southern Europe as regards immigration and emigration is more mixed. Spain, Portugal and Italy were traditional exporters of labour, and in Spain and Italy that remained the case until fairly recently. Today, however, these countries have become immigration destinations. This varied picture of immigration and emigration past and present is reflected in the diversity of efforts made to substantiate integration policy quantitatively by means of registers, research and monitoring. There is still a marked lack of infrastructure for monitoring integration processes in a reliable and regular way. It is not clear in many European countries where responsibility lies for data-gathering, there is by no means always a responsible ministry which coordinates the information and prescribes what information is needed. Or responsibility is spread across different levels of policy, with independent roles for regions or cities, sometimes in turn leading to confusion of interpretation because of the lack of a uniform language.

In the individual country chapters, therefore, the authors explore the question of whether and how data on migrant integration are gathered in their country. Who has taken the initiative; who actually carries out the data-gathering; and who monitors the quality of the data? The answers to these questions are important in determining whether monitoring is regarded as a serious contribution to policy in a given country, or whether it is merely an initiative of academics. Ideally, monitoring should be part of a policy cycle, in which the need for knowledge is formulated on the basis of observed problems in the integration and social participation of migrants. How are migrants faring, and what effect have the efforts made by governments or other bodies produced?

The authors then describe the form and content of the monitoring activities in their countries. What material is available? Can time series be constructed or are only cross-sectional data available? The question also arises here of what criteria are used to distinguish between migrants, foreigners or ethnic minorities. We have already touched on some of the problems in this regard.

Which areas of life are analysed, and which indicators are used? The list published by the EU (see table 1.1 above) is a minimum list of indicators, but are the different countries able and willing to incorporate other domains and indicators? It is interesting in this regard to investigate the views that underlie the choice of indicators used for monitoring. These are after all political choices, not neutral selections from a set of relevant indicators. The views in a given country about what constitutes successful integration are reflected in the indicators applied. Does the emphasis lie on structural integration, or is socio-cultural integration also considered important? And is an attempt made to measure the reciprocity of the integration process and the role of the host society? Directly linked to this is the question of whether benchmarks are used. Have policy goals been formulated, are their targets for measuring successes in integration? To what extent is a distinction made between different groups of migrants, different generations, different migration motives, different age groups and different genders? As we have seen, there is no such thing as 'the' migrant, but is this reality also reflected in the monitoring activities in the various countries?

The different chapters in this book present a kaleidoscopic overview of the opinions about integration and the efforts to make integration measurable in practice in seventeen European countries. If we are realistic, we have to accept that harmonisation in the monitoring of immigrant integration in Europe is still a long way away. The different speeds and developments in relation to immigration and emigration in the various countries are too great for this. There is also a divergence of interests. The numbers of migrants in the different European countries alone vary enormously. Why should a country be concerned about and invest in developing an integration monitor if the numbers of migrants are minimal and there is no policy urgency? There is also a practical point here: setting up a monitoring system takes time and money, and the latter in particular is not available to an equal degree in all countries.

However, an important – perhaps the most important – factor is the importance attached by a society to the integration of minority groups. Where a society – and as a consequence its political leaders – attaches great importance to equivalence in the position and participation of migrants in that society, activities to monitor that participation over time are often already in place, even where the numbers of migrants in the population are relatively small. In countries where this view is not so deep-rooted, there is generally little willingness to invest in a knowledge infrastructure in relation to integration.
More generally, we would argue that reliable policy information is important both where there are relatively high percentages of immigrants and where the numbers are relatively small. And that is not just because agreements have been made about this at European level, but above all because experience has shown that new and sometimes sizeable migration flows can arise , dry up or change direction within a short space of time. Moreover, it is difficult if not impossible to predict how temporary or permanent migration will be and what impact immigrants will have on the receiving society. In order to assess the magnitude of this influence and to be able to make a substantiated judgment

about whether or not an immigration or integration policy should be constructed, reliable policy information is essential. The situation is different in countries which are already pursuing an integration policy; here, monitoring information is indispensable in order to establish whether developments are moving quickly enough to achieve the agreed policy objectives on time, or whether adjustments are needed. An evidence-based approach to integration policy, conducted at European level or nationally, is of great importance here.

However, it is anything but certain that an EU-wide, uniform monitoring system will become available in the short term. Because although a number of correspondences emerge if we compare the seventeen countries described in this book, Europe is also characterised by great diversity. For example, there is on the one hand a relatively broad consensus about the importance for integration of having a good command of the language of the country where migrants build their – second – life, or about the great importance of a good education and having work in the ability to play a full part in the host society. There also appears to be a broad development in (policy) views about the role and position of newcomers in the receiving society, with a clear shift in the recent period away from a multiculturalist view, in which integration was seen as a two-way process and newcomers were able to integrate into the host society 'without relinquishing their own culture', to a more assimilationist approach in which newcomers are expected to adapt much more to the dominant national culture. We also see this development in the terms used in relation to immigration and integration policy: whereas in recent decades the talk was often of 'rights and duties', the emphasis today is much more on 'obligations' (on the part of migrants) and 'own responsibility'.

At the same time, in addition to these agreements, wide differences can also be observed between the European countries. For example, some countries have experience of immigration stretching back decades, while for others it is a relatively new phenomenon. There is also great variation in the background and characteristics of the immigration flows: in some countries these flows consist mainly of immigrants originating from the host country's former colonies or overseas territories, who were already more or less familiar with the language and culture of the destination country before they migrated. At the same time, there are migrant flows for which this does not apply: for example, for the labour migrants of the past, but also the recent labour migration which has taken place in (and within) Europe in the 21st century, or the large groups of refugees and asylum-seekers. We also see that – partly connected to the differences in migration history – there are wide differences in the policy traditions between the different countries of Europe. Some countries have pursued an integration policy for many years, though even then there is variation between countries in the administrative level at which this policy is pursued; in other countries, integration policy is a relatively new phenomenon, or is *de facto* (virtually) non-existent. Partly related to this, we also see wide differences in the tradition and technique of policy information systems and policy monitoring between European countries. Where a number of Northern European countries in particular have advanced systems in operation, in which accurate and reliable information on the progress of the integration of migrant groups is available based on the linking of registration data (and in which all manner of subcategories can be distinguished), other countries use periodic censuses or specific (or non-specific) sample surveys as a basis; yet other countries have only very limited quantitative information available about the integration of migrants.

The conclusion is that there are wide differences and that there is still a long way to go before a standardised and cohesive picture of the integration of migrants in Europe becomes available. However, this does not alter the fact that many promising developments can be observed.

References

Council of the European Union (2004). *EU Common basic principles for immigrant integration policy* (14615/04). Brussels: Council of the European Union.

European Commission COM (2011) 455. *European Agenda for Integration 2011*. Brussels: European Commission.

European Commission COM (2010). *EUROPE 2020. A strategy for smart, sustainable and inclusive growth* (2020 final). Brussels: European Commission.

European Commission (DG for Justice, Freedom and Security) (2010). *Handbook on integration for policy-makers and practitioners* (third edition). Brussels: European Commission.

European Council (2010). *The Stockholm Programme – An open and secure Europe serving and protecting citizens* (2010/C 115/01). Brussels: European Council.

European ministerial Conference on Integration in Zaragoza, 15 and 16 April, 2010. *Declaration*.

EUROSTAT/European Commission (2010). *Demography Report 2010. Older, more numerous and diverse Europeans*. Brussels: EUROSTAT/European Commission.

EUROSTAT/European Commission (2011). *Indicators of Immigrant Integration. A pilot study.* Brussels: EUROSTAT/European Commission.

Gijsberts, M., W. Huijnk & R. Vogels (eds.) (2011). *Chinese Nederlanders. Van horeca naar hogeschool*. The Hague: The Netherlands Institute for Social Research | SCP.

King, R. (2010). Towards a new map of European migration. In: M. Martiniello & J. Rath (eds.), *Selected studies in international migration and immigrant incorporation* (p. 111-140). Amsterdam: Amsterdam University Press.

Lucassen, L., D. Feldman & J. Oltmer (eds.) (2006). *Paths of integration. Migrants in Western Europe (1880-2004)*. Amsterdam: Amsterdam University Press.

Martiniello, M. & J. Rath (eds.) (2010). *Selected studies in international migration and immigrant incorporation*. Amsterdam: Amsterdam University Press.

Oblak Flander, A. (2011). Immigration to EU Member States down by 6% and emigration up by 13% in 2008. In: *EUROSTAT, Statistics in focus*, no. 1.

UNHCR (2011). *2010 Global Trends report*. Geneva: UNHCR.

UNHCR (2011). *Asylum Levels and Trends in Industrialized Countries*. Geneva: UNHCR.

Vasileva, K. (2010). Foreigners living in the EU are diverse and largely younger than the nationals of the EU Member States. In: *EUROSTAT, Statistics in focus*, no. 45.

Vasileva, K. (2011). 6.5% of the EU population are foreigners and 9.4% are born abroad. In: *EUROSTAT, Statistics in focus*, no. 34.

PROMINSTAT/European Commission (2010). *Statistics on migration, integratin and discrimination in Europe. Final report*. Vienna: International Centre for Migration Policy Development (ICMPD).

2   Monitoring integration in Austria

Albert Kraler and David Reichel

2.1   Introduction

The integration of immigrants in Austria has been part of the political agenda since the 1990s, and in terms of actual practices at local level can be traced back to the 1980s. However, it is only since the turn of the millennium that integration has become a major focus of national policymaking. Since integration is an elusive term, discussions on integration have always been accompanied by debates about the meaning of integration and how it should be measured. While research on integration dates back to the early 1980s, it is not until very recently that measurement or monitoring of integration of immigrants and their descendants has received more systematic attention from researchers and policymakers. These recent efforts resulted in the definition of national integration indicators published in 2010. In the same year the city of Vienna launched its own official integration monitoring system.

This chapter provides a descriptive analysis of integration monitoring in Austria. Section 2.2 begins with a brief overview of Austria's migration history and describes basic features of the resident population in terms of immigrant status and selected socioeconomic characteristics. Section 2.3 summarises the national integration policy framework, while section 2.4 reviews existing studies focusing on the integration of immigrants and their descendants in Austria. In the second part of the chapter – sections 2.5 and 2.6 – we take a closer look at statistical monitoring of integration in Austria. Section 2.5 provides contextual information on data collection in relation to immigrants in Austria and describes the main data sources for measuring migration and integration, as well as overall data availability. Section 2.6 goes on to describe the two recently established integration monitoring systems in more detail, the national integration monitoring system and the Viennese integration and diversity monitor, both launched in 2010. Section 2.7 presents the conclusions.

2.2   Austria – a diverse country with a diverse population

2.2.1   Immigration in Austria in a nutshell

Austria's 20th-century migration history largely reflects the experiences of other Central and Northern European states, though with some particularities. In the late 19th and early 20th century the two predominant forms of migration were rural-urban migration within the territory of the Habsburg Empire, and large-scale emigration to overseas destinations. Following the collapse of the Habsburg Empire, people who were formerly internal migrants became international migrants and non-citizens. Against the backdrop of the persistent economic crisis following World War I, labour migration came to an almost completely halt. The genocidal policies pursued by the Nazis, World War II and its aftermath led to massive displacement and forced migration, which continued to shape migration patterns well into the 1950s. Since the 1960s, labour and related family migration have been the dominant patterns of migration, while Austria has also received considerable numbers of refugees. Migration to Austria since the 1950s can be divided into four phases: the period 1950 to 1973, characterised by Cold War refugees and 'guest-worker' migration; 1973 to 1989, with mainly 'spontaneous' labour migration, family reunification and refugee-related migration, overwhelmingly from Eastern Europe; 1989 to 2004, consisting mainly of family related migration, more limited labour migration (especially between 1989 and 1993) and conflict refugees (Kraler & Stacher 2002: 51); and from 2004 onward. In the fourth phase, since 2004, immigration from the new EU countries increased, following EU enlargement, while immigration from non-EU countries decreased. Generally, trends in net migration closely correspond to economic cycles. However, political factors, including migration policy decisions, have played an important role, too.

Figure 2.1

Net immigration to Austria by citizenship category, 1961-2009

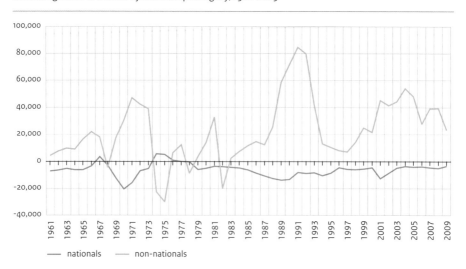

Sources: Chart produced by the authors based on data from Statistics Austria. Figures for 1961 to 1995 are estimates based on intercensus population estimates. Figures for 1996 to 2001 are based on aggregate migration statistics derived from municipal population registers. Figures for 2002 to 2009 are calculated on the basis of the Population Register (POPREG) (revised figures). For data see www.statistik.gv.at).

In terms of types of migration, a majority of immigrants in Austria have migrated for family-related reasons (53.3%) and employment (25.7%), while some 9.2% have migrated as refugees (Statistik Austria 2009b).

Since 1945, Austria has received several waves of refugees and asylum-seekers, including ethnic Germans (*Volksdeutsche*) in the wake of World War II, Hungarians in 1956, Czechoslovakians in 1968 and Poles in 1981/82. After the breakdown of the Soviet Union, the numbers of asylum-seekers in Austria increased sharply at the end of the 1980s and reached a first peak in 1991, with 27,300 asylum applications (Fassmann & Münz 1995: 35-37; Kraler & Stacher 2002: 55-56). In the 1990s, asylum-related migration mainly involved asylum-seekers from former Yugoslavian countries, although most were eventually admitted on an ad hoc basis under a 'temporary protection' scheme. Most of the 85,000 displaced war refugees from Bosnia – some 70,000 – were eventually granted long-term residence status at the end of the 1990s (Kraler & Stacher 2002: 57; Kraler & Reichel 2009). One of the largest recent refugee groups in Austria are refugees from Chechnya; between 1997 and 2006 over 22,000 asylum applications from Russian citizens (mostly from Chechnya) were recorded in Austria, a high proportion of which were granted. This means that almost three-quarters of decisions on Chechen asylum applications were positive between 2002 and 2006 (Hofmann & Reichel 2008).

However, both in quantitative terms and as regards its long-term impact, labour and family-related immigration from the Former Yugoslavia and Turkey has been the single most important migration movement to Austria in the past 50 years or so.

2.2.2 The Austrian population by country of origin

At the beginning of 2009 over 15% of the Austrian population were foreign-born. Of this foreign-born population, 41% were born in another EU/EEA country or Switzerland. About half of the EU-born population were born in one of the EU-15 countries (excluding Austria), the other half in the EU-12 (countries that have been member states since 2004 and 2007). The main country of birth of immigrants in Austria is Germany, at 187,000 persons or around 2.2% of the total Austrian population. The majority of the Austrian population who were born in a third country originate from the Former Yugoslavia, at over 375,000 persons, with Bosnia and Herzegovina being the most important country in this group. Finally, the population born in Turkey make up a considerable share of the Austrian population, at almost 158,000 persons or just under 2% of the total population. However, when speaking about integration, not only immigrants but also their descendants are of importance. Statistics Austria estimates the share of persons with a migration background – defined as either persons who have migrated to Austria or persons who were born in Austria but both of whose parents were born abroad – at 17.8% of the total population in 2009 (Statistik Austria & KMI 2010).

The importance of the city of Vienna is worth mentioning with regard to the immigrant population. Since it is by far the largest city in Austria, many immigrants select Vienna as their destination. 20% of the total Austrian population live in Vienna, but this rises to almost 40% of the foreign-born population. Persons born in Serbia and Montenegro, in particular, are more likely to be found in Vienna; this population group totalled more than 100,000 persons at the beginning of 2009.

Table 2.1

Austrian population on 1 January 2009 by country of birth (in numbers and percentages)

country of birth	total Austria	% of total	% of total foreign-born	Vienna	% of total Austria (row %)
total	8,355,260	100.0	–	1,687,271	20.2
Austria (native-born)	7,078,162	84.7	–	1,182,728	16.7
not-Austria (foreign-born)	1,277,098	15.3	100.0	504,543	39.5
EU, EEA and CH	522,288	6.3	40.9	170,999	32.7
Germany	187,023	2.2	14.6	38,276	20.5
EU-10 2004	182,802	2.2	14.3	82,644	45.2
EU-12 2007	70,298	0.8	5.5	25,659	36.5
third countries	754,810	9.0	59.1	333,544	44.2
Former Yugoslavia (excl. SI)	375,278	4.5	29.4	153,553	40.9
Bosnia and Herzegovina	133,585	1.6	10.5	33,811	25.3
Croatia	34,830	0.4	2.7	9,231	26.5
Macedonia	18,612	0.2	1.5	8,906	47.9
Serbia and Montenegro	188,251	2.3	14.7	101,605	54.0
other European countries	196,101	2.3	15.4	81,494	41.6
Russian Federation	26,002	0.3	2.0	11,005	42.3
Turkey	157,750	1.9	12.4	65,044	41.2
Ukraine	6,797	0.1	0.5	3,196	47.0
Africa	39,657	0.5	3.1	21,980	55.4
America	29,083	0.3	2.3	12,195	41.9
Asia	103,302	1.2	8.1	61,914	59.9
Oceania	2,649	0.0	0.2	952	35.9
unknown	8,740	0.1	0.7	1,456	16.7

Source: own presentation based on data from Statistik Austria Website, Statistik des Bevölkerungsstandes (accessed April 2010)

2.2.3   Immigrants' socioeconomic status

Detailed information on the socioeconomic characteristics of immigrants is available from the 2008 *Mikrozensus* – the Austrian version of the Labour Force Survey. In the second quarter of 2008, some 690,000 foreign-born persons aged between 15 and 64 years were members of the economically active population in Austria (i.e. were employed or seeking employment), constituting 16.5% of the total active population. The share of active persons within the total native-born population is 4.4 percentage points higher than that of foreign-born citizens (75.7% native-born vs. 71.3% foreign-born). The difference in employment rates (i.e. the share of persons employed as a percentage of the total population aged between 15 and 64 years) is even higher, at 7 percentage points (73.5% vs. 66.5%). However, there are major differences in the employment rates for different countries of birth. The employment rate among foreign-born persons originating from an EU-15 country (in practice mainly originating from Germany) is relatively high; however, the highest employment rates occur among persons born in Bosnia and Herzegovina, with some 80% being employed. By contrast, the employment rates among persons born in Serbia and Turkey are considerably lower (66.1% and 60.1%, respectively). One of the main reasons for these differences in employment rates is the low employment rate among foreign-born women; while the employment rate among Austrian-born men was 17.3% higher than that for women, the employment rate among foreign-born men exceeded that for women by 35%. However, the gender gap in employment rates also varies considerably between different countries of birth. The employment rates among women and men born in an EU-15 country are comparable to those among the Austrian-born population; employment rates among both men and women from Bosnia and Herzegovina are higher among people born in Austria, and the gender gap is also smaller. The gender gap is widest for the Turkish-born population; male immigrants from Turkey have almost the same employment rate as Austrian-born men (78.3% vs. 79.3%), but only 40.7% of Turkish-born women are employed compared to 67.6% of native Austrian females. Unemployment among immigrants is significantly higher than in the native-born population. Unemployment rates are higher in all immigrant groups than in the Austrian-born population. The unemployment rate of Turkish-born women is especially high, at 11.5% (cf. Statistik Austria 2009b: 35-38).

It is however important to note that the general differences in employment indicators can be largely explained by the different composition of the immigrant and native populations. When comparing unemployment rates among non-nationals and Austrian citizens, Biffl finds that the characteristics age, education and gender explain 64% of the differences (Biffl 2007: 280). As in other European countries of immigration, immigrants are overrepresented among the lower educated and higher educated and underrepresented among those with medium skill levels. EU-born migrants are dominant among those with higher skill levels, whereas those of non-EU origin account for the majority of low-skilled migrants (Münz et al. 2007: 32). While the majority of the Austrian-born population are employed as white-collar workers (60.3%), this applies for only 42.2% of the immigrant population, and almost half of immigrants are employed as blue-collar workers. Some 25.9% of immigrants are unskilled workers, compared to only 8.4% within the native-born population (Statistik Austria 2009b: 43-44).

However, while this picture shows significant inequality between migrants and non-migrants and between different groups of migrants on a number of key indicators, these differences do not necessarily fully explain labour market outcomes. Additional factors that need to be taken into account include the mismatch between supply and demand, limited transferability of skills acquired in the country of origin, language difficulties, lack of local social networks and discrimination (Biffl 2007: 280).

2.3   National integration policy

2.3.1 A multiplicity of actors? The sectoral nature of integration policy

As a social policy concern, integration cuts across several policy domains, including labour market policy, education policy, protection of fundamental rights, non-discrimination, immigration policy, housing policy, social security and other welfare policies, policies relating to political participation as well as citizenship issues. As a result, measures are often adopted in the context of these sectoral policies. At the same time, sectoral integration policies may not necessarily be framed as integration policies explicitly targeting migrants, but rather as policies targeting specific vulnerable groups using more general criteria (unemployment, poverty, low qualifications, etc.). Indeed, the prevailing view among labour market authorities in the 1990s was that there was no need for targeted (labour market) integration policies for immigrants.[1] More recently, partly under the influence of EU programmes and policies (Equal, National Employment Plans, etc.), public authorities have abandoned any specific targeting of immigrants in their programmes, even if the design of such programmes may not differ fundamentally from those carried out in the 1990s. Given the nature of integration policy as a cross-cutting policy field, it is also clear that competences on matters relating to integration are scattered across a large number of different ministries at national level and are moreover divided between national, provincial and local levels of government. Nevertheless, as an only weakly federalised state, the main competence in relation to setting the overall legal framework is vested at the federal level (Thienel 2007). Provinces and municipalities do play an important role in the implementation of policies, and can thus have a significant impact on the actual shape of measures 'on the ground', while for certain issues provinces also have legislative powers. At federal level, the Ministry of the Interior, which is responsible for immigration, residence and citizenship matters, and the Ministry of Labour, Social Affairs and Consumer Protection, which has responsibility for all employment-related issues, including labour market access for non-citizens, are the most important actors in integration policymaking. In addition, the Austrian Integration Fund – a formally independent agency under the Ministry of the Interior – has become an increasingly important institution during the last decade, though mainly for operational purposes. Apart from these institutions, a host of other bodies are involved in integration policymaking. While an advisory council on migration and asylum made up of representatives from relevant ministries, the 'social partners' (trade union, the Chamber of Labour, the Chamber of Commerce and the Federation of Austrian Industries), representatives of provinces and municipalities had already been established in the late 1990s, charged with advising the government on all matters concerning migration and asylum, including integration, in 2010 a new, specific expert committee on integration was established by the Minister of the Interior, which is charged with advising the government in relation to the National Action Plan on Integration (NAP); this is discussed in more detail below.[2]

Following the resignation of Vice-Chancellor, Finance Minister and leader of the Austrian People's Party (ÖVP), Josef Pröll, in April 2011 and the ensuing reshuffling of ministers and state secretaries nominated by the ÖVP an office of a state secretary for integration was created within the Austrian Ministry of the Interior. Sebastian Kurz was appointed as the first state secretary for integration. According to the state secretariat's mission statement, the primary task of the state secretariat is to actively deal with the opportunities and challenges of integration and contribute to a more objective debate on the topic.[3] Politically, the new state secretariat is expected to improve the coordination of integration policy making between different ministries, while also reinforcing the leading role of the Ministry of the Interior in integration policy making.

2.3.2 The emergence of integration policy and the shift towards language testing

Integration became a key issue in debates on migration policy in the early 1990s. The immediate context was the perception of a looming immigration crisis, with unprecedented levels of immigration, high numbers of asylum applications and a growing politicisation of immigration. Integration was closely linked to immigration in this context, as expressed in the slogan 'integration before new immigration'. While restrictions were indeed quickly imposed on new immigration in the early 1990s, however, measures to promote integration did not follow until the late 1990s, most notably through improving the legal status of long-term residents (König & Stadler 2003: 231; Nowotny 2007: 68-69); but there was still no overall integration strategy. At the same time, integration became the subject of increasing debate in terms of the characteristics that migrants needed to possess in order to qualify for citizenship or 'denizenship' (long-term residence status). As a first expression of the changing philosophy on integration, the 1998 amendment to the nationality law[4] introduced integration conditions which applicants had to meet in order to acquire citizenship. The commentary to the law framed citizenship as the culmination of a 'successful integration process', rather than a means of (legal) integration. According to the nationality law, applicants must demonstrate their 'personal and professional integration'. In addition, the law stipulates knowledge of a minimum level of German as a precondition for acquisition of Austrian citizenship (Cinar & Waldrauch 2006: 28-29). Under the 1998 law, language proficiency was only assessed by the administration through a simple interview, and without clear guidelines as to what level of German proficiency would be required. In an amendment to the law that entered into force in 2006, a formal citizenship test was introduced and level A2 according to the European Framework of Reference for Languages was set as the minimum level of German language proficiency to be attained.

After a change of government in 2000, and modelled on the Dutch integration policies, Austria subsequently introduced mandatory civic integration courses for immigrants in 2002. The so-called 'integration agreement'[5] mainly includes compulsory language courses which must be attended by new immigrants and which culminate in a test. If the requirements of the 'integration agreement' are not fulfilled, immigrants can be sanctioned. As part of a major overhaul of the immigration legislation in 2005, the requirements of the 'integration agreement' were tightened up considerably, both as regards the hours of teaching to be attended and the level of German language proficiency to be attained (Bauböck & Perchinig 2006: 737; Bruckner et al. 2005: 343-349; König & Stadler 2003: 238). Currently, the 'integration agreement' affects immigrants who intend to stay in Austria for an extended period and who have arrived since 2006. Immigrants need to achieve level A2 of the common European Framework of Reference for Languages within five years. In addition, the Minister of the Interior has announced the introduction of language tests before entry to Austria, for which level A1 would be required and which would mainly affect family members of settled migrants and citizens.

In 2008, over 3,900 persons successfully participated in a German test at the end of an integration language course, of whom 50% were citizens of Former Yugoslavian countries and a quarter held Turkish citizenship (Austrian Integration Fund 2009: 12).

2.3.3 The National Action Plan on Integration – changing paradigms of integration policymaking?

In 2009, a consultation process for the first National Action Plan on Integration (NAP) was launched by the Ministry of the Interior; it was adopted by the Council of Ministers in January 2010. The main outcome of the Action Plan was the definition of major challenges, principle policy positions and measures with regard to seven areas (language and education; employment and occupation; rule of law and values; health and social affairs; intercultural dialogue; sports and leisure; housing; and the regional dimension of integration). The NAP reports included a report on integration measures, a study on opinions and attitudes toward integration in Austria as well as a report on integration indicators at national level (see below for more detail).[6] The NAP defined its target groups in broad terms – including both the native population as well as immigrants (Ministry of the Interior 2010).

In many ways, the NAP marked a departure from established thinking on integration, with its preoccupation with the language skills of immigrants and related language conditions in immigration law. While the language proficiency of immigrants remains an important issue within the NAP, integration and integration policy are seen as being about much more than just language. In addition, while the perception of integration as a 'two-way process' was already an issue accompanying the debates surrounding the introduction of mandatory integration courses in the early 2000s, the responsibility of the mainstream population (or the State, for that matter) was not a particularly prominent concern in integration policy through the decade. By contrast, the NAP puts more emphasis on the dual responsibility of both the migrant and the host society, and among other things, stresses the need to provide opportunities for migrants and to counter discrimination and xenophobia. Nevertheless, the NAP still tends to emphasise the obligations of migrants, rather than those of the State or the mainstream population.

The NAP process was not uncontested, and in particular some municipalities and provinces, especially Vienna, were critical of the way the process was managed and of the Action Plan that resulted from it. Partly in the light of this, Vienna established its own immigration commission in 2009, which was presented in 2010.

2.3.4   The role of data and research in integration policymaking

While scientific evidence and relevant statistical data became increasingly important in migration and integration policymaking since at least the early 1980s, when the first large studies on integration were conducted, it is only relatively recently that the need for regular and systematic data collection and reporting on migration and integration has been recognised at political level. The publication of the first and second Austrian reports on migration and integration (Fassmann & Stacher 2003; Fassmann 2007) – a semi-regular report addressing medium-term developments from a scientific perspective and in depth – the launch of a statistical yearbook on migration and integration in 2008 and the launch of a national integration monitoring system all reflect this trend. In addition, the regular availability of statistical data on the population with a migration background has greatly expanded since the late 1990s, both in terms of the groups on which information has become available – the variables 'country of birth' and, more recently, 'country of parents' birth' became systematically available only after 2001 – and in terms of the topics on which data are collected.

At the same time, however, the importance of scientific evidence for policymaking is still rather limited. While scientific evidence or statistical data are used increasingly often to justify policy decisions, more systematic scientific evaluations of policy measures or ex-ante impact analyses of planned measures take place to rather a limited extent.[7] That said, the organisation of the legislative process – all legislative proposals issued by the government are subject to a consultation process – ensures that scientific evidence does play a role in policy evaluation, at least indirectly, as many commentaries to legislative proposals do not just address technical legal issues but also use scientific evidence to assess impacts. Nevertheless, because of the open nature of the consultation process, any commentaries to legislative proposals are treated almost by definition as partisan opinions and scientific evidence does not necessarily carry more weight than less well-founded opinions. In addition, the contested nature of integration as a policy field, and the fact that integration issues often impinge on deeply held beliefs about rights and wrongs in particular areas of policymaking means that scientific evidence itself often becomes part of political struggles between different parties to a debate, as is evident, for example, in the debates about the results of the PISA study. While everyone agrees about the below-par performance of Austrian pupils compared to other countries, the question of who is to blame and what policy conclusions should be drawn from the study is hotly debated. Nevertheless, the very format of the National Action Plan and the definition of specific aims (though not yet necessarily measurable targets) as well the related definition of integration indicators suggests that the role of data will increase in the future.

2.4   Integration reporting and related research in Austria

It was not until the early 1980s that integration became a topic for systematic scientific investigation. Nevertheless, integration remained a fairly marginal issue for much of the 1980s and 1990s, to some degree reflecting the marginality of migration studies in general (Perchinig 2005). The main initial impetus for integration research came from a two-year study on foreign workers, commissioned by the Ministry of Social Administration and the Ministry of Economics and Social Affairs and carried out by a group of researchers at the Institute of Advanced Studies (IHS) in Vienna between 1982 and 1984 (cf. Wimmer 1986). It was not until the mid-1990s that a second major empirical study, similarly based on a large-scale survey but only implemented in Vienna, was conducted, this time no longer focusing on selected groups of non-citizens, but on the broader category of foreign-born persons (cf. Hofinger et al 1998).

An important impetus for integration research also came from a research programme on xenophobia launched by the Austrian Ministry of Science in the mid-1990s, under which some 30 research projects involving more than 70 researchers were funded (König & Menasse-Wiesbauer 2002). Subsequent research programmes launched by the Ministry of Sciences, such as the NODE research programme (*New Orientations in Democracy in Europe*)[8] as well as the increasing availability of European funding, including framework research programmes, funding from the European Refugee and Integration Fund and the Equal and Progress programmes, also had a major impact on integration and migration research in Austria and contributed to a considerable expansion and consolidation of integration research, including quantitative research.[9] In addition, following the launch of the European Migration Network in 2002, several 'state of the art' reports on integration, migration and its impact were published (Ministry of Interior & IOM 2005; IOM & National Contact Point within the European Migration Network 2006), again reflecting the increased interest of government agencies in systematic data collection on migration and integration. Nevertheless, both migration studies as a discipline as well as government reporting on integration and migration remained only weakly institutionalised well into the mid-2000s and continued to depend on individual initiatives and one-off projects.

An important milestone was the publication of the first Austrian report on migration and integration in 2003 (Fassmann & Stacher 2003). Financed by the Ministry of the Interior and the Ministry of Science, its chapters addressed a wide range of issues, including demographic and socioeconomic trends, living conditions, health, family issues and gender, the legal framework for immigration, xenophobia, civic participation and mobilisation of immigrants . The second edition, published in 2007, covered a similarly broad range of topics and reviewed developments since the launch of the first edition. In addition, it also featured a wide range of specific topics covered by recent research projects (cf. Fassmann 2007). At the same time, migration and integration also became increasingly mainstreamed in other government reports, such as the report on the position of women (Bundeskanzleramt 2010)[10] or the report on families (Bundesministerium für Umwelt, Jugend und Familie 1999; Bundesministerium für Wirtschaft, Jugend und Familie 2010). The launch of a statistical yearbook on migration and integration in 2008 (see Statistik Austria & KMI 2011 for the most recent edition), as well as the implementation of a large integration survey between 2007 and 2009, all reflect the mainstreaming of the monitoring of integration and migration and the increasing relevance of statistical data collection (Ulram 2009).

2.5 Data on the integration of immigrants – practices, possibilities and limitations of national statistical data

The Austrian statistical system for migration, integration and discrimination data has been developing rapidly in the past two decades or so. Not only have a variety of new statistical datasets emerged, but the range of available information has also expanded massively.

Citizenship is still the main variable for the identification of persons with a migrant background in migration and integration statistics, although country of birth has become increasingly available in a number of key datasets, including the Mikrozensus/LFS (as of the mid-1990s), the EU-SILC (since its introduction in 2004) and the population register (POPREG, with country of birth available since 2007). In addition, information on country of birth was also collected in the 2001 census. Nevertheless, a variety of administrative datasets still use citizenship as the sole criterion for the identification of persons with a migration background. Except in the case of indigenous ethnic minorities, ethnicity is not used as a statistical concept, although with the concept of 'person with a migration background' that was introduced with the introduction of the variable *parents' country of birth* in the 2008 *Mikrozensus*, a closely related concept has been adopted (Kraler et al. 2009: 8-9). In terms of the monitoring and measurement of the migrant population, Statistics Austria now uses three basic concepts:

1 foreign citizens;
2 persons with a foreign background (non-citizens born in Austria + foreign-born); and
3 persons with a migration background (defined as persons both of whose parents were born abroad).

The first two concepts are available both from surveys and the population registers, while the latter is only available from the *Mikrozensus*.

The main sources for core demographic data and migration control[11] are maintained by Statistics Austria and the Ministry of the Interior, and include data on the total population, migration movements, naturalisations, asylum, the legal status of immigrants and irregular migration. Until the new millennium, the population census (the last of which was conducted in 2001) was a core element of population and social statistics in Austria. While it is still one of the most robust and comprehensive – if somewhat dated – data sources, however, the increasing availability of register-based information in intercensus years and the improved availability and reliability of the *Mikrozensus* (see below) as regards information on immigrants has reduced the central function of the census as a source of information. Moreover, the 2011 census is being conducted as a register-based census. To facilitate this, several new registers have been introduced in the last few years by linking existing registers.

Since the establishment of a Central Register of Residence in 2001, the main data source for the size and structure of the population is the population register (POPREG), in turn based on the Central Register of Residence. The register holds information on the population stocks, migration flows and naturalisations, including information on gender, age, citizenship and country of birth of the person included in the database. Integration-related statistics relating to employment, income, housing, health, education and family characteristics are mainly collected and disseminated by Statistics Austria and/or relevant line ministries. The register on social insurance cases that is maintained by the Main Association of the Austrian Social Insurance Institutions (*Hauptverband der österreichischen Sozialversicherungsträger*) is the main source register for employment and incomes, while the Austrian Public Employment Service (AMS) maintains registers on unemployed persons and on non-nationals whose employment in Austria is subject to approval. The registers on social insurance cases and the unemployment register form the basis for the so-called Labour Market Database (AMDB), which contains information on the employment status, annual income and employer/company of all persons in receipt of social security in Austria (Kraler et al. 2009: 17-18). Other important registers are kept by the Ministry of Health (on child allowance, hospital statistics), while the Federal Provinces (*Bundesländer*) collect statistics on social security benefits (cf. Kraler et al. 2009). While the tax register is already used for national income statistics, it is currently underexploited as regards information on the incomes of immigrants. The planned linkage of the *Mikrozensus* (see below) with tax records is however expected to provide more robust data on individual incomes of immigrants in the future.[12]

While administrative records have many advantages, including their comprehensive coverage and regular updating, the administrative purpose they serve also implies a number of limitations. In particular, the reliability of information that is not essential for the purpose of a particular register is often limited. This applies particularly to country of birth, but also to citizenship. Information on citizenship in the register of social insurance cases, for example, appears not to be updated upon naturalisation and subsequently leads to an overrepresentation of non-citizens in the register and the Labour Market Database that is derived from it (cf. Reichel 2010). A second limitation of registers is the relatively limited range of variables included. In principle, this limitation can – to some extent – be overcome by systematic linkage of different registers. In the Austrian context, however, register linkage is subject to major legal constraints and is only permitted for census purposes. In addition, some information is not available at all from registers.

Against this background, surveys provide an important alternative to register-based information, although they have limitations, too, such as low sample sizes and consequent low numbers of immigrants in the samples, as well as higher non-response rates among immigrants (cf. Kraler & Reichel 2010: 11-13). In Austria, the *Mikrozensus* (LFS) is by far the most important survey in terms of its relevance for issues related to integration

and migration. The survey is conducted quarterly and the sample includes some 22,500 households per quarter. The survey contains rich information on labour market performance, housing and education. Apart from citizenship, country of birth and year of immigration, since 2008 the survey has also provided information on parents' country of birth. A particularly rich source of information on migration and integration is provided by the 2008 ad hoc module on migrants on the labour market.
Other important surveys for migration and integration-related statistics include the EU-SILC survey[13], the Austrian Health Survey (which forms part of the European Health Interview Survey – EHIS) and PISA. In addition, several special surveys targeting only immigrants or certain groups of immigrants and their descendants have been conducted in Austria. Information on attitudes of the general population and xenophobia is available from the European Social Survey and the Eurobarometer (Kraler & Reichel 2010) as well as, albeit more infrequently, from national surveys.

Generally, the introduction of new registers and the related move to a register-based statistical system present new opportunities regarding the availability of data. A major gap to date, however, is the lack of longitudinal datasets, and more particularly longitudinal surveys.[14] In addition, the scope and quality of statistical information on certain topics such as incomes, social security benefits, political participation and crime and justice is currently rather limited and unsatisfactory (Kraler et al. 2009).

2.6 Integration monitoring in Austria

2.6.1 Integration indicators at national level

In 2010, the first report including standardised integration indicators as defined in the NAP was published by Statistics Austria and the Commission for Migration and Integration Research of the Austrian Academy of Science (Statistik Austria & KMI 2010). The aim of the report is to provide frequent measurements of integration in Austria over the long term. Prior to 2010, two yearbooks on migration and integration at national level had already been published by the Austrian Integration Fund in collaboration with Statistics Austria. The 2010 yearbook includes statistical information corresponding to the integration indicators as described below. Areas covered include population size and structure, migration, language and education, employment and occupation, social affairs and health, security, housing and spatial distributions, immigrants' identification with Austria, aspects of immigrants' perception of integration and attitudes of the mainstream population towards immigrants. In addition, the report provides an overview of key characteristics at the level of the Austrian *Bundesländer* (provinces) (Statistik Austria & KMI 2010).

A detailed proposal for integration indicators developed within the framework of the National Action Plan on Integration (NAP) preceded the publication of the Statistical Yearbook on Migration and Integration 2010 (cf. Fassmann 2010). The proposal suggested that the national integration monitoring system be built on three pillars:

1   indicators for basic demographic characteristics of immigrants and their legal status ('framework indicators');
2   a set of core social indicators; and
3   indicators for various specific topics. In so doing, the report attempts to operationalise the areas and topics addressed by the main report resulting from the NAP process.

The framework indicators include statistics on the general population by citizenship, migration background, age, gender, legal status of third-country nationals and length of residence. In addition, the indicators include a variety of flow statistics, including migration flows, asylum applications and decisions, immigration by legal status, births and deaths, fertility rates and naturalisations by citizenship (Fassmann 2010: 48-49).

Table 2.2
Framework indicators

no.	indicator
	stocks
1	resident population by citizenship/MB in the reporting year
2	resident population by citizenship/MB and country of birth in the reporting year
3	resident population by age, gender and citizenship/MB in the reporting year
4	legal residence status of third-country nationals in the reporting year
5	long-term residence (share of non-citizens with a length of residence longer than x years)
	flows
6	immigrations to Austria and emigrations from Austria in the reporting year
7	asylum applications and positive decisions by citizenship in the reporting year
8	legal categorisation of immigration in the reporting year
9	births and deaths by citizenship in the reporting year
10	naturalisations by previous citizenship in the reporting year
11	total fertility rate by citizenship in the reporting year

MB = migration background.

Source: Fassmann 2010: 49 (own translation)

The core indicators on social characteristics of immigrants refer to language and education, employment and occupation, social affairs and health, rule of law and values, housing and spatial context, the social and identification dimension, as well as questions concerning immigrants' and the majority population's perception of integration. Five out of the total of 25 social indicators suggested are regarded as essential in a monitoring system (highlighted in bold in table 2.3). Indicators 1 to 19 can be assigned to certain areas of activity of the NAP. Indicators 20 to 25 do not belong to any of the seven NAP fields, while the areas intercultural dialogue, sports and leisure and rule of law and values (under the heading 'security') are not well covered due to a lack of data on these aspects (Fassmann 2010: 50-52).

Generally, the availability of the statistical data varies greatly between different areas. However, the data basis for several indicators is expected to improve considerably in the near future. Certain statistics are not yet available in the desired form, but the availability of data is expected to improve in the near future, especially following the 2011 census.

Table 2.3
Core indicators on social characteristics of immigrants

no.	indicator	data source (2010 reporting)
	language and education	
1	preschool care rates by age of the child and citizenship	kindergarten statistics ZMR/POPREG
2	children (age 5) with MB and good/inadequate German skills as percentage of all children with MB	BIFIE statistics
3	school students by school type and citizenship	school statistics ZMR/POPREG
4	university/college[15] students by citizenship	statistics of higher education ZMR/POPREG
5	**highest level of education by citizenship/MB**	**register of education /Mikrozensus**
6	share of adolescents (age 15-20) without education by citizenship/MB	school statistics
	employment and occupation	
7	**employment rate by gender, age and citizenship/MB**	**Mikrozensus**
8	self-employment rate by gender and citizenship/MB	Mikrozensus
9	**unemployment rate by gender, age and qualification by citizenship/MB**	**AMS Austria**
10	employed persons by highest level of education and citizenship/MB	AMS Austria
11	long-term unemployed (> 1 year) as percentage of active population by citizenship/MB	AMS Austria
12	youth unemployment – share of persons with MB among unemployed persons younger than 25 years	AMS Austria
	social affairs and health	
13	**net annual income (median) by citizenship/MB**	**statistics Austria/general income report**
14	**risk of poverty and manifest poverty by citizenship/MB**	**EU SILC**
15	life expectancy at birth by gender, citizenship and country of birth	statistics of natural population movement and from the social insurance institutions
16	use of preventive health services (vaccinations, preventive examinations, breast-cancer screening)	Health Interview Survey

Table 2.3 (continued)

no.	indicator	data source (2010 reporting)
	security (rule of law and values)	
17	criminality by age and citizenship (relation of convicts to population of same age and same citizenship)	crime statistics and POPREG
18	victims of crimes by citizenship	Ministry of Interior, police statistics
	housing and spatial context	
19	size of dwelling per capita by citizenship/MB	Mikrozensus
20	relative living costs by citizenship/MB	EU SILC
21	legal status of dwelling by citizenship/MB of head of household	Mikrozensus
22	population by origin and proportion of immigrants in spatial units (municipalities and lower level)	POPREG
	social and identification dimension	
23	marriage statistics by citizenship and country of birth	statistics of marriages
24	naturalisations as percentage of the number of non-nationals with required minimum residence by citizenship	POPREG and naturalisation statistics
	subjective questions on the 'integration climate'	
25	sample surveys with persons with and without MB	opinion polls

MB = migration background. The exact definition of migration background (place of birth, one parent or both immigrated) is still under discussion and also depends on the data source.
Primary core indicators emphasised in bold.

Source: Fassmann 2010 (own translation from German)

Finally, the report proposes four topics for additional in-depth analyses, namely
1 institutional integration capacity;
2 political participation;
3 'integration climate', i.e. immigrants' subjective assessments of their integration in Austria and attitudes of the mainstream population; and
4 education.
The report suggests that these topics be alternated in future editions of the yearbook. The first topic, institutional integration capacity, refers to the capacity of public institutions to deal with a diverse population and, specifically, the recruitment of staff with a migration background. Political participation is suggested as an additional topic both in its own right and because it is considered to be a strong indicator for overall integration. The report proposes the development of research instruments for measuring political participation by persons with a migration history, and possibly the creation of an indicator that could become part of the core indicators on social characteristics of immigrants in future editions of the yearbook. In addition, the report suggests the migration background of political functionaries, notably parliamentarians, as an

additional possible indicator. As regards 'integration climate' and xenophobia, the report suggests developing indicators that measure both xenophobic attitudes of the mainstream population and experiences of hate crimes and harassment. On education, the report suggests using existing major student assessment surveys such as PISA and PIRLS as possible sources for indicators (Fassmann 2010: 56-58).

Even before the development of integration indicators at national level, the city of Vienna had started to develop its own integration monitoring system. Given the key role of Vienna as the largest municipality and province, and its prominent role in debates on integration and migration, we will describe the Viennese integration monitor in rather more depth. Vienna is not the only province which began to develop an integration monitoring system. However, Vienna's 'integration and diversity monitor' is the most elaborate initiative, and in many ways is more comprehensive than the national monitoring system.

2.6.2 The Viennese integration and diversity monitor

The Viennese 'integration and diversity monitor' was launched in April 2010, after more than three years of preparation. It follows a major shift from a classical, minority-oriented integration policy based on special measures to include disadvantaged minorities, to a diversity-oriented integration policy based on the mainstreaming of migration and integration issues across different policy fields. The basic premise of the diversity policy is that inclusion of disadvantaged minorities must go hand in hand with an awareness and acceptance of diversity along the lines of ethnicity, class, gender, sexual orientation and other aspects as a basic condition of contemporary societies. Integration is thus always to be understood as integration into a pluralistic society (cf. Europaforum Wien 2010: 3, 7). The Viennese integration and diversity monitor is a twofold system including an integration monitor that focuses on ongoing integration processes in the city of Vienna, and a diversity monitor that systematically monitors the successful implementation of Viennese diversity management.

The *integration monitor* aims at systematically monitoring key dimensions of integration. For the purpose of the monitoring system, integration is defined as the incorporation of all sections of the population into central domains of society and their active participation in these domains. The areas selected for the integration monitoring system are:

1 basic demographic information;
2 immigration, integration and legal status;
3 education;
4 employment and labour market;
5 income and social security;
6 housing;
7 health;
8 societal and political participation; and
9 general social 'climate', co-existence and security.

Indicators have been defined for each area in order to describe the status quo of the Viennese population as a basis for the strategic development of policies. Altogether, 75 indicators have been defined, which are listed in the Appendix to this chapter. Not all selected indicators were implemented in the first monitoring round, since the basic data for several indicators were not available. The missing indicators are scheduled to be included in future monitors as soon as the required data become available. A major challenge for the first integration monitor was the clarification of the availability of data. The main data sources used are the population register (POPREG), the *Mikrozensus*, the Labour Market Database and the '*Sozialwissenschaftliche Grundlagenforschung Wien*',[16] which is a survey of a total of 8,700 persons. In addition, the integration monitor drew on data from other sources for certain areas, such as the registers of the Ministry of the Interior, the PISA survey and the Austrian Health Survey (Europaforum Wien 2010: 7-10, 17).

Against the background of the results of the integration monitor, the *diversity monitor* is an instrument for measuring how far the Viennese administration has implemented its proposed integration-orientated diversity policy. The diversity monitor is split up into seven areas of activity:
1 'city of diversity' strategy;
2 education, youth and women;
3 employment and entrepreneurship;
4 housing and co-existence;
5 health and social affairs;
6 infrastructure and services; and
7 culture and public space.
For each of these areas of activity, selected administrative units of the city were assessed in terms of:
− their service delivery and customer orientation;
− training and competence of staff; and
− strategy and organisation.

The results of the integration and diversity monitor are presented in a demand profile for integration-oriented diversity policy in each of the thematic areas covered, along three dimensions. The first dimension – 'demography and society/status quo and future' – presents the results of the integration monitoring; the second dimension – 'policy and programmes' – presents the city's basic policy approach towards individual themes, while the third dimension – 'organisation and action' – presents the results of the diversity monitor and is concerned with specific measures and practices of individual parts of the city administration. The objective of the Vienna integration and diversity monitor is to enable systematic monitoring of policy implementation and the identification of future challenges (cf. Europaforum Wien 2010: 11). The integration and diversity monitor is scheduled to be conducted every two years. To sum up, the Vienna integration and diversity monitor goes well beyond the integration monitoring at national level and links integration monitoring more closely to actual policymaking. Its impact on actual policymaking, however, remains to be seen.

2.7   Conclusions

Reflecting broader European trends, integration monitoring has received increasing attention from policymakers, academics and practitioners in Austria in recent years, at both national and regional level. On the national level, the Ministry of the Interior has emerged as the lead actor in integration policymaking and as such has driven the process leading to the National Action Plan on Integration and the related definition of integration indicators. These indicators were first published in 2010 and a second edition was published in July 2011. At the same time, the city of Vienna began developing an alternative model for integration monitoring at provincial level in the form of an integration and diversity monitor, based on a total of 75 indicators and with a specific format designed to support the systematic monitoring of diversity policies at city level. In this sense, the Viennese integration monitoring system goes much further than the national integration monitor.

Apart from the challenge of defining and operationalising integration – the differences between the national and Viennese monitoring systems have arguably mainly to do with different views on how to define integration – one of the main challenges in measuring integration is the availability of relevant data, and in particular the regular availability of relevant indicators between census dates. While data availability has considerably improved, particularly since the turn of the millennium, large gaps remain. In addition, the implementation of a register-based census in 2011 implies that certain data, including information on family members and households, religion, colloquial language use at home and educational attainment will no longer be comprehensively available for the whole population, as such information is either not available at all, or not in sufficient quality from the source registers. While the population register, in common with most large-scale surveys conducted in Austria, now permits the identification of migrants by citizenship and country of birth, many registers still use only citizenship as the main variable to identify migrants. In addition, the quality of information on citizenship is often deficient.

Measuring immigrant integration according to a predefined list of indicators also raises methodological and ethical issues. First, bivariate statistics on socioeconomic outcomes disaggregated by citizenship, country of birth or migration background are suggestive – they suggest that migration status is indeed the main explanatory factor for any particular outcome, whereas in reality other demographic characteristics such as age, sex, education and qualifications may be more important. The correlations between migration background and socioeconomic outcomes may thus be spurious and in fact due to other background factors that are not included in the analysis. Although researchers might be aware of these conceptual and methodological issues, the broader public may not, and may incorrectly understand differences in terms of migration background. Any presentation of statistics should therefore always be combined with theoretical discussions and explanations. Secondly, the selection of categories for indicators that are to be produced frequently has the effect of institutionalising certain categories of persons, such as non-nationals or immigrants. Although a monitoring system might not be a source for categorisations, its repeated use contributes to the manifestation of certain population groups and consequently to stereotyping.

On the other hand, the institutionalisation of integration monitoring also has a major positive effect, namely that the integration of immigrants remains on the political agenda, something that has not always been the case in the past.

Annex: List of indicators in the Viennese integration monitor 2009[17]

Note: Where possible, all indicators are broken down by gender, age, citizenship, country of birth, and parents' country of birth.

no.	indicator

demography: basic information on the Viennese population

1	foreign-born persons
2	foreign-born persons by length of residence
3	foreign nationals by length of residence
4	distribution of foreign-born persons by age at beginning of residence
5	persons by age groups by country of birth and gender
6	immigrations and emigrations by country of birth as a share of the population with the same country of birth
7	immigrations and emigrations by country of citizenship
8	live births by mother's and father's country of birth, respectively
9	live births by citizenship of the child
10	deaths by citizenship
11	number of deceased persons by country of birth
12	marriages by citizenship
13	existing cohabitations by country of birth of both partners
14	divorce rates
15	population by country of birth in the smallest spatial units

immigration, integration and legal status

16	persons by legal status (residence/immigration)
17	number of residence titles/permits by length of residence
18	number of asylum-seekers in Vienna with/without basic care (*Grundversorgung*)
19	number of persons with subsidiary protection status by length of residence
20	number of persons living in Vienna with asylum status granted
21	non-nationals born in Austria as a percentage of all naturalisations
22	naturalisations as a percentage of all foreign nationals
23	naturalisations by age groups
24	non-nationals born in Austria as a percentage of all foreign nationals/total population
25	number of valid permanent work permits (*Befreiungsscheine or similar*)

education

26	population by highest education level attained
27	share of persons aged 15-24 years who are currently in education higher than compulsory education by country of birth of parents
28	school students by school types
29	children aged 2-5 years attending Kindergarten or similar institution
30	apprentices by citizenship and country of birth
31	children with need for support (*Förderbedarf*)
32	annual number of persons completing an apprenticeship

no.	indicator
33	school students with mother tongue other than German in the 8th grade of grammar school (*ahs*)
34	school students without Austrian citizenship in the 8th grade of grammar school (*ahs*)
35	university students by citizenship (educational residents)
36	teachers and lecturers (*Lehrkräfte*) not born in Austria/not holding Austrian citizenship by school types

employment and labour market

37	employment rate among population of working age
38	employment rate by country, in which highest education level was attained
39	working time of the population broken down by country, in which the highest education level was attained
40	population of working age with compulsory social insurance
41	annual average share of employed persons and share of persons in education
42	marginally employed persons (*geringfügig Beschäftigte*)
43	average number of days employed with social insurance per year, employed persons
44	employed persons by legal status of employment (blue-collar (*ArbeiterInnen*), white-collar (*Angestellte*), civil servants (*öffentlich Bedienstete*))
45	employed persons by economic sector
46	self-employed persons
47	share of all employed persons employed through temporary staffing agencies/leasing agencies
48	unemployment rate

income and social security

49	average annual gross income of blue and white-collar workers
50	net equivalent income (standardised non-household income)
51	persons in receipt of unemployment allowances and social security benefits (*Notstandshilfe*)
52	retired persons with additional social allowances (*Ausgleichszulage*)

housing

53	population by categories of standard of dwellings (categories A, B, C and D)
54	population by legal status of dwellings
55	size and number of household members of dwelling (square metres per person, number of rooms/ square metres of dwellings)
56	receipt of housing allowances (*Wohnbauförderung and Wohnbeihilfe*)
57	total housing costs as percentage of income

health

58	average age at time of death
59	relative number of causes of death
60	use of preventive health examinations
61	main clinical diagnoses
62	average sick leave days per year/length of hospital stays
63	use of care services

no.	indicator
	societal and political participation
64	persons entitled to vote in local elections (*kommunalem Wahlrecht*)
65	voter turnout
66	members of district representative bodies, municipal council /national parliament
67	members of *Interessensvertretungen* (elected representatives in several official Austrian employer and employee associations – *Kammern, oegb-FunktionärInnen, BetreibsrätInnen*)
68	elected students' representatives by school type
69	households with access to the Internet
	societal climate, co-existence and security
70	persons who are (not) satisfied with their quality of life
71	persons satisfied with residential area/neighbourhood
72	persons who (do not) feel secure in Vienna
73	persons feeling discriminated against/persons who have experienced discrimination
74	victims of crimes
75	number of convictions

Notes

1   However, in the 1980s the Ministry of Social Affairs and, more specifically, the labour market administration (then a unit of the Ministry) pursued a more proactive integration policy, though this was limited to unemployed 'guest workers' and to labour market programmes (Interview with Heidi Fenzl, former Head of the Integration Unit at the Ministry of the Interior, 29 August 2006). These programmes were discontinued in the 1990s.

2   'Fekter richtet Expertenrat für Integration ein', OTS press release, 10.6.2010. Consulted online on 4 December 2010 at http://www.ots.at/presseaussendung/OTS_20100610_OTS0158/fekter-richtet-expertenrat-fuer-integration-ein.

3   Cf. http://www.bmi.gv.at/cms/BMI_staatssekretaer/ Consulted online on 06 July 2011.

4   Staatsbürgerschaftsgesetznovelle 1998: BGBl. I Nr. 124/1998.

5   *Integrationsvereinbarung.*

6   See http://www.integrationsfonds.at/de/nap/ Consulted online on 6 February 2010.

7   Evaluations or impact analyses are usually carried out by policy units of relevant ministries themselves and do not necessarily investigate impacts in a systematic manner.

8   See http://www.node-research.at (2002-2007).

9   Three notable recent studies which are based on large-scale surveys and investigate various dimensions of integration include the FP5 project LIMITS (Immigrants and Ethnic Minorities in European Cities: Life-courses and Quality of Life in a World of Limitations, see https://www.zsi.at/en/publikationen/349/2013.html); the TIES project (see http://www.tiesproject.eu/) focusing on the second generation; and the Six Country Immigrant Integration Comparative Survey (SCIICS, see http://www.wzb.eu/zkd/mit/projects/projects_sciics.en.htm), all of which were international comparative projects with Austria/Austrian cities as case studies.

10 The report contains a separate chapter on the situation of female migrants. By contrast, the first report on the situation of women in 1995 did not consider migration background as a key social characteristic (see Bundesministerium für Frauenangelegenheiten/Bundeskanzleramt 1995).

11 See for more detail: Kraler et al. (2009).

12 Personal communication, Josef Kytir (Statistics Austria), November 2010.

13 EU-SILC stands for European Union Statistics on Income and Living Conditions.

14 Many registers are in principle usable as longitudinal databases, but have so far not been adapted for longitudinal research purposes.

15 *Fachhochschule.*

16 Literally translated: Basic Research in the Social Sciences Vienna.

17 Free translation from German by authors, the full list is taken from the full report on the Viennese Integration Monitoring, p. 13-15. Consulted online at http://www.wien.gv.at/integration/monitor.html in April 2010.

References

Austrian Integration Fund (2009). *Migration & Integration. Zahlen, Daten, Fakten 2009*. Vienna: Ministry of the Interior, Statistics Austria, Austrian Integration Fund (Consulted online in February 2009 at www.integration.at).

Bauböck, Rainer & Bernhard Perchinig (2006). Migrations- und Integrationspolitik. In: Herbert Dachs et al. (eds.), *Politik in Österreich. Das Handbuch*. Vienna: Manz.

Biffl, Gudrun (2007). Erwerbstätigkeit und Arbeitslosigkeit: die Bedeutung von Einbürgerung, Herkunftsregion und Religionszugehörigkeit. In: Heinz Fassmann (ed.), *2. Österreichischer Migrations- und Integrationsbericht. 2001-2006. Rechtliche Rahmenbedingungen, demographische Entwicklungen, sozioökonomische Strukturen* (p. 265-282). Klagenfurt: Drava.

Bundesministerium für Umwelt, Jugend und Familie (1999). *Familie – zwischen Anspruch und Alltag. Österreichischer Familienbericht 1999*. Consulted online in December 2010 at www.bmwfj.gv.at/Familie/Familienforschung/Seiten/4Familienbericht1999.aspx.

Bundesministerium für Wirtschaft, Jugend und Familie (2010). *5. Familienbericht 1999-2009. Die Familie an der Wende zum 21. Jahrhundert*. Consulted online in December 2010 at http://www.bmwfj.gv.at/Familie/Familienforschung/Seiten/5Familienbericht.aspx.

Ministry of the Interior/IOM (2005). *Integrationspraktiken in Österreich. Eine Landkarte über Integrationspraktiken and –philosophien von Bund, Ländern und Sozialpartnern*. Vienna: Ministry of the Interior/IOM.

Bruckner, René et al. (2005). *Fremdenrechtspaket. Asylgesetz 2005, Fremdenpolizeigesetz 2005, Niederlassungs- und Aufenthaltsgesetz*. Vienna/Graz: Manz.

Cinar, Dilek & Harald Waldrauch (2006). Austria. In: Rainer Bauböck et al. (eds.), *Acquisition and Loss of Nationality. Volume 2: Country Analyses. Policies and Trends in 15 European Countries* (p. 19-62). Amsterdam: Amsterdam University Press.

Europaforum Wien (2010). *Integrations- und Diversitätsmonitor der Stadt Wien 2009*. Prepared on behalf of the city of Vienna/MA 17.

Fassmann, Heinz & Rainer Münz (1995). *Einwanderungsland Österreich? Historische Migrationsmuster, aktuelle Trends und politische Maßnahmen*. Vienna: Jugend und Volk / Dachs Verlag.

Fassmann, Heinz & Irene Stacher (2003). *Österreichischer Migrations- und Integrationsbericht. Demographische Entwicklungen, sozioökonomische Strukturen, rechtliche Rahmenbedingungen*. Klagenfurt: Drava.

Fassmann, Heinz (2007). 2. Österreichischer Migrations- und Integrationsbericht. 2001-2006. Demographische Entwicklungen, sozioökonomische Strukturen, rechtliche Rahmenbedingungen. Klagenfurt: Drava.

Fassmann, Heinz (2010). Integrationsindikatoren des Nationalen Aktionsplans für Integration. Begriffe, Beispiele, Implementierung. Consulted online in March 2010 at www.integration.at

Hofinger, Christoph et al. (1998). Einwanderung und Niederlassung II. Soziale Kontakte, Diskriminierungserfahrungen, Sprachkenntnisse, Bleibeabsichten, Arbeitsmarktintegration und Armutsgefährdung der ausländischen Wohnbevölkerung in Wien (research report). Vienna: IHS/SORA.

Hofmann, Martin & David Reichel (2008). Chechen Migration Flows to Europe – a Statistical Perspective. In: Alexander Janda, N. Leitner & Matthias Vogl (eds.), Chechens in the European Union (p. 9-26). Österreichischer Integrationfonds / Austrian Federal Ministry of the Interior.

IOM / National Contact Point within the European Migration Network (2006). The Impact of Immigration on Austria's Society. Vienna: IOM (Consulted online in December 2010 at http://www.emn.at/studien.html).

König, Ilse & Elisabeth Menasse-Wiesbauer (2002). Vorwort. In: Heinz Fassmann (ed.) et al. Zuwanderung und Segregation. Europäische Metropolen im Vergleich (p. 7-8). Klagenfurt: Drava.

König, Karin & Bettina Stadler (2003). Entwicklungstendenzen im öffentlich-rechtlichen und demokratiepolitischen Bereich. In: Heinz Fassmann & Irene Stacher (eds.), Österreichischer Migrations- und Integrationsbericht. Demographische Entwicklungen, sozioökonomische Strukturen, rechtliche Rahmenbedingungen (p. 226-260). Klagenfurt: Drava.

Kraler, Albert & Irene Stacher (2002). Austria – Migration and Asylum Patterns and Policies in the 19th and 20th Century. In: Historische Sozialkunde. Geschichte – Fachdidaktik – Politische Bildung, International Migration. Problems – Prospects – Policies, vol. 51-65, no. 32 (special issue 2002).

Kraler, Albert et al. (2009). Prominstat. Country Report Austria. National Data Collection Systems and Practices. Consulted online in February 2010 at www.prominstat.eu

Kraler, Albert & David Reichel (2009). Austria. In: Martin Baldwin-Edwards & Albert Kraler (eds.), REGINE. Regularisations in Europe (p.175-185). Amsterdam: Pallas Publications.

Kraler, Albert & David Reichel (2010). Quantitative data in the area of migration, integration and discrimination in Europe – an overview (Prominstat Working Paper No. 01). Consulted online in March 2010 at www.prominstat.eu

Lebhart, Gustav & Stephan Marik-Lebeck (2007). Demographische Strukturen und Entwicklungen. In: Heinz Fassmann (2007), 2. Österreichischer Migrations- und Integrationsbericht. 2001-2006. Demographische Entwicklungen, sozioökonomische Strukturen, rechtliche Rahmenbedingungen (p. 145-162). Klagenfurt: Drava.

Ministry of the Interior (2010). Nationaler Aktionsplan für Integration. Bericht. Consulted online in March 2010 at http://www.integrationsfonds.at/de/nap/bericht/

Perchinig, Bernhard (2010). Migration Studies in Austria – Research at the Margins? (KMI Working Paper 4/2005). Consulted online at http://www.oeaw.ac.at/kmi/working-papers.htm.

Reichel, David (2010). Einbürgerungen in der österreichischen Arbeitsmarktdatenbank – eine Evaluierung der Erfassung des Merkmals –Staatsbürgerschaft– auf Basis von HV- und AMS-Daten (report prepared for the Ministry of Work, Social Affairs and Consumer Protection. ICMPD Working Paper 3). Consulted online at http://research.icmpd.org.

Statistik Austria (2009a). Wanderungsstatistik. Revidierte Ergebnisse für 2005 bis 2007. Erstellt am: 27.05.2009. Consulted online on 12 January 2010 at http://www.statistik.at/web_de/statistiken/bevoelkerung/wanderungen/index.html

Statistik Austria (2009b). Arbeits- und Lebenssituation von Migrantinnen und Migranten in Österreich. Modul der Arbeitskräfteerhebung 2008. Vienna: Statistik Austria.

Statistik Austria (2009c): *Modul Arbeitsmarktsituation von Migrantinnen und Migranten in Österreich. Technicher Bericht*. Vienna: Statistik Austria.

Statistik Austria/KMI (2010). *Migration & Integration. Zahlen. Daten. Indikatoren 2010*. Vienna: Statistik Austria/ KMI.

Statistik Austria/KMI (2011). *Migration & Integration. Zahlen. Daten. Indikatoren 2011*. Vienna: Statistik Austria/ KMI.

Thienel, Rudolf (2007). Integration als rechtliche Querschnittsmaterie. In: Heinz Fassmann (2007). *2. Österreichischer Migrations- und Integrationsbericht. 2001-2006. Demographische Entwicklungen, sozioökonomische Strukturen, rechtliche Rahmenbedingungen* (p. 83-126). Klagenfurt: Drava.

Ulram, Peter (2009). *Integration in Österreich. Einstellungen, Orientierungen, und Erfahrungen von MigrantInnen und Angehörigen der Mehrheitsbevölkerung*. Vienna: Gfk Austria / Ministry of Interior.

Wimmer, Hannes (ed.) (1986). *Ausländische Arbeitskräfte in Österreich*. Frankfurt/Main/New York: Campus.

3   Monitoring integration in Belgium

Towards comprehensive and structural outcome measurement

Didier Boone

3.1   A history of immigration and integration policies in Belgium

By 1945, following World War II, Belgian coal production had declined drastically.
Despite efforts to improve the working conditions and salaries for coal miners, domestic recruitment dried up, forcing the authorities to look to foreign labour – a policy the
government had pursued before the War. Beginning with Italy in 1946, and continuing
with Spain (1956), Greece (1957), Morocco (1964), Turkey (1964), Tunisia (1969), Algeria
(1970) and Yugoslavia (1970), the government pursued several bilateral agreements.
When a crisis struck the coal industry in the early 1970s, these immigrant workers left to
find employment in other industries such as iron and steel, chemicals, construction, and
transportation.

In the early 1960s, when the demand for labour was still strong, the Ministry of Justice
stopped strictly applying the legislation governing immigration. A work permit was no
longer considered a prerequisite for a residence permit. In this sense, the market and
public policy conspired to encourage clandestine immigration. Many immigrant workers arrived in Belgium as tourists, looking for a job. Only later did they formalise their
residence in the country. This arrangement was implicitly accepted by employers and
tolerated by the immigration authorities.

The worsening economic situation and rising unemployment in the late 1960s, however, demanded a new response. In 1967, the government ended this clandestine route
of entry by returning to a strict application of immigration legislation. New laws were
passed to control the granting of work permits; the goal was to control and regulate the
flows of immigrants into the country in line with economic needs.

At the end of the 1960s, an economic recession and a rise in unemployment once again
forced the government to review its policy on allowing immigrants to enter the employment market. In March 1969, the Ministry for Employment and Work proposed three
measures designed to cut the awarding of work permits. In one fell swoop, the government refused to grant new work permits and to regularise foreigners who had arrived as
tourists but continued to stay in the country as workers. Next, the government pushed
forward with legislation that would prevent immigrants from gaining employment in
any other industry apart from the one for which they had been authorised to stay. It also
wanted to expel unemployed foreigners.

Nonetheless, these measures did not stop the arrival of immigrant workers. As a result
of the rise in unemployment and economic difficulties faced by some industries that
used a great deal of foreign labour, the government hardened its immigration policy by
introducing two new measures: an official ban on immigration and an increase in the
sanctions on employers who sought out new immigrant workers.

On 1 August 1974, by means of a simple decision of the Belgian Cabinet, the government imposed a strict limit on new immigration, allowing entry only for people with qualifications that were not already available in the host country. This decision, which was similar to the official ban on immigration, was also accompanied by a policy on legalising foreigners residing clandestinely in Belgium. This latter measure benefited some 9,000 foreigners, who were granted residence permits in 1975.

As in other European countries, officially halting all new immigration of foreign workers did not stop immigration. Furthermore, the government's various initiatives to persuade certain immigrant workers to return to their country of origin were also not successful. Thus, in the case of Belgium, the official ban on recruiting new unqualified foreign workers that was adopted in 1974 never resulted in complete closure of the borders. In fact, Belgium has never ceased to be a country of immigration, although immigration happens to a lesser extent than in the past. The nature of immigration has simply changed since 1974, especially with regard to the types of immigration and the national origins of the migrants.

One of the modern-day types of immigration involves nationals from member states of the European Union. Thanks to the free movement of labour in the EU, many people come to live and work in Belgium. For example, the number of French and Dutch people residing in Belgium has been constantly rising since 1991. European nationals account for a significant share of the increasing number of foreigners in Belgium.

It was only in the mid-1980s that the government began to develop policies to encourage immigrants to settle in Belgium and to foster their inclusion in society. Three distinct periods characterise the new focus on integration.

In December 1980, the law on the entry, residence, settlement and return of foreigners, which is still in force, was passed unanimously. This law provided more legal security regarding residence. Most importantly, it introduced a legal process for foreigners to contest measures questioning the legality of their residency. This culminated in the passage in 1981 of a law to curb racism, and the refusal to grant voting rights to foreigners at community level.

In the mid-1980s, immigrants had become the political scapegoats for persistent unemployment during election periods. It was clear, however, that a policy of expulsion was politically unacceptable. In an effort to achieve a compromise, the government implemented a policy to encourage immigrants to return to their home countries (which had no notable effect), whilst at the same time establishing an integration policy. With tensions at their peak, the government introduced the new Nationality Code in 1984, reforming the Code dating from 1932, which established the principle of *jus soli* and simplified the procedure for naturalisation. Children born on Belgian soil of foreign parents who themselves were born in Belgium became Belgian citizens. Although simplified, the naturalisation process still required individuals to demonstrate a 'desire to integrate', which was measured arbitrarily by the administration.

The third period began in 1989 with the creation of the Royal Commissioner for the Policy on Immigrants. The position was introduced following the large electoral gains by the extreme right in Flanders and Antwerp. In fact, the centre of gravity of the 'immigrant problem' shifted. While the problems of coexistence between Belgians and immigrants in Brussels had made headlines in the 1980s, immigration flared up as a problem in Flanders in the 1990s. The upswing in support for the extreme right and the revolt in certain Brussels neighbourhoods by young immigrants denouncing discrimination, in particular by the police, forced the government to introduce new social policies aimed at improving relations between Belgians and foreigners and at improving conditions in the neighbourhoods where many immigrants lived. The new policies covered fields as wide-ranging as regional planning, culture, education, professional training and combating petty crime. In the 1990s, the Centre for Equal Opportunities and Opposition to Racism was created and entrusted with the task of fighting all forms of racial discrimination. It took over from the Royal Commissioner for the Policy on Immigrants.

3.2 Migrants in Belgium: facts and figures

In 2009, the number of foreign citizens in Belgium was 971,000 in absolute values. This corresponds to 9.1% of the total population. The major countries of origin were Italy (169,000, 17.4%), France (130,000, 13.4%), the Netherlands (123,500, 12.7%), Morocco (79,900, 8.2%) and Spain (42,700, 4.4%).

3.3 Belgian integration policies: regional competencies in a federal context

In the 1980s, integration of foreigners became the competence of the three Belgian Communities (the French, Flemish and German-speaking Communities). Since then, important institutional changes have occurred. In the Brussels-Capital Region, the Flemish Community Commission and the French Community Commission have been the competent body with regard to the integration of foreigners since 1989. In 1994, the French Community transferred parts of its competence with regard to the integration of foreigners in the French Community to the Walloon Region and to the French Community Commission of the Brussels-Capital Region. Meanwhile, the federal authority retains overall responsibility for a number of relevant policy programmes (e.g. funds for urban policies and security); some of those programmes provide support and funds for integration policies designed by the Region and Communities (e.g. Federal Impulse Funds for Immigrant Policy). As a consequence, different authority levels can (and do) espouse different integration policies, which implies that any description of the 'Belgian integration policy' consists of a presentation of the different policy options taken at every level.

The overall objectives as set out in the Flemish Decrees on Integration and Civic Integration (*inburgering*) aim towards the active participation of all citizens (irrespective of their origin) in society, while developing social cohesion. Therefore, the Flemish Integration Policy (*integratiebeleid*) targets the whole of society. Every individual (first and second generation, Western and non-Western, etc.) is expected to cooperate in order to attain active and shared citizenship for all. Simultaneously, special attention is given to:

1 citizens with legal and long-term residence status who did not have Belgian national-ity at birth – or have at least one parent without Belgian nationality at birth; and
2 citizens without a legal residence permit who require specific guidance.

The Flemish Civic Integration Policy (*Inburgeringsbeleid*) targets all foreigners with resi-dence rights in Belgium (except for asylum-seekers whose procedure has not exceeded four months and people residing in the territory with a specific and temporary purpose) and Belgians born abroad who have at least one parent born abroad.

The Walloon Decree on Integration underlines the importance of defining the specific needs and developing the required strategies for foreigners and all people of foreign origin. The overall aim of this Integration Policy is to achieve social cohesion, with par-ticular attention for underdeveloped neighbourhoods and precarious living conditions.

3.4   What does the 'integration package' offered to foreigners contain?

In Flanders (excluding the Brussels Region) the integration programme (*inburgeringstra-ject*)[1] consists of a primary training programme which is coordinated by the reception centre (*onthaalbureau*)[2] and complemented by individual guidance. The training pro-gramme comprises a Dutch language course, a social orientation course and a career orientation course. Additionally, individual guidance is provided throughout the pri-mary integration programme by one reference person from the reception centre, which means that the training programme is tailored in terms of length and content to the needs of each person on the programme.

The secondary programme consists of assistance, education or training delivered by public services, educational institutions or social aid providers following success-ful completion of the primary programme. As part of the secondary programme, the Flemish Public Office for Employment (VDAB) has developed training programmes for migrant job-seekers (*inwerking*) which include job-specific language training.

The package offered in the Brussels-Capital Region is similar to that in Flanders. However, the amount of social orientation hours differs and the participation is never obligatory.

In addition to integration programmes, the Flemish Community develops policy with regard to empowerment and participation of ethnic and cultural minorities. In this respect key actors have been officially recognised and receive structural funding.

In addition to offering the standard Flemish integration programme, the Flemish Com-munity Commission of the Brussels-Capital Region supports a number of non-profit organisations that assist, valorise and help organise migrants and ethnic minority communities.

Following the initiatives by the French Community Commission of the Brussels-Capital Region, many public and private initiatives are financially supported to improve the gen-eral social cohesion and the integration of migrants and ethnic minorities. The overall objectives of this social cohesion policy are to enhance active citizenship and maintain social cohesion in a socially and culturally diverse society. This implies that social links have to be created between individuals and between groups. Proximity is therefore a key dimension that has to be taken into account when designing projects.[3] Reception of newcomers is approached as a global issue that is to be addressed through networking with existing social care providers, health care providers, guidance services, etc. Particular attention is given to French language courses.

The Walloon Region launched the creation of seven Regional Integration Centres in Wallonia (*Centres Régionaux d'intégration*). Within its respective regional territory, each Integration Centre can develop initiatives such as individual guidance with respect to training, vocational orientation and integration of foreigners and people of foreign origin (including assistance and orientation with housing, health, employment and social integration); promotion of social and cultural participation of foreigners and promotion of intercultural dialogue; support for public services and non-profit organisations who have to deal with a foreign public (e.g. through staff training); networking and consultation with local actors; statistical data collection and creation of statistical indicators; dissemination of useful information (including statistical information) for the integration of foreigners and people of foreign origin; and evaluation of local integration initiatives subsidised by the Walloon Region.

In addition to the above policies specifically targeting foreigners, these target groups are also entitled to access adult education, literacy classes, vocational training, regional public offices for employment, public centres for social aid, etc. in all Communities and Regions. All these educational institutions, training providers and public services are open to everyone, although legal residence on the Belgian territory is often required.

3.5 Which categories of foreigners can benefit from the integration measures?

In Flanders (excluding the Brussels Region), the following categories of foreigners are *entitled* to take part in primary integration programmes: foreigners aged 18 and over who reside permanently in Flanders or in the Brussels-Capital Region; and Belgian nationals who were not born in Belgium and at least one of whose parents was not born in Belgium. This means that both the nationality and residence criterion are applied.
Within the two categories described above, participation in a primary integration programme is *compulsory* for foreigners who receive their first residence permit valid for more than three months; people who acquired Belgian nationality abroad and settle in the Belgian territory for the first time; asylum-seekers who claimed asylum longer than four months ago (they only have to attend the social orientation course); foreign religious personnel of officially recognised religions in Belgium.
In addition, all foreigners and persons of foreign origin can *benefit*, on a voluntary basis, from integration measures related to empowerment and participation of ethno-cultural minorities, which sometimes includes undocumented migrants. If residing in the Brussels-Capital Region, all foreigners entitled to take part in the primary integration

programme (as described above) can benefit from all or part of the programme without any obligation.

As regards the initiatives by the Flemish Community Commission and the French Community Commission of the Brussels-Capital Region, all foreigners and persons of foreign origin – which might include undocumented migrants – can benefit from the offer. The same applies to the Walloon Region.

It should be added that in both the French and the Flemish Communities, school-age children[4] of newcomers (including undocumented migrants) can benefit from adapted programmes when they enrol in schools for the first time. Reception classes (also called 'welcome classes' or *classes passerelles*, or *onthaalklassen*) are transitional classes for new-comers with a special focus on language learning and individual guidance.

3.6 Belgian monitoring instruments: unity in diversity

A quick view of the monitoring instruments currently constructed in Belgium (federal and regional level), reveals the existence of different approaches aimed at comparable goals.

On the *federal level*, a first monitoring project is the Socioeconomic monitoring of the labour market by national origin.[5] This monitoring proposes a methodology based on objective, anonymous and aggregated data stemming from existing administrative data-bases. It is important to stress each of these characteristics, as this monitoring aims to be a recurrent administrative process applied to the entire active population. This means that no registration (for example by 'self-identification') would take place.

A second project has been labelled the 'Diversity Barometer', a tool for measuring diversity which is currently being developed by the Centre for Equal Opportunities with support from the federal and the different regional Belgian authorities. A combination of research methodologies such as discrimination testing, statistical analysis of existing data, surveys, etc. is proposed for the future analysis and measurement of the degree of discrimination faced by different minority groups. The objective will therefore be to identify the difficulties which might be encountered by ethnic minorities, people with a disability, lesbians, gays, bisexuals and transgenders, people within certain age categories, women/men when accessing the labour market, education and housing. Additionally, a 'Tolerance Survey' based on a quantitative poll of 1,400 test subjects measures the attitudes of native Belgians towards ethno-cultural diversity, as well as feelings, behaviour and negative (racism, xenophobia, ethnocentrism) or positive (tolerance, trust, etc. opinions about ethnic minorities.[6]

On the *Flemish Regional level*, another longitudinal instrument is the 'Integration Map' (Vlaamse Integratiekaart).[7] The purpose of this instrument is to map out the current status and highlight possible trends in integration in Flanders on a regular basis.[8]

The 'Integration Map' is constructed on different pillars. It consists of:
- monitoring of existing databases (linking data on social security to the National Register);
- a face-to-face survey on integration.

Additionally, case studies are used to underpin the results of the research.

At the *Walloon Regional level*, a 'Synthetic indicator for access to fundamental rights' proposes to measure the degree of social cohesion in every Walloon municipality. For the moment, this indicator only evaluates the current situation in accessing those rights (e.g. a decent income, health care, housing, labour market). However, indicators for evaluating the practical success of social cohesion policies will be constructed together with local actors in the near future. Evaluation will then be carried out on an annual basis.

As regards the *Brussels Capital Region*, there is as yet no consensus on indicators that are likely to be developed and on how monitoring should be conceived. For the moment ad hoc evaluations are carried out in different policy domains.

The above summary may provide a first insight into the monitoring instruments and indicators currently being developed in Belgium.

3.7 Putting monitoring into practice: organising the collection of data on origin

Given the fairly comprehensive and structural approach to integration monitoring in Belgium, it would be of particular interest to explain the procedures relating to the centralised data collection in the National Register.

Specific procedures have been set up for the administrative data collection. Data applications must be submitted to a Sectoral Committee of the National Register. This Committee, which includes representatives of the Belgian Privacy Commission, will assess the application in order to formulate its opinion. If a positive opinion is formulated, authorization is given to the 'Crossroads Bank for Social Security' for data collection and data structuring. Anonymised data will then be delivered to the client. It goes without saying that this Crossroads Bank plays quite an important role in the delivery of integrated statistical information for research purposes.

In the assessment of data applications, the Sectoral Committee will usually attach certain conditions relating to privacy protection and proportionality.

In order to respect the private life of individuals, the risks of re-identification must be excluded throughout the entire monitoring process. Therefore, the proposed methodology needs to be clearly defined and must rule out the possibility of revealing an individual's identity through their National Register Number. Only then will data be considered to be fully anonymous. It must not be possible to retrieve the identity or original personal data of an individual from the results generated. Although the privacy conditions still have to pass the Sectoral Committee assessment, they are already covered in the Crossroads Bank procedures. The Crossroads Bank is authorised to link data on origin to socioeconomic data on the basis of the National Register Number, but will remove this identification key when delivering the requested data linkage.

In addition, the requested data must be proportionate to the objectives set by the monitoring system. This means that the requested data should not be excessive in relation to the ultimate objective and must not be used by the researchers for other purposes. For example, the objective of the socioeconomic monitoring has been clearly defined as 'better combating the discrimination on the labour market', starting from the legal basis of each of the institutions involved. The relevant variables have then been identified on this basis.

3.8   Making monitoring systems work: what are the first results and what is the added value?

At the present time, in 2011, it could be said that Belgium has made a fair amount of progress in terms of methodology-building. The design of the various instruments currently under construction is fairly robust. Although the first results may appear quite provisional, they form a good basis for the further implementation of indicators and monitoring systems.

With regard to the proposed methodology for the *socioeconomic monitoring of the labour market*, a technical working group[9] has submitted a data request to the National Register as a means of pre-testing the availability and relevance of the data on the origin of the entire population (2009). Among other variables (period of registration in the National Register, period of naturalisation), the National Register was requested to supply data on the first nationality of the person concerned, their place of birth, the first nationality of both parents and the place of birth of both parents.[10]

These National Register data were analysed in May 2010. This initial analysis showed that data on origin are available for about 90% of the entire active population (aged 20-60 years). This leads to the clear conclusion that there is sufficient information for linking variables on origin to socioeconomic variables as contained in the Data Warehouse of the Crossroads Bank for Social Security.[11]

The high reliability of the pre-test results (including a favourable prognosis for the growing quality of data over time) affirms the methodological choice for a recurrent administrative process which relies mainly on existing National Register data and does not require additional data production. During the coming months, the monitoring working group will therefore seek to remove potential institutional obstacles to the structural implementation of the proposed methodology.

At this stage, the aim is to make the instrument fully operational by the end of 2011. In order to draft a consistent authorisation request to the Sectoral Committee, the working group will have to apply for further guidelines from the Privacy Commission / National Register / Crossroads Bank for Social Security. If a positive opinion is received, the first implementation of the labour market monitoring could begin. In the longer term, it would be reasonable to call for the introduction of variables on origin in the Data Warehouse of the Crossroads Bank, making permanent monitoring on origin even more operable and transferable to other policy domains.

Publication of the first *Diversity Barometer* results is scheduled for 2011.[12] The second 'Barometer' is scheduled to appear in 2013 (focus: housing) and a third is scheduled for 2015 (focus: education). The cycle will restart in 2017, with another Barometer on the labour market.

The results of the first *Tolerance Survey*, conducted in 2009, show that native Belgians tend to have a tolerant attitude towards ethnic minorities, although explicit intolerance does seem to occur. On the negative side, survey respondents agreed that racist reactions can be justified under certain circumstances and that minorities come to Belgium to take advantage of the social security system. Furthermore, a substantial proportion of native Belgians link the increasing crime rates to immigration. Positive trends highlighted in the survey are that respondents value the presence of other cultures and religions in society, while almost the same percentage report having had positive experiences with persons from ethnic minorities. The overall conclusion could be that Belgians seem to be more tolerant towards ethnic minorities where there is frequent interaction with them, thus confirming the contact hypothesis (also referred to in Common Basic Principle 7)[13]. In any event, these provisional results underline the two-way nature of the integration process (Common Basic Principle 1)[14]. The next Tolerance Survey is likely to be conducted in 2011.

At *regional level*, the Flemish Authority has published the first results of its *Integration Map* in April 2009, commissioned by the Flemish Regional Minister for Integration in order to inform policy decisions[15].

The first findings of the monitoring part of the project relate to education, employment, poverty and income, housing and health.

As regards education, the monitoring reveals that:

- Students of foreign origin exhibit more educational arrears (starting at preschool age).
- Their educational arrears are generally greater.
- Students of foreign origin will more often move into vocational training and the lower tracks of secondary education.
- Participation in higher education remains very limited.

Results in the area of employment show that:

- Persons of foreign origin are more often non-employed.
- If they participate to the labour market, the risk of unemployment is usually greater.
- They are at higher risk of having precarious jobs.

As regards income, the monitoring reveals:

- A greater risk of precarious income and poverty for people with an immigrant background.
- Income inequality and vulnerable income position for Turkish and Moroccan households.

As regards housing, the monitoring indicates that:
- Non-EU citizens more often rent their homes.
- Non-EU citizens are usually found in lower-quality segments of the rental and owner-occupied housing markets.
- This lower-quality housing might explain the higher housing mobility.

On health, the monitoring reports on:
- physical complaints and impairments;
- infant mortality;
- medications use and use of preventive measures.

The researchers in the Flemish Integration monitoring system make a number of important comments on these first results. They stress that dimensions and indicators on integration are dynamic and always have to be clarified in accordance with the definition of 'integration' (for example: they raise the question of whether or not health indicators should be included in an Integration Monitor).

Once a decision has been made as to which dimensions and indicators should be included, these still have to be populated with available data. One option might be to use administrative databases, although these seem to have their own limitations. Nationality, for example, is often used as a distinguishing criterion, whereas data on origin are currently not fully available. Moreover, the available databases do not always allow conditional comparisons (based on gender, aged, education level, etc.), since they are structured differently.

3.9 Monitoring integration policies: back to the future

By way of final reflection, a few important remarks and questions on monitoring integration policies need to be raised. Given the current choices in favour of comprehensive and structural outcome measurement, these remarks are very relevant in the Belgian context.

First, it should always be borne in mind that the development of indicators and monitoring systems is a dynamic process. At all times, this work in progress needs to take into account aspects of suitability and feasibility as well as the quality and periodicity of the collected data.

Secondly, the choice of dimensions and indicators implies some agreement between the expert point of view and the policy point of view. Findings generated by evaluation instruments should in the end be useful for informing integration policies.

A third question is 'who do we represent?'. Do monitoring systems approach target groups as uniform entities or do they make allowance for a degree of diversity?

Finally, the instruments developed should always take into account the quality, relevance and comparability of the available data, as well as the limitations of the data generated.

Based on the currently developed projects and their first provisional results, the choice in favour of comprehensive and structural outcome monitoring of integration policies in Belgium looks rather promising. Naturally, some methodological, institutional and political issues need to be further clarified, but it may reasonably be argued that all the assets needed for the robust implementation of a sustainable integration monitoring system are in place.

Notes

1   Detailed information is available at http://www.binnenland.vlaanderen.be/inburgering/ (consulted on 20 November 2008). References from the Flemish Integration Decree: *Decreet van 28 februari 2003 betreffende het Vlaams inburgeringsbeleid, SB 8 mei 2003, gewijzigd bij decreet van 14 juli 2006 en gewijzigd bij decreet van 1 februari 2008.*

2   Eight reception centres have been established in the territory of the Flemish Community (which includes Brussels).

3   A regional support centre (CRACS) has been created for projects funded within the framework of the so-called 'Social Cohesion Decree'. It evaluates the practical application of the Decree. The French Community Commission has also recognised one regional centre for intercultural relations in the Brussels-Capital Region, the *Centre bruxellois d'action interculturelle (CBAI)*.

4   School is mandatory for children aged 6-18 years.

5   http://www.diversiteit.be/?action=onderdeel&onderdeel=234&titel=Initiatieven+van+het+Centrum

6   http://www.diversiteit.be/?action=publicatie_detail&id=70&thema=2&setLanguage=3 (including a link to the English survey report)
http://www.diversite.be/?action=publicatie_detail&id=70&thema=2 (including a link to the French survey report)
http://www.diversiteit.be/?action=publicatie_detail&id=70&thema=2&setLanguage=1 (including a link to the Dutch survey report)

7   Vlaamse Integratiekaart, Steunpunt Gelijkekansenbeleid – Policy Research Centre on Equal Opportunities – Consortium Universiteit Antwerpen & Universiteit Hasselt, K. Vancluysen, M . Van Craen, M. Lamberts, A. Morissens, F. Pauwels, L. Sannen, J. Ackaert, 2009.

8   De Vlaamse Integratiekaart Deel III:
L. Sannen, M. Lamberts, A. Morissens & F. Pauwels (2009). *De Vlaamse Integratiekaart Deel III: Naar een Vlaamse integratiemonitor* (Steunpunt Gelijkekansenbeleid). Consulted at: http://www.steunpunt-gelijkekansen.be/main.aspx?c=*SGK&n=60386
De Vlaamse Integratiekaart Deel II:
S. Van den Eede, J. Wets & F. Levrau (2009). *De Vlaamse Integratiekaart Deel II:Exploratieve literatuurstudie van het concept integratie* (Steunpunt Gelijkekansenbeleid). Consulted at: http://www.steunpunt-gelijkekansen.be/main.aspx?c=*SGK&n=77523&ct=71437
De Vlaamse Integratiekaart Deel I:
K. Vancluysen, M. Van Craen, M. Lamberts, A. Morissens, F. Pauwels, L. Sannen & J. Ackaert (2009). *De Vlaamse Integratiekaart Deel I: Conclusies en beleidsaanbevelingen* (Steunpunt gelijkekansenbeleid). Consulted at: http://www.steunpuntgelijkekansen.be/main.aspx?c=*SGK&n=60391

9   Technical working group comprising the Crossroads Bank for Social Security, the Federal Public Service for Employment, the National Institute for Statistics and the Centre for Equal Opportunities.

10 Socioeconomic monitoring of the labour market by national origin – extract from the data request to the National Register as a means of pre-testing the availability and relevance of the data concerning the origin of the entire population (2009).

11 Socioeconomic monitoring of the labour market on national origin – extract from the analysis on the availability of National Register data on origin.

12 The Centre for Equal Opportunities requested three studies in the light of the 2011 report: a large-scale study of discrimination based on correspondence testing, a survey of employers and HR personnel, a statistical study using both a set of equality indicators proposed by the EC Directorate-General for Employment, Social Affairs and Equal Opportunities, and regression analysis. The final report is expected in October 2011.

13 Common Basic Principle 7: 'Frequent interaction between immigrants and Member State citizens is a fundamental mechanism for integration. Shared forums, intercultural dialogue, education about immigrants and immigrant cultures, and stimulating living conditions in urban environments enhance the interactions between immigrants and Member State citizens' – A Common Agenda for Integration, COM (2005) 389 final.

14 Common Basic Principle 1: 'Integration is a dynamic two-way process of mutual accommodation by all immigrants and residents of Member States' – A Common Agenda for Integration, COM (2005) 389 final.

15 Vlaamse Integratiekaart, Steunpunt Gelijkekansenbeleid – Policy Research Centre for Equal Opportunities – Consortium Universiteit Antwerpen & Universiteit Hasselt, K. Vancluysen, M. Van Craen, M. Lamberts, A. Morissens, F. Pauwels, L. Sannen, J. Ackaert, 2009.

4 Monitoring integration in the Czech Republic

Selma Muhič Dizdarevič

4.1 Introduction and integration policy changes in the Czech Republic

In this chapter, integration is considered as a process of gradual inclusion of immigrants[1] with various statuses into the host society; it reflects both given societal settings and attitudes and activities of the host country and immigrants. It is not possible within the scope of this chapter to go into detail about the discussion of the concept or include other, similar ideas such as acculturation (as used by Bauböck 1998: 40) or the private and public dimension of the integration process (as discussed by e.g. Rex 1997: 207-208). The chapter focuses on how the term is operationalised in integration policies in the Czech Republic (CR), and on whether and how it is measured using available data.

When it comes to measuring integration, the crucial issue is how to define what will be monitored and measured. Kymlicka suggests the adoption of measures that celebrate and publicise ethnocultural diversity, reduce legal constraints on immigrant groups whilst maintaining their identity and culture, and which represent forms of active support for immigrant communities and individuals (Kymlicka 2009: 241). It is safe to say that none of these integration measures are applied in the CR, or at least not fully. This is however due to a process of change, which Baršová and Barša see as indicative of the situation across the EU and in the USA, Canada, etc. This change entails a shift away from the idea of multicultural integration, which focused on ethnic groups and allowed for unlimited cultural specifics to be developed within those groups, towards the 'civic integration' of individuals, which stresses more adoption of the shared, common, members-of-polity approach (Baršová & Barša 2005: passim).

It is worth noting here the close connection between immigration and integration policies; however, this connection will be addressed only indirectly in this chapter, in order to focus more on integration. Baršová and Barša also note that post-communist nations are more likely to define themselves in ethnic rather than civic terms, and have difficulties with the integration of their national minorities, making the integration of immigrants more challenging (ibid.: 166). Any discussion of integration in the various segments of the public space in the CR will in the vast majority of cases be concerned with Roma integration. Similarly, reports about racism and discrimination in the CR are almost exclusively related to the treatment of Roma, who are also more likely to be targets of physical violence.[2] From a comparative perspective it may be argued that the socioeconomic status of immigrants in the old EU countries is much closer to that of Roma in the CR than to CR immigrants, including in terms of spatial segregation, early drop-out from education, unemployment rates and dependency on benefits, to name just a few examples. Organisations concerned with the integration of minorities tend to concentrate mainly on the Roma population, and to focus on social exclusion rather than on integration in a broader sense (Horáková & Bareš 2010: 107). Bearing this in mind, we will focus here on changes in integration policies for immigrants in the three phases of migration[3] and three phases of integration policy as suggested by Baršová and Barša (ibid: 221-240).

The first phase of migration policy, which lasted from 1990-1995, was characterised by a *laissez faire* attitude towards immigration and integration policy. The authors see this as libertarian and stemming from a (post-Velvet) revolutionary ethos. The policies were liberal – it was for example possible to apply for a residence permit without leaving the country – but at the same time the prevailing attitude towards immigrants was one of tolerance, rather than acceptance. During this phase it was possible for the foreign nationals to submit applications for a long-term stay in the Czech territory, which – combined with the fact that the Czech Republic had visa-free relations with the most major countries of origin of immigrants – meant there were virtually no bureaucratic obstacles to a foreigner's legal stay in the Republic, creating a situation that was described by commentators as both liberal and chaotic (Čižinský 2008: 188)

The second phase, lasting from 1996 to 1999, was characterised by a need to adopt *acquis* and integrate into the EU. As a result, the policy became more restrictive and at the same time limited the scope for the Czech Republic to focus on creating its own migration policy. Although more restrictive, the new legal framework also made it possible to obtain a permanent residence permit after ten years of long-term residency, which was not the case in the previous period. This change also had direct consequences for the citizenship policy. In the previous period, citizenship could only be obtained through marriage to a Czech national (since permanent residency status is a condition for obtaining citizenship and in the first phase that permanent status could only be granted on humanitarian grounds, not on the basis of the accumulation of a certain number of years' residence in the CR). In the second phase, by contrast, this was possible through naturalisation. In the third phase, which lasted from 1999-2005 (when Baršová and Barša's book was published) the state became a major player in the migration policy, regulating all aspects of it. The period of waiting to be upgraded from long-term to permanent status was reduced to five years (under pressure from the EU) and according to Baršová and Barša was not accompanied by any integration requirements. They see it as a negative development that all what was required to obtain a permanent residence permit was to 'survive' for five years. According to the authors, this period saw the beginning of the creation of complex migration (immigration + integration) policies (an example of this was the launch by the Ministry of Labour and Social Affairs of a pilot project in collaboration with other ministries and an inter-governmental organisation under the title 'Selection of Qualified Foreign Workers' in 2003) and the first steps towards not only conforming to the EU rules but trying to influence them, as reflected in the production of the Principles of Conception of Integration of Foreigners in 1999.[4]

Baršová and Barša also focus on three phases of Czech integration policy – the first phase (1990-1998) is characterised by a rather narrow focus on specific groups (refugees and Czechs returning from former Soviet Republics, for example) and is partial in nature. The second phase (199-2003) saw expansion of the integration policy under the auspices of the Ministry of the Interior (MI), which played the role of 'enlightened moving force' (ibid.: 231), the third phase started in 2004 when the integration agenda was taken up by the Ministry of Labour and Social Affairs. (We may add that from August 2008 the agenda was returned to the MI.) The first phase focused on the provision of material help and lacked any wider conception of integration. Since it was focused on such specific groups, it was not financially or administratively possible to expand it to other groups. The second phase, which began in the wake of societal developments which showed that immigrants were here to stay and because of an initiative by the Council of Europe as well as the MI, brought an increase in activities: non-governmental organisations were included and financially supported, there was an ambition to transfer responsibilities for integration to local bodies, other ministries and stakeholders were assigned specific duties, support was provided for data collection and research, and the Commission for Integration of Foreigners and Community Relations was established at the MI. Not all of these steps were successful in this phase (e.g. transfer to local authorities), but in conceptual terms this was the period in which multicultural (community-based) and civic (individual-based) concepts of integration clashed. In Baršová and Barša's view, the former was represented by the Council of Europe and the latter by the EU. The latter approach signals clearly that some community practices, for example those violating gender equality, cannot be tolerated in the host society regardless of the fact that some community members might see them as essential. However, as the authors hint (p. 233), the former approach has never really happened in the CR. Unlike in some old EU member states, there was no multicultural 'honeymoon' during which the flourishing of immigrant cultures was celebrated or promoted. Nevertheless, civic integration, requiring individuals to adapt to the host country culture, came into focus and the only remaining scope for multiculturalism was in the field of multicultural education. The third phase saw some critical reflections, as the concept of integration was found to be too general, lacking in operationalisation; the system did not support those who wanted to integrate, nor did it put adequate pressure on those who did not, and the institutional and legal framework seemed to make integration harder rather than easier. The authors conclude their account by suggesting that for integration to be successful, integration tests should be required for obtaining permanent residency and an integration contract should be introduced.

However, considering that the majority of immigrants in the CR are labour migrants, and therefore financially self-sufficient, my own feeling is that integration policy should focus more on removing segmentation of the job market and discrimination in housing, followed by combating xenophobia in some government bodies (such as the aliens police) and supporting the education of immigrant children. The CR was the last country to adopt an Anti-Discrimination Act implementing the Racial Equality Directive (Council Directive 2000/43/EC) and the Employment Equality Directive (Council Directive 2000/78/EC), and did so by outvoting a year-old presidential veto by Václav Klaus. The usefulness of introducing integration tests has been quite ambiguous so far (see e.g. Joppke 2007). It is questionable whether immigrants are offered fair integration conditions in the CR such as those to which, according to Kymlicka, they are entitled in liberal democracies (Kymlicka 2001: 162).

The final measure suggested by Baršová and Barša, namely the establishment of integration centres and courses, could move us towards the fourth phase, which started with the return of the integration agenda to the authority of the MI in 2008. The integration priorities as laid down in the Conception of Integration of Foreigners dating from 2000 (and updated annually since) have not changed essentially, but have now moved towards the development of integration centres. Their establishment, which signals an ambition to decentralise integration, to move it towards regions and districts, was funded by The European Fund for the Integration of Third-country Nationals. There are currently six integration centres, and although the original intention was to decentralise integration, by awarding four out of six centres to its own organisation, namely the Administration of Refugee Facilities of the Ministry of the Interior, the opposite effect was achieved, namely reinforcing the central role of the MI (Tošnerová 2009: 7). According to some studies, there is no local strategy for the integration of immigrants, among other things because their numbers are low, they typically do not use the social security benefits system and the local authorities who should be dealing with the issues are understaffed (Rákoczyová & Trbola 2008: 51).

Another step in the direction of strengthening the demands placed on integrating immigrants was taken by a legal provision which made knowledge of the Czech language a requirement for obtaining permanent residency status. Although previously this condition applied only in the case of citizenship applications, it was extended to permanent residence applications from 1 January 2009. The required level is A1 as per the Common European Framework of Reference for Languages, which is the least demanding level. The MI issues special vouchers to finance taking one such exam; in the event of failure, it is up to immigrants to pay for taking further exams.

The Report on Implementation of the Conception of Integration of Foreigners (KIC) for the year 2009 shows that in this phase of the integration policy, integration was expanded to include not only immigrants living in the CR for at least a year, as previously, but also newly arrived third-country nationals. In addition, the Report devotes special attention to the integration of immigrant children and young people (KIC 2010: 2) .
However, when analyzing Czech immigration and integration policies it is important to keep in mind that foreigners are categorised in various ways, and based on this categorisation there are different policies, different stakeholders and different goals in this field. All foreigners, i.e. persons without Czech or EU documents, are divided according to their status into:
— asylum-seekers (now called applicants for international protection);[5]
— refugees i.e. persons granted international protection (including persons under subsidiary protection);
— immigrants (i.e. legally residing foreigners, either temporarily or permanently, again divided into subcategories of foreigners with a visa not exceeding one year, with a long-term visa not exceeding one year[6] and, after five years of a long-term visa, with permanent residence);

– persons staying for a period not exceeding 90 days;
– irregular migrants.
Since the groups vary in terms of their status, rights and position in Czech society, it is understandable that their treatment in various governmental policies also differs. I will now sketch out the different policies after introducing some basic figures on the numbers of foreigners in general and those with permanent residence (see table 4.1).

Table 4.1
Total number of inhabitants, total number of foreigners, foreigners with permanent residence, top 10 countries of origin of all foreigners up to 30 November 2010

country of origin	number of foreigners	permanent residence	total number of inhabitants in the CR (up to 30 June 2010)
total	425,568	187,840	10,515,818
Ukraine	126,521	46,183	
Slovakia	71,676	28,543	
Vietnam	60,605	36,434	
Russia	31,297	13,445	
Poland	18,328	10,980	
Germany	13,577	4,428	
Moldavia	9,136	2,591	
Bulgaria	6,800	3,109	
USA	6,031	2,743	
Mongolia	5,559	2,030	

Source: Based on data from the Czech Statistical Office: http://www.czso.cz/csu/cizinci.nsf/t/
DC0053CB0B/$File/c01t01.pdf (consulted 4 December 2010). Permanent residence data have been selected because this is the most integrated stage of residence before obtaining citizenship, and hence comes closest to full citizenship rights.

4.2   Different target groups for specific integration policies

4.2.1 Immigrants

In the case of immigrants, referred to as aliens in government documents, the process of integration has to have a different perspective because their position, status and opportunities are different. This agenda was also in principle a competence of the Ministry of the Interior (MI); it was transferred to the Ministry of Labour and Social Affairs (MLSA) on 1 January 2004, only to be transferred back to the competence of the Ministry of the Interior again in 2008.
Since the MI was responsible for the coordination of policies related to the integration of immigrants until 2004, we find basic policy formulation documents within their agenda. These documents consist of Principles of the Conception of Integration of Aliens in the Territory of the Czech Republic (adopted in 1999) and Conception of Integration of Aliens in the Territory of the Czech Republic (adopted in 2000).

The Principles stress some very important points, revealing Czech government policy thinking in this field: the state takes responsibility for the condition of a precisely defined group of foreign citizens (legally residing long-term residents of foreign origin), but it also stresses the responsibility and effort required on the part of immigrants, which is a basis for policy formulation. Mutual responsibility opens the way for other principles mentioned in the text, namely integration without self-segregation or discrimination.

The Conception report states that during the year 2000, and based on the Principles adopted in the previous year, the Ministry of the Interior's Commission for Integration of Foreigners was divided into working groups focusing on the following topics: employment, entrepreneurship, housing; social security and health care; education; culture, traditions, religion; residence status, naturalisation and political participation. The goal of the working groups was to gather available material and information within their fields and compare it with the Principles already adopted in order to identify the current status and possibilities in relation to migration and the integration of foreigners. The fields in which the working groups were engaged were similar to the indicators adopted at the conference 'Indicators and Monitoring of the Outcome of Integration Policies' in Malmö in December 2009, which included: employment, education, social inclusion and active citizenship.

As stated in the Conception, the fundamental goal in relation to integration, which is to be achieved gradually taking into account the specific conditions of the migratory phenomenon in the CR, is to bring the legal status of long-term legal foreign residents in the CR more into line with the status of the citizens of the CR. This goal is seen as complying with EU requirements in this regard. It is very important to keep in mind that this is the overriding idea governing the whole Conception; gradual harmonisation of the legal regulation with those of the EU and contributing to the creation of a common European integration policy are seen as guiding principles towards achieving the goal making the status of residents and citizens more equal.

In the case of the naturalisation process, the Ministry holds that naturalisation is a matter of choice for the foreigner concerned. According to the Conception, however, the state policy should be predicated on awareness that citizenship status is the best route to equality in society, and therefore the best route to solidarity. Naturalisation should therefore be regarded as beneficial for Czech society, and it is in the interests of the state to secure favourable conditions for it. To this we may add that citizenship currently tends to be perceived by foreigners as a goal that is rather difficult to attain and that is governed by arbitrary and ambiguous conditions.[7] From 2004 onwards, the number of naturalised immigrants started to decline, falling from 5,020 to 1,837 in 2008. It is mostly Slovak and Ukrainians who become Czech citizens.[8]

The target group of the Conception comprises not only foreigners, but also Czech citizens. In a similar way to The Hague Programme, the Conception sees integration as a two-way process of mutual accommodation between the majority and minorities. The main contribution of the Conception lies in its focus on the crucial issue of integration: its connection to European policies; its pioneering character; its awareness of the weaknesses of legislation, policy and the practical situation; its comprehensiveness; its call for mobilisation of all the relevant stakeholders (government agencies at all levels, citizens, foreigners, experts, non-governmental nonprofit organisations); its call for decentralisation and its long-term character.

If we now move from general political declaration to the level of practical integration in Czech society, we should first look at statistical data on foreigners combined with various aspects of integration, mainly in the jobs market but also in the areas of health, education and obstacles posed by legal requirements. The scope of integration incorporates four fields (social, economic, cultural and political) of integration, each of which contains other dimensions to be researched. It is not the aim of this chapter to present them all, however, but to focus only on the most important.

Today, foreigners make up approximately 4% of the total population and 6% of the jobs market in the CR. The percentage of foreigners in the population rose from 0.75% in 1993 to 4.22 by the end of 2009 (Horáková 2010: 17). The CR thus counts as one of the EU member states with a low percentage of foreigners.[9] Third-country nationals make up 68% of all foreigners in the CR, with the remainder being citizens of the EU, EES and Switzerland. Naturalised foreigners and second and third-generation immigrants are not statistically reported (Horáková & Bareš 2010: 105-106). The number of residence permits issued rose from 1993 to reach a peak in the first half of 2009, but in the second half of the latter year the number fell by 9,021 residence permits in the wake of the economic crisis. However, this downward trend masks an increase in the number of foreigners with permanent residency status (+5,279), while the number of long-term visas decreased (−14,480) in the first half of 2009. The percentage of people with permanent residency rose to 42% by the end of 2009, the second highest percentage since 2006 (43%) (Horáková 2010: 18). The total number of third-country nationals (TCN) decreased only slightly by the end of 2009 (−195); the remaining fall of 9,006 was due to a decline in the number of EU citizens, leading Horáková to conclude that the economic crisis did not prompt the TCN to leave (whereas it did in the case of EU citizens), presumably in part because the conditions in their countries of origin are often worse than the conditions in the CR, even during a period of crisis (ibid.: 24). We may therefore conclude that it is TCN who stay permanently in the CR, rather than EU citizens. Most foreigners are concentrated in Prague (11.9%), followed by Karlový Vary (6.4%) and Plzeň (4.8%) (ibid: 34).

The rising trend in the percentage of foreigners in the labour market, which reached a peak of 6.4% in 2008, began falling during the economic crisis, and stood at 5.4% at the end of 2009. At the same time, the number of foreigners whose residency status was not based on a work permit but on a trading licence increased, as always happens when there is drop in demand for labour from the market (ibid.: 41). Up to 2009, foreigners with work permits were dependent on a specific company and job to extend their residence permit, which meant that if they did not find another job immediately (something that is made almost impossible by the lengthy administrative procedures), they had to leave the country. This restrictive measure was removed in 2009 with the introduction of the 'protection period', which lasts for 60 days. Together with this liberalisation, the green card system was introduced for selected countries, with three types of visas. The medical check requirement was also abolished as a condition for obtaining a work permit. At the same time, it was no longer necessary in 2009 for an employer to apply for permission to employ a foreigner; it was sufficient for this to by the foreigner only; the procedure up to 2009 required both the employer and the foreign worker to apply for permission. Finally, the groups not requiring a work permit were expanded to include students studying at Czech colleges. The trading licence visa (which is to be restricted from 2011) is easier to obtain but the visa-holder has to pay for their health and social benefits and taxes, and is not protected by the Act on Employment. This is especially worrisome because some foreigners may be in a job which requires a work permit but, since it is difficult to obtain one, they pretend to be in a trading licence regime. It is not uncommon for employers to prefer this arrangement, which is less legally demanding for them than a traditional employment contract. Since the employment rate among foreigners is extremely high (in 2008, the peak year for foreign employment, the employment rate among Czech citizens was 66.8%, compared with 93.8% among foreign nationals (ibid.: 85)), the main reason for not entering into a traditional employment contract is the administratively demanding and lengthy process of obtaining work permits for foreigners. Despite the crisis, according to the World Migration Report 2010, the difference in the growth of unemployment rates among migrants and nationals in the Czech Republic was 0.1 percentage points (WMR 2010: 272).

Most foreign nationals residing in the CR are aged 25-39 years, and there are more men than women, though the number of women is rising slightly (currently 39.7%). 29.3% of foreigners registered with the Employment Office work in manufacturing industry, followed by the construction industry (20.3%); these are followed in turn by repair of motor vehicles, motorcycles and personal and household goods (10.6%), professional, scientific and technical activities (6.8%), and administrative and support services activities 5.9% (ibid.: 63).[10] Table 4.2 shows the educational profile of foreign nationals registered with the Employment Office for 2009 and, according to their type of residence, the top three most frequent levels of education.

Table 4.2

Top three levels of education according to type of residence, with percentages

EU, EES and Switzerland	long-term visa	permanent visa
1. secondary education with vocational certificate, 31.45%	1. basic, practical education, 55.12%	1. basic, practical education, 28.89%
2. basic, practical education, 15.51%	2. secondary education with vocational certificate, 18.04%	2. secondary education with vocational certificate, 21.83%
3. university education, 12.56%[11]	3. secondary education with no vocational or graduation certificate, 7.01%	3. university education, 17.44%

Source: Horáková 2010: 77, selected by the author

According to The International Standard Classification of Occupations (ISCO) 88, most foreigners who are employees are employed in ISCO groups 7, 8 and 9, which are the least demanding (in terms of education/training), the worst paid and the least secure type of jobs. 75.1% of foreigners who are employees in the CR occupy jobs in this 'tertiary' or 'external' jobs market[12], with the majority being in group 9 requiring little or no qualification. The only group in which there is constant demand for labour is group 1 (the most highly qualified) (Pořízková 2010: 19). In group 9, by contrast, there are more jobseekers than jobs, but due to their low prestige and financial unattractiveness coupled with the national social benefits system, these jobs are taken by foreign workers and rejected by the domestic labour force. It is important to stress that some qualitative studies report discrimination on the labour and housing markets. According to one of these studies, as soon as a person is identified as a foreigner, the vacancy suddenly becomes occupied or, in case of housing, the price is raised (Tollarová 2009).

The legal framework defining access to public health insurance has been criticised repeatedly because in the category of foreigners with a long-term visa (foreigners with a permanent visa are almost equal to Czech citizens generally, and in this case are fully equal) only those who have an employment visa are entitled to access the public health system, but not those with a trading licence visa or the dependents of the employment visa-holder. These people are referred to commercial health insurance providers. However, this insurance is voluntary for both parties, which in some instances means that companies do not provide health insurance. Consequently, if a sick or disabled child is born, it might be uninsurable. The positive aspect of the integration effort, on the other hand, is that from 2008 all children have access to compulsory education regardless of their status. The difficulties in integration policies in relation to housing, health and education are too complex to be addressed in any more detail here.

4.2.2   Persons under international protection (recognised refugees, persons under subsidiary protection)

Generally, refugees have the same rights as permanent residents in the CR. The recognition rates in the CR are consistently low, however, and the number of refugees is therefore also low. According to the Czech Statistical Data for 2008, there were 2,110 refugees.
There is a set of policies and approaches defined by law for refugees, called the State Integration Programme (SIP). The SIP falls under the authority of the Ministry of the Interior in collaboration with the Ministry of Labour and Social Affairs on issues relating to the jobs market, and with the Ministry of Education on issues relating to Czech language courses. However, the priority for those refugees who enter the integration process through the SIP is to secure housing. The Czech government approves the quota and financial resources for the SIP.
Within the SIP there is an Individual Action Plan, implemented in 2005, which also includes the offer of retraining schemes, but with a very limited scope. Refugees are reluctant to enter the scheme if courses are not financed by a future employer.

Consequently, the general question that remains is whether the schemes are efficient, and there is a major paradox whereby refugees with university degrees are retrained to become manual workers. Since refugees´ previous work experience is typically not recognised, even after they have completed retraining courses, employers are still reluctant to employ them because of lack of experience. Another problem is that the housing on offer tends to be in rural areas with high unemployment rates. The situation is particularly desperate for disabled refugees. The SIP also includes persons under subsidiary protection, except in housing.

4.3 Data monitoring system

As the earlier sections of this chapter make clear, the term 'integration' must be linked to a specific group rather than used as a general concept. To sum up, there are integration policies for national minorities (i.e. Roma), for refugees and for foreigners with residence status.[13] Monitoring data on foreigners in general, and more specifically data on integration, is therefore rather complex. I will first list the kinds of data that are monitored in relation to foreign nationals and then comment on those that are related to integration. The benchmarks of integration as formulated by the Ministry of the Interior are almost impossible to monitor, either because it is hard to define what or how should be monitored or because there is no data available. In the Ministry's view, these benchmarks should be:
- knowledge of the Czech language;
- economic self-sufficiency;
- orientation within Czech society;
- mutual relations between foreigners and the indigenous majority.

While information on economic self-sufficiency can be gleaned from the Czech Statistical Office (CSO) data, while knowledge of the Czech language has recently been standardised and become obligatory for permanent residence and citizenship applications, the latter two aspects are genuinely hard to define and thus to measure. In such cases we can only rely on reports from non-governmental organisations and academic research which produce partial results related to the extent to which the integration of foreigners is successful.

The major source of data on the foreign population can be found through the CSO, which is obliged by legal and political conditions to gather data and regularly publishes the results in the form of a brochure and on its website. Some of the data on the website, including the total number of foreigners excluding refugees, data on asylum applicants and asylum proceedings and employment of foreigners, are updated on a monthly basis. The other statistical data are updated annually. The brochure is a joint product of the CSO, Ministries (of Labour and Social Affairs, Justice, Interior, and Industry and Trade), research institutions (Research Institute for Labour and Social Affairs, Institute for Information on Education, and Institute of Health Information and Statistics of the Czech Republic)[14] and the General Directorate of the Prison Service. The brochure is distributed free of charge to libraries, schools, research institutes, non-governmental organisations and of course to various state bodies at central and regional level, as well as to journalists and anyone who is interested.

The sources of information for each of the areas monitored in relation to foreigners are individual Ministries, which collect information for their own needs and could be labelled as the owners of the data. However, the data are publicly available to everyone. They present a picture of the foreign nationals who come into contact with the state administration in general; these constitute the majority, but the data leave out irregular migrants (for whom only estimates are available) and EU citizens, who generally do not report their residence in the CR. There is no difficulty in accessing the data; on the contrary, CSO makes them available to everyone in a user-friendly form, with publications in both electronic and physical format which it appears to distribute very actively. If we look more deeply into the question of who collects the data, the answer would be the CSO, which conducts a Population and Housing Census every ten years (the next one will be in 2011), which are of crucial importance. However, in terms of international migration the 2001 census offers somewhat incomplete information (only about 60% of foreigners who should have been counted were in fact counted) (Drbohlav & Lachmanová-Medová 2009: 4). The Labour Force Survey and the European Union Statistics on Income and Living Conditions include foreigners in negligible numbers, and are therefore not particularly useful. All the other data relating to foreign nationals are collected by various government agencies, the two most important being the Ministry of the Interior and the Ministry of Labour and Social Affairs. They also decide which data are given to the CSO (based on legal regulations or their interpretations) and are therefore available to public. Drbohlav and Lachmanová-Medová stress what in their view is the rather detrimental role played by the Office of Personal Data Protection in linking the various databases, making the data unavailable for comparison (2009: 8).[15] The MI administers the most comprehensive population register, the ISEO, which contains data on all Czech citizens, foreign nationals with residence permits including 90-day visas, EU citizens registered in the CR and refugees (with asylum and subsidiary protection). The system is however not available for research. In addition, the MI operates the Alien Information System and the system for asylum-seekers. The MLSA administers Information System of Employment Services, a register of persons who have contacted employment offices, and the System of State Social Support Benefit, which also includes foreigners entitled to social benefits (permanent, long-term residence permit or refugees).

The monitoring takes into account both structural (legal, educational and occupational) aspects and socio-economic dimensions (economic activity, health care, crime rates). Irregular migration (termed 'illegal' by the CSO and the Ministries) is also monitored, both as regards illegal entry to the country and overstaying or irregular residence status. Table 4.3 shows the most important types of data monitored.
The list of data monitored appears comprehensive. The data are cross-sectional. This particular database did not include any cohort-based research, though it is likely that both longitudinal and cohort-based research do form part of academic research; however, the

impact of this research is much more limited, being used for specific policymaking decisions (if financed from the state budget). Some indicators can be tracked over time (e.g.
foreigners according to residence type, number of acquired citizenships, etc.). In the
case of the data collected by the CSO, these data are provided on the basis of legal regulations and government requirements, but also as a result of EUROSTAT requests.
The data gathering is based on registration data collected by the various ministries and
the general state administration. This is the only comprehensive database available for
monitoring data on immigrants, and it can serve as a basis for monitoring the factors
that influence integration. Direct monitoring of integration, based on pre-defined indicators, is not carried out, at central level, but involves a combination of partial monitoring of specific groups or factors by stakeholders other than the state. Examples include
non-governmental organisations and academic research focusing either on specific
group or specific indicators (or a combination of the two, as in the case of monitoring
health care among foreigners with long-term residence status). One recommendation
for improving integration monitoring would therefore be to create a comprehensive
system based pre-defined factors, which would be monitored separately or given special
attention. To achieve that, however, it would be necessary to operationalise the integration goals set by the government, which were discussed earlier.

Table 4.3

Area and the type of data monitored by the CSO in relation to foreign nationals in the CR

area	type of data	type of data	type of data	type of data	type of data	type of data
demographic aspects	total no. of foreigners by citizenship	by area, region and district by citizenship	by category of residence	by sex and age	by acquired citizenship and the previous citizenship	by marriage, divorce, births, abortions, deaths
asylum and asylum proceedings	new applicants, initial procedure, procedure at regional courts, before the Supreme Administrative Court	applicants by age and sex, citizenship and place of residence	unaccompanied minors	granted asylum and number of refugees by age and sex	citizenship granted to refugees	
economic activity	employment and residence permits by area, region and district	employment of foreigners by citizenship and sex	foreigners registered at employment offices by area, region, district, citizenship and sex	foreigners with trade licence by citizenship, sex and area, region, district	foreigners in main employment by sector, by CZ-NACE classification, age, sex, nationality	
education	foreign children by citizenship on all levels of education (from nursery schools to universities)	foreign students by fields and type of study and study programme	foreign graduates	foreign students by area/region		
health care	health insurance contracts with the General Health Insurance (joint-stock company)	utilisation of health care by foreigners by country of origin, age, source of payment and total costs of health care	foreigners treated in hospitals by reason for hospitalisation	abortions for foreigners including by locality	new notified cases of TBC by patient's country of birth	
crime rates	prosecuted, accused and convicted by citizenship	expulsion from the CR by citizenship				
irregular migration	illegal border crossing	illegal stay				foreigners caught working illegally

Source: Based on data from the CSO

There is no subdivision of statistics on migrants by the first and second generation, possibly partly due to the limited period of immigration in the CR (from 1989) and the changed character of migration in this period, most notably the transformation of the CR from transit to target country in the 1990s. This subdivision might be of interest in the future, but tracking citizens of foreign origin, as is being done in some EU countries, does not seem a plausible idea since it undermines the concept of citizenship as such; citizenship should entail full equality. The above statistical data allow for the subdivision of migrants by asylum, labour and marriage. Unlike the country of origin (i.e. citizenship), country of birth is not registered.

The owners of the data are various state bodies which are obliged to submit the data to the CSO. The data are available to everyone and to date there have never been any restrictions in accessing the data. On the other hand, linking the registration data to the micro-level of individual persons is not possible due to privacy protection laws. For the data owner/collector, such as Ministry of the Interior, however, it should be possible to drill down to the micro-level from the general statistical data.

4.4 Interpretation issues and recommendations

Turning to the question of the quality (reliability and validity) of the data and improving the monitoring system as such, the data are organised by the CSO and collected by various state bodies as part of their regular work. However, while the database is impressive in terms of data quantity it totally lacks the qualitative dimension which is provided by research and surveys by the academic, non-profit or profit sector. Would it be possible to connect the data, not just through juxtaposition but also in terms of interpretation? Combining the qualitative approach of the CSO and the Ministries for the selected indicators with the qualitative dimension offered by research in other sectors is unlikely to be undertaken by the government sector, but could be done (and is indeed being done, albeit partially) through joint efforts by the other sectors. The context of the data is also important. This is illustrated by the crime rates among foreign nationals, which have remained remarkably stable since 1993 at around 5-6% of the total crime rate. The highest percentage of foreign nationals charged with criminal offences had unauthorised residence status (28.2%), followed by EU citizen status without a residence permit for the CR (23.3%) and permanent residence status (10.8%) (Koncepce 2007: 82). The threat of terrorism figures very low among the criminal activities, as Conception report makes clear. However, the printed version of the book 'Foreigners in the Czech Republic' (Cizinci 2009:173-187) provides meticulous data on crime rates among foreigners as compiled by the Ministry of Justice; more research would be needed in order to reach any conclusions about the crime rate among foreign nationals relative to the overall crime rate, which might not be a very public-friendly way of presenting the data. We need to consult the Conception of the Integration of Foreigners to ascertain the actual rate and its interpretation, and we know that crime rates among foreign nationals are seen as one of the most sensitive issues in media reports concerning this group. It could therefore be said that, while there are no taboo subjects in the CR in relation to official data monitoring, the presentation of the data could be improved in some respects.

In technical terms, Drbohlav and Lachmanová-Medová cite the inaccessibility of some datasets as well as linking of the various datasets, but also state that data collection is more of a by-product of the collection of data on the population as a whole and is therefore not necessarily useful for monitoring the /integration of immigrants (2009). More specifically, they identify the following shortcomings in relation to specific data: 'Moreover, it is inevitable that there will be a broadening of the information on certain variables tied to immigrants´ basic characteristics (e.g. level of education at the time of arrival) and their integration into the economic sphere, i.e. on remittances, income and unemployment. Also, more specific characteristics that are related to immigrants with permanent residence permits should be made available and accessible. Furthermore, in the statistics of the Aliens Police it is still not possible to distinguish between immigrants who are arriving in the country for the first time and those who are just renewing their permit or moving between different permits/visa categories. There is a further shortcoming – no statistics allow us to link members of one family.' (ibid. 22-23). Varečková and Baštýř (2010:13) also refer to a lack of data at the levels of completed education on the part of foreign nationals and premature school drop-out by TCN children. Moreover, the European Union Statistics on Income and Living Conditions EU-SILC, as well as containing little information on TCN, does not include research in group accommodation facilities, such as hostels where considerable numbers of TCN live. At EU level, the indicators for which comparable data are missing are self-employment, language proficiency, experience with discrimination, trust in public institutions, voter turnout and feeling of belonging to the host society, as well as more general longitudinal data.

With regard to data quality, Vavrečková and Baštýř argue that a 'system of monitoring instruments for evaluation of the course of integration of the third country nationals in the CR has only started to be created recently.' (2010: 12). They also warn that there is a need for a broad political consensus on how integration should be monitored and the sets of indicators that should be used. At this stage, however, they consider the administrative databases of ministries and other similar government institutions to be very valuable for obtaining significant data on the type of residency, employment, education and social status of TCN.

The comprehensive system of monitoring data on foreigners, although it includes some aspects of integration, is not focused primarily on integration. This means that data from the database can be selected and interpreted by selecting integration indicators depending on their definition. For example, while we find data on the acquisition of citizenship, the database tells us nothing about the number of rejected applications (or this would require additional research), nor about the reasons for the rejection of applications. Another example is family reunion, where the basic problem is not that data on marriage to foreign nationals are not available, but that the new (legally embedded) policy has weakened the position of spouses of Czech nationals by denying them permanent residence status and entitling them only to long-term residence, and also that the Czech legal system allows reunion only between nuclear family members, whereas the wider family can be a valuable source of integration for newcomers. This then raises the problems mentioned earlier with health insurance, social security and access to mortgages and other types of loans. The positive change lies in the possibility for permanent residents to vote and run for office at local elections, but only if stipulated by the international treaties, which is not in accord with the European Convention on the Participation of Foreigners in Public Life at Local Level,[16] and has been repeatedly criticized.

It is hard to imagine how the concept of integration as a two-way process would be measured. Some elements could be derived by studying the increasingly multicultural dimension of education as the second generation of migrants (who are however not classified as such) enters the education system. However, even if we find data on the composition of the school population, we need more research to determine whether there has been any accommodation on the part of the majority population in response to increasingly multicultural dimension of education. In order to study the mutual influence further, we would need to turn to the workplace, provided the concentration of immigrants in certain occupations such as construction or cleaning is not the only pattern of work available to immigrants. It is also crucial – and currently not done at EU level – to monitor and measure the various roles of the majority in the integration process.

Generally speaking, the issue as such is not seen as a priority at all in the CR: not by the media not by political parties and not by people in 'everyday' life. The Czech Republic still sees itself as a predominantly homogenous country in national terms, and is in fact partly justified in doing so when we consider the number of foreigners in the country compared with the population as a whole and allowing for the number of foreigners who are EU nationals (see table 4.1). If there are any such questions that do stir public debate at all, they are more likely to be related to the question of Roma rather than immigrants, and very rarely concern asylum-seekers or refugees. This does not however rule out the occasional sensationalist reports in the media, especially concerning topics such as the crime rate among foreigners or, more recently, the fall into the illegal circuit of some foreigners due to the economic crisis. It is not possible within the scope of this chapter to discuss in any serious way the situation with regard to racism and xenophobia in the CR in general, and more specifically in the media, but it is nonetheless useful to look at the shadow report written for ENAR (European Network Against Racism 2010), which repeatedly identifies the group most susceptible to racism as being the Roma population, not immigrants. This once again brings to the fore with great clarity the difference, often discussed among social scientists, between Western and Central and Eastern Europe, namely the difference in the vulnerability of ethnic minorities in the former countries as opposed to the vulnerability of national minorities in the latter (see e.g. Kymlicka 2001). According to a policy paper by Baršová and Barša (2006: 8), Czech immigration and integration policies are still a predominantly administrative but not public matter, and hence are still relatively closed to public dialogue and inclusion in the mainstream political process. The positive side of this is a lack of populist abuse of anti-immigration discourse, but the negative flipside lies in a lack of responsibility on the part of citizens for migration and its consequences. According to Günter (2007: 10), there is no public debate on integration in Czech society because there is no debate about the nature of Czech society as such, about how it should be structured and under what conditions Czechs are prepared to share their social space. In my view this is then mirrored in the definition and measurement of integration and the corresponding policies.

Notes

1   I use the term 'immigrant' in this chapter to denote every person without Czech citizenship who holds some type of residence permit and is not a refugee, asylum-seeker or irregular migrant. Although this also includes EU nationals, the context or explicit reference should imply third-country nationals (TCN). Czech administrative and academic language uses the term 'foreigner'; where the original text uses this term, I will also do so.
2   See Muhič Dizdarevič & Valeš (2010).
3   The authors use the term 'migration policy' to describe both immigration and integration policies.
4   Ministry of the Interior at: http://www.mvcr.cz/azyl/integrace2.html#zasady (consulted 10 January 2008)
5   I will use the term 'asylum applicants' in this chapter since I see it as more readily understood, and also because it has been traditionally used.
6   In 2009 the extension period for this type of visa increased to two years.
7   For details about the shortcomings of the citizenship law, see the report by the Czech Helsinki Committee (in Czech) (Zpráva 2006).
8   http://www.czso.cz/csu/cizinci.nsf/kapitola/ciz_nabyvani_obcanstvi (consulted 5 December 2010)
9   Compared to e.g. Luxembourg 40 %, Spain 20 %, Latvia 19 %, Estonia 18 %, Ireland, Austria cca 10 %, Germany cca 9 % in 2007 (Horáková 2010: 17).
10   Data for 2009.
11   In this category for 12.78% there are no data.
12   See more in labor market segmentation theory.
13   There is also an integration policy for Czech nationals returning to the CR, e.g. from former Soviet states.
14   It is important to stress that these research institutes are typically founded by the respective Ministries and therefore do not represent the classic academic research institutes.
15   For the details on which Ministries and other institutions gather data on foreigners, and using which methods see the report in question. I am focusing here only on information that is available to the public through the CSO.
16   See http://www.worldlii.org/int/other/treaties/COETSER/1992/2.html

References

Bauböck, R. & J. Rundell (eds.) (1998). *Blurred Boundaries: Migration, Ethnicity, Citizenship*. Hants: Ashgate Publishing House.

Baršová, A. & P. Barša (2005). *Přistěhovalectví a liberální stat*. Brno: Masaryk University.

Černík, J. (2007). Czech Republic. In: A. Triandafyllidou & R. Gopas (eds.), *European Immigration: a sourcebook* (p. 59-70). Hampshire: Ashgate.

Český Helsinský Výbor (Zpráva 2006). *Zpráva o stavu lidských práv 2006*. Consulted online on 22 January 2008 at: http://www.helcom.cz/view.php?cisloclanku=2007021901

Český Statistický Úřad (2009). *Cizinci v České Republice [Foreigners in the Czech Republic]*. Prague: Czech Statistical Office.

Čižinský, P. (2008). Czech Republic Report. In: *Comparative Study of Laws in the 27 EU Member States for Legal Migration*. Consulted online on 5 December 2010 at: http://www.iom.int/jahia/webdav/shared/shared/mainsite/law/legal_immigration_en.pdf

Drbohlav, D. & L. Lachmanová-Medová (2009). *Prominstat Report on the Czech Republic*. Consulted online on 10 March 2010 at: http://www.prominstat.eu/drupal/?q=system/files/PROMINSTAT_Country_Report_Czech_Republic.pdf

Günter, V. (2007). *Cizinci v ČR – přehledová studie*. Consulted online on 5 December 2010 at: http://caat.cz/attachments/150_150_Vladislav_Gunter_Cizinci_v_CR.pdf

Horáková, M. (2010). *Vývoj pracovních migrací v České Republice v období hospodářské recese*. Prague: Research institute for labour and social affairs (VÚPSV). Consulted online on 5 December 2010 at: http://praha.vupsv.cz/Fulltext/vz_320.pdf

Horáková, M. & P. Bareš (2010). Intercultural Opening of the Labor Market and Employment Institutions in the Czech Republic. In: *Moving Societies towards Integration*. Consulted online on 5 December 2010 at: http://www.cizinci.cz/files/clanky/708/Moving_societies.pdf

Joppke, C. (2007). *Policy Brief 8. Do Obligatory Civic Integration Courses for Immigrants in Western Europe further Integration?* Consulted online on 5 December 2010 at: http://www.focus-migration.de/uploads/tx_wilpubdb/PB08_IntegrationCourses_02.pdf

KIC (2010). *Zpráva o realizaci Koncepce integrace cizinců v roce 2009*. Consulted online on 5 December 2010 at: http://www.google.com/cse?cx=015489265366623571386%3Aizzrwg3bmqm&as_q=zprava+o+realizaci+koncepce+integrace+cizincu&ok.x=0&ok.y=0&ok=ok

Kymlicka, W. (2001). *Politics in the Vernacular*. Oxford: Oxford University Press.

Kymlicka, W. (2009). The Multicultural Welfare State? In: P. Hall & M. Lamont (eds.), *Successful Societies*. New York: Cambridge University Press.

Muhič Dizdarevič, S. & F. Valeš (2010). ENAR *Shadow Report 2009/2010, Racism and Discrimination in the Czech Republic*. Consulted online on 18 July 2011 at: http://cms.horus.be/files/99935/MediaArchive/publications/Czech%20Republic.pdf

Pořízková, H. (2010). Segmentace trhu práce jako faktor integrace cizinců na trhu práce. In: M. Rákoczyová & R. Trbola (eds.), *Vybrané aspekty života cizinců v ČR*. Prague: Research institute for labour and social affairs (VÚPSV). Consulted online on 5 December 2010 at: http://www.cizinci.cz/files/clanky/710/Vybrane_aspekty.pdf

Rákoczyová, M. & R. Trbola (2008). *Lokální strategie integrace cizinců v ČR I*. Prague: Research institute for labour and social affairs (VÚPSV). Consulted online on 5 December 2010 at: http://aa.ecn.cz/img_upload/224c0704b7b7746e8a07df9a8b20c098/Lokalni_strategie_integrace_cizincu_v_CR.pdf

Rex, J. (1997). The Concept of a Multicultural Society. In: M. Guibernau & J. Rex (eds.), *The Ethnicity Reader* (p. 205-220). Cambridge: Polity Press.

Tollarová, B. (2009). *Praktické potíže cizinců v* ČR. Consulted online on 5 December 2010 at: http://aa.ecn.cz/ img_upload/224c0704b7b7746e8a07df9a8b20c098/вTollarovaPraktickeproblemycizincuvcR.pdf

Tošnerová, B. (2009). *Podoba integrace cizinců v českých krajích – Krajská integrační centra.* Consulted online on 5 December 2010 at: http://aa.ecn.cz/img_upload/224c0704b7b7746e8a07df9a8b20c098/ вTosnerova_PodobaIntegraceCizincuvceskychKrajich.pdf

Usnesení vlády č. 126 ze dne 21.2.2007 – Zpráva o realizaci Koncepce integrace cizinců v roce 2006 a návrh dalšího postupu (Koncepce 2007). Consulted online on 28 January 2008 at: http://www.cizinci.cz/files/clanky/423/ koncepce.pdf

Vavrečková, J & I. Baštýř (2010). Vytváření systému monitorování a hodnocení výsledků integrace cizinců z třetích zemí. In: *Fórum sociální politiky*, roč. 4/2010, p. 10-15. Prague: Research institute for labour and social affairs (VÚPSV).

WMR (2010). *World Migration Report 2010.* Geneva: International Organization for Migration. Consulted online on 5 December 2010 at: http://publications.iom.int/bookstore/free/WMR_2010_ENGLISH.pdf

5 Monitoring the integration process in Denmark

Line Møller Hansen

5.1 Introduction

This chapter describes how integration is measured and monitored by the Ministry of Refugee, Immigration and Integration Affairs in Denmark (Ministry of Integration for short)[1]. The purpose of measuring and monitoring is not only to show politicians that the legislation and initiatives are working effectively, but also to show citizens that their tax money is being used effectively. Moreover, the objectives that are set are used as a management tool to bring together the work of all actors so that everyone is pulling in the same direction, making the collective effort more effective. Finally, the indicators can contribute to efforts to communicate that a positive development is taking place and that integration is improving daily.

The Danish integration policy's development and status in the year 2010 are reviewed in sections 5.2 and 5.3. How immigrants and their descendants are defined in Denmark and which databases we have built around the measuring of the integration process are then described in sections 5.4 to 5.6. Subsequently, section 5.7 describes what types of analyses, assessments and performance measurements are included in the monitoring of integration in Denmark. Section 5.8 describes the development of a change theory and the setting up of key objectives and indicators for the integration process. In conclusion, the status of the monitoring system is discussed in section 5.9.

5.2 Danish integration policy since 1999

Denmark's first Integration Act was introduced in 1999. At the time of writing, this was 11 years ago and a lot has happened since then. The Integration Act fundamentally changed the frameworks for integration work in Denmark, especially as regards who was included, who was responsible and the scope and character of the integration efforts. For instance, it was a completely new task for many municipalities in 1999 to have to contribute to the integration of newly arrived immigrants.

Many legislative amendments and adjustments have since been implemented as a result of the intense political focus. The purpose of all these changes has been to ensure that refugees and reunified families would be met with challenges and requirements at an early stage after they had received residence permits. As such, a more active integration policy had to be pursued, both with regard to the new citizens themselves and with regard to Danish society as a whole. Among the issues prior to the implementation of the Act were that far too many immigrants in Denmark were outside the labour market, and only after many years' residence could they speak Danish well enough to cope in Danish society.

In 2001, the work was further intensified after the conservative/liberal coalition govern-ment came to office. One of the initial actions was the establishment of a Ministry for Refugee, Immigration and Integration Affairs, with the aim of bringing the administra-tion of foreigners and the integration policy into one place. The focus was now directed mainly towards helping newly arrived immigrants into jobs quickly through simplifica-tion of job training, improved efficiency of Danish language training, better utilisation of the qualifications of newly arrived immigrants and making integration a common issue.

On the employment front, the purpose of a range of new initiatives was among other things to establish personal contact between individual immigrants and employers through wage subsidy, company work experience and similar schemes. Danish language training became more flexible and now offers scope for immigrants to work and fol-low Danish language lessons at the same time. A number of other initiatives were also launched, for example for immigrant women, children and youngsters.

The incentives for individual immigrants were strengthened. Thus, a lower allowance – the starting/introduction allowance – was introduced in 2002 for those persons who had been in the country for less than seven years. The aim was to further strengthen the incentives to work. A proper integration contract was introduced, which obliges indi-viduals to participate actively in the integration programme and to be active citizens. Newly arrived immigrants who participate actively in the integration programme and who find employment quickly can obtain permanent residency status earlier than would otherwise be the case.

Municipalities also had to have incentives to make an extra effort, e.g. the perform-ance grant was introduced in 2004, under which the municipalities which achieved the best results were rewarded financially by the Ministry of Integration. More recently, in 2008, a more comprehensive funding reform was introduced, which further strengthens municipalities' financial incentives to make an effective integration effort.

Simultaneously with the changes on the integration front, a number of changes have also taken place in relation to immigration, primarily aimed at limiting the number of newly arrived immigrants. The purpose was to be able to manage the integration proc-ess better in relation to those immigrants who were already in the country and to man-age more intensive integration efforts in relation to future immigrants in Denmark. As a result of these changes, the pattern of immigration to Denmark has changed.

5.3   Danish integration policy in the year 2010

The Integration Act and the law on Danish courses for adult aliens are the primary basis of the Danish integration policy in relation to newly arrived immigrants. After newly arrived immigrants have completed the three-year integration programme, they become subject to the normally applicable legislation with regard to matters such as unemploy-ment, etc.

In recent years there has also been a tremendous focus on the integration of immigrants who have resided in the country for a longer period of time and who are not fully inte-grated, including a focus on their children (descendents). This target group is addressed through special initiatives and projects, which are developed and implemented in inter-action between the Ministry of Integration, other ministries, municipalities and other actors in the field. Among other things, efforts are made to break down barriers in voca-tional education so that more youngsters with foreign backgrounds can complete an education. In addition, a number of initiatives have been launched in relation to equal-ity between the sexes among immigrants, prevention of 're-education trips', prevention of crime among children and youngsters in ghetto areas and homework help schemes. The following section outlines the current integration policy in relation to newly arrived immigrants.

5.3.1   Housing

When a refugee receives residency status in Denmark, The Danish Immigration Service decides in which municipality the refugee will live. With regard to housing, the Dan-ish Immigration Service first takes into account the general integration of refugees in Denmark to ensure an even geographical distribution of newly arrived immigrants takes place to all municipalities in the country. The distribution of refugees takes place in accordance with agreements between the regions and, within the regions, on the basis of agreements between municipalities. With regard to housing, the Danish Immi-gration Service takes into consideration the refugee's own requirements and personal circumstances, but also the individual's opportunities in the future municipality of residence. It thus matters, for example, whether the individual has any form of attach-ment to a municipality in advance, but the opportunities for employment can also be of great importance. When the municipality has taken over responsibility for a refugee, the municipality must assign a home to the person concerned.

5.3.2   Integration programme

After arrival, municipalities must offer an integration programme to all refugees and reunified families over 18 years of age. This integration programme can run for three years at the most and consists of at least 37 hours per week on average.
The integration programme includes Danish language training for up to three years, which is described further below. In addition, the programme includes a number of offers directed towards employment. It is estimated that about 61,000 persons have participated in an integration programme from 1999 to 2010 (of whom about 15,000 are refugees).
The extent and content of the integration programme's individual elements are deter-mined in an integration contract, which is entered into between the newly arrived refugee/immigrant and the municipality. The contract is entered into on the basis of a complete assessment of the individual's situation and needs with a view to securing regular work as soon as possible. Included in the assessment are, among other things, the individual's skills and prerequisites as well as the needs of the labour market. In this connection, it is essential that an effective competence assessment is carried out so

that the individual's current competences and qualifications are utilised as effectively as possible.

Newly arrived refugees and reunified families who receive an introduction allowance must be offered Danish language training and participate in job training. Newly arrived refugees/immigrants who do not receive an introduction allowance must be offered Danish language course and can chose to participate in offers aimed at employment.
Newly arrived refugees/immigrants who are offered an integration programme are obliged to participate actively in the individual parts of the programme. If a newly arrived refugee/immigrant does not participate, this can have consequences for the payment of benefits and ultimately on the chance of achieving permanent residency.

In April 2010 the government entered into a new political agreement with the Danish People's Party, which among other things contains an agreement that the rules for indefinite residency will be simplified so that immigrants can obtain permanent residency if they make an active effort to integrate and develop a genuine attachment to Denmark. At the same time, the rules for permanent residency will be changed so that immigrants who make an active effort to be a part of Danish society can obtain an indefinite residence permit faster – though at the earliest after having had legal residency in Denmark for four years.

In future, the conditions for obtaining an indefinite residence permit will be based on the results of the individual's integration into Denmark and, to a lesser degree, on how much the person concerned has followed his or her integration programme. To this end, a points system will be introduced that motivates immigrants to become integrated in Denmark, e.g. through work, education, language skills and citizenship. In future, an indefinite residence permit will be an indication that the person concerned has developed a genuine affiliation with Denmark through actual results, and has not rejected Danish society either through criminality or debt to the public sector.

5.3.3 Offers directed towards employment during the integration programme

Danish municipalities are currently able to offer three types of job training: guidance and upgrading of skills, company internships and subsidised employment.
Newly arrived refugees/immigrants who need to have their competences assessed or upgraded may be offered guidance and upskilling programmes. These might include courses, introduction to specific industries or municipal employment projects.
Newly arrived refugees/immigrants whose employment opportunities need to be assessed or who lack the necessary skills to become employed under normal wage and working terms may be offered a company internship. During an internship, the individual's professional, linguistic or social competences at the workplace will be trained and the intern must acquire an increased understanding of Danish society.

Ultimately, employment with wage subsidy can be offered. This entails employment at a public or private company with a view to training the individual's social, linguistic or professional competences. In the event of wage subsidy, the unemployed person is employed, for example in a private company, and receives a regular wage subsidy (for a maximum of 6-12 months).

These job training offers can be combined with a mentor scheme. Here, the municipality provides a subsidy so that an employee in the company or an external consultant can take responsibility for the induction, guidance or training of the newly arrived immigrant.

A systematic effort including among other things Danish language courses, fast competence assessment and skills upgrading, as well as the use of company-specific training, is an effective way of helping newly arrived refugees/immigrants into the labour market.

5.3.4   Danish language training

Immigrants who live in Denmark have the right to Danish language training for three years. This applies to both newly arrived immigrants covered by the Integration Act (refugees and reunified persons) and other immigrants, e.g. EU citizens. Municipalities are responsible for providing Danish language courses. These courses must provide participants with linguistic qualifications to enable them to hold their own on the labour market and become active citizens. To date, the courses have included tuition in culture and societal understanding. From August 2010, an independent course on Danish societal conditions and Danish history and culture will be introduced. The course will be offered to everyone as part of the integration programme in order to improve the individual's ability to participate actively in Danish society. The course will also become a criterion for awarding points in the future in the event of obtaining permanent residency, providing evidence that the immigrant has passed a citizenship test that demonstrates their familiarity with Danish society and thus their degree of integration.

There are three Danish language courses – language course 1, 2 and 3 – which are geared towards the participants' educational background. All three Danish language courses are split into six modules and culminate in a national test (test in Danish 1, 2 or 3). The Danish language courses must be adapted to the participants so that the tuition can be combined with other activities, such as work or other forms of education.

Box 5.1   Danish language courses 1, 2 and 3

In 2008, there were approximately 38,500 participants registered for the three Danish language courses:
- Danish language course 1 is aimed at participants who cannot read or write the Latin alphabet.
- Danish language course 2 is aimed at participants who have a short schooling and educational background from their home country.
- Danish language course 3 is aimed at participants who have a medium or long schooling and educational background from their home country.

From 1 July 2010, a new Danish language course directed towards the labour market (so-called intro-Danish) will commence. This Danish language course is offered to newly arrived immigrants who have entered Denmark and have regular employment.

5.3.5   Funding of the integration efforts

The Ministry of Integration provides subsidies and refunds for municipalities' expenses on Danish language courses, introduction allowances and the integration programme. The rules regarding funding were changed on 1 January 2008 in order to simplify the system and increase municipalities' economic incentives to provide effective integration. Before the funding reform, municipalities' expenses on the integration programme were financed among other things through programme subsidies. From 1 January 2008, this system was replaced by a 50% refund of municipalities' integration programme expenses.

Additionally, the state provides a performance grant to municipalities; municipalities receive a grant of approx. DKK 42,000 (€ 5,600) for each person who gains regular employment or starts an education programme during the course of the three-year introduction period, and a grant of DKK 32,000 (€ 4,300) for each person who registers for and passes a Danish language test within the introduction period.

5.4   Definition of integration

The Danish integration policy does not use a set definition of integration. In a political programme for better integration (2003), the government formulated the following strategy and vision for the integration policy; the aim is:

1   to create a framework for a society where *diversity* and *personal freedom* thrive and where there is *solidarity about fundamental values*; a society where the right to choose and shape one's own life is respected, where there is scope for cultural and religious display and where the individual contributes as an active citizen; and a society in which violation of its basic values carries consequences.

    An important prerequisite for this to succeed is that all citizens, regardless of ethnic or cultural background, have equal opportunities to participate in and contribute to society.

2 to create a framework such that immigrants and refugees receive a better *education* and *good knowledge of the Danish language*. These are not just important gateways to the labour market; they also increase the opportunities for participating as active citizens in a social and democratic context and for understanding and connecting with society and the community of which the individual is a part.

3 to create a framework such that everyone has *access to the labour market* and thus the opportunity not only to be self-supporting, but also to contribute to positive societal development in a broad sense. Full employment and self-sufficiency among immigrants and refugees is not just a question of improving the socio-economics; it is also about showing the individual human respect as a full member of society.

In addition, four preambles are included in the Integration Act; see also box 5.2. In brief, these can be described as a participation objective, a self-sufficiency objective, a value objective and an inclusion objective. These objectives are key to the Ministry's work.

Box 5.2 The aim of the Integration Act

The aim of the Integration Act (§1) is to:

1 assist in ensuring that newly arrived aliens can participate in the life of society in terms of politics, economy, employment, social activities, religion and culture on an equal footing with other citizens;

2 assist in making newly arrived aliens self-supporting as quickly as possible through employment; and

3 impart to the individual alien an understanding of the fundamental values and norms of Danish society.

Another object of the Act is to promote the opportunities for citizens, enterprises, authorities, institutions, organisations, associations, etc. in society to contribute to the integration effort.

The recent political agreement means the preamble in the Integration Act will be revised in order to clarify the individual's responsibility for successful integration. Thus, it is emphasised that anyone who has residence in Denmark is expected to contribute to Danish society and to participate in the life of society in accordance with society's fundamental norms and values.

5.5 Definition of immigrants and descendants

A definition of immigrants and their descendants in Denmark was drawn up in the 1980s. There has been consensus about the use of this definition ever since. This is a purely statistical definition, which does not say anything about whether or not the persons concerned are integrated in Denmark.

All persons whose parents have a foreign background are defined as either immigrants or descendants. The definition is based on the parents' citizenship and the person's place of birth. This definition provides the possibility of changing the status across generations, whereby a person at least one of whose parents is *both* a descendant of immigrants in Denmark (i.e. was born in Denmark) and who is a Danish citizen will be defined as Danish for statistical purposes.

In the statistics, *immigrants* are defined as persons who were born abroad to parents who are *both* foreign citizens. If there is no information about either of the parents and the person in question was born abroad, the person is categorised as an immigrant.

In the statistics, *descendants* are defined as persons who were born in Denmark to parents, neither of whom is a Danish citizen *born* in Denmark. If there is no information about either of the parents and the person in question is a foreign citizen *born* in Denmark, the person is categorised as a descendant. Descendants are also described as second-generation immigrants.

Immigrants and descendants include both foreigners and Danish citizens with a foreign background. Table 5.1 shows immigrants, descendants and Danes distributed over foreign and Danish citizenship, as at 1 January 2010.

Table 5.1
Immigrants, descendants and Danes by foreign and Danish citizenship, 1 January 2010
(in absolute numbers)

	immigrants	descendants	Danes	total
foreign citizens	284,297	38,756	6,887	329,940
Danish citizens	130,125	89,560	4,985,113	5,204,798
total	414,422	128,316	4,992,000	5,534,738

Source: Statistics Denmark

As of 1 January 2010, there were 330,000 foreign citizens in Denmark, representing 6% of the total population. All in all there were 543,000 immigrants and descendants in Denmark, some of whom had obtained Danish citizenship. 40% of all foreigners in Denmark were Danish citizens (31% of immigrants had Danish citizenship, 70% of descendants).

Whether one uses the 'stock of foreign citizens' or 'immigrants and descendants' as a definition depends on the purpose. When measuring the integration of immigrants and their descendants in Danish society, it is often most appropriate to focus on persons of foreign origin; i.e. immigrants and their descendants, and not just people with foreign citizenship. In Denmark we are able to use both definitions when analysing the foreign population.
Most analyses on integration are carried out on immigrants and descendants from non-Western countries, since this is where the major challenges lie. Many analyses focus on the ten largest immigrant groups in Denmark, namely Turkey, Iraq, Lebanon, Bosnia-Herzegovina, Pakistan, Yugoslavia, Somalia, Iran, Vietnam and Afghanistan.

Western countries: EU member states, Iceland, Norway, USA, Canada, Australia,
                            New Zealand, Andorra, Liechtenstein, Monaco, San Marino,
                            Switzerland and Vatican City.

Non-Western countries: All other countries.

Table 5.2 shows the number of male and female immigrants and descendants in
Denmark as at 1 January 2010.

Table 5.2
Immigrants and descendents, 1 January 2010 (in absolute numbers)

	immigrants		descendants		total
	men	women	men	women	
Western countries	79,449	82,961	8,731	8,240	179,381
non-Western countries	123,331	128,681	56,773	54,572	363,357
total	202,780	211,642	65,504	62,812	542,738

Source: Statistics Denmark

As of 1 January 2010, there were 543,000 immigrants and descendants in Denmark, representing 10% of the total population of 5.5 million. 414,000 were immigrants and 128,000
were descendants. 363,000 persons, or 67% of all immigrants and descendants, were
from non-Western countries, thus constituting by far the majority of all immigrants and
descendants. The proportions of men and women appear to be almost equal, regardless
of country of origin, except for immigrants from Western countries where the number of
women exceeds the number of men.

All statistical analyses are conducted at national and municipal level. It is essential to
analyse integration at municipal level as the municipalities are responsible for the three-
year integration programme which all newly arrived refugees and reunified families
must complete. Moreover, municipalities are responsible for providing job training,
Danish language training and other skills upgrading to all unemployed persons, including foreigners with a residence permit in Denmark. It is irrelevant in a Danish context to
analyse the integration at regional level.

5.6   Statistical basis for monitoring

Since 1999, the Ministry of Integration has had access to statistical information about
immigrants and descendants in Denmark. When the Integration Act came into force in
1999, a database with information about immigrants and descendants was established.
The database is held at Statistics Denmark under the name 'Foreigner database' as
Statistics Denmark collects a large amount of statistics on the population. The Ministry

has direct access to the information, which is used exclusively for analytical purposes. During the processing of data, discretion is used and private information is not disclosed.
The database is based on the personal ID number register, which is constantly updated with information about people's gender, age, country of origin, citizenship, etc. Based on this information, it is possible to define immigrants and descendants (see the definition in section 5.5). Subsequently, the personal ID register is linked to information about people's occupation, education, settlement, etc. This linkage makes it possible to conduct analyses of occupation, education, settlement and much more of immigrants and descendants in comparison with native Danes.

In collaboration with Statistics Denmark, the Ministry of Integration has constantly developed the foreigner database by adding indicators about the integration of immigrants and descendants. The Ministry works with a large number of indicators, which among other things are based on information from the foreigner database, but also from other sources (assessments and other ad hoc analyses). The indicators are used to retrieve information about the development in integration, but also to monitor compliance by municipalities with the provisions of the Integration Act. This is thus a comprehensive monitoring system, which is described further in the following section.

5.7   Monitoring through analysis, assessment and effectiveness measurement

The Ministry of Integration carries out analyses, assessments and effectiveness measurements on an ongoing basis on a large number of aspects of integration. The following section describes how the effects of the Integration Act are measured.

5.7.1   Measuring the effects of the legislation

It is particularly essential to measure the effects of the legislation. In 2004, the first effectiveness measurement of the municipalities' integration efforts was published in 2004, and March 2009 saw publication of the fifth measurement[2].

As described in section 5.3, since the Integration Act came into force in 1999 municipalities have been responsible for the integration of newly arrived refugees/immigrants. The core of the integration work is the special three-year integration programme, which municipalities must offer to newly arrived refugees and reunified persons. The aim of the programme is to give newly arrived immigrants better opportunities to gain employment or enter education or training, and thus to put them on equal terms with other citizens in society.
Experience shows that it takes time for the majority of newly arrived refugees/immigrants to gain employment or enter education. However, in recent years significant progress has been made in raising the number of refugees/immigrants who have done so. The assessment is that this is due both to a more focused approach by municipalities and the positive economic development in Denmark.

The effectiveness measurement compares municipalities based on which is the fastest to help newly arrived refugees and reunified families into employment or education as required, under the Danish Integration Act. As far as possible, the measurement takes into account a number of key differences between municipalities, including differences in the characteristics of the refugees and reunified persons. The selected background variables can explain 70% of the differences between municipalities' success in helping refugees/immigrants into employment or education.

The purpose of measuring the of municipalities' integration efforts is to create a basis for the exchange of experiences between municipalities so that those municipalities that perform less effectively can learn from those municipalities which are providing an effective service. Ongoing exchange of experiences makes it possible to streamline and improve the work.

The latest effectiveness measurement shows that 15%of refugees or reunified persons who arrived in 2000have found employment or entered education after one year in Denmark; the corresponding figure for those who arrived in 2006 is 29% (see table 5.3). This means that the percentage of refugees and reunified persons who arrived in 2006 and have found employment or entered education after one year in Denmark has doubled compared to those who arrived in 2000. The progress is also significant when considering the percentage who are in employment or education after two, three, four, five and six years' residency. This progress is partly the result of a more effective approach to integration, but also of positive economic development.

Table 5.3

(Observed) percentage of refugees and reunified persons who commenced employment or a course of education (for at least six months) in the period 1999-2007, distributed between the year of obtaining a residence permit and the number of years after receiving a residence permit[a]

year of obtaining residence permit	number of years after receiving residence permit							
	1	2	3	4	5	6	7	8
1999	18.7	30.2	39.5	47.2	52.0	56.0	60.0	64.0
2000	15.2	26.4	36.7	43.8	50.4	55.3	60.0	
2001	15.7	26.4	38.0	46.4	53.3	59.5		
2002	17.7	30.6	42.7	52.3	59.9			
2003	18.4	35.0	48.7	59.8				
2004	24.1	41.0	55.5					
2005	25.4	44.0						
2006	29.0							

a   The figures have not been adjusted for those foreigners who arrive over the years who may have different characteristics.

Source: Benchmarking analysis of integration in municipalities measured by employment of foreigners, 1999-2007, AKF, January 2009.

For the country as a whole, 47% of the integration cases culminated in employment or education in the period from 1999 to 2007, while one out of every two cases was uncompleted in the period (see table 5.4). This represents a significant improvement compared to the preceding effectiveness measurement (1999-2004), in which only one in every three cases concluded with employment or education.

Table 5.4

Number of integration processes culminating in employment or education (for at least six months) in the period 1999-2007 for male and female persons under the Integration Act (in percentages and absolute numbers)

		employment (%)	education (%)	neither employment nor education (%)	number of processes
employment or	men	49	4	46	18,351
education	women	34	8	58	27,081
for at least six months	total	40	7	53	45,432

Source: Benchmarking analysis of integration in municipalities measured by employment of foreigners, 1999-2007, AKF, January 2009.

On average, for the country as a whole it takes 45 months for refugees and reunified persons to gain employment or enter education (for at least six months). In the fastest municipalities it takes 9.4 months less than expected and in the slowest municipalities 7.1 months longer than expected before refugees and reunified persons gain employment or enter education. In other words, there is 16.5 month difference between the fastest and slowest municipalities[3].

Table 5.5

Distribution of municipalities across five categories, in alphabetical order, according to how successful they are in helping newly arrived persons into employment or education as per the Integration Act, 1999-2007[a]

very good	good	average	poor	very poor
Allerød	Albertslund	Brøndby	Assens	Dragør*
Ballerup	Bornholm	Fredensborg	Bogense	Faxe
Billund*	Faaborg-Midtfyn	Gladsaxe	Brønderslev-Dronninglund	Frederiksberg*
Egedal	Glostrup	Helsingør	Esbjerg	Haderslev
Frederikshavn*	Gribskov	Herning	Favrskov	Langeland*
Frederikssund	Guldborgsund	Holstebro	Fredericia	Lemvig*
Greve	Herlev	Hvidovre	Furesø	Lolland*
Halsnæs*	Kerteminde	Ikast-Brande	Gentofte	Lyngby-Taarbæk
Hedensted*	Middelfart	Kalundborg	Holbæk	Mariagerfjord
Hillerød	Odder	**Copenhagen**	Kolding	Nyborg*
Hjørring	Ringsted	Køge	Lejre	Odsherred*
Horsens*	Roskilde	Næstved	Morsø	Ringkøbing-Skjern
Høje-Taastrup*	Rudersdal	Rebild	Norddjurs	Skive*
Hørsholm*	Rødovre	Stevns	**Odense**	Sorø*
Ishøj*	Silkeborg	Struer	Randers	Svendborg
Jammerbugt	Slagelse	Varde	Solrød	Tønder*
Skanderborg	Sønderborg	Vesthimmerland	Syddjurs	Viborg
Tårnby*	Vejen	Vordingborg	Thisted	**Århus**
Vallensbæk*	Vejle	Åbenrå	**Ålborg**	

a   There must be a minimum of 80 refugees and reunified families in the municipality for it to be included in the ranking.
*   Marks the ten fastest and the ten slowest municipalities in the categories 'very good' and 'very poor'.

Source: Benchmarking analysis of integration in municipalities measured by employment of foreigners, 1999-2007, AKF, January 2009.

Table 5.5 shows the distribution of municipalities' success in integrating persons under the Integration Act in five categories. The four largest municipalities in Denmark are marked in bold. All score average or below average in the measurement with regard to helping newly arrived immigrants into employment or education. However, it should be noted that, due to the housing placement policy, these municipalities basically only accept reunified persons, and not refugees. Compared to reunified persons, who usually do not receive any benefits from the public sector, the programme is not as comprehensive as for persons who do receive benefits. In practice, this results in a less active integration effort since municipalities are not obliged to offer the same comprehensive effort, but can choose to do so.

However, it should be noted that two of the municipalities that are right at the top of the ranking in table 5.5 are among the municipalities that have the highest percentage of immigrants in Denmark (and which therefore also accept many reunified persons), namely the municipalities of Ishøj and Høje Taastrup; other municipalities can draw inspiration and motivation for a successful effort from these two municipalities.

Other assessments of municipalities' performance show that since 2001 they have focused more on employment initiatives. As a consequence, newly arrived refugees and reunified persons find work faster than in the past.

In September 2008 the Ministry published an effectiveness measurement of Danish language providers showing which providers were the fastest and most effective in teaching Danish. The measurement indicates that the effectiveness of Danish language tuition has risen sharply under the new law on Danish courses for adult aliens (2004). From 2004 to 2006, substantially fewer lessons were required to complete the individual Danish course modules than previously, and language training has thus become more effective.

5.8 Monitoring through performance management

In addition to the effectiveness measurements, the Ministry of Integration also uses performance management, or result-based management. The aim is to continually monitor the development of central parts of the integration effort to determine whether the envisaged effects/results are feasible. The following section describes how the Ministry has applied performance management.

5.8.1 The aim of performance management

Performance management is a new initiative for public sector management, which places the performance of a municipality, an organisation or a ministry in focus. This means that management of the integration process is based on outcome rather than output. The method is used to show citizens that the integration effort is working – and thus that tax-payers' money is being used effectively – and also to continually monitor the development of central parts of the integration effort to determine whether the envisaged effects/results are feasible.

As described in section 5.3, the integration effort in Denmark is organised in such a way that it is carried out locally in the municipalities. This implies that municipalities are responsible for the actual implementation of the Integration Act for newly arrived immigrants. A central task for the Ministry is therefore to create a common understanding of the goals of the integration efforts across organisational boundaries so that all players work towards the same objectives. This can be done through result-based management, where the focus is on ascertaining what works effectively. The aim is to inform and motivate municipalities and other players to implement their integration efforts to maximum effect.

5.8.2   The development of performance management

As a new management tool, performance management has gained ground year by year in
the public sector in Denmark. Currently, it is used in a number of other ministries and in
selected domains in a number of large municipalities, e.g. Copenhagen and Aarhus.
The inspiration for the use of performance management comes mainly from the USA,
where its use a management tool for state institutions was introduced by law in 1993.
The USA has thus gained a good deal of experience in the organisation of performance
management in practice. At the same time, the US administration differs greatly from its
counterpart in Denmark, and it is therefore essential to find the right model for the Danish context.
The demand for a management tool that focuses on performance has been on the
increase for the last five years. That demand comes from politicians, citizens, the media
and bodies such as the National Audit Office of Denmark, which among other things
audits the accounts and administration of the laws passed by Parliament. The National
Audit Office has also begun to focus more attention on how ministries measure the
effects of legislation, based on whether the laws' objectives (see box 5.2) are being
achieved.
The Ministry of Integration was among the first ministries in Denmark to use performance management, and has actively worked with the idea as well as trying to motivate
others to adopt a management system based on outcome rather than output. Among
other things, the Ministry co-organised a major conference on performance management in Copenhagen in 2005, and a number of employees have been on study trips to
the USA to gain experience about performance management. Additionally, the Ministry
is co-author of a book (in Danish) containing examples of the use of performance management. Currently, the Ministry has organised a network together with municipalities
focusing on effectiveness measuring and performance management, to inspire and
motivate municipalities to embrace this way of thinking. The network is also aimed at
sharing existing experiences with all stakeholders.

5.8.3   The change theory

As part of the move towards performance management, a change theory has been established. This is used to visualise which steps and initiatives will be used to achieve the
desired overall effect. The change theory shows how the Ministry's resources and activities contribute to achieving the envisaged objectives and ultimately lead to the overall
desired effect. It thus provides a roadmap showing the path towards the common goals.

Box 5.4   How the change theory works as a method

Fundamentally, the change theory is a tool for the development of a performance management tool. By basing the theory on the envisaged long-term effects (impact/effect), it is then
possible to move backwards through the model to formulate the outcome required in the
longer term in order to achieve the long-term effects.

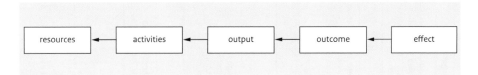

The output/products that need be achieved in the *shorter term* in order to secure the desired
effect are also formulated, as well as the activities and resources that are needed in order to
achieve this.

Since it has been the pioneering institution for this way of thinking in relation to integration, the Ministry of Integration is also the place where the first change theory
was formulated. The theory is based on the experiences gained by the Ministry since
its establishment in 2001 and the mechanisms underlying the integration process. It is
also adapted to the political visions and requirements in this area. The change theory is
thus not simply a theoretic model, but also relates to the current political goals, making
its implementation as a management tool directly possible. The intention is that it will
be regularly updated and adapted to the current challenges and political visions and be
adjusted as new knowledge is gained on what works most effectively.

The change theory contains six key objectives for the integration process in Denmark
and 14 intermediate objectives for the Ministry of Integration's contribution in moving towards the overall objectives. The theory illustrates how the Ministry's activities,
legislation and cooperation with central players impact on integration. The goals are
described further in the following section.

During the preparation phase, the change theory and the objectives as well as proposals
for indicators were presented to a large number of external parties in the integration
field. These parties contributed key input to the development and utilisation of the
theory.

Figure 5.1
Theory of change

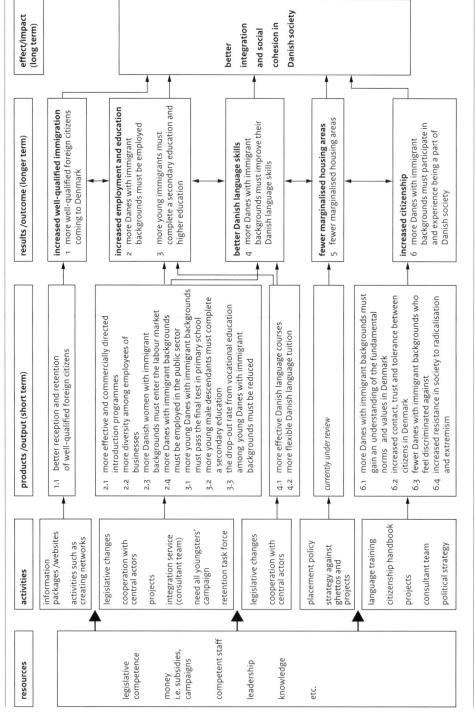

resources

legislative
competence

money
i.e. subsidies,
campaigns

competent staff

leadership

knowledge

etc.

activities

information
packages /websites

activities such as
creating networks

legislative changes

cooperation with
central actors

projects

integration service
(consultant team)

need all youngsters'
campaign

retention task force

legislative changes

cooperation with
central actors

placement policy

strategy against
ghettos and
projects

language training

citizenship handbook

projects

consultant team

political strategy

products /output (short term)

1.1 better reception and retention
of well-qualified foreign citizens

2.1 more effective and commercially directed
introduction programmes
2.2 more diversity among employees of
businesses
2.3 more Danish women with immigrant
backgrounds must enter the labour market
2.4 more Danes with immigrant backgrounds
must be employed in the public sector
3.1 more young Danes with immigrant backgrounds
must pass the final test in primary school
3.2 more young male descendants must complete
a secondary education
3.3 the drop-out rate from vocational education
among young Danes with immigrant
backgrounds must be reduced

4.1 more effective Danish language courses
4.2 more flexible Danish language tuition

currently under review

6.1 more Danes with immigrant backgrounds must
gain an understanding of the fundamental
norms and values in Denmark
6.2 increased contact, trust and tolerance between
citizens in Denmark
6.3 fewer Danes with immigrant backgrounds who
feel discriminated against
6.4 increased resistance in society to radicalisation
and extremism

results /outcome (longer term)

increased well-qualified immigration
1 more well-qualified foreign citizens
coming to Denmark

increased employment and education
2 more Danes with immigrant
backgrounds must be employed

3 more young immigrants must
complete a secondary education and
higher education

better Danish language skills
4 more Danes with immigrant
backgrounds must improve their
Danish language skills

fewer marginalised housing areas
5 fewer marginalised housing areas

increased citizenship
6 more Danes with immigrant
backgrounds must participate in
and experience being a part of
Danish society

effect/impact (long term)

**better
integration
and social
cohesion in
Danish society**

116

5.8.4 Objectives

Currently, 14 intermediate objectives for the Ministry's short-term activities and six general, long-term objectives have been established. The long-term objective for the integration efforts is 'Better integration and cohesion in Danish society'.

Since 2001, the government has made it clear that the goal is to conduct a firm and fair immigration policy, i.e. to reduce the number of new immigrants so as to make it possible to give those immigrants who are in Denmark a fair chance to become integrated. A strict immigration policy is therefore conducted in order to strengthen the basis for positive integration. In several government presentations employment, Danish language skills and education (goals 2-4) have been central elements in the integration efforts. In its strategy to combat ghettoisation, the government has also focused on immigrants' settlement (goal 5). In addition, a new bill tabled in 2007 placed more importance on working towards better integration by focusing on citizenship and inclusion in society of newly arrived immigrants (goal 6).

Additionally, Denmark faces a shortage of labour. The declining size of the younger generations and the growing number of older people makes it necessary to attract labour from abroad in order to maintain the welfare society. The focus in the government's 2007 proposal was thus mainly on the possibilities for facilitating increased, controlled immigration to Denmark with a view to alleviating the shortage of labour as well as retaining the new potential labour force. The focus was therefore on strengthening the integration of the new labour force in order to ensure that they would play an active part in Danish society from the outset (goal 1).

The envisaged long-term effect of this approach is better integration and cohesion in Danish society. Integration is a multifaceted process in which the most essential elements are employment, education, Danish language skills, settlement and the experience of being citizens in society. Moreover, when there is no financial crisis, there is a shortage of qualified labour in Denmark, which makes the attraction and retention of more well-qualified labour necessary.

The six key objectives thus reflect the government's main focus and visions. However, the objectives can only be achieved if all stakeholders cooperate and pull in the same direction.

In addition, 14 intermediate objectives have been established, which describe how the Ministry of Integration can contribute to the achievement of the general objectives. These intermediate objectives show the main areas on which the Ministry is focusing in order to contribute to the achievement of the six key objectives. The Ministry's focus areas are thus addressed through legislative amendments, initiatives and support of good integration projects. The 14 intermediate objectives were established according to an internal development process.

Box 5.5   Overview of the six key objectives and the 14 intermediate objectives

six key objectives	14 intermediate objectives for the Ministry of Integration
1 more well-qualified foreign citizens coming to Denmark	1.1 better reception and retention of well-qualified foreign citizens
2 more Danes with immigrant backgrounds originating from non-Western countries must be employed	2.1 more effective and commercially directed integration programmes
	2.2 more diversity among employees of businesses
	2.3 more Danish women with immigrant backgrounds must enter the labour market
	2.4 more Danes with immigrant backgrounds originating from non-Western countries must be employed in the public sector
3 more young Danes with immigrant backgrounds originating from non-Western countries must complete a secondary education and higher education	3.1 more young Danes with immigrant backgrounds originating from non-Western countries must pass the final test in primary school
	3.2 more young male descendants must complete a secondary education
	3.3 the drop-out rate from vocational education among young Danes with immigrant backgrounds originating from non-Western countries must be reduced
4 more Danes with immigrant backgrounds must improve their Danish language skills	4.1 more effective Danish language courses
	4.2 more flexible Danish language training
5 fewer marginalised housing areas	*objectives currently under review*
6 more Danes with immigrant backgrounds originating from non-Western countries must participate in and experience being a part of Danish society	6.1 more Danes with immigrant backgrounds originating from non-Western countries must gain an understanding of the fundamental norms and values in Denmark
	6.2 increased contact, trust and tolerance between citizens in Denmark
	6.3 fewer Danes with immigrant backgrounds originating from non-Western countries who feel discriminated against
	6.4 increased resistance in society to radicalisation and extremism

5.8.5   Indicators

Behind all objectives, one or two indicators have been established to measure progress. These indicators have been selected on the basis of the experience built up by the
Ministry measuring integration and external input. The indicators draw on a large number of mainly quantitative data sources.

The Ministry has not, at the time of writing, gained much experience in measuring citizenship and is only at the start of this process. The indicators in relation to this area will
therefore develop continuously as experience is gained. On the other hand, the Ministry
has comprehensive experience in measuring employment and education, and also has
good data sources for these areas.

See Box 5.6 for an overview of the indicators for all objectives. There are 11 indicators for
the six key objectives and 20 for the 14 intermediate objectives, i.e. a total of 31 indicators.

When establishing the indicators, the focus was mainly on measuring performance as
opposed to the activity and in ensuring that they were measurable without having to use
a great deal of resources. Moreover, the indicators must make sense to those who work
within the area and must be able to be communicated to outside parties. It is also very
important that the indicators are as current as possible so that progress is continuously
measured and the process can be adapted if that progress falls short of what is desired.

Box 5.6 Overview of indicators for measuring objectives

key objectives	Ministry's intermediate objectives	indicators
1 increased well-qualified immigration		
1 more well-qualified foreign citizens coming to Denmark	1.1 better reception and retention of well-qualified foreign citizens	– number of work permits – period of residency in Denmark of well-qualified immigrant workers – number of immigrant workers receiving Danish language training
2 increased employment		
2 more Danes with immigrant background originating from non-Western countries must be employed	2.1 more effective and commercially directed integration programmes	– percentage of 16-64 year-old immigrants and descendants from non-Western countries in employment – employment rate among non-EU immigrants – number of performance grants granted to municipalities for-employment – percentage of introduction allowance recipients in job training – percentage of introduction allowance recipients in combined Danish language training and job training
	2.2 more diversity among employees of businesses	– percentage of businesses with 5% of employees from non-Western countries
	2.3 more Danish women with immigrant backgrounds must enter the labour market	– percentage of 16-64 year-old female immigrants and descendants from non-Western countries in employment
	2.4 more Danes with immigrant backgrounds originating from non-Western countries must be employed in the public sector	– percentage of immigrants and descendants from non-Western countries employed in the public sector

Box 5.6 (continued)

3 increased level of education

3 more young immigrants originating from non-Western countries must complete a school education and higher education

– percentage of 20-24 year-old immigrants and descendants from non-Western countries who have completed a school education
– percentage of 25-29 year-old immigrants and descendants from non-Western countries who have completed a higher education

3.1 more young Danes with immigrant backgrounds originating from non-Western countries must pass the final test in primary school

– grades obtained in the final test in primary school

3.2 more young male descendants must complete a school education

– percentage of 15-24 year-old male descendants from non-Western countries who complete a school education

3.3 the drop-out rate from vocational education among young Danes with immigrant backgrounds originating from non-Western countries must be reduced

– drop-out rate from vocational education among immigrants and descendants from non-Western countries

4 better Danish language skills

4 more Danes with immigrant backgrounds must improve their Danish language skills

– number of immigrants who pass a Danish language course
– average grades in Danish language courses 1, 2 and 3
– personal opinion of immigrants about their Danish language skills

4.1 more effective Danish language courses

– progression in Danish language courses 1, 2 and 3
– satisfaction with Danish language skills among businesses

4.2 more flexible Danish language tuition

– satisfaction with Danish language courses among participants

5 fewer marginalised housing areas

5 fewer marginalised housing areas *currently under review*

121

Box 5.6 (continued)

6 increased citizenship

6   more Danes with immigrant backgrounds must participate in and experience being a part of Danish society

- percentage of immigrants who feel integrated
- percentage of immigrants who are members of an association, political party or interest group
- electoral participation by immigrants

6.1 more Danes with immigrant backgrounds originating from non-Western countries must gain an understanding of the fundamental norms and values in Denmark

- the understanding by immigrants of democracy, equality, freedom of speech and other fundamental values and norms in Denmark

6.2 increased contact, trust and tolerance between citizens in Denmark

- percentage of immigrants who are friends with other Danes
- percentage of Danes who are friends with immigrants
- percentage of immigrants who marry a Dane or another immigrant in Denmark

6.3 fewer Danes with immigrant backgrounds originating from non-Western countries who feel discriminated against

- percentage of immigrants who feel discriminated against

6.4 increased resistance in society to radicalisation and extremism

- trust in social institutions

5.9   Discussion

For many years, the Ministry of Integration has worked purposefully to analyse, assess and measure the performance in the area of integration in Denmark. Surveys and indicators are used to monitor the integration process and to continuously adapt legislation and other initiatives. It has been a long process to arrive at where we are today and there is still a need to refine and improve the analyses and indicators.
Among other things, we would like in the future to do more to clarify socioeconomic background factors, something that is not done to any great extent today. The only area where this is done systematically is in the statistics on crime. When this is done, some of the difference in the crime rate between native Danes and immigrants disappears, though not all of it; immigrants – and especially young refugees – commit crimes more frequently than others. Crime statistics are included as an indicator in the overall monitoring system, but are not among the indicators used to measure the key objectives.

To date, the reactions to the change theory, the objectives and the indicators have been predominantly positive. However, these have not been introduced on a wide scale; once they have been introduced more widely, a more general discussion can follow. It has been apparent among other things from international presentations that the objectives, to a greater extent than at present, should illustrate that integration is a two-way process, which Denmark is trying to strengthen further.
Over the years, municipalities have reacted to the measurements of the effectiveness of their integration efforts. In particular, they have criticised the fact that the analyses cover a period that is always between a year and eighteen months out of date. However, it is not possible to produce the more up-to-date analyses they would like since those analyses are based on register data.
Large municipalities such as Copenhagen and Aarhus have developed their own local monitoring systems. Here, key objectives have also been established which are measured using a number of indicators. The Ministry has taken the initiative to establish a network together with all Danish municipalities on effectiveness measuring and performance management in order to motivate and inspire the municipalities to adopt this approach. The aim of the network is to enable experiences to be shared about methods and data sources so that, together, Denmark can become better at measuring and monitoring the integration process.
A major recommendation here is to begin with a small number of key objectives and as few indicators as possible. In an overly comprehensive measuring system, it is easy to lose the overview and the ability to use it as a genuine management tool may be lost. At the same time, it is also crucial to be able to communicate both objectives and indicators; this means they must be clear, simple, relevant and broadly accepted.

In Denmark, negative stories about immigrants generally flourish in the media, and the challenge for the Ministry of Integration is to convey the message that there are positive developments with regard to the integration of our new citizens. Never have so many new citizens been in employment and education, and more and more are becoming better at speaking Danish and seeing themselves as active citizens in Danish society. Successfully increasing the focus on these positive developments could contribute greatly to strengthening the integration process further.

Appendix to chapter 5

Results for key indicators
The following shows the results for selected key indicators.

Increased employment and education
The key indicator for goal 2 on increased employment is the employment rate. In 2008, the employment rate for 16-64 year-old immigrants and descendants originating from non-Western countries was 57%, compared with 79% for native Danes. The number of immigrants and descendants from non-Western countries who have gained employment shows an upward trend since 2001. From 2006 to 2007, the employment rate increased from 50% to 55%, a large increase within just one year, and from 2007 to 2008 the rose further to 57%. The increase applies for both men and women.

Figure 5.2
Trend in employment rate for 16-64 year-old immigrants and descendants from non-Western countries and native Danes, 2001 to 2008 (in percentages)

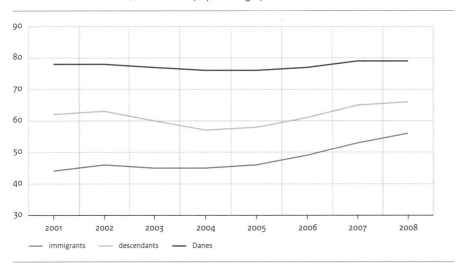

Source: Ministry for Integration Affairs' Foreigner database from Statistics Denmark

Goal 3 regarding increased education is measured among other things by how many youngsters have completed a (secondary) school education. In 2009, 22% of 20-24 year-old immigrants from non-Western countries and 47% of descendants originating from non-Western countries completed a maximum of secondary school education in Denmark. By comparison, this applied for 61% of their native Danish counterparts.

The trend from 2005 to 2009 shows a slight increase in the percentage of 20-24 year-old immigrants and descendants completing a secondary school education, while the percentage of native Danes in this category is declining. The difference between native

Danish youngsters and descendants of the same age reduced from 19 percentage points in 2005 to 14 percentage points in 2009.

Notes

1   The Ministry of Integration was closed in October 2011, when a new government took office. A wide range of law amendments are expected in the field of immigration and integration.
2   The analysis may be found at www.nyidanmark.dk/en-us/publications, dated 12 June 2009.
3   These periods are however calculated against the background of the limited average period studied of up to six years. This means that the differences between municipalities would actually be bigger if a longer period was studied, because some processes are not concluded within those six years. Municipalities' relative positions in relation to each other would however be the same.

6   Monitoring integration in Estonia[1]

Kristina Kallas

6.1   Introduction

In early 2008 the Estonian Minister of Population Affairs presented the national integration strategy for the years 2008-2013 to the government. The strategy was the result
of years of work by different stakeholders that resulted in a comprehensive and, more
importantly, measurable integration policy. However, just one year later, in May 2009,
the Bureau of the Estonian Minister of Population Affairs closed its doors for good. Faced
with the need for extensive expenditure cuts caused by the global economic crises, the
coalition government under Prime Minister Andrus Ansip decided to let the ministry
and its twelve employees go, saving a meagre total of € 650,000 per year. The tasks of the
Bureau were divided between different ministries, with the Ministry of Culture as the
coordinator for integration policy. The government rushed to reassure minority communities and other stakeholders, dissatisfied with the decision, that the rearrangement
would not result in cuts in the scope of planned policy measures; however, this move did
represent a symbolic event – integration policy was among the first policies to face cuts
in times of economic hardship.

The ease with which the government let the ministry go reflects how little value is placed
on integration policy by the ruling coalition. This is perhaps not surprising, given that
the drive to develop national integration policy came first from social scientists and
international donors such as UNDP and the Nordic Council of Ministers, not the government. By the late 1990s, Estonia was in what some prominent Estonian social scientists
called a situation of societal 'separation' (Lauristin & Heidmets 2003: 15). As a result of
a range of legislation put in place after 1991, the segregation into ethnic Estonian and
Russian-speaking communities that had already developed during the Soviet era became
even more pronounced and new lines of separation were established – in addition to
fully-fledged citizens of the re-established Estonian state, there was a group of former
citizens of the Soviet Union who did not possess citizenship of any state.[2] Furthermore,
lack of knowledge of Estonian as the newly established official language of the state
resulted in exclusion of this group from the political, economic, social and cultural life
of the new republic. Throughout the 1990s the government practised what analysts have
called the policy of alienation (Pettai & Kallas 2009) by putting into practice a raft of laws
and policies that adversely affected the Russian-speaking minority. It was only after the
aforementioned group of social scientists had pointed out the segregationist tendencies
in society, and under some pressure from the European Union and international organisations, that the government changed its approach and embarked, rather unenthusiasti-
cally, on the path of integration by developing a national integration programme and
establishing governmental structures for its operation.[3]

6.2   Background: history of immigration and integration

European countries differ widely in their immigration history. The history of migration greatly influences the integration process and this is especially true in the case of Estonia, where the question of national minorities and immigrants is very much tied to the historical background and current political context. A heated debate about the origins of different ethnic groups began once Estonia regained its independence in 1991. More specifically, the question arose as to whether post-war immigration of mostly Russian citizens from other parts of the Soviet Union was an instrument of Moscow's efforts to colonise effort a troublesome republic, as is often stated in domestic political rhetoric, or whether immigration was the outcome of the industrialisation of the USSR. In official government policies, settlers from the Soviet era are classified as immigrants from an occupying regime, and in this way their legal status in the re-established Estonian republic became that of foreigners. However, the significant difference is that most of these Russians do not see themselves as immigrants. Although they have had migrated from one geographical location to another, this move took place within the borders of one state. It was the border which eventually moved in 1991.

For most of its recent history, Estonia has been a country of emigration. The largest wave of emigration happened shortly before and during the Second World War, when large numbers of people, mainly the political and economic elite of the republic, emigrated to Western European countries and later to the USA, Canada and Australia. During the Second World War Estonia lost almost 25% of its population (Parming 1978: 34, Misiunas & Taagpera 1993: 358). Given these dramatic losses, the labour force vacuum created by accelerated post-war industrialisation initiated by the Soviet rulers could not be replaced without immigration. As a result, after the War, Estonia turned into an immigration country.
The first decade of Soviet rule was characterised by the influx of large numbers of people from other parts of the Soviet Union, mainly from the neighbouring Russia. These people crowded the emerging industrial centres of the northern part of the country, filling the vacuum in blue-collar labour created by the War and emigration. Although the ethnic composition of immigrants was heterogeneous, in reality there was just one ethnic dividing line, between Estonians and non-Estonians (or Russian-speakers).[4] By the time the Soviet Union came to its end, the share of ethnic Estonians in the population had fallen from 88% in 1934 to 61% in 1989 (Hallik 1998: 14).
One of the characteristic features of post-war migration was its high turnover,
more than double the total Estonian population at the time (Katus et al. 2002: 144).[5]
Having the smallest population among the Soviet Union republics, Estonia could hardly integrate such a great number of immigrants in such a short period of time. Integration was further complicated by the high concentration of immigrants in the urban centres of north Estonia: in the towns in the north-east of the country, immigrants constituted four-fifths of the urban population; in the north-west, around half (Kulu 2001: 2388).

In everyday life, it meant the segregation of the Estonian population into northern urban-industrial Russian-dominated communities surrounded by the agricultural Estonian countryside. This situation led to tensions between the two groups, one Estonian and the other Russian-speaking. The lack of control over the population processes, accompanied by the loss of independence and experience of repression and violence exercised by Russian-speaking KGB officers and the Soviet army turned the majority of Estonians against newcomers. The immigrants were viewed as 'Soviet henchmen' and treated as representatives of an occupying regime. Deliberate ignorance of the emergence of ethnic conflict by the Soviet rulers that was based on the official doctrine of 'brotherly friendship' of all Soviet people deepened the segregation further.

The independence movement that emerged in the second half of 1980s took the issue of control over immigration as one of its main tenets. It ran slogans that promised to stop the immigration that had resulted in a situation where ethnic Estonians were slowly becoming a minority in the capital of the republic. Right after the collapse of the Soviet Union in 1991, the Estonian parliament, where different fractions of nationalist independence movements held a firm majority, passed a resolution stating that all Soviet-era immigrants and their descendants (around 35% of the population in 1991) would not be accorded automatic citizenship in the restored Republic of Estonia. This policy was part of the broader Estonian political doctrine of *legal restoration*, which viewed Estonia's independence in 1991 as a direct restoration of its pre-1940 statehood.[6] This legal restoration principle soon became the dominant political doctrine and as a consequence all Soviet-era settlers were considered as the by-products of 50 years of illegal Soviet rule, and thus were expected to re-migrate to their countries of origin.

In 1992 a new citizenship law was adopted that turned this resolution into policy. As a result, roughly a third of the population (32%), mostly Russian-speaking Soviet-era settlers, were left without Estonian citizenship and as a result were excluded from the political life of the new republic. In reality, they had two choices: either to become naturalised Estonian citizens after passing language and civic tests, or to take the citizenship of the newly independent Russian Federation or their country of origin. In reality, many of them did not choose either of these options and remained citizens of the extinct USSR. As time passed and their passports expired, they re-registered as stateless people with permanent residence permits in Estonia (persons with 'grey passports').

During the 1990s the alienation process deepened. Some time earlier, in 1989, the Estonian Supreme Soviet (or local parliament) had already passed a language law that declared the Estonian language to be the sole official language on the territory of the republic and classed Russian, which had previously enjoyed the status of official language, as a 'foreign language'. This further excluded Russian-speakers, whose knowledge of Estonian was rather modest, from the labour market, higher education (which was slowly turned into Estonian-language only), the state administration and the pubic and cultural life of the country. There were no Estonian language courses for adults financed by the state, and even teaching the official language in Russian-medium schools remained under-funded for most of the first decade. Restructuring of the economy and

bankruptcy of large, state-owned factories left large numbers of Russian-speakers unemployed with little or no hope of finding a job in the Estonian language-dominated labour
market.

The adoption of new laws was often accompanied by exclusionist rhetoric calling on
Soviet-era settlers either to fully assimilate into Estonian ethno-national culture or
emigrate. Any suggestion made to the Estonian government by international organisations, mainly the Organisation for Security and Cooperation in Europe (OSCE) and the
European Union, to adopt a more integrationist approach towards its Russian-speaking
population, was met with hostility and considered to be against the vital interests of the
Estonian state.

By the end of the first decade of independence, the segregation of Estonian society extended to all aspects of social life (Lauristin & Heidmets 2003). Politically, the Estonian
population was divided into three categories:

1   those with Estonian citizenship (1,115,000 persons), totalling 80% of the population,
    who enjoyed full political rights;
2   those with the citizenship of another country (around 100,000, nearly 7%), mainly the
    Russian Federation, whose political rights remained limited; and
3   around 13% of the population (175,000 people) with 'undetermined citizenship', i.e.
    essentially stateless permanent residents with significant restrictions on their politi-
    cal rights (Eesti Statistikaamet 2002).

Linguistically, society was divided into Estonian-speaking and Russian-speaking public
spheres – a division that was inherited from the Soviet time, but which became even
deeper as a result of the policies implemented in 1990s as described above. It was against
this backdrop that the impulse began for the formation of a real integration policy.

6.3   The birth of Estonian integration policy under EU conditionality pressures

Among the first group to highlight the dangers of further segregation were social
scientists, an interuniversity research group called 'VERA', established in 1996 on the
initiative of the Ministry of Education and in collaboration with the Estonian Association of Sociologists. The research group warned the government, that according to
their research results, the dominant model of separation could develop just as easily
in the direction of deepening conflict as towards intercultural integration (Lauristin
& Heidmets 2002). Similarly, Max van der Stoel, OSCE High Commissioner on National
Minorities, on his numerous monitoring visits to Estonia throughout the 1990s, called
on the Estonian authorities to soften their approach towards the Soviet-era settlers.
Few of his recommendations, however, were immediately fulfilled. It was not until 1997,
when the process of Estonia's accession to the European Union and the consequent pressure on the Estonian government to adopt measures to curb the process of alienation
began, that official steps were taken towards the establishment of a national integration
policy. The same year, the government appointed a Minister without Portfolio for Population Affairs, whose task it was to deal (among other things) with integration issues.
The Minister drew on the work done by the social scientists cited above and formulated

an initial set of policy principles declaring minority integration to be a central political goal of Estonia. In 2000, a full-scale policy programme for the period 2000-2007 was completed and approved by the cabinet. For the implementation and monitoring of the policy, the Non-Estonian Integration Foundation was established.[7]

Thus, by the turn of the century an institutional and policy structure for integration policy was in place. The first strategy described the desired outcome of an integration process as

> the Estonian model of a multicultural society, which is characterised by the principles of cultural pluralism, a strong common core and the preservation and development of the Estonian cultural domain.
>
> (my emphasis, State Programme 2000)

This putative contradiction in the vision – the aspiration for cultural pluralism in society in parallel with the desire to preserve the Estonian cultural domain – illustrates the pressure of two political processes in which the formulation of the policy took place. The course towards 'Estonianisation' of the state and society was firmly set, legally and politically, and was strongly supported by the majority ethnic Estonian population. On the other hand, Estonia's integration with European institutions, which had began by then, introduced alternative visions of multiculturalism and integration as an outcome of the democratisation and nation-building processes. The tension between these diverging visions characterised Estonia's integration efforts in the following decade.[8]

The formulation of the policy, and especially the conceptual basis of the integration, took place through discussions between social scientists and experts and as a result was more of an analytical concept rather than an outcome of political and public dialogue. Integration was conceptualised as a two-way process where harmonisation of society towards 'a common core' was taking place in the public sphere in parallel with valuing ethnic differences and acceptance of cultural rights of minorities in the private sphere (State Programme 2000). A common (public) core was envisioned as the Estonian cultural domain, with the Estonian language and national history dominating while ethnic identities were pushed into the private sphere. Thus, the vision of an 'Estonian model of multiculturalism' called for recognition of the diversity of cultural identities in society, but did not open up the public space for their representation. Furthermore, it became clear fairly quickly that an 'Estonian model of multiculturalism' is difficult to operationalise and even more difficult for policymakers to follow as a policy guide. How social unity in the public sphere was to be achieved at the same time as preserving cultural differences in the private sphere remained unclear.

The document envisioned the integration to take place in three structural domains: linguistic, legal-political and socioeconomic. However, the emphasis was placed heavily on linguistic integration, on which more than half the programme budget was spent (Lõpparuanne 2009). Knowledge of the Estonian language was regarded as a prerequisite for any integration process, be it naturalisation or integration into the labour market. Taking into consideration the low levels of self-reported knowledge of Estonian by Russian-speakers – according to the population census in 1989 only 15% of

Russian-speakers declared that they had a command of the Estonian language (Eesti Statistikaamet 2002) – it was only logical that the focus was placed on mastering the official language. However, the decision to spend public money on teaching Estonian to Russian-speakers had as much to do with putting things right as with practical necessity. At the time of immigration, no pressure was put on settlers by the Soviet authorities to learn the local language, while the pressure on Estonians to use Russian as the language of interethnic communication grew each decade. This left ethnic Estonians vulnerable to the issue of the survival of their language; as time passed the Estonian language, although formally enjoying the status of official language in Soviet Estonia, was losing its position as the language of administration and everyday services in some regions of the country. Thus, when re-establishing political control over the state, the goal was to reassert the position of the Estonian language, and the integration policy was seen as a means of achieving this goal.

The running of the programme was highly centralised and networking between central government, local authorities and civil-society organisations was rather weak during the whole implementation period. In effect the decision-making powers were concentrated in the hands of a few ministries and as a result no awareness and knowledge about the challenges of integration was developed at local level. This shortcoming became especially apparent in the case of the Ida-Viru region, where the Russian-speaking population constituted some 80% of the population, but where no specific integration policy was developed locally to deal with the problems of the region.

However, the main criticism of the policy was not focused on its overly analytical concepts, heavy centralisation or strong focus on Estonian language teaching. Strong disagreement was voiced by the Russian-speaking community, which pointed to the assimilative tendencies of the policy (Ernst & Young 2006). Despite the conceptual promise of integration as a two-way process, a limited number of policy measures were planned to include the majority population in the process. Responsibility for the success of integration was placed almost exclusively on the shoulders of the Russian-speaking population and identified as the goal to be attained by them within their daily lives, without much participation by ethnic Estonians.

Regardless of its flaws, the emergence of the policy was itself a major change in the field of minority affairs. By embracing the concept of integration as a two-way process that strives towards mutual accommodation and even multiculturalism, the government backed away from the alienation policy that characterised the legislation on minorities in the previous decade.

6.4   Successes and failures of the first integration programme

The difficulties with which all the subsequent Ministers of Population Affairs struggled while soliciting public support for their policy were caused by the conceptual problems introduced into the policy that I discussed at some length above. The job of the Ministers was further complicated by the fact that the first integration programme did not include clearly defined milestones or markers of success.[9] The desired outcomes of the integration process were formulated in general terms, leaving the interpretation of the programme's success rather arbitrary.[10]

Monitoring of the integration process nevertheless started almost immediately. As one of its first tasks as early as 1999, the Integration Foundation commissioned a study that aimed to measure the integration process in the social, economic, cultural and political domains. Based on an analysis of a survey of around 1,000 respondents, the study measured the levels of tolerance, understanding of integration and expectations towards the integration policy, appraisal of the citizenship policy, and self-professed knowledge of the Estonian language. It also used available survey data to analyse aspects of structural integration such as education levels and occupational structure, employment and income as well as media consumption of ethnic Estonians and non-Estonians (Monitoring 2000). Thus, attention was paid to both structural and socio-cultural integration.

In the course of the first integration programme, the monitoring study was repeated three more times at intervals of three years (2002, 2005 and 2008). These studies, which became known as *Integration Monitoring*, attempted to correct the lack of measurable indicators in the national integration programme and to operationalise the outcome of the integration process. The first monitoring exercise in 2000 identified the social domains where integration takes place, as well as the data that need to be gathered; the subsequent studies built on this.

The approach was largely designed to measuring the progress made by Russian-speakers in achieving linguistic, legal-political and socio-economic indicators as compared with ethnic Estonians. Little attention was paid to comparing Russian-speaking people with each other based on their social, economic or political standing. This had two major consequences for the integration outcome: first, well-integrated Russian-speakers disappeared from the view of policymakers and remained out of the scope of the policy; second, and even more importantly, due to this disappearance the perception among ethnic Estonians about the successes and failures of the integration process were shaped by less-integrated groups. Monolingual, unemployed Russian men with criminal records became the symbol of the failure of integration. The potential of well-integrated Russian-speakers to drive the integration process remained unused.

The first and each subsequent monitoring survey brought to the attention of the policymakers the deficiencies resulting from the lack of attention to political and socioeconomic integration. By the time of the launch of integration programme in 2000, naturalisation rates had fallen from a high of 22,773 in 1996 to 3,090 in 2001 (Kodakondsus- ja Migratsiooniamet 2006: 19) and the monitoring survey further revealed that among young Russian-speakers it was not so much the lack of knowledge of Estonian but rather the low motivation and psychological barriers that prevented them from acquiring Estonian citizenship (Vetik 2002: 75). Monitoring surveys found that the 'integration is at its greatest disadvantage in the social-economical sphere' (Lauristin & Vetik 2000), reflecting the fact that throughout the entire period after the restoration of independence the highest unemployment rates were primarily among Russian-speakers, and the occupational division between majority Estonians and minority Russian-speakers was consistently detrimental for integration (Pavelson 2002). While some positive changes could be observed by 2005, the socioeconomic disparities remained large, with the average job satisfaction of Russian-speakers, for example, two times lower than that of Estonians (Pavelson 2006). Problems of political and socio-economic exclusion were brought to light in the public discussion and consequently, it could be argued, paved the way for paying more attention to these issues in designing the next integration programme.

However, although *Integration Monitoring* studies declared their objective as being to monitor the 'integration processes to determine the changes in relations and notions of different national groups in the course of the implementation of the National Integration Strategy' (Lauristin & Vetik 2000), the outcomes of the studies cannot be directly linked to the evaluation of the impact of the national integration programme. *Integration Monitoring* studies monitored the integration processes in society, but did not measure the impact of the activities implemented in the framework of the national integration programme. The studies thus served as a good data source, setting the background and defining base indicators for determining the future direction of integration policy, while the impact of programme activities was never really evaluated.

Regular *Integration Monitoring* studies provided data on the socioeconomic, political and cultural-linguistic integration processes taking place in the Russian-speaking minority. The monitoring process itself was a good stimulus for the policy process. The planning of surveys brought together social scientists, policymakers and programme managers from the Integration Foundation. The public presentations and seminars for the interpretation of the survey data played an important role in raising awareness of integration in Estonian society. They trained journalists and policymakers to use structured data and analytical concepts rather than emotional stereotypes when speaking about minority issues. However, studies were methodologically weakly linked to the objectives defined in the integration programme and thus could not be used as an assessment tool to evaluate whether Estonia was moving towards its avowed goal of integration. The problems for policymakers with measuring the success or failure of Estonia's integration process were twofold: first, the conceptualisation of integration in national policy was rather analytical and did not provide a specific and measurable objective towards which to aspire; second, no measurable targets were set that would guide them in their work. Thus, lack of measurable objectives left the evaluation of the success or failure of the programme dependent largely on people's prior expectations. Even in cases where integration monitoring studies showed progress, such as Estonian language acquisition, it was still up to each evaluator to see it either in terms of success or not enough progress.

6.5   National integration programme 2008-2013

In 2005 a third monitoring report was written in a rather positive vein compared to the previous two. Following Estonia's accession to the EU in 2004, the number of naturalisations per year had risen above 7,000 again and the number of stateless persons had fallen to around 130,000 (Kodakondsus- ja Migratsiooniamet 2006: 18-19). Among

Russian-speakers, the number of people who claimed to have a 'good' knowledge of Estonian had reached 42%; moreover, among Russians aged 15-29, only 8% reported not knowing any Estonian (Proos 2005: 22). Estonia's economy continued to boom and socioeconomic disparities between Estonians and non-Estonians seemed to be decreasing (Pavelson 2006).

It was in the light of these positive developments that the riots in Tallinn on 26-27 April 2007 took so many people by surprise. Prime minister Andrus Ansip's determination to relocate a Soviet-era memorial known as the Bronze Soldier from a site in central Tallinn to a more distant military cemetery brought to the surface an issue that neither Estonia's integration policy nor any international organisations had dealt with sufficiently: history. While Estonians saw the monument – erected to commemorate the Soviets' recapture of Tallinn in 1944 – as a painful reminder of the Soviet occupation of their country, Russian-speakers generally viewed the statue as an essential element of their historical identity – the Soviet Union's victory in the Second World War. This 'monumental' conflict over the interpretation of history became the leading issue that the public expected integration policy to solve.

The development of a new national integration policy that had started just few months before the conflict was now brought into the public eye from behind the closed doors of expert groups. As a result of the conflict, the public attitude towards integration had become rather negative, especially among the minority population, nearly 60% of whom stated that integration policy has failed and had largely been a waste of money (Saar Poll 2007: 41). Ethnic Estonians remained more optimistic, expressing the opinion that the crises had engendered a public debate about the integration challenges and that there was a need for a more focused integration policy (ibid.).

Despite the public pessimism and rather adversarial political environment, the development of a new integration policy continued under the direction of a new Minister of Population Affairs.[11] Almost a year after the riots, and following a series of discussion and consultation rounds with interest groups, analysis of large-scale needs and a feasibility study, and a good deal of debating and disputing among politicians and policymakers, the new State Integration Strategy 2008-2013 was signed by the government in April 2008.[12] The vision, objectives and expected outcomes were defined in working groups composed of politicians, policymakers and experts and led by the Minister of Population Affairs (Praxis 2008).

Although taking the previous programme as the starting point, the new strategy represents a step forward compared to its predecessor in terms of agreeing on a vision, defining the desired objectives and developing measurable indicators to evaluate the success or failure of the policy. It lists six core objectives that Estonia's integration process needs to achieve by 2013: a diminishing of the inequalities in employment and income between people with different ethnic backgrounds; an increase in the knowledge of Estonian among non-native speakers; a steady decrease in the number of stateless residents; an increase in the contacts between people from different ethnic backgrounds; an increase in the trust in the state and its political institutions as well as between the different ethnic communities; and last but not least, an increase of the use of and trust in the Estonian-language media among the Russian-speaking population (Eesti lõimumiskava 2008-2013: 15). It thus devotes attention to structural integration (employment and income, acquisition of language, acquisition of citizenship, increase in use of Estonian media) as well as to socio-cultural integration (increase in social contacts and trust).

A significant change has taken place in the conceptualisation of integration. Where the first policy aspired to the amalgamation of two large communities and the creation of a common public sphere based on Estonian cultural values, the new programme abandons the community-centred approach altogether and aims instead for integration through building trust, a sense of security and a feeling of belonging on the part of all individuals residing in Estonia (Eesti lõimumiskava 2008-2013). Significant is the absence from the policy of the concept of multiculturalism. Estonian policymakers have thus followed the same path as their colleagues and the general public in other European multi-ethnic democracies who have declared multiculturalism to be dead.[13] Instead, the new policy follows the 'integration trends' in Europe and defines the objective of integration process as achieving social cohesion. It derives its priorities from universal European principles such as respect for fundamental rights, non-discrimination, creation of equal opportunities, political participation, combating social exclusion and the development of a strong sense of belonging through a common national identity (Eesti Lõimumiskava 2008-2013: 4).

Each of the six core objectives is accompanied by measurable, specific and time-bound indicators that include a baseline level and an outcome level (Eesti lõimumiskava 2008-2013: 15-17). These core indicators use statistical register data[14] for the majority of structural indicators; different survey data are used for the more subjective socio-cultural indicators. Although it is not specified how the data for outcome indicators will be gathered, it may be assumed that the same sources will be used as for the declared baseline indicators, i.e. *Integration Monitoring* surveys.

More critically, however, the programme document does not define the system for the collection and analysis of the indicators' data. The coordinating ministry is the Ministry of Culture, which is responsible for the measurement and analysis tasks; however, it is not specified how the data from different registers will be obtained, nor who will be responsible for conducting surveys and analysing the results.

To correct this deficiency, the Integration Foundation commissioned an analytical study aimed at developing a comprehensive set of indicators and establishing a structure for gathering and analysing the data. The work was carried out by the audit company Ernst & Young Baltic in 2008 and resulted in a wide-ranging system of indicators: instead of fourteen programme outcome indicators, the newly developed system presented 69 impact indicators (Ernst & Young 2009). Each indicator was provided with a data source and quantifiable measurements. It elaborated the system for gathering, analysing and evaluating the data.

However, this new system has yet to be put into practice. According to the undersecretary of the Ministry of Culture, Anne-Ly Reimaa, the monitoring system developed by Ernst & Young includes too many indicators, making the process of gathering and analysing the data too complicated and too expensive. According to Ms. Reimaa, the Ministry has no plans to abandon these indicators entirely; however, the mid-term evaluation of the integration policy based its analysis on the original indicators as first defined in the integration programme.[15] The monitoring survey was carried out at the end of 2010 and measured the progress towards meeting the core indicators. Despite the fact that it did not have quantifiable measurements against which to evaluate progress, the study concluded that satisfactory progress was being made on most of six core objectives. The exception was the use of Estonian media by the Russian-speaking population, which had remained at the baseline level or in some instances had even decreased (Lõimumiskava monitoring 2010: 8-10). The monitoring study did not set out to test the core indicators, although considering that it was the first such exercise, attention should have been given to the functionality and operationalisation of the defined core indicators.

The functionality of the integration indicators is to be tested in 2014 when the current programme comes to an end; however, there are some significant shortcomings in the system developed to measure the integration process. The core indicator system does not define which information should be included in the gathered data: whether the data should be gathered based on citizenship, mother tongue, age, geographical location, nationality or a combination of these.[16] While it is clear that, for the naturalisation process, data need to be collected on changes in the citizenship status of stateless persons, it is not apparent which data are required in order to assess progress in command of the Estonian language among Russian-speakers. This latter aspect is complicated further by the inconsistency and incomparability of the data on knowledge of Estonian language among the Russian-speaking population as gathered in different studies and censuses. The 2000 population census asked respondents of different nationalities to list the languages they speak and did not differentiate between whether the language stated was spoken as the mother tongue or as a foreign language. The outcome of the census is not comparable with the first *Integration Monitoring* study that was conducted in the same year and assessed the (self-reported) knowledge of Estonian as a second language among the Russian-speaking respondents. Furthermore, the *Integration Monitoring* study analysed the results based on the citizenship status of the respondents rather than their nationality. The monitoring studies of 2002, 2005, 2008 and 2010 used citizenship, age and region variables to differentiate the Russian-speaking community; however, the use of these characteristics has not been consistent, as not all variables were used each year. This inconsistency and incompatibility of the data gathered and analysed has prevented researchers and policymakers from making a comprehensive evaluation of the progress achieved in Estonian language proficiency by the Russian-speaking population.[17] However, the failure to differentiate the core outcome indicators between different generations of the immigrant population constitutes the biggest shortcoming of the current system. While in total 24% of the Estonian population have an immigrant background, only 11% belong to the first generation of immigrants, i.e. those persons who were born abroad (Järv 2009: 37).[18] In other words, the majority of the immigrant population were born in Estonia. Furthermore, an entire generation of Russian-speakers has emerged who have reached adulthood predominantly in the independent Estonia. Taking into consideration these population changes, monitoring integration in different immigrant generations is important because, as Niessen points out, "over time, migration-related distinctions become less significant as immigrants and their descendants acquire full citizenship and become active citizens and other more socio-economic and cultural distinctions gain importance" (Niessen 2009: 2). *Integration Monitoring* studies have consistently shown that the knowledge of the Estonian language among the younger generation of Russian-speakers is much better than that of their parents or grandparents. According to a recent monitor, 82% of young people aged 15-19 years declared that they can communicate in Estonian, compared to 59% of their parents' generation (aged 40-49 years) and only 24% of their grandparents' generation (aged 60 years and over) (Lõimumiskava monitoring 2010). Similarly, the younger generation of Russian-speakers are overrepresented among naturalised citizens. Over the last ten years, half of all naturalised citizens have been children under the age of 15 (PPA 2010). While the integration policy towards the first generation of immigrants needs to be focused on structural integration, such as teaching the Estonian language and promoting naturalisation, the integration challenges for the second and third generations of immigrants lie in other areas such as social and cultural integration, a feeling of belonging and a sense of identity. Failure to monitor the integration processes among different generations of Russian-speakers results in the neglect of the needs and challenges of integration, which differ significantly between the younger and older generations of Russian-speakers. Furthermore, the issue of consistency and comparability of data gathered through consecutive *Integration Monitoring* and other surveys needs to be addressed in parallel with the incomparability caused by the plurality of definitions used in those studies to classify the immigrant population.

6.6   Conclusions

In 2010 Estonia celebrated ten years of the implementation of its integration policy. A decade is a long enough period to enable an in-depth evaluation to be carried out of the integration process and policy outcomes. *Integration Monitoring* studies carried out since 2000 have provided an insight into these processes, mostly within the Russian-speaking community. For the authors of the integration policy, whose aims are generally supported by the majority ethnic Estonian population, the policy has had positive outcomes: the most recent monitoring study concluded that self-professed knowledge of the Estonian language has improved among the Russian-speaking population: the share of people who do not speak the language at all has decreased and the share of active users of the language has increased (Vihalemm 2008: 71). The progress in language proficiency is especially noticeable among the younger generation of Russian-speakers, enabling the evaluation of integration to be concluded on a positive note. However, progress has been less favourable in several other domains. The naturalisation process has almost come to a standstill and integration of the immigrant population into the labour market and political life remains problematic. While the strong focus on structural integration processes, and especially on language acquisition, have paid off to a degree, the challenge for the future lies more in socio-cultural integration, where issues have emerged relating to a sense of belonging, trust and security.

In order to be able to arrive at far-reaching conclusions about the success or failure of the integration policy, however, a comprehensive framework of specific, measurable and time-bound indicators needs to be used. In Estonia, work has only recently started on developing such indicators. The first integration programme for the years 2000-2007 defined a number of indicators, but did not include measurable milestones and did not provide policymakers with a specific and assessable conceptual ideal of integration to which they could aspire. *Integration Monitoring* studies that were launched in parallel with the programme implementation were methodologically not designed to evaluate the programme's successes and failures but rather to monitor the integration processes in society. The current integration programme represents a step forward in terms of a consensus of vision, defining the desired goals and developing measurable indicators to evaluate the success of the policy. Even more work has been carried out recently on developing indicators, resulting in a fairly comprehensive and systematic set of integration indicators. However, in addition to some technical and methodological shortcomings, the main deficiency of the current system lies in the failure to recognise the plurality of integration processes that are taking place within the Russian-speaking community. Like any other community, Russian-speakers adopt a variety of integration strategies achieve diverse outcomes. Age and country of birth need to be included as variables in each indicator data set in order to grasp the differences in the integration needs and challenges of the Russian-speaking population. Furthermore, a system has yet to be established for the collection and analysis of data. With the dissolving of the previous structure of integration policy management, work on developing the indicators has come to a halt. However, the need for policy making paired with the pressure from integration experts and other stakeholders to devise a comprehensive system for measuring and evaluating the outcomes of the current integration programme, along with the requests from the European Union for Member States to develop comparable integration indicators, is putting pressure on the coordinating Ministry of Culture to have a system in place by 2013, when the new programme will be in place.

Notes

1   I would like to thank two anonymous reviewers for helping me to explain, tighten and sharpen my arguments in an earlier version.
2   It should be noted that the citizenship laws adopted in 1992 and 1995 did not include any ethnic criteria for obtaining citizenship, but were rather based on the restitutionist principle. Nearly 75,000 ethnic Russians whose parents or grandparents had been citizens of the Estonian Republic prior to Soviet occupation automatically acquired Estonian citizenship.
3   For further discussion about the role of the international community and the impact of EU conditionality on Estonia's integration policy, see Kelley 2004; Jurado 2008; Pettai & Kallas 2009.
4   A wide array of definitions has been used to describe the ethnic composition of Estonian society. While the majority population is often referred to as Estonians or the titular/native population,

several definitions are applied for Soviet era settlers: Russians, Estonian Russians, Russian-speakers, immigrants. While each of them has some minor characteristic that sets them apart from the others, in a broader sense these terms are used to describe that part of the population whose common attribute is a history of recent migration into Estonia and the use of Russian as the language of communication. In this analysis the term 'Estonians' is used to describe the native population while Soviet-era settlers, irrespective of their ethnic background, are all categorised in one group of 'Russian-speakers'.

5   For instance, over the period 1946-1991, the migration turnover comprised 2,900,000 persons, whereas net migration was only 337,000. Approximately seven out of eight immigrants have emigrated at one time or another (Katus et al. 2002: 145).

6   More on legal restoration principle may be found in Pettai 2004 and Pettai & Kallas 2009.

7   The name of the foundation, referring to exclusion (non-Estonian) rather than inclusion, came under criticism from the minority community. It was changed a few years later to the Integration Foundation and in 2010 merged with the Migration Foundation under the name Migration and Integration Foundation 'Our People' (MISA).

8   This structural tension was also recognised by Raivo Vetik, one of the leading researchers in the working group for the integration strategy. In his analysis he points out that

    [...] the main structural contradiction in the current phase of Estonian national development lies in reality where two in some ways incompatible processes need to be matched: on the one hand [there is a need to continue] the nation-building process that Soviet rule cut short. On the other way there is a need to acknowledge the emergence of multiculturalism globally and follow humanistic principles of promotion of fundamental rights, protection against discrimination and guaranteeing equal rights to all members of society. (Vetik 2002: 72; Vetik 2007: 4)

9   The programme included a definition of indicators for objectives, but no targets were set for evaluating the success or failure in achiving those objectives. The only target was set for language proficiency for basic school graduates (to achieve intermediate-level fluency in the Estonian language by 2007).

10 For example, in the area of language learning the programme stated that as a result of integration process, the 'non-Estonian's knowledge of the Estonian language shall improve considerably.' Similarly, in the area of legal-political integration the programme prescribed that 'the naturalisation process shall become more productive and effective.' (State Programme 2000:19)

11 It should be noted here that the author was a member of the team of researchers that was contracted by the Minister of Population Affairs to carry out research on the needs and feasibility of future integration policy.

12 More on the process of development of new national integration programme for 2008-2013 may be found in Eesti Lõimumiskava 2008-2013. (Consulted online at: http://www.kul.ee/webeditor/files/integratsioon/Loimumiskava_2008_2013.pdf on 26 January 2011.); on public consultations with interest groups, see *Avalikkuse ja sihtgruppide kaasamine Eesti lõimumiskava 2008-2013 koostamisse*, Policy Research Centre PRAXIS, September 2008. (Consulted online at http://www.meis.ee/raamatukogu?book_id=194 on 31 January 2011.)

13 This is a rephrasing of the now famous headline in Britain's *Daily Mail* newspaper on 7 July 2006. For more on multiculturalism losing ground, see Vertovec & Wessendorf 2010.

14 The basic socioeconomic data are gathered by *Statistikaamet* (Statistics Estonia) for different survey databases such as the Estonian Employment Survey or the European Social Survey; language examination data are gathered by the National Examinations and Qualifications Centre; naturalisation

statistics are gathered by the Citizenship and Migration Department of PPA (Police and Border Guard Board).

15 Author's interview with Anne-Ly Reimaa conducted on 25 January 2011. Transcript available from the author upon request.

16 The new and improved integration indicator set developed by Ernst & Young Baltic addresses this shortcoming and defines the following dimensions on which data need to be collected: geographical region, age, citizenship and nationality (see Ernst & Young 2009). However, this new system has not yet been put into practice.

17 For more on the incomparability of the data on the language proficiency of Russian-speakers, see Vihalemm 2008.

18 People with immigrant background are defined here as those who have been born abroad or whose parents have been born abroad. If one parent was born abroad, but the other parent was born in Estonia, the person is not included in this category. More on the definitions of people with immigrant background see Krusell 2009. It also merits to note here that in public and political discourse Estonian population is often divided along ethnic lines between Estonians and non-Estonians where the latter group is automatically equated with the 'Soviet time immigrants' without further differentiating them based on the time of migration into Estonia and current citizenship status. While the dominant perception is that the immigrants constitute of total 30% of the population, only one third of them (or 35%) have actually migrated to Estonia while the rest has been born in the country (Järv 2009: 37). For more on the public and political discourse about immigrants and minorities in Estonia, see Kallas & Kaldur 2010.

References

Eesti lõimumiskava eesmärkide saavutamise monitooring 2010. Uuringu kokkuvõte. Lead contractor: Prof. Raivo Vetik. Consulted online on 2 February 2011 at: http://www.kul.ee/webeditor/files/integratsioon/ ELK_monitooring_2010_kokkuv6te.pdf

Eesti lõimumiskava 2008-2013. Kinnitatud Kinnitatud Vabariigi Valitsuse 10.04.08 korraldusega nr 172. Consulted online on 31 January 2011 at: http://www.kul.ee/webeditor/files/integratsioon/ Loimumiskava_2008_2013.pdf

Eesti Statistikaamet (2002). Rahvaloendus 2000. Tallinn: Kodakondsus ja emakeel.

Jurado, Elena (2008). Complying with the European Standards of Minority Protection: the Impact of the European Union, OSCE and Council of Europe on Estonian Minority Policy, 1991-2000. Saarbrücken: VDM Verlag Dr. Müller.

Järv, K. (2009). Recent Immigrants in Estonia. In: Immigrantrahvastik Eestis. Immigrant Population in Estonia. Tallinn: Statistics Estonia.

Hallik, K. (1999). Ethnically divided Estonia. In: R. Vetik (ed.), Estonian Human Development Report 1999. Tallinn: United Nations Development Programme.

Hallik, K. (1998). Vene küsimus ja Eesti valikud. Tallinn: TPÜ Kirjastus.

Kallas, K. & K. Kaldur (2010). Estonia: A Post-Soviet Predicament. In: Katrine Fangen, Kirsten Fossan & Ferdinand Andreas Mohn (eds.), Inclusion And Exclusion Of Young Adult Immigrants: Barriers and Bridges. London: Ashgate.

Katus, K., A. Puur & L. Sakkeus (2002). Immigrant population in Estonia. In: W. Haug et al. (eds.), *The demographic characteristics of immigrant populations* (Population Studies no. 38). Strasbourg: Council of Europe Publishing.

Kelley, J. (2004). *Ethnic Politics in Europe: The Power of Norms and Incentives*. Princeton: Princeton University Press.

Kodakondsus- ja Migratsiooniamet (2006). *Citizenship and Migration Board 2006*. Tallinn: Kodakondsus- ja Migratsiooniamet.

Krusell, S. (2009). Data and General Characterisation of Immigrant Population. In: *Immigrantrahvastik Eestis. Immigrant Population in Estonia*. Tallinn: Statistics Estonia.

Kulu, H. (2001). Sõjajärgne sisseränne Eestisse võrdlevas perspektiivis (Post-war immigration to Estonia in comparative perspective). In: *Akadeemia*, vol. 13, no. 11.

Lauristin, M. (ed.) (2008). *State Integration Programme 2008-2013 Final Report on Needs and Feasibility Research*. Tallinn: Integration Foundation.

Lauristin, M. & M. Heidmets (eds.) (2003). *The Challenge of the Russian Minority. Emerging Multicultural Democracy in Estonia*. Tartu: Tartu University Press.

Lauristin, M. & R. Vetik (eds.) (2000). *Integration of Estonian Society: Monitoring 2000*. Tallinn: MEIS. Consulted online on 29 January 2011 at: http://www.meis.ee/raamatukogu?book_id=94

Lõpparuanne. Riikliku programmi –Integratsioon Eesti ühiskonnas 2000-2007– rakendamine (Final Report. Implementing National Programme 'Integration in Estonian society 2000-2007'). Approved by the Government on 27 May 2010.

Misiunas, R. & R. Taagepera (1993). *The Baltic States. Years of Dependence 1940-1990*. London: Hurst & Company.

Monitoring (2000). *Integration into Estonian Society: Monitoring 2000*. Tallinn: MEIS.

Niessen, J. (2009). *Developing and Using European Integration Indicators. With Mary-Ann Kate and Thomas Huddleston, Migration Policy Group*. Consulted online on 7 February 2011 at http://www.migpolgroup.com/publications_detail.php?id=259

Parming, T. (1978). *A Case Study of a Soviet Republic: The Estonian SSR*. Colorado: Westview Press.

Pavelson, M. (2006). The Social-Economic Condition of Estonians and Estonian Russians: Expectations and Changes. In: *Integration of Estonian Society: Monitoring 2005*. Tallinn: Mitte-Eestlaste Integratsiooni Sihtasutus.

Pavelson, M. (2002). Work, income and coping: socio-economic background of integration. In: *Integration in Estonian Society: Monitoring 2002*. Tallinn: TPÜ Rahvusvaheliste ja Sotsiaaluuringute Instituut.

Pettai, V. & K. Kallas (2009). Estonia: Conditionality Amidst Legal Straightjacket. In: B. Rechel (ed.), *Minority Rights in Central and Eastern Europe*. London/New York: Routledge.

Pettai, V. (2004). *Framing the Past as Future: The Power of Legal Restorationism in Estonia* (PhD dissertation). New York: Department of Political Science, Columbia University.

PPA (2010). *Politsei ja Piirivalveamet*. Consulted online on 2 April 2010 at: http://www.politsei.ee/et/organisatsioon/avalik-teave/statistika/index.dot

Praxis (2008). *Avalikkuse ja sihtgruppide kaasamine Eesti lõimumiskava 2008-2013 koostamisse*. Tallinn: Policy Research Centre PRAXIS. Consulted online on 31 January 2011 at http://www.meis.ee/raamatukogu?book_id=194

Saar Poll (2005). *Määratlemata kodakondsusega isikute suhtumisest Eesti kodakondsuse saamisesse: teadmised ja soovid*. Projekt 'Määratlemata kodakondsusega isikute integratsiooni toetamine Eestis' 2004/006-270.05.02.0001.

Saar Poll (2007). *Rahvussuhted ja integratsioonipoliitika väljakutsed pärast pronkssõduri kriisi*. Commissioned by Rahvastikuministri Büroo (Office of Minister of Population Affairs). Consulted online on 7 February 2011 at www.erl.ee/index.php?doc_id=206

State Programme (2000). *Integration in Estonian Society 2000-2007*. Approved by the Government of Estonia on 14 March 2000. Consulted online on 29 January 2011 at: http://www.kul.ee/index.php?path=0x2x1424x1596

Vertovec, S. & S. Wessendorf (2010). *The Multiculturalism Backlash. European Discourses, Policies and Practices*. London/New York: Routledge.

Vetik, R. (2002). About the Formation of a Common Foundation in Legal-Political Integration. In: *Integration in Estonian Society: Monitoring 2002*. Tallinn: TPÜ Rahvusvaheliste ja Sotsiaaluuringute Instituut.

Vetik, R. (2007). *Eesti ühiskonna integratsiooniprogrammi 2008-2013 üldideoloogia kontseptuaalne põhjendamine. Integratsiooni Sihtasutus*. Consulted online on 31 January 2011 at: http://www.meis.ee/raamatukogu?book_id=156

Vetik, R. (2003). Multicultural Democracy as a New Model of National Integration in Estonia. In: Marju Lauristin & Mati Heidmets (eds.), *The Challenge of the Russian Minority* (p. 55-65). Tartu: Tartu University Press.

Vihalemm, T. (2008). Keeleoskus ja hoiakud. In: *Eesti ühiskonna integratsiooni monitooring. Uuringu aruanne*. Consulted online on 9 February 2011 at http://www.meis.ee/raamatukogu?book_id=196

7   Germany: Monitoring integration in a federal state[1]

Lisa Brandt and Gunilla Fincke

7.1   Becoming a country of immigration

For many years, Germany was one of the most significant immigration countries world-wide. At times second only to the USA in absolute terms, Germany received considerable inflows of labour migrants and their families, asylum-seekers and ethnic German repatriates from the middle of the twentieth century onwards. Immigration reached a peak in 1992, with an influx of 1.2 million people (Bundesregierung 2010). Around 15.6 million people with a migrant background live in Germany today, accounting for about 19% of the total population (Statistisches Bundesamt 2010a).

Yet, although among the world's most significant countries of immigration, Germany constitutes a somewhat special case. Unlike the USA or Canada, where migration has traditionally formed an integral part of nation-building, until the turn of the century Germany's approach to immigration and its immigrant population was encapsulated in the notion that 'Germany is not a country of immigration' (Bade & Münz 2002). At least partially, this notion was rooted in a traditional ethno-cultural understanding of German nationhood. Immigration of non-Germans took place against this background of being not perceived, or at least not publicly promoted, as a viable option (Brubaker 1992). So-called 'guest workers', mainly from Turkey, the former Yugoslavia, Italy, Greece and Spain and their descendants therefore experienced significant disadvantages in terms of integration conditions compared with ethnic German repatriates (Spät-/Aussiedler), 4.4 million of whom migrated to Germany between 1950 and 2005. In line with the 'ostentatious ignorance' (Bade 2007) of Germany's status as a de facto immigration country, access to citizenship remained highly restricted for non-German immigrants until the turn of the century. Despite flourishing initiatives at the local level, explicit political efforts to promote integration were not made. Thus, while Germany witnessed neighbouring countries like the Netherlands and France developing specific mindsets and practices for how to incorporate their respective immigrant populations, this was lacking in Germany (Michalowski 2004). Ausländerpolitik ('aliens policy') was in practice limited to labour market policies, in line with the delusion that large parts of Germany's migrant population would eventually return to their respective countries of origin (Expert Council of German Foundations on Integration and Migration 2010).

The 1998 federal elections marked an important turning point in the German approach to immigration and the immigrant population. The new coalition government of the Social Democratic Party (SPD) and the Green Party (Bündnis 90 – Die Grünen) publicly acknowledged Germany as an immigration country for the first time. This cleared the way to bring in a number of reforms that had already been partly taken into consideration by the previous government.

As a first crucial step in the year 2000, access to nationality for foreign residents was eased and the acquisition of citizenship by birth was enabled. Thus, elements of *ius soli* were incorporated in German law – albeit in quite a restrictive manner, which was due to intense political friction over the issue. Children born to foreigners residing in Germany now acquire dual citizenship at birth but have to choose between the foreign and German nationality when they are between 18 and 23 years of age. The legal change marked an important move away from an ethnicity-based towards a republican perception of nationhood and thus towards a closer approximation of the mindsets of other European immigration states. Heightened requirements for the immigration of 'ethnic Germans', such as language prerequisites, pointed in the same direction.

The acknowledgement of the existing immigration situation in Germany and changed perceptions of immigration to Germany in general meant that, finally, the question of integration could also be addressed politically at the federal level. In fact, the question of how to support immigrant integration experienced a significant rise up the political agenda and after years of being bypassed, the role of policy intervention to promote integration processes was strongly underlined. Tangible reforms were introduced mainly with the passing of the 2005 Immigration Law, which included mandatory integration courses for newly arrived migrants and foreign welfare recipients. The course comprises a comprehensive language module and civic instruction classes. Significant institutional changes further emphasized the new importance of integration as a political topic. The Federal Office for Migration and Refugees, before 2005 only responsible for determining refugee status, was allocated further responsibilities in the area of integration, including the implementation of integration courses, the development of further integration mechanisms and the restructuring of migration advice structures in Germany. Furthermore, the post of Commissioner for Migration, Refugees and Integration was upgraded with the additional function of Minister of State in the Chancellery.

Under the Merkel administration, an annual 'Integration Summit' between representatives of government, media, migrant organizations, employers' organizations and trade unions was introduced. Based on the first summit in 2006, a 'National Integration Plan' was drawn up in 2007, and a first progress report was published in 2008. In 2011, the Plan has been developed further into a 'National Action Plan' aimed at achieving measurable and binding goals for integration.

With changes in the field of integration policy, such as obligatory language instruction and mandatory language tests for family reunification, Germany has in recent years been part of a European trend towards policy convergence. Beyond strictly assimilationist or multicultural ideologies, European states have recently assumed rather pragmatic approaches to integration with regard to long-term immigrants, focusing particularly on migrants' socioeconomic and civic integration.

Integration monitoring then serves to assess progress for different groups of immigrants, to identify trends and to ascertain which issues are in greatest need of policy intervention.

7.2   Integration as participation

The Independent Commission on Migration to Germany (*Unabhängige Kommission Zuwanderung*), put in place in the year 2000 to develop immigration reforms, defined the goal of integration as being to

> facilitate the equal participation of immigrants in social, economic, cultural and political life, while at the same time respecting cultural diversity.

(Unabhängige Kommission Zuwanderung 2001: 196)

The Commission stressed that efforts from both the majority and the immigrant population are needed in order to achieve this and that integration policy should therefore not target the immigrant population alone, but rather society as a whole.

Despite considering integration to be 'one of the most important domestic tasks' (2010a), the government has not issued one standardized definition of integration. However, while definitions vary and are quite vague at times, official accounts generally pick up on the Independent Commission's recommendations. The Federal Office for Migration and Refugees (*Bundesamt für Migration und Flüchtlinge* – BAMF) refers to integration as a long-term process, its aim being to

> include everyone in society who lives in Germany on a permanent and legal basis [...]. Immigrants should have the opportunity to participate fully in all areas of society on an equal footing. Their responsibility is to learn German and to respect and abide by the Constitution and its laws.

(BAMF 2010a)

The Ministry of the Interior (*Bundesministerium des Innern* – BMI) also stipulates among other things that 'integration should allow for equal opportunities and actual participation in all areas, especially in social, economic and cultural life' (BMI 2010a). Like the BAMF, the Ministry also points to a 'two-way-process' that is necessary to accomplish successful integration, including efforts on the part of the immigrant population to learn the language and to gain a basic civic education, and on the part of the majority population a willingness to live in a tolerant and intercultural society.

7.3   Goals of monitoring

With integration being increasingly understood as a major political task, efforts to monitor integration processes and progress have multiplied.

At a basic level, monitoring helps to compare the outcomes of persons with and without a migrant background. Comparisons can also be drawn between diverse subgroups of the immigrant population, allowing for a more differentiated understanding of the latter. For instance, differences can be detected between first and second-generation migrants, male or female migrants or members of various nationalities and ethnic backgrounds.

If multivariate analysis is performed, explanations of why some groups perform better or worse than others may be deduced (e.g. the socioeconomic status of parents affecting children's upward mobility).

Monitoring also serves as an important tool for political agenda-setting. Thus, monitoring is crucial for the determination of political targets and goals in the field of integration, for capturing the status quo of immigrant integration in various fields, for identifying problematic areas or for observing trends. Finally, monitoring helps to set benchmarks and to guide long-term progress towards them.

The Federal Government views integration monitoring as essential for a successful integration policy in the sense that knowledge on the progress and deficits of integration is needed for the development of effective integration measures (Beauftragte der Bundesregierung für Migration, Flüchtlinge und Integration 2008).

7.4 Data sources

With large numbers of immigrants having naturalized, acquiring dual citizenship at birth or having acquired German citizenship as ethnic German repatriates (*Spät-/Aussiedler*), the former distinction between foreign and German citizens in the official statistics becomes skewed. Immigrants with German citizenship are on average better educated and more successful in the labour market. Therefore, integration is thought of in terms of a much larger group of persons with a 'migrant background'.

According to the Federal Statistical Office (*Statistisches Bundesamt*), a person has a migrant background if they:
- migrated to Germany's present-day territory after 1949;
- were born in Germany as a foreigner; or
- were born in Germany and have at least one parent who migrated to or was born in Germany as a foreigner (Statistisches Bundesamt 2010b).

According to this definition, children born in Germany with German citizenship have a migrant background if at least one of their parents immigrated. Even where a child's parent was born in Germany, but does not hold German citizenship, the child would be considered to have a migrant background. Part of the third generation is thus included in the definition.

The first survey to take up this new distinction was the microcensus in 2005. This change provided an important impetus for integration monitoring activities at the federal, regional and local level. However, the adaptation of this definition and according of survey characteristics to other datasets has been slow, meaning that many datasets still differentiate only between foreigners and Germans. Furthermore, not every organization or authority agrees with the above definition of a 'migrant background'. In the field of education, for instance, falling under the competence of the *Länder*, Ministers have agreed that the primary language spoken in the homes of children should serve as an indicator for a migrant background. The following provides an overview of official and non-official data that are relevant to immigrant integration in Germany.

7.4.1   Official statistics

Microcensus

One of the most important databases for monitoring immigrant integration is the microcensus, an annual representative household survey coordinated by the Federal Statistical Office. This multi-topic survey has been in place since 1957[2]. Based on a one-percent random sample of all German households[3], it is the largest annual household survey in Europe. Households remain in the sample for four consecutive years, allowing for longitudinal analysis.

The purpose of the microcensus is to provide structural and social data on the population and the labour market[4] in Germany. The survey contains comprehensive questions on household and family structures, (continuing) education/training, employment, forms of income and housing. Some variables are covered at four-yearly additional programme intervals only, for example questions on health. Due to the statutory obligation to provide information, the non-response rate among the households covered (unit non-response) is very small, at about 5% (Statistisches Bundesamt 2010c). Given its representativeness and reliability, as well as the low non-response rate, it is the best dataset available; on the downside, immigration-related questions such as place of birth and current and former citizenship of parents are only asked every four years. In addition, its socioeconomic focus means that data on social relations, identifications or attitudes are not available.

Central Register of Foreigners

The Central Register of Foreigners (*Ausländerzentralregister* – AZR) has been kept by the Federal Office for Migration and Refugees (BAMF) since 2005. It contains data on all foreign nationals who stay or stayed in Germany for a period longer than three months. The dataset comprises basic personal data but also further information on things such as the last place of residence in the country of origin and marital status. Data relating to immigration status (e.g. legal status, decisions of the Federal Employment Agency regarding admission to employment) are also collected. The Register contains a separate visa file, containing data on foreigners who have applied for a visa at a German diplomatic representation abroad.

The AZR is among the largest registers of public administration in the Federal Republic of Germany, containing about 20.4 million personal records (Bundesverwaltungsamt 2010). Its purpose is to provide information for over 6,500 authorities performing tasks in the field of immigration and asylum law, including aliens offices, employment agencies and the police. More specifically, its purpose is to 'aid the administrative authorities in performing tasks under the law on foreigners and on asylum', to serve a 'supporting function as a tool of domestic security', to aid 'planning policy on foreigners' and to 'ascertain figures on foreigners that are relevant to management' (BAMF 2010b). In terms of measuring integration, the AZR can serve as a useful tool for providing data on the residence statuses of the foreign population, for example, the share of persons with a long-term residence status.

School registers

Due to the constitutionally anchored sovereignty of the *Länder* in the area of education, school statistics are retrieved annually at *Länder*-level and differ according to specific regional education structures. However, the Standing Conference of the Ministers of Education and Cultural Affairs of the *Länder* in the Federal Republic of Germany and the Federal Statistical Office regularly publish summarized data, seeking to draw cross-regional comparisons. For this purpose a set of core data to be collected in every Bundesland was agreed by the Standing Conference of Cultural Ministers in 2000, to make the statistics more comparable (Halhuber 2007: 67).

Until recently, in terms of gathering information on students with a migrant background, *Länder* statistics mainly differentiated between students with German and non-German citizenship. However, in 2008, more variables were included in the core dataset. A migrant background is now defined by:
 – non-German citizenship;
 – a foreign country of birth; or
 – the use a foreign language as the main language of communication in the student's family (Sekretariat der Ständigen Konferenz der Kultusminister in der Bundesrepublik Deutschland 2008).

The decision to introduce the criterion 'migrant background' mainly stems from the introduction of *ius soli* components in the citizenship law, through which the share of foreign students in the registers was significantly reduced and the identification of children with a migrant background rendered more difficult (Sekretariat der Ständigen Konferenz der Kultusminister in der Bundesrepublik Deutschland 2009). This was perceived as problematic, especially with regard to identifying special language needs. Education experts have thus argued that the language spoken at home is more influential on immigrant children's schooling careers than their nationality or parental place of birth. Against this background, school statistics/registers provide information on things such as the share of children with a migrant background in various school types and their diplomas.

Child and Youth Services Registers

The Child and Youth Services Registers monitor the competence areas of the youth welfare offices and are coordinated by the Federal Statistics Office. Among other things they include data on family support services, youth support programmes and day care institutions. Additionally, since 2006 data on children and employees themselves in day care institutions are collected against the background of the increasing relevance of early childhood education (Statistisches Bundesamt 2010d).

The statistics on children in day care institutions differentiate between children with and without a migrant background. A child has a migrant background if at least one of its parents' country of origin is not Germany; neither the citizenship of the parents nor of the child plays a role in this regard. Additionally, the Child and Youth Service Register gathers data on the primary language spoken at home (German or non-German) (Statistisches Bundesamt 2010e). The statistics allow for the identification of interrelationships between a migrant background and the age of children, daily care time and special educational needs and thus provide useful information in terms of integration monitoring.

The other datasets do not contain information on migrant background, but some differentiate between Germans and foreigners. Statistics on children and adolescents who have been taken into care differentiate between Germans and foreigners. Statistics on educational support for families, on the other hand, do not contain information on migrant backgrounds.

Vocational training statistics

Since 1977, data on training facilities and trainees themselves have been collated on an annual basis. The purpose is to evaluate particular support programmes and identify areas where state intervention is needed. The statistics provide data on things such as the length of traineeships, early termination of training contracts, examination successes and the commercial sector in which the training facilities are situated.

Data are transmitted to the Statistical Federal Office by all regional chambers of commerce, which ensures comprehensive samples. The statistics do not yet include variables for migrant background, but distinguish between German and non-German nationals.

Employment statistics

The Federal Employment Office is bound by law to publish monthly statistics on a broad range of topics surrounding employment and the labour market, for example the development in employment by economic activity, unemployment, recipients of unemployment benefits and vocational support measures. The statistics are based on data drawn from the regular records of the Employment Office.

In September 2010 a decree was passed which stipulates that information on migrant background has to be sampled in the employment statistics. The sampling started in 2011 and the data is expected to be available in 2012.

Previously, data differentiated between Germans and foreigners only. A person is considered to have a migrant background if he or she:

– does not have German citizenship;
– was born outside the present territory of the Federal Republic of Germany and immigrated after 1949; or
– has at least one parent who was born outside the present territory of the Federal Republic of Germany and immigrated after 1949.

Contrary to the definition of the Federal Statistics Office, according to this definition third-generation migrants would not have a migrant background unless they hold foreign nationality themselves.

Integration course statistics

The Federal Office for Migration and Refugees publishes statistics on integration courses (*Integrationskursgeschäftsstatistik*) which are updated on a quarterly basis. Information is provided on entitlements granted to participate in integration courses, on participant structures, completion rates and integration course providers. On this basis, information may be obtained with regard to things such as the share of course repeaters, the number of persons participating in various types of integration courses[5], the number of participants who are German citizens, EU citizens or immigrants who have not newly arrived in Germany[6] or the share of foreigners obliged to participate as beneficiaries of social aid (BAMF 2010c).

Statistics on criminality / Statistics on politically motivated crime

Since 1953, the Federal Criminal Police Office *(Bundeskriminalamt)* has published statistics on criminality annually *(Polizeiliche Kriminalstatistik)*, reporting on all documented criminal offences. The statistics include data on criminal suspects which allow for a differentiation between German and foreign citizens. However, these data need to be interpreted with caution. First, the statistics report criminal *suspects* as opposed to criminal *convicts*, meaning that the figures do not necessarily represent the number of people eventually convicted of crimes. Furthermore, the statistics comprise documented offences only, which means the data need not be representative for all criminal offences committed. In terms of comparing the crime rates of Germans and foreigners, it has to be borne in mind that some crimes, such as breaches of immigration or asylum regulations, can only be committed by foreigners. In addition, the foreign population also includes transients who do not reside in Germany but may be involved in criminal activities. Finally, the foreign population in Germany is on average younger, poorer and more urban than the native population – three factors that increase the propensity for crime (BMI 2010b).

Data on politically motivated crimes (PMK – *Politisch motivierte Kriminalität*) are collected by the police authorities of the *Länder*, who also compile annual reports. Data are also submitted to the Federal Criminal Police Office for an annual nationwide analysis. The statistics distinguish between rightist and leftist politically motivated criminality, politically motivated foreigner criminality (crimes motivated by political developments abroad) and other politically motivated criminality (BMI 2010c). In terms of integration, the statistics are particularly useful in shedding light on xenophobic, racist or anti-Semitic tendencies within the majority population.

7.4.2 Survey data

Official statistics lack information on social relations, perceptions and values, but also longitudinal data that would allow individuals to be tracked over time. They therefore need to be supplemented by non-official survey data. The following non-official data sources are relevant here.

German Socio-Economic Panel (GSOEP)

The German Socio-Economic panel is a representative longitudinal panel study of private households, conducted by the German Institute for Economic Research *(Deutsches Institut für Wirtschaftsforschung – DIW)*. The panel survey started in 1984 and was expanded in 1990 to include the Eastern *Länder*. It is held on an annual basis and – to the extent possible – surveys the same sample of private households[7]. Currently, the sample comprises

11,000 households, involving a total of around 20,000 adult persons. Every household member older than 16 years is asked questions about objective living conditions (e.g. household composition, employment and health), but also on subjective issues such as perceptions, values, life satisfaction or the willingness to take risks.

Since 1984, the GSOEP has contained a disproportionately large 'foreigner sample', comprising households whose head is of Turkish, Spanish, Italian, Greek or former Yugoslavian origin. In 1994, a further 'immigrant sample' was added, reflecting the changed demographic composition of the West-German *Länder* due to relatively large-scale immigration from Eastern Europe at the time. This sample includes households in which at least one household member moved from abroad to West Germany after 1984. The GSOEP thereby constitutes the largest regular survey of foreigners and immigrants in the Federal Republic of Germany (DIW 2010). The survey includes questions on nationality, year of immigration, language skills, motives for migration, relatives in the home country, remigration intentions and attachment to Germany (Sander 2009).

Overall, the GSOEP offers detailed information on a broad range of integration-related issues and links those to comprehensive data on socioeconomic status and perceptions.

Panel Study on Labour Market and Social Security (PASS)

PASS is an annual household panel study which was introduced in 2006 and is conducted by the Institute for Employment Research *(Institut für Arbeitsmarkt und Berufsforschung – IAB)*, the research institute of the Federal Employment Agency. It aims to examine the individual and social consequences of the implementation of the Unemployment Benefit II *(Arbeitslosengeld II)* scheme, the new assistance scheme for long-term unemployed persons. During the latest wave of the panel study between December 2008 and July 2009, approximately 13,400 persons in more than 9,500 households were interviewed, including 11,300 persons and 8,200 households for the second time. Households chosen include recipients of the Unemployment Benefit II as well as households with a low income which run an increased risk of becoming beneficiaries. In addition to structural questions on employment or receipt of social security benefits, the survey includes questions on life satisfaction, worries, attitudes towards gender roles, subjective social standings and subjective evaluations of health status.

The study proves to be a useful tool for measuring labour market integration as it takes into account both the nationality and the migrant background of interviewees. The latter is determined by questions about the interviewee's, their parents' and grandparents' country of birth. The panel study focuses on this group, as it is assumed that immigrants find themselves in precarious living situations more often than other sections of the population. Interviews are conducted in German, English, Turkish and Russian. Personal interviews (CAPI) are employed where telephone interviews (CATI) are not successful (IAB 2010; IAB 2009).

Other relevant surveys

A *Volunteer Survey* has been conducted every five years since 1999. Within the scope of this survey, 20,000 persons are interviewed about their civic engagement on behalf of the Federal Government. Questions asked relate to former and current nationality, year of immigration and country of birth. Information is also collected on religious affiliation. The volunteer survey provides information on social engagement within and outside the family for persons with and without a migrant background. (Bundesministerium für Familien, Senioren, Frauen und Jugend 2010; Geiss and Gensicke 2006)

The *Youth Survey* by the German Youth Institute (Deutsches Jugendinstitut – DJI) is a representative study of adolescents and young adults aged from 12 to 29 years. It was carried out in 1992, 1997 and 2003 among 9,000 interviewees, a quarter of whom have a migrant background. Among other things, the youth survey examines educational background, friendships, political orientations and values (Moser 2010).

The *German Health Interview and Examination Survey for Children and Young Adolescents* (Kinder- und Jugendgesundheitssurvey – KiGGs) by the Robert Koch Institute covers a broad range of issues regarding the development and physical as well as mental health of a representative sample of 17.641 children aged from 0 to 17 years. It includes a written survey, a medical examination and an interview and is designed as a longitudinal study. Migration-related items include nationality, year of parents' immigration, country of birth and languages spoken at home. The study is optionally conducted in German, Turkish, Russian, Serbo-Croat, Arabic, English and Vietnamese (Schenk et al. 2007).

The German broadcasting corporations ARD and ZDF conducted a representative study in 2007 on the use and significance of German and foreign-language media by persons with a migrant background. A total of 3,010 immigrants aged 14 years or older were interviewed in order to identify preferences and barriers regarding the use of public media (ARD/ZDF Medienkommission 2007).

The Federal Ministry for Education and Research (Bundesministerium für Bildung und Forschung – BMBF) has conducted the *Reporting System on Further Education* (Berichtssystem Weiterbildung) since 1979, providing information on participation in further education by persons between 19 and 64 years. The study is conducted every three years and is based on a nationwide sample of 7,000 interviewees. It is supplemented by Länder-specific surveys with 1,500 participants in each Land. Since 1997, the sample has included foreigners but not Germans with a migrant background. Due to its repetitive design, changes in attitudes towards lifelong learning can be discerned (Bundesministerium für Bildung und Forschung 2006).

7.5 Monitoring integration at federal level

In a first step towards a systematic monitoring of integration at the federal level, the Federal Government published its first 'Report on Integration Indicators' in June 2009, which presented and tested a set of indicators to measure integration (Beauftragte der Bundesregierung für Migration, Flüchtlinge und Integration 2009).

Within the framework of the 2007 National Integration Plan, both federal and *Länder* representatives had stressed the importance of integration monitoring systems and accordingly the need to develop appropriate indicators to capture and monitor integration processes and to assess the impact of new integration policies.

In preparing the report, relevant federal ministries together with experts from academia, politics and civil society and under the leadership of the Federal Government

Commissioner for Migration, Refugees, and Integration work up 100 relevant integration indicators spread across twelve thematic areas:
1   Legal status and demography;
2   Early childhood education and language support;
3   Education;
4   Vocational training;
5   Labour market;
6   Social integration and income;
7   Civic and political participation and equal opportunities;
8   Housing;
9   Health;
10 Media;
11 Intercultural openness of the public sector and social services; and
12 Crime, violence and discrimination.
The Institute for Social Research in Cologne (ISG Köln) and the Social Science Research Center Berlin (WZB) were contracted for the completion of the report. More than analyzing actual integration progress and results, the first Report on Integration Indicators aimed at presenting the newly developed integration indicators and assessing their suitability for measuring integration. A second report with a reduced set of 65 indicators is scheduled for 2011.
Simple comparisons between the outcomes of the immigrant and native population are complemented in some thematic areas by multivariate analyses using data from the microcensus, the volunteer survey and the PISA-survey. This additional analysis allows for the assessment of the degree to which divergences between groups derive from the criterion 'migrant background' or from general socioeconomic factors.
The report concludes with an overview of the complete indicator set and evaluates their suitability for future integration monitoring activities.

Positive results in language acquisition through integration courses and small improvements in drop-out rates on the part of persons with a migrant background contrast with persistently lower rates in vocational training and higher rates of unemployment (as compared to the native population).
Results show that persons with an individual or familial history of migration are in many respects still in an unfavourable position compared to the native population. However, progress is also detected in many areas, especially for the second generation of immigrants. After controlling for socioeconomic factors, divergences between the population with and without a migrant background prove less significant or even disappear.
The monitoring report does not distinguish between different ethnic origin groups, but provides separate information only for first and second-generation immigrants and for immigrants with or without German citizenship. Singling out data, for example for immigrants of Turkish or Russian origin, was considered to be politically too controversial. The efforts of the majority population are only measured in one indicator (intercultural openness). Given that integration is often referred to as a 'two-way process', further data on the willingness of the majority population to integrate should be

introduced. On the other hand, the strengths of the federal monitoring system are the
inclusion of multivariate regression analysis and laying the foundation for analyzing
integration trends: If the same set of indicators is used consistently, the federal monitoring system will help to evaluate developments in the field of integration and to identify
ongoing problem areas.

7.5.1   Monitoring integration at Länder-level

Integration monitoring activities have likewise been developed at the *Länder* level in
recent years, both in the individual *Länder* and within an overarching 'Interregional
Working Group on the Development of Indicators and Monitoring' *(Länderoffene Arbeitsgruppe – Indikatorenentwicklung und Monitoring –)*. The *Länder* stress their wish to monitor – in
addition to nationwide developments – particular integration situations and progress
within their respective regions, with the ability to define their own indicators and definitions.

The Interregional Working Group

The Interregional Working Group was set up in 2008 by the Integration Minister Conference *(Integrationsministerkonferenz – IntMK)*, which has brought together ministers and
senators responsible for regional integration portfolios on a regular basis since 2007.
The integration ministers had previously stressed the importance of standardized
integration monitoring systems in the framework of their contribution to the National
Integration Plan, and reiterated this in their contribution to the First Progress Report
on the National Integration Plan (Bundesregierung 2008). Against this background, the
Interregional Working Group was established with the aim of:
– working out in consultation with the Federal Government a single definition of the
  aspect 'migrant background' in all *Länder*;
– harmonizing integration indicators; and
– identifying any necessary changes in statistics.
The Working Group published its first report in 2008, in which it proposed a standardized definition of 'migrant background / immigration history' for the purposes of cross-
regional analyses. The definition comprises:
– persons who immigrated after 1949;
– foreigners;
– naturalized persons; and
– children with at least one parent who was either born abroad and immigrated, or was
  naturalized or holds a foreign nationality.
It is thus in accordance with the definition employed at federal level (Länderoffene
Arbeitsgruppe „Indikatorenentwicklung und Monitoring" 2009). A set of integration
indicators was then put forward in a second report in 2009. The latter differs from the
catalogue of integration indicators employed at federal level mainly in terms of its nar-
rower scope, which was also explicitly envisaged by the group. The report sought to
'prevent [...] the listing of numerous characteristics and indicators without a secure database' and to choose where possible only those indicators for which valid and sufficient

data are available and which take stock of migrant background as opposed to nationality only. On this basis, seven core subject areas with a total of 50 indicators were selected. The core subject areas include:

1   Basic data on the population of migrant background (population quota, legal statuses, naturalization rates etc.);
2   Early childhood education and language support;
3   Education and vocational training;
4   Work and income;
5   Health;
6   Housing; and
7   Crime, violence and discrimination.

The report then includes a set of optional indicators for some of the core subject areas as well as two further subject areas (civic engagement and intercultural openness the public administration), which *may* but do not have be considered by the *Länder*, as the available databases are less suitable and reliable.

After the indicators had been tested in practice and evaluated in the framework of a pilot study (2010) in seven *Länder*, the Working Group issued its first report on integration monitoring on the basis of the stipulated indicator set in 2011 (Länderoffene Arbeitsgruppe „Indikatorenentwicklung und Monitoring" 2011). Allowing for a comprehensive comparison between integration data in the sixteen *Länder*, it is however explicitly stressed in the report that a ranking is not envisaged, as the demographic and socio-cultural features of the population with a migrant background would not be comparable. In the future, a report of this type will be published on a two-yearly basis.

Länder monitoring systems: Examples from Berlin and North-Rhine Westphalia

In recent years, some *Länder* have developed their own integration concepts and monitoring systems. By taking over this pioneering role they hoped to generate attention for their integration policies and to build momentum for the development of monitoring at the federal level.

As an example, in 2009 Berlin published the 'First Implementation Report on the Berlin Integration Concept 2007-2009', containing a specific 'Berlin Integration Monitor' (Beauftragter des Senats von Berlin für Integration und Migration 2009). The Monitor employs indicators from differing datasets, some providing information on foreigners and some on persons with a migrant background. Two indicators on the integration of 'tolerated' migrants (persons without a legal status who cannot be deported immediately – *Geduldete* in German) are also included. In addition, the Berlin Integration Monitor contains a comparatively large set of indicators focusing on the intercultural openness of majority institutions, such as the share of staff who have undergone intercultural training or the share of cultural organisations with multilingual marketing.

North-Rhine Westphalia published a first 'Integration Report' in 2008 (Ministerium für Generationen, Familie, Frauen und Integration 2008) and was thus pioneering in drawing on the newly available, differentiated data on the immigrant population from the 2005 microcensus. The report differentiates between two separate categories of integration, namely social and structural integration, emphasizing that integration can be successful in one sphere while being unsuccessful in the other.

7.6   Monitoring at the local level

Municipalities and larger cities have been the first to develop integration monitoring systems. In Wiesbaden, capital of the *Land* Hesse, an indicator-based monitoring system of integration was introduced as early as in 2003 for the purposes of 'sensitization', 'early warning' and 'evaluation' with regard to immigrant integration (Amt für Wahlen, Statistik und Stadtforschung Wiesbaden 2008). The monitoring system comprises 22 indicators on structural, cultural, social and identificational integration and is based in addition to official statistics on a special citizen survey (Beauftragte der Bundesregierung für Migration, Flüchtlinge und Integration 2007 / Amt für Wahlen, Statistik und Stadtforschung Wiesbaden 2008).

Many municipalities have followed their lead. In 2006, the Municipal Community Office for Public Management *(Kommunale Geschäftsstelle für Verwaltungsmanagement – KGSt)*, a management centre supported by cities, towns and counties, together with 15 communities developed an indicator set for communal integration monitoring based on the Wiesbaden concept. The brochure on integration monitoring developed by this group was sent to all German municipalities and serves as an important basis for the development of local monitoring systems (Beauftragte der Bundesregierung für Migration, Flüchtlinge und Integration 2007). A further important basis for the development of local integration monitoring systems is the 'Key Index' on integration indicators developed by the Bertelsmann Foundation and put forward in 2008 *(Bertelsmann Stiftung)* (Bertelsmann Stiftung 2008).

These handbooks and networking opportunities have helped some cities to build on the experiences of other municipalities when developing their own monitoring systems. Stuttgart, for example, introduced an integration monitoring concept in 2008 that has strong parallels to the Wiesbaden and KGSt concepts. Other cities, however, continue to introduce their own approaches; the city of Solingen, for instance, launched a distinct monitoring concept in 2007 which is based on integration policy targets (Beauftragte der Bundesregierung für Migration, Flüchtlinge und Integration 2007).

7.7   Monitoring experiences and perceptions

The monitoring systems established in recent years at federal, regional and local level have led to significant improvements in the available data on immigrant integration in a broad range of fields. However, these instruments focus on structural integration results and generally compare the outcomes of immigrants to those of natives. Reducing and finally eliminating the gap in educational outcomes, participation in the labour force, etc., by improving immigrants' outcomes is the stated long-term goal. The focus is therefore mainly on the immigrant population and its alignment with the outcomes of the native population. The dynamics of integration processes on an everyday level are for the most part neglected.

In view of the Expert Council of German Foundations on Integration and Migration (SVR), however, the inclusion of data on these subjects is crucial, as everyday experiences and evaluations of integration have consequences for the willingness of individuals to invest in integration and thus influence the success of integration processes. The SVR has therefore developed an Integration Barometer, which for the first time measures experiences and empirically based personal assessments of integration both within the native population and in the different immigrant groups. Observing these interdependent dynamics of integration processes helps create a better understanding of the immigration society and constitutes a useful supplement to existing monitoring systems.

In the first Integration Barometer, 5,600 persons were interviewed in the autumn of 2009 in three selected metropolitan regions (Rhine-Ruhr, Rhine-Main, Stuttgart). These regions have a long-standing immigration history. The randomly selected sample was stratified and the immigrant population was overrepresented, allowing for a deeper analysis of social and demographic factors: 80.5%[8] of individuals had a migrant background and 19.5% were natives. Data were weighted for the analysis. If an interviewee or one of their parents was born abroad, he or she was considered to have a migrant background. Currently, the survey is being re-administered as a longitudinal study and extended to include the larger region of Berlin as well as Halle/Leipzig, thus including data on East Germany.

In the survey, persons with and without a migrant background are asked the same questions. Interviewees are first asked about their contacts and experiences with immigrants/natives in four thematic areas (the neighbourhood, education, work and social relations), followed by their assessment of the norms and the performance of the system in dealing with integration, and finally about future behavioural tendencies. Other questions touch on evaluations of current integration policies, trust in various population groups and everyday life in an immigration society.

The results of the Integration Barometer support the notion that monitoring experience-based perceptions of integration plays an important role in evaluating integration in Germany. Everyday experiences of integration in neighbourhoods, schools, at the workplace and in social relations are fairly good. Immigrants and natives share this cautiously optimistic appraisal. While some problem areas are identified (particularly the educational performance of mixed schools), overall assessments are satisfactory and more positive than evaluations that are not based on the respondents' personal experiences. The native and immigrant populations alike are relatively satisfied with the developments in integration policy over recent years and the majority expect further progress: 50% of all respondents expect that integration policy will improve the degree of integration in the coming years; only 10% to 15% anticipate a deterioration. The majority and migrant populations have the same understanding of what integration entails and whose responsibility it is, and abstain from scapegoating. Trust is a decisive factor for social peace in an immigration society. Contrary to the widespread belief of mutual distrust between the native and immigrant populations, the Integration Barometer shows a satisfactory level of trust: nearly two-thirds (62%) of the immigrants surveyed trust natives 'fully' or 'more often than not'. The majority population's trust towards immigrants varies with the different immigrant groups, and oscillates between 40% and 55%.

The results show that in addition to the structural indicators largely employed in the current monitoring systems, experience-based indicators should also be taken into consideration in the future in order to comprehensively monitor integration and to gain a full and realistic picture of the integration climate.

7.8   Summary

In recent years, a range of useful mechanisms has been introduced in Germany to monitor immigrant integration at federal, regional and local level. This development has been driven particularly by the upgrading of integration as a major political task in Germany and the introduction of a broad range of more or less explicit integration policies, namely language training, early childhood education, anti-discrimination laws and actions, measures to combat school drop-out and better employment offers as well as vocational training for individuals aged under 25 years. With this has come a move away from presenting separate data only on foreign nationals to monitoring integration of the larger population with a migrant background, including German citizens who were born abroad or at least one of whose parents was born abroad. The emergence of various monitoring mechanisms has therefore also been accompanied and driven by new possibilities for obtaining data on the population with a migrant background, notably those covered by the microcensus, for example. Although many datasets do not yet include the criterion of migrant background, recent years have brought increasing discussions and efforts aimed at harmonizing definitions and indicator sets at federal, regional and local government levels.

Without doubt, the monitoring systems established in recent years have led to significant improvements regarding the available data on immigrant integration in a wide range of fields, albeit certain improvements such as the inclusion of experience-based indicators (and the mutual perceptions of the immigrant and native populations) as well as further harmonization would considerably improve the quality of monitoring. Care should be taken to limit monitoring systems to those indicators that are clearly linked to integration and to abstain from requiring assimilation. Indicators on religious behaviour or the language spoken at home are thus not good measures, while support for constitutional norms and German language skills are.

Another challenge will be to present integration results separately for different groups of origin (e.g. Russian, Turkish) while avoiding trying to compare apples and oranges and falsely attributing differences to cultural incompatibilities that are mostly rooted in socioeconomic background. Measuring the integration of the immigrant population also becomes more difficult as the diversity within the immigrant population increases. In 2007, 50% of all immigrants in Germany belonged to an immigrant group whose share of the immigrant population was less than 2% (BAMF 2010d). Furthermore, people immigrate with diverse statuses, for example as refugees, family migrants or work migrants. Also, the immigration population exhibits a very wide-ranging variety of social backgrounds. Monitoring systems will need to take better account of this 'super-diversity'

(Vertovec 2007) of the immigrant population in terms of ethnic and social background as well as legal status.

Finally, when monitoring integration the results should not be too hastily misinterpreted as measuring the effect of integration policies. Government bodies at all levels tend to trace positive integration results back to new integration policy measures, while the media lean towards attributing remaining problems to the failure of that same integration policy. However, both causal attributions will most likely be flawed as integration is a complex long-term process that is affected by several general structural developments (e.g. economic growth). The results of integration monitoring should thus not be misunderstood as short-term judgments of various policies, but rather as valuable indicators of medium and long-term trends. It is in this light that they are of greatest help to policymakers and the general public.

Notes

1   We thank Esra Kücük for valuable research for this chapter.

2   In the new *Länder* (including East-Berlin) since 1991.

3   All households have the same probability of selection. Within the territory of the Federal Republic of Germany, areas (or sampling districts) are selected in which all households and persons are interviewed (one-stage cluster sample). Every year, a quarter of the households (or sampling districts) included in the sample are exchanged. This means that each household remains in the sample for four years.

4   The Labour Force Survey of the European Union (EU Labour Force Survey) forms an integral part of the microcensus.

5   In addition to the general integration course, there are special integration courses, e.g. for women, parents, illiterate persons, young persons or persons with special needs (BAMF 2010c).

6   These persons do not generally have an entitlement to participate in an integration course but may be admitted under §44(4) of the Immigration Act. An entitlement to participate, which at the same time constitutes an obligation, is allocated to beneficiaries of social aid and to newly arrived migrants unless they have sufficient knowledge of German, low integration needs or are still subject to scholastic education §44(3) Immigration Act.

7   The GSOEP displays a fairly high degree of stability over time. In 1984, 5,921 households containing a total of 12,245 individual respondents were included in the West German sample. 3,154 of these households, with 5,626 respondents, were still participating in 2008 (DIW 2010).

8   The diversity of the immigrant population in Germany was accounted for by selecting a very diverse survey sample: 15.6% of the full sample were persons who came to Germany as ethnic German repatriates, 17.5% had a Turkish background, 23.8% were from European Union countries, 11,1% originated from European countries outside the European Union and 12.5% were of Latin American, African or Asian descent.

References

Amt für Wahlen, Statistik & Stadtforschung Wiesbaden (2008). *Monitoring zur Integration von Migranten in Wiesbaden. Bericht 2008.* Wiesbaden: Amt für Wahlen, Statistik und Stadtforschung. Consulted online on 10 December 2010 at: www.stuttgart.de/img/mdb/publ/17932/52045.pdf

ARD/ZDF Medienkommission (2007). *Migranten und Medien 2007. Ergebnisse einer repräsentativen Studie der ARD/ZDF-Medienkommission.* Mainz/Frankfurt: ARD/ZDF Medienkommission. Consulted online on 12 December 2010 at: www.unternehmen.zdf.de/fileadmin/files/Download_Dokumente/DD_Das_ZDF/Veranstaltungsdokumente/Migranten_und_Medien_2007_-_Handout_neu.pdf

Bade, Klaus J. & Rainer Münz (2002). Einführung: Migration und Migrationspolitik – Säkulare Entscheidungen für Deutschland. In: Ibid. (eds.), *Migrationsreport 2002: Fakten, Analysen, Perspektiven.* Frankfurt a.M./New York: Campus Verlag.

Bade, Klaus J. (2007). *Leviten lesen: Migration und Integration in Deutschland* (farewell lecture 27 June 2007 in Osnabrück). Consulted online on 13 December 2010 at: www.kjbade.de/bilder/LevitenHomepage.pdf

BAMF (2010a) *Integrationslexikon.* Berlin: Federal Office for Migration and Refugees (BAMF). Consulted online on 12 December 2010 at: www.integration-in-deutschland.de/cln_116/nn_278852/SubSites/Integration/DE/04__Service/Lexikon/__Function/glossar-catalog,lv2=278880,lv3=974684.html

BAMF (2010b) *Ausländerzentralregister.* Berlin: Federal Office for Migration and Refugees (BAMF). Consulted online on 10 February 2011 at: www.bamf.de/DE/DasBAMF/Aufgaben/FuehrungAZR/fuehrungazr-node.html

BAMF (2010c) *Bericht zur Integrationskursgeschäftsstatistik für das erste Halbjahr 2010.* Berlin: Federal Office for Migration and Refugees (BAMF). Consulted online on 13 December 2010 at: www.integration-in-deutschland.de/SharedDocs/Anlagen/DE/Integration/Downloads/Integrationskurse/Kurstraeger/Statistiken/2010__Integrationskursstatistik__BL__Halbjahr_202010,templateId=raw,property=publicationFile.pdf/2010_Integrationskursstatistik_BL_Halbjahr%202010.pdf

BAMF (2010d) *Migrationsbericht 2008.* Berlin: Federal Office for Migration and Refugees (BAMF).

Beauftragte der Bundesregierung für Migration, Flüchtlinge und Integration (2007) *7. Bericht der Beauftragten der Bundesregierung für Migration, Flüchtlinge und Integration über die Lage der Ausländerinnen und Ausländer in Deutschland.* Berlin: Beauftragte der Bundesregierung für Migration, Flüchtlinge und Integration. Consulted online on 10 December 2010 at: www.bundesregierung.de/Content/DE/Publikation/IB/Anlagen/auslaenderbericht-7-barrierefrei,property=publicationFile.pdf

Beauftragte der Bundesregierung für Migration, Flüchtlinge und Integration (2009) *Integration in Deutschland. Erster Integrationsindikatorenbericht: Erprobung des Indikatorensets und Bericht zum bundesweiten Integrationsmonitoring.* Berlin: Beauftragte der Bundesregierung für Migration, Flüchtlinge und Integration. Consulted online on 12 December 2010 at: www.bundesregierung.de/Content/DE/Publikation/IB/Anlagen/2009-07-07-indikatorenbericht,property=publicationFile.pdf

Beauftragter des Senats von Berlin für Integration und Migration (2009) *Erster Umsetzungsbericht zum Berliner Integrationskonzept 2007-2009.* Berlin: Beauftragter des Senats von Berlin für Integration und Migration. Consulted online on 10 December 2010 at: www.berlin.de/imperia/md/content/lb-integration-migration/publikationen/berichte/umsetzungsbericht_ik_2007_bf.pdf?start&ts=1288694030&file=umsetzungsbericht_ik_2007_bf.pdf

Bertelsmann Stiftung (2008). *Kennzahlen Integration.* Consulted online on 10 December 2010 at: www.bertelsmann-stiftung.de/cps/rde/xbcr/SID-3300A512-C60BE0A3/bst/xcms_bst_dms_18441_27411_2.pdf

BMI (2010a). *Integrationspolitik*. Berlin: Federal Ministry of the Interior (BMI). Consulted online on 10 December 2010 at: www.bmi.bund.de/DE/Themen/MigrationIntegration/Integration/Integrationspolitik/integrationspolitik_node.html

BMI (2010b). *Polizeiliche Kriminalstatistik 2009*. Berlin: Federal Ministry of the Interior (BMI). Consulted online on 13 December 2010 at: www.bmi.bund.de/cae/servlet/contentblob/1069004/publicationFile/65239/PKS2009.pdf

BMI (2010c). *Politisch motivierte Kriminalität im Jahr 2009*. Berlin: Federal Ministry of the Interior (BMI). Consulted online on 12 December 2010 at: www.bmi.bund.de/SharedDocs/Pressemitteilungen/DE/2010/03/politisch_motivierte_kriminalitaet.html?nn=106342

Brubaker, Rogers (1992). *Citizenship and Nationhood in France and Germany*. Harvard: Harvard University Press.

Bundesministerium für Bildung und Forschung (2006). *Berichtssystem Weiterbildung IX. Integrierter Gesamtbericht zur Weiterbildungssituation in Deutschland*. Bonn/Berlin: Bundesministerium für Bildung und Forschung. Consulted online on 9 December 2010 at: http://www.bmbf.bund.de/pub/berichtssystem_weiterbildung_neun.pdf

Bundesministerium für Familie, Senioren, Frauen und Jugend (2009). *Hauptbericht des Freiwilligensurveys 2010. Zivilgesellschaft, soziales Kapital und freiwilliges Engagement in Deutschland 1999-2004-2009*. Berlin: Bundesministerium für Familie, Senioren, Frauen und Jugend. Consulted online on 14 December 2010 at: http://www.bmfsfj.de/RedaktionBMFSFJ/Broschuerenstelle/Pdf-Anlagen/3._20Freiwilligensurvey-Hauptbericht,property=pdf,bereich=bmfsfj,sprache=de,rwb=true.pdf

Bundesregierung (2010). *Zuwanderungsland Deutschland*. Berlin: Federal Government (Bundesregierung). Consulted online on 29 December 2010 at: (http://www.bundesregierung.de/Content/DE/Artikel/IB/Artikel/Geschichte/2009-05-23-zuwanderungsland-deutschland.html

Bundesregierung (2008). *Nationaler Integrationsplan. Erster Fortschrittsbericht*. Berlin: Federal Government (Bundesregierung). Consulted online on 10 December 2010 at: (http://masgff.rlp.de/fileadmin/masgff/Aktuelles/int_mk/1__Fortschrittsbericht_zum_Nationalen_Integrationsplan__NIP__2008.pdf

Bundesverwaltungsamt (2010). *Ausländerzentralregister*. Berlin: Federal Office of Administration (Bundesverwaltungsamt). Consulted online on 13 December 2010 at: http://www.bva.bund.de/nn_372236/DE/Aufgaben/Abt__III/InnereSicherheitAuslaender/AZR/azr-node.html?__nnn=true

DIW (2010). *Übersicht über das SOEP*. Berlin: German Institute for Economic Research (DIW). Consulted online on 10 December 2010 at: http://www.diw.de/de/diw_02.c.222508.de/uebersicht_ueber_das_soep.html

Expert Council of German Foundations on Integration and Migration (2010). *Einwanderungsgesellschaft 2010. Jahresgutachten 2010 mit Integrationsbarometer*. Berlin: Expert Council of German Foundations on Integration and Migration. Consulted online on 14 December 2010 at: http://www.svr-migration.de/wp-content/uploads/2010/05/einwanderungsgesellschaft_2010.pdf

Geiss, Sabine & Thomas Gensicke (2006). Freiwilliges Engagement von Migrantinnen und Migranten. In: Thomas Gensicke, Sibylle Picot & Sabine Geiss (eds.), *Freiwilliges Engagement in Deutschland 1999-2005*. Berlin: Bundesministerium für Familie, Senioren, Frauen und Jugend.

Halhuber, Werner (2007). Die Schulstatistik der Kultusministerkonferenz. In: BMBF (ed.): *Migrationshintergrund von Kindern und Jugendlichen: Wege zur Weiterentwicklung der amtlichen Statistik*. Berlin: Bundesministerium für Bildung und Forschung. Consulted online on 10 December 2010 at: http://www.bmbf.de/pub/bildungsreform_band_vierzehn.pdf

IAB (2010). *Panel Study –Market and Social Security– (PASS)*. Nürnberg: Institute for Employment Research (IAB). Consulted online on 12 December 2010 at: http://www.iab.de/en/befragungen/iab-haushaltspanel-pass.aspx

IAB (2009). *Design and stratification of PASS – A New Panel Study for Research of Long Term Unemployment* (IAB Discussion Papers 5/2009). Nürnberg: Institute for Employment Research (IAB). Consulted online on 12 December 2010 at: http://doku.iab.de/discussionpapers/2009/dp0509.pdf

KGSt (2006). *Integrationsmonitoring (M2/2006)*. Köln: KGSt.

Länderoffene Arbeitsgruppe 'Indikatorenentwicklung und Monitoring' (2009). *Zweiter Bericht der Länderoffenen Arbeitsgruppe –Indikatorenentwicklung und Monitoring* (paper presented at the Integration Minister Conference on 26 June 2009 in Hannover).

Länderoffene Arbeitsgruppe 'Indikatorenentwicklung und Monitoring' (2010). *Ergebnisse der Pilotstudie. Indikatorenentwicklung und Monitoring 2005-2008.* Consulted online on 10 December 2010 at: http://www.statistik-berlin-brandenburg.de/einzelseiten/integ_buch.pdf

Länderoffene Arbeitsgruppe 'Indikatorenentwicklung und Monitoring' (2011). *Erster Bericht zum Integrationsmonitoring der Länder 2005-2009.* Consulted online on 21 August 2011 at: http://www.statistik-berlin-brandenburg.de/Einzelseiten/Integrationsbericht_Teil1_2011-02-10-Lesezeichen.pdf

Michalowski, Ines (2004). Integration Programmes for Newcomers: A Dutch Model for Europe? In: *Migration and the Regulation of Social Integration. Themenheft Institut für Migrationsforschung und Interkulturelle Bildung Osnabrück*, no. 24, p. 163-75.

Ministerium für Generationen, Familie, Frauen und Integration des Landes Nordrhein-Westfalen (2008). *Nordrhein-Westfalen: Land der neuen Integrationschancen. 1. Integrationsbericht der Landesregierung.* Düsseldorf: Ministerium für Generationen, Familie, Frauen und Integration des Landes Nordrhein-Westfalen. Consulted online on 10 December 2010 at: http://www.mags.nrw.de/08_PDF/003_Integration/001_aktuelles/aktuelles_1_Integrationsbericht_25_09_2008.pdf

Moser, Sonja (2010). *Beteiligt sein. Partizipation aus der Sicht von Jugendlichen.* Wiesbaden: VS Verlag für Sozialwissenschaften.

Sander, Monika (2009). *Migration and Health – Empirical Analyses based on the German Socio-Economic Panel Study (SOEP)* (inaugural dissertation). Bamberg. Consulted online on 12 December 2010 at: http://www.opus-bayern.de/uni-bamberg/volltexte/2009/196/pdf/Sander2009.pdf

Schenk, Liane, Ute Elltert & Hannelore Neuhauser (2007). Kinder und Jugendliche mit Migrationshintergrund in Deutschland. Methodische Aspekte im Kinder- und Jugendgesundheitssurvey (KiGGS). In: *Bundesgesundheitsblatt*, vol. 50, no. 5/6, p. 590-599.

Sekretariat der Ständigen Konferenz der Kultusminister in der Bundesrepublik Deutschland (2008). *Definitionenkatalog zur Schulstatistik (2).* Consulted online on 14 December 2010 at: http://www.kmk.org/fileadmin/pdf/Statistik/Defkat2008_2__m_Anlagen.pdf

Sekretariat der Ständigen Konferenz der Kultusminister in der Bundesrepublik Deutschland (2009). *FAQ's: Frequently Asked Questions zum Kerndatensatz und zur Datengewinnungsstrategie.* Consulted online on 12 December 2010 at: http://www.kmk.org/fileadmin/pdf/Statistik/FAQ_Januar09.pdf

Statistisches Bundesamt (2010a). *Anteil der Einwohner mit Migrationshintergrund leicht gestiegen.* Wiesbaden: Statistisches Bundesamt. Consulted online on 12 December 2010 at: http://www.destatis.de/jetspeed/portal/cms/Sites/destatis/Internet/DE/Presse/pm/2010/01/PD10__033__122,templateId=renderPrint.psml

Statistisches Bundesamt (2010b). *Personen mit Migrationshintergrund*. Wiesbaden: Statistisches
    Bundesamt. Consulted online on 21 December 2010 at: http://www.destatis.de/jetspeed/portal/
    cms/Sites/destatis/Internet/DE/Content/Statistiken/Bevoelkerung/MigrationIntegration/
    Migrationshintergrund/Aktuell,templateId=renderPrint.psml

Statistisches Bundesamt (2010c). *Microcensus*. Wiesbaden: Statistisches Bundesamt. Consulted online on
    9 December 2010 at: http://www.destatis.de/jetspeed/portal/cms/Sites/destatis/Internet/EN/press/
    abisz/Mikrozensus__e,templateId=renderPrint.psml

Statistisches Bundesamt (2010d). *Kinder- und Jugendhilfe*. Wiesbaden: Statistisches Bundesamt. Consulted
    online on 10 December 2010 at: http://www.destatis.de/jetspeed/portal/cms/Sites/destatis/Internet/
    DE/Content/Statistiken/Sozialleistungen/KinderJugendhilfe/Aktuell,templateId=renderPrint.psml

Statistisches Bundesamt (2010e). *Kinder- und Jugendhilfestatistiken: Kinder und tätige Personen in*
    Tageseinrichtungen und in öffentlich geförderter Kindertagespflege am 1.3.2010. Wiesbaden: Statistisches
    Bundesamt. Consulted online on 9 December 2010 at: https://www-ec.destatis.de/csp/shop/sfg/bpm.
    html.cms.cBroker.cls?cmspath=struktur,vollanzeige.csp&ID=1026418

Statistisches Bundesamt (2010f). *Berufsbildungsstatistik 2009*. Wiesbaden: Statistisches Bundesamt.
    Consulted online on 10 December 2010 at: http://www.destatis.de/jetspeed/portal/cms/Sites/
    destatis/Internet/DE/Content/Publikationen/Qualitaetsberichte/BildungForschungKultur/
    BeruflicheBildung/QBBeruflicheBildung,property=file.pdf

Unabhängige Kommission Zuwanderung (2001). *Zuwanderung gestalten – Integration fördern. Bericht der*
    Unabhängigen Kommission –Zuwanderung–. Berlin: Unabhängige Kommission Zuwanderung. Consulted
    online on 11 December 2010 at: http://www.bmi.bund.de/SharedDocs/Downloads/DE/Themen/
    MigrationIntegration/AsylZuwanderung/Zuwanderungsbericht_pdf.pdf;jsessionid=A0797BD28313D
    A7FB3E3AB3252FC88B5.1_cid183?__blob=publicationFile

Vertovec, Steven (2007). Super-diversity and its implications. In: *Ethnic and Racial Studies*, vol. 29, no. 6,
    p. 1024-54.

8   Monitoring integration in Ireland

Nanette Schuppers and Steven Loyal

8.1   Introduction

Discussions of migrant integration policy and measurement in Ireland have interest-ing parallels with discussions in other Western European countries. However, Ireland's peculiar migration history also exhibits a number of unique characteristics, specifically its 'lateness' in becoming a country of immigration and the preponderance of migrants from Western Europe and Central Europe.

We will begin this chapter by discussing Irish migration patterns. The last fifteen years have seen a remarkable increase in immigration, with the vast majority coming from within the European Union (EU). Immigrants are primarily of working age and many are well educated. The recent recession, however, has led to increased unemployment, es-pecially among immigrants from the accession states. We will then highlight the State's integration policies, which we argue effectively leave migrants responsible for their own integration. Establishing a coherent view of the State's understanding of its integration goal and how best to achieve it is a difficult endeavour. The chapter then moves on to discuss the data available to migration and integration researchers. While there is a large amount of descriptive data available, it often lacks detail and generally is inadequate for monitoring integration precisely. The chapter concludes by giving a short overview of the limited research that has been carried out on integration in Ireland. Again, the research tends to lack detail, is descriptive rather than explanatory, and is difficult to generalise.

The term 'integration' is a contested concept. There is, as elsewhere, a wide discrepancy among actors in their interpretations of the term. While the State focuses on integra-tion as a means for migrants to become independent and self-sufficient, scholars tend to concentrate more on migrants and the host population becoming more equal in rela-tion to health, housing, employment and education, as well as on the absence of racism and discrimination. This chapter focuses on all these aspects and on the extent to which monitoring these areas of integration in Ireland is taking place.

8.2   Migration in figures

Ireland has historically been a country of emigration, but 1996 marked a major turn-ing point: for the first time in its history, Ireland became a country of net immigration. Between 1999 and 2008, Ireland's population increased by 18% – the highest rate in the 27 countries comprising the EU. The vast majority of this increase was a result of immi-gration. The number of immigrants entering Ireland has grown rapidly over a very short period. The 2002 Census recorded that non-Irish nationals made up just under 6% of the population. The most recent Census in 2006, which is probably the most accurate measurement of the non-Irish population so far, recorded 419,733 non-Irish nationals, constituting about 10% of the population. As many European countries have a longer history of immigration it is difficult to compare Irish migration figures with those of other countries. However, if we look at the case of Italy, also a relatively new country of immigration, it is estimated that in 2006 6.2% of the population were migrants, according to the Catholic charities Caritas and Fondazione Migrantes. The next Census in Ireland in 2011 will be of particular interest, as it will be the first reliable dataset on migration since the beginning of the recession that marked the end of the Celtic Tiger boom.

The Census estimates that 275,775 individuals from the EU-25 were resident in Ireland in 2006, making up 66% of the non-Irish population. Almost 120,000 of these migrants were from the accession states that joined the EU in 2004. The EU nationals who had migrated to Ireland were followed by nationals from Asia (11%), Africa (6%), and North and South America (5%). Although 188 different nationalities are estimated to be residing in Ireland, almost 70% are estimated to originate from just ten countries (CSO 2008: 8). The predominance of European migrants was reflected in the Census question on ethnic and cultural background; 95% of the population identified themselves as white, while only 1.3% identified themselves as Asian and 1% as black. Many, however, would consider the Census to underestimate factual racial diversity.

Table 8.1

Source countries of non-Irish nationals (in absolute numbers and percentages)

country	number of non-Irish nationals	percentage of all non-Irish nationals
United Kingdom	112,548	26.8
Poland	63,276	15.1
Lithuania	24,628	5.9
Nigeria	16,300	3.9
Latvia	13,319	3.2
USA	12,475	3.0
China	11,161	2.7
Germany	10,289	2.5
Philippines	9,548	2.3
France	9,046	2.2

Source: Census 2006

The population of non-Irish nationals is predominantly of working age. Only 12% of immigrants are children, while those over the age of 65 account for about 3.5%. Overall, 53% of non-Irish nationals recorded in the Census were male, while 47% were female. Yet the gender ratio varies quite markedly by nationality. Thus 64% of the Poles are men, compared to only 37.4% of the Swedes. Despite a decline, Ireland is still predominantly a Catholic country, counting 87% of the total population as Catholics. A relatively high proportion – 51% – of non-Irish nationals described themselves as belonging to this religion. The increase in the number of Muslims, from 19,000 in 2002 to 33,000 in 2006, made Islam the third-largest religion, with more Muslims than Presbyterians now residing in the country.

Migrants in Ireland are often categorised on the basis of their legal status. The major distinction made is between EU citizens and non-EU citizens, because the rights granted to these two groups differ greatly. Secondly, the State has created a number of categorical and policy distinctions between labour migrants, international students, and asylum-seekers and refugees. Among the labour migrants a further subdivision is made between work permit-holders, work visa-holders and Green Card holders. The last group that is identified are dependants of non-EU migrants. The consequences of this division will be discussed further later in the chapter, when we shall discuss access to public services.

Socioeconomic status
Many of the immigrants are comparatively well educated. While they reported higher overall levels of education than the Irish population – 38% were thought to have a tertiary education, compared to 28% of Irish nationals – this was primarily a demographic effect caused by the older age profile of the Irish population. When those aged 15 to 44 years from both groups are compared, educational differences largely disappear – about 31% have a tertiary education. However, it should be noted that there are wide differences between nationalities. Census data indicate that approximately three-quarters of people from the EU-15, excluding Ireland and the United Kingdom, were educated to tertiary level. The equivalent figure for people from the rest of the world was just under 50% (CSO 2008: 18).
As most migrants came to Ireland in pursuit of work, we find a higher level of economic activity among migrants than the average labour participation rate in Ireland (CSO 2008: 19). However, there is also significant evidence from the Census indicating high levels of ethnic labour market segmentation. For example, over half of Polish and Lithuanian males, two of the biggest groups of non-Irish nationals in the country, are recorded as working in construction and manufacturing, while half of all females from these countries work in shops, hotels and restaurants.

Migration, work, and recession
Since Ireland has primarily been a country of emigration, it is well accustomed to emigration functioning as a pressure release valve for the labour market in times of economic downturn, and evidence of this pattern can be seen again today. In September 2009, more people began to leave Ireland than to enter it for the first time in more than a decade. The Central Statistics Office (CSO) calculated that the number of emigrants in the year to April 2009 had increased by over 40%. Of the 65,100 who emigrated during that period, almost half were accession state nationals, while approximately 30% were Irish nationals. Immigration declined, with those from EU accession states showing the biggest fall. Figures from the CSO indicate that more than half the foreign nationals who registered for PPS numbers (Public Personal Service numbers – tax numbers) in 2004 no longer appeared in the employment or welfare statistics in 2008, suggesting that many

had left the country. Whether this emigration was due to unemployment caused by the economic downturn or to other reasons cannot be determined from the available data.

Throughout the recession, the high labour market participation rate of migrants has fallen dramatically, which is reflected in the unemployment data. Those data show that, although the numbers of people claiming either jobseeker's allowance or jobseeker's benefit rose by more than half for Irish nationals, it tripled from 8,000 to 25,000 for non-Irish nationals in the year to December 2008. Various factors account for immigrants' overrepresentation in the unemployment figures. The concentration in specific sectors and in low-pay occupations means that they were the hardest hit during the recession. This was particularly the case for accession state nationals, who were heavily concentrated in construction, hotels and restaurants, and manufacturing. Three-quarters of all nationals from the EU accession states, for example, were concentrated in four industries: manufacturing, construction, wholesale and retail trades, and hotels and restaurants.

Figure 8.1

Unemployment rates for Irish and non-Irish nationals, 2004-2009 (in percentages)

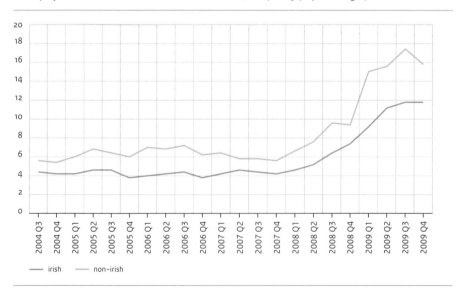

Source: QNHS 2010

8.3   Integration policy

The integration of migrants into Irish society has to be understood as involving their inclusion in a number of overlapping processes and spheres, each of which follow diverse paths and possess their own logic and specific temporality. It can be argued that four broad interconnected processes have significantly shaped and account for the patterns of incorporation or integration of various migrant groups in Ireland. Firstly, the mode of entry and legal status of the migrant; secondly, the conditions of reception in the host country, including racism and discrimination from the state and host population; thirdly, the characteristics, background, and outlook of the migrant, including, age, gender, ethnicity, socioeconomic background, language proficiency, etc.; and fourthly, the shape of government policies towards migrants in terms of providing language classes, recognising qualifications, but also the state's policy with respect to the resident population as a whole in terms of providing a basic economic infrastructure.

Here, we will examine the state's integration policy and legislation. A very limited policy of integration was initially developed by the Irish state in the 1990s for Bosnian refugees. However, with the rapid increase in migration after the European expansion in 2004, a broader focus on immigrants, and specifically those who came to work, was established with the appointment of a Minister for Integration Policy in 2007. Nevertheless, the Office of the Minister of Integration was established in such a way that integration policy remained separated from migration policy. There was no attempt to develop any systematic state-run monitoring of integration. This absence was reinforced with the onset of the recession in 2008 and the funding cuts that ensued.

The Irish state attempted to address the issue of discrimination and racism, both through specific legislation and more general legislation aimed at the population as a whole. Examples include the introduction of the Prohibition of Incitement to Hatred Act (1989), the establishment of the Reception and Integration Agency (2001), the goal of which was to ensure service provision to asylum-seekers, the creation of the Irish Naturalisation and Immigration Service (2005), which looks to aid the integration of all legal migrants, and the National Action Plan Against Racism (Cross & Turner 2006: 220). All of these initiatives were aimed specifically at the migrant population. The Equal Status Act (2000) and the Employment Equality Act (2004), by contrast, aimed to create a level and non-discriminatory playing field for all residents of the state.

In terms of governmental reports dealing with integration, two were of special importance. *Integration: A Two Way Process* (1999), and *Planning for Diversity: National Action Plan Against Racism* (2005) were especially significant for facilitating the placing and establishment of integration on the national agenda. The appointment of Conor Lenihan as Minister for Integration Policy in 2007 was a further indication of the state's move towards an integration agenda. Both reports on integration tended to define the term in a way that was close to multiculturalism, making them particularly attractive to NGOs and immigrant support groups. *Integration: A Two Way Process* stated that migrants needed to adapt to the culture of the host society, without having to give up their cultural identity. The report was however concerned with access to state services for refugees only. The National Action Plan Against Racism took a similar, though more broadly applicable, multiculturalist view, imposing obligations and duties both on minority groups and on the state, and applying this not only to refugees, but also to other migrants and to Travellers. The Department of Social and Family Affairs refers to integration in its report on social protection and social inclusion 2008-2010. It states that integration can be facilitated by enabling participation in employment, access to services, education and training, as well as language support (Office for Social Inclusion 2006: 24).

An influential policy document produced by a semi-state think-tank, the National Economic and Social Council (NESC), set out the goals of the state. The NESC report argued that integration can be discussed in relation to three main areas: socioeconomic, structural and cultural integration (2006b: 184). It provided a list of requirements that migrants need to meet in order to facilitate these forms of integration. The most important requirement is English language proficiency. This is followed by economic independence and employment at a level that is appropriate to the migrant's educational attainment. It also argued that migrants need to obey the law, respect democratic values, pay taxes, participate in the political process and, finally, develop empathy with the Irish society. Conversely, the host society needs to ensure that migrants have access to housing and transportation, as well as to services, especially health care and education (NESC 2006b: 184).

The NESC report emphasised the importance of social and human capital in the integration process and advocated selection of migrants before arrival. It argued that a larger proportion of migrants with higher levels of human capital and social capital would help create a more cohesive society from the start. However, it recognised that Ireland was also in need of migrants who were willing to fill less-skilled positions. In line with these assumptions on social and human capital and its relationship to integration, Ireland combined the need for less-skilled migrants with the freedom of labour granted to EU nationals, and limited non-EU migration to higher-skilled migrants as much as possible (NESC 2006a: 155-159). The issuing of work permits (aimed at lower-skilled jobs) was curtailed and these jobs were instead to be offered to EU nationals. Only when a labour market test could prove that the employer had been unable to recruit an EU national were they able to apply for a work permit and hire a non-EU employee. In addition to this change to the Permit scheme, Ireland has now also introduced a Green Card system under the Employment Permits Act (2006), aimed at migrants earning more than €60,000 annually or working in specifically targeted sectors. The Green Card does not offer permanent residence, but does offer residency for the first two years, after which it is indefinitely renewable. It also means that the migrant has the right to immediate family reunification (Mac Einri & White 2008: 154-155). There were at least two motives for introducing the Green Card. First of all, it was assumed that a sense of permanency would offer both the migrants and the host population a sense of belonging, which would benefit integration (NESC 2006a: 167). On a less altruistic note, it was also intended to make Ireland a more attractive destination for highly skilled potential migrants (Boucher 2008: 21).

It appears that the Irish state has adopted a fairly liberal approach to migrant integration, in which the cultural identity of the migrant is not seen as an obstacle to integration. The governmental and NESC reports, however, failed to discuss what resources and material infrastructure would be provided to facilitate integration. Rather, the attitude of the Irish state was one of *laissez faire*, instead placing the emphasis and responsibility on the individual migrant to adapt (Boucher 2008: 7-8; Gray 2006). Though the state legislated on issues of racism, no particular attention was paid to the problem of institutional racism and exclusion. The state also overlooked the fact that its policies of differentiating migrant statuses, limiting family reunification, and its immigration legislation impact negatively on the chances of integration for migrants. The integration reports were emblematic of state discussions of integration.

Next, we will look at the practical side of state policies by investigating the access to state services for migrants. We will examine access to welfare, employment, political participation, education, health, and housing. Migrants do not have automatic entitlements to social welfare. The Irish social welfare system has two schemes: social insurance and social assistance. The former operates on the basis of pay-related social insurance (PRSI) contributions. To qualify, workers must have made the required number of payments into the scheme; immigrants are eligible if they have done so and if they have a valid residence stamp. If migrant workers build up a sufficient quantity of stamps over a number of years they may become eligible for jobseeker benefits. Social assistance is means-tested and does not depend on PRSI contributions. However, the Habitual Residence Condition (HRC) means that many migrants remain ineligible for social welfare payments. The government of Ireland introduced HRC in 2004 to prevent 'welfare tourism'. Individuals had to demonstrate they had been habitually resident in Ireland – usually for over two years – and intended to remain there. These requirements apply to Irish nationals who have lived abroad, as well as to EEA and non-EEA nationals. Many unemployed migrants are denied welfare benefits because they do not meet the Habitual Residence Condition. Fewer than 5,000 individuals were refused in 2005, while over 10,500 were refused in 2009. Moreover, claiming social welfare often means that an application for citizenship or long-term residency is refused (ICI 2009). For this reason many migrants do not apply.

There are a number of restrictions on migrant access to the labour market. Despite the fact that Romania and Bulgaria have joined the EU, Ireland has not extended the freedom of labour to nationals of these two countries; instead they have to apply for a work permit. Work permits are also required for non-EEA migrants who are looking to work in a job that pays over €30,000 annually (and in exceptional cases less than €30,000) and that is on the list of eligible jobs. A person can only apply for a work permit when a labour market test has shown that there are no EEA nationals available to fill the position. For jobs that pay more than €60,000 annually the state has created Green Cards. Both the work permit and the Green Card are employer-specific, but employees are – in theory – allowed to change jobs after twelve months as long as a new application is made for a Permit or Card. The labour market test is not required in this case. Work permit-holders are able to apply for family reunification after one year, while Green Card-holders are immediately eligible. A permit-holder can apply for permanent residency after five years, while this is two years for a Green Card-holder. Spouses of Green Card-holders, work permit-holders and work visa-holders can apply for a Spousal Work Permit; only then are they allowed to work. In order to apply for this permit they have to be legally resident in Ireland. No labour market test is required and all jobs are eligible for this permit. Many migrants who hold a student visa, which is required for all non-EEA students of Irish educational institutions, are active on the labour market. Holders are allowed to work up to twenty hours weekly (and forty hours outside of term). After graduation the visa-holder may remain in Ireland for six month in order to apply for a work permit or a Green Card. During this time they are allowed to work a maximum of forty hours per week. Voting rights are granted to all legal residents in Ireland who are aged 18 years or older. Non-EU residents are allowed to vote for local elections and EU migrants in local and European elections. In order to be able to vote, every resident has to register for the elections. In order to be eligible to register a resident must have been legally resident in Ireland since at least 1 September of the year preceding registration.

Tertiary education is currently free for the majority of Irish students. However, the situation is different for migrants. In order to be eligible for free education one must be an EU national and have been living in an EU member state for three of the past five years. For non-EU migrants or those do not meet the HRC, fees apply. EU nationals who do not meet the HRC, refugees, and non-EU nationals who do meet the HRC are liable for EU fees. All other students have to pay non-EU fees. Non-EU fees are on average twice or three times the amount of the EU fees.

Access to public health care is dependent on a number of criteria. Migrants are subject to the common means test that determines whether a person is granted a medical card or merely medical services. Medical card-holders are granted free visits to a General Practitioner and to public hospitals and they are supported in other medical costs. Those who do not qualify for a medical card have to contribute financially to GP visits, to medication, and when being admitted to a public hospital. In addition to this means test, which is standard for all residents of Ireland, migrants have to hold a residency visa or permit and provide proof of residency through rental or property purchase.

Finally, as regards access to housing, EEA nationals are in a position quite similar to Irish nationals, as long as they are in employment, when they apply for housing support. Non-EEA nationals are much more limited in their eligibility. Only non-EEA migrants, whose legal status provides for long-term residency in Ireland, such as refugee status, are eligible for housing support. Work permit-holders and asylum-seekers are not eligible for this support.

As the above discussion of access to state services shows, the Irish state opens up many of its services to EU migrants and to those who have been resident in Ireland for a substantial period of time. Non-EU migrants and recent arrivals have much more limited access to the labour market, education, the welfare system, housing, health care or the political arena.

The state has not communicated any plans for installing its own national monitor for integration. This gap in integration research is filled by other sources. The Office of Integration, for example, has acknowledged that it has to rely on intermittent CSO data and academic research to measure the progress in and obstacles to migrant integration

(Office of the Minister for Integration 2008). However, no adjustments have as yet been made to policies stemming from CSO and academic data.

8.4   Data sources in Ireland

One of the biggest obstacles faced by Irish immigration and integration research is the lack of a population register. Although the absence of a register ensures personal data protection, a register could provide researchers with a wealth of data, as well as a good source for samples in their own research. A consequence of having no register is that all available migration and integration data are based solely on samples, whose representativeness cannot be guaranteed or tested. The most comprehensive set of data on migration in Ireland is the total number of PPS numbers issued per nationality. Although this gives a complete overview of migrants who have applied for legal work, and therefore needed a tax number, this information does not take into consideration migrants who do not work, migrants who work informally, or migrants who used to work in Ireland but have since left. Ireland also lacks any form of longitudinal studies, which could have provided an insight into the integration processes rather than the integration outcome.

In addition, statistical and Census data are available and are used by the Office of the Minister for Integration. The CSO is arguably the main source of data in Ireland. It was set up in 1949 and is responsible for gathering official statistical data. As well as general statistical data, the CSO carries out a Census every five years and a Quarterly National Household Survey (QNHS) four times a year based on a sample of 39,000 households. In 2004, the CSO executed a QNHS module devoted to equality and discrimination. It also gathers data on employment in the National Employment Survey.

Table 8.2

Available data on migrants by cso

cso general	QNHS	Census
people on the Live Register	labour force participation rates	religion
religion	sectoral breakdown	economic status
number per country of origin	persons in employment classified by occupation	industrial group/sector
number per nationality	family composition	occupational group
PPS allocation		socio-economic group
economic activity: employment and welfare		social class
industrial sector		educational attainment
risk of poverty (Irish vs. non-Irish)		number per nationality
hourly and annual earnings		number per country of birth
weekly paid hours		marital status
		ethnic/cultural background[a]
		housing type
		ethnic/cultural background[a] and marital status
		ethnic/cultural background[a] and town
		ethnic/cultural background[a] and country of birth
		ethnic/cultural background[a] and nationality
		ethnic cultural background[a] and religion
		ethnic/cultural background[a] and economic status
		ethnic/cultural background[a] and education
		Irish speaking by ethnic group[a]
		Irish speaking by nationality

a   Self-reported ethnic or cultural background.

The limited availability of data on integration in Ireland has not been helped by the fact that the different datasets cannot be linked. The QNHS data from different modules can be compared so that changes over time can be tracked, but QNHS data and Census data cannot be linked for analysis. The CSO has made available much of the data collected, but those data are limited to Irish/non-Irish, which hampers integration research. All the CSO data are descriptive, and the CSO does not provide many explanations for the correlations found.

Although the state makes no systematic attempts to monitor integration, there have been some academic and independent reports that have analysed, measured and moni- tored integration in Ireland. However, much of the data mentioned in this chapter is affected by problems with validity and reliability. The Population Census is the most extensive database. Unfortunately, it did not contain a question about nationality until 2002, and a question on ethnic and cultural background was not added until 2006. This recent addition to the Census is illustrative of the novelty of migration as an issue in Ireland. Most evidence suggests that Census data from 2006 seem to underestimate the number of migrants in the country. Although the Census was available in several lan- guages, respondents had to request or download a form in their own language, and this information was not widely available. In addition, many migrants may not have been aware that the Census was taking place. There were also issues of migrants' housing arrangements that might make them unwilling to be registered (e.g. too many people in one house), or their legal and employment status might have made them unwilling to complete the Census. In addition to the Census, the CSO is also the collector and owner of the QNHS data and of the National Employment Survey data. The CSO has indicated that the representation of migrants in the QNHS remains difficult due to language issues (Barrett & Kelly 2008). Other data available and only partly related to migration and integration studies are the data collected on cases that come before the Equality Tribu- nal and the Garda Síochána Ombudsman Commission (Irish Police Force Ombudsman Commission). While these data give an indication of the number of cases that are related to race or religion and what the outcomes of these cases are, the data are too limited to contribute significantly to the integration debate.

8.5   Integration research

Ireland does not have a state-run monitor for integration, and all forms of monitoring are left to NGOs, think-tanks and academic researchers. At international level there is a monitor that does not investigate the level of integration achieved by migrants, but which instead focuses on scrutinising the policies put in place by the government. This monitor was developed by Niessen et al. in the Migrant Integration Policy Index (2007). The performance of 25 EU member states and three other countries (Canada, Norway and Switzerland) were measured against each other and against international best-practice policies. The report found that, while Ireland scored around the average on issues such as anti-discrimination, labour market access, family reunification and political partici- pation, its policies on long-term residency were below par. Figure 8.2 shows how the Irish policies compare to the best-practice policies.

Figure 8.2
Irish integration policies (in percentages)

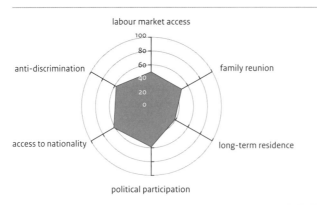

Source: Niessen et al. (2007: 92)

The report also made some key findings in relation to how Irish policies have impacted on integration. On the one hand, migrants have gained some independence from their employer since the new legislation of 2006, as renewal of their work permit is no longer dependent on one specific employer. On the other hand, those who have applied for family reunification have few opportunities to appeal a negative outcome and the relative's status remains dependent on the status of the sponsor. This dependency limits access to education and employment for the relative (Niessen et al. 2007: 94). Thirdly, while electoral rights and political freedom in Ireland meet best practice, political participation does not. Whereas some local authorities consult migrant organisations, at national level migrant NGOs are not consulted. Funding is available for the few organisations involved at a local level, but the criteria do not match those in place for other associations (Niessen et al. 2007: 95). Next, the chance of success for applications to Irish citizenship is dependent on the judgement as to whether the applicant earns enough money and is of 'good character'. Appealing a negative decision is not possible. An important change in the position of migrants in Ireland followed a public referendum held in 2004: Irish citizenship for children born in Ireland to migrants was subsequently no longer automatic after January 2005; their legal citizenship was now dependent on their parents' legal status. Finally, in relation to fighting discrimination and racism, there is a strong factor working against migrants' interests. In cases of incitement of hatred, the burden of proof that the alleged behaviour did indeed incite hatred among third parties lies with the complainant. In addition, the state does not get involved in public dialogue about racism and discrimination, but leaves this task to the Equality Authority (Niessen et al. 2007: 96). The Migrant Integration Policy Index shows that while Ireland is performing well in certain areas and making improvements in others, policies in relation to long-term residency, family reunification and labour market access are not aiding integration.

Next, we will move from monitoring governmental policies to monitoring integration processes. Taken as a whole, the research done in Ireland in relation to migrant integration is limited and lacks depth. Most projects look at only one domain of integration, for example the labour market, or look at only one national group. Integration research in Ireland is therefore in its infancy and a great deal of development is still required.

We can begin by examining the number of cases related to race or religion that have come before the Equality Tribunal and the Garda Síochána Ombudsman Commission. These data provide an insight into the prevalence of discrimination in Ireland. However, the data do suffer from an important shortcoming, because not enough information is available to gain a real understanding of the cases presented. Although the reliability of the data is undisputed, the validity of the data for measuring racist incidents in Ireland is not. Data show that of the 1,208 cases that came before the Equality Tribunal between 2003 and 2009, only 190 were race-related. Of those cases, almost a third were judged in favour of the complainant. From May 2007 until June 2010, the Garda Síochána Ombudsman Commission received 8,091 complaints, a hundred of which referred to discrimination on grounds of race or religion. Of these hundred cases, three were ruled in favour of the complainant and sanctions were imposed, and 55 cases were ruled in favour of the defendant. Race and religion are in the minority when it comes to the grounds of cases brought before the Equality Tribunal or the Garda Síochána Ombudsman Commission. Whether this means that discrimination on these grounds is rare or that these incidents tend not to be reported cannot be determined on the basis of the data presented here.

A QNHS module from 2004 that focused on experiences with discrimination found that non-white respondents had the most experiences of discrimination, at 31%. It was found that the groups who had suffered the greatest level of discrimination were the least likely to take action against it and were least aware of their legal rights. Ethnicity was not the most frequently cited ground for discrimination as stated by the respondents; rather, gender and age were more common grounds. In work-related discrimination nationality, skin colour and ethnicity were most commonly cited by the victims. When these grounds for discrimination are compared in different settings, ethnicity, nationality and skin colour were common grounds for discrimination on public transport (28.1%), in shops, pubs and restaurants (26.5%), in looking for work (23.1%) and in looking for housing (20.4%) (CSO 2005).

A report undertaken in 2005 by the Economic and Social Research Institute (ESRI) which looked at discrimination and xenophobia in Ireland bore striking similarities to the findings of the special module of the QNHS. Harassment on the street or on public transport were the most commonly experienced forms of discrimination. Of the entire sample, 35% had experienced such discrimination, while among black Africans the figure was over 50%. The second most frequent form of discrimination was harassment at work, which was followed by discrimination when applying for employment; around a third of African migrants had faced difficulties with discrimination when applying for a job. Discrimination is not just shown by the host population and by employers: over 17% of respondents complained about bad treatment by the state's immigration service (McGinnity et al. 2006). The ESRI report combined with the data collected in the 2004 QNHS indicates that discrimination on the basis of race, ethnicity or nationality is not uncommon in Ireland and that black African migrants, in particular, face discrimination regularly. While the majority of incidents related to harassment and racism by individuals, the national immigration service is also mentioned as taking part in poor treatment of migrants.

Using the Quarterly National Household Survey from 2005, Turner et al. (2008) studied the membership of trade unions by migrants in Ireland. Trade union involvement is indicative of integration because it specifies the level of representation of migrants in labour relations. Since migrants are more likely to work for larger companies, and since employees of larger companies are 70% more likely to be union members, this should have a positive effect on the level of membership among the migrant population. On the other hand, trade union membership among migrants would be limited by the fact that they are overrepresented in the private sector, while trade union membership is more widespread in the public sector (Turner et al. 2008: 486). After controlling for all other variables, Irish employees are almost four times more likely to be unionised than immigrant workers (Turner et al. 2008: 489). This is an important fact, as it indicates severe underrepresentation of migrant workers in Irish trade unions.

Studying integration in the labour market, Barrett and Duffy (2008) also used the data collected for the QNHS 2005. They tested whether migrants and the host population performed similarly in the labour market and whether any differences could be explained by the length of time migrants had spent in Ireland, assuming that increasing knowledge of the Irish labour market, and therefore greater social capital, would allow migrants to climb the labour market ladder and end up at a level that was appropriate for their educational attainment. The first comparison, looking at migrants and the host population and their employment levels, showed that migrants were doing much worse than natives (Barrett & Duffy 2008: 604). However, this picture was distorted by the dominance of recent arrivals, who had lower educational levels compared to the older arrivals, potentially impacting on their employment level (Barrett & Duffy 2008: 606). When focusing solely on immigrants from the accession states, it was found that the employment gap for older arrivals was no smaller than that for more recent arrivals. This means that there are no signs of integration into the labour market for this group (Barrett & Duffy 2008: 611). Small cell sizes and the limited time frame cannot be overlooked when examining this finding, and it should therefore be approached with care. Besides investigations into the opportunities for migrants to increase their employment level over time, it is also interesting to compare the pay levels of Irish and non-Irish employees in the Irish labour market. These data were brought together in the National Employment Survey of 2007. The data show that migrants work more hours per week than their Irish colleagues in all sectors, with the exception of public administration and the defence sector. At the same time, the hourly wages of migrants are lower than those of Irish employees, as can be seen in figure 8.3 (CSO 2009: 45). The data show that the position of migrants in the Irish labour market is not equal to that of Irish employees. Combined with the information disclosed by Barrett and Duffy (2008) that the employment gap does not decrease with time, this means that we cannot speak of full integration of migrants in the Irish labour market.

Figure 8.3

Hourly wages (in euro's per hour)

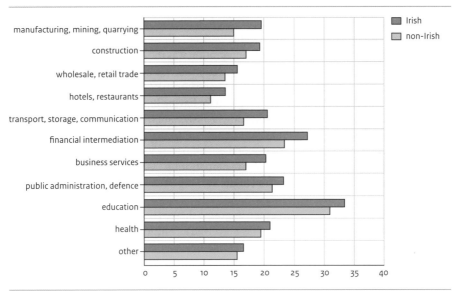

Sheringham investigated the integration of Brazilian migrants in the western Irish town of Gort. While the investigation was very thorough, it has to be asked whether the findings of this research can be generalised to other national groups and to other areas in Ireland. Sheringham found many positive signs of integration in Gort. While strong friendships between national groups were rare, most respondents did have many Irish acquaintances (Sheringham 2009: 97). The host population welcomed Brazilians into their community, partly because their presence improved the economy, created employment and led to property development opportunities. Although there is some spatial segregation, the small size of the town means that this segregation is limited and that Brazilians and Irish use the same shops and schools (Sheringham 2009: 99). The schools facilitated Brazilian children by having at least one Portuguese-speaking teacher. A large proportion of the Brazilians have overstayed their visas, but the local police force is lenient. State policy, however, is not, and migrants cannot rely on the continuation of this local compassion (Sheringham 2009: 100). This research shows that in a small community the social relations between migrants and the host population are generally good; however, the contribution made to the local economy by the migrants is very important in the positive reception they have received, and the recession may dampen the enthusiasm of the Irish population. Only future research will be able to test this hypothesis.

The last set of data in relation to integration of migrants in Ireland comes from the Migration and Citizenship Research Initiative (MCRI 2008), which is in some ways the most comprehensive collection of data. This research focused on the political, cultural, economic and social integration of Chinese, Indian, Nigerian and Lithuanian migrants (MCRI 2008: 7-8). An important obstacle to integration identified by the MCRI report was the lack of family reunification. It led to feelings of isolation, but also impacted on labour market participation, as one parent often felt the need to stay at home and look after the children because grandparents were not allowed to join the family in Ireland. Another important hindrance to integration was the lack of awareness among migrants about their political rights. Lack of awareness was the most important cause for migrants not to register for elections (MCRI 2008: 10-11). Lack of financial resources and time were the most common reasons given for having limited social contacts. In addition to these factors, the lack of childcare facilities and lack of confidence to speak English also played an important role (MCRI 2008: 14). Verbal and physical harassment were also a problem, particularly for respondents who were visibly recognisable as migrants because of their skin colour. Those perpetrating the harassment were often teenagers, and the abuse often occurred in the evening (MCRI 2008: 15).

The MCRI report found that migrants with very little certainty about their stay in Ireland, asylum-seekers and undocumented migrants showed the lowest levels of integration, followed by migrants whose stay was perceived as a little more stable but still very dependent on employment, and by migrants who held an Irish or EU passport and were free to travel in and out of the country. The group with the highest levels of integration were those whose stay in Ireland was fairly secure, either because they held refugee status, because they were long-term residents, or because they were on a work visa.

Table 8.3

Integration by legal status (in percentages)

level of integration	EU/Irish	work visa, refugee, long-term resident	work permit, student visa, dependent, leave to remain	asylum, undocumented	total
very low	9	0	4	0	4
low	29	4	30	73	26
medium	39	47	45	27	43
high	23	49	21	0	27

Source: MCRI 2008: 179

The MCRI report showed that the legal status of migrants and certain individual characteristics determine many aspects of integration. Lack of family reunification hampers people in accessing the labour market and in establishing social contacts. Racism on the basis of skin colour takes away from the sense of safety among migrants. And lack of financial resources and limited English proficiency stand in the way of interacting with the Irish population. However, a central flaw of the MCRI report was the sampling method deployed. Since a snowball sample was used for this project, representativeness could not be guaranteed.

In assessing the research discussed here, we can make certain statements about integration data in Ireland. First of all, the data are limited in both amount and quality. Secondly, the data show that discrimination and racism are prevalent, but that legal action against discrimination is rather scarce. Thirdly, labour market participation is unequal, both in the sense of level of employment and in the sense of remuneration. Fourthly, while social contact is good at a local level, current research does not allow statements to be made about larger urban areas or situations where the economic contribution of migrants is less significant. And finally, the legal status of migrants and the possibilities it offers them is of significance to their position in the integration process.

8.6 Conclusion

Contrary to many other European countries, Ireland has only become a destination country for migrants in the last two decades. It is only in the last fifteen years that the number of immigrants entering Ireland has outstripped the number of emigrants leaving. Another difference between many European countries and Ireland is that the vast majority of Ireland's immigrants are EU citizens and that a large number are well educated. Ireland has applied its migration legislation to safeguarding the high educational standard of its migrants, by limiting non-EU immigration to those who are well educated and those working in professions where Ireland has a shortage of staff. The recentness and rapidity of immigration to Ireland has meant that the state has generally responded to increasing numbers in an ad hoc manner. Initially it focused on the integration of refugees, only much later including the integration of labour migrants on the government agenda. In its policy documents, the Irish state allowed a great deal of cultural diversity, but in practice this diversity was not always accommodated and infrastructure and services for social and structural integration were not provided by the government. For example, language classes are not provided by the state, even though it is very aware that language proficiency lies at the core of integration possibilities.

Currently, Ireland does not have a state-run monitor of integration, and statistical and academic publications will for the time being have to suffice as a stand-in for a monitor. The data are scarce and often lacking in detail, preventing a comprehensive measurement of integration. The data show that racism is common in Ireland, but that legal action against it is not. It is also evident that labour market integration is lacking and that social integration, while successful in certain small communities, is dependent on the goodwill of the host society.

A number of NGOs concerned with integration issues have consolidated to form the Integration Centre. This Centre aims to be involved in integration monitoring, advocacy and planning at all bureaucratic levels. Although this is only a first step in the direction of integration monitoring, and the first monitor has not been executed to date, it is expected that the focus of the Integration Centre on education, employment, active citizenship and social inclusion should generate more integration data that can be examined on a comparative basis.

References

Barrett, A. & D. Duffy (2008). Are Ireland's Immigrants Integrating into Its Labor Market? In: *International Migration Review*, no. 42, p. 597-619.

Barrett, A. & E. Kelly (2008). How Reliable is the Quarterly National Household Survey for Migration Research? In: *The Economic and Social Review*, no. 39, p. 191-205.

Boucher, G. (2008). Ireland's Lack of a Coherent Integration Policy. In: *Translocations*, no. 3, p. 5-28.

Cross, C. & T. Turner (2006). Irish Workers' Perceptions of the Impact of Immigrants: A Cause for Concern? In: *The Irish Journal of Management*, no. 27, p. 215-245.

CSO (2005). *Quarterly National Household Survey. Equality. Quarter 4 2004*. Dublin: Central Statistics Office.

CSO (2008). *Census 2006. Non-Irish Nationals Living in Ireland*. Dublin: Central Statistics Office.

CSO (2009). *National Employment Survey 2007*. Dublin: Central Statistics Office.

Department of Justice, Equality and Law Reform (2005). *Planning For Diversity. The National Action Plan Against Racism 2005-2008*. Dublin: Department of Justice, Equality and Law Reform.

Gray, B. (2006). Migrant Integration Policy: a Nationalist Fantasy of Management and Control? In: *The Irish Migration, Race and Social Transformation Review*, no. 1, p. 121-141.

ICI (2009). *Citizenship processes in need of overhaul: Immigrant Council of Ireland*. Dublin: Immigrant Council of Ireland.

Interdepartmental Working Group on the Integration of Refugees in Ireland (1999). *Integration. A Two-Way Process*. Dublin: Interdepartmental Working Group on the Integration of Refugees in Ireland.

Mac Einri, P. & A. White (2008). Immigration into the Republic of Ireland: a Bibliography of Recent Research. In: *Irish Geography*, no. 41, p. 151-179.

McGinnity, F., P.J. O'Connell, E. Quinn & J. Williams (2006). *Migrants' Experience of Racism and Discrimination in Ireland*. Dublin: Economic and Social Research Institute (ESRI).

MCRI (2008). *Getting on: From Migration to Integration. Chinese, Indian, Lithuanian, and Nigerian Migrants' Experiences in Ireland*. Dublin: Immigrant Council of Ireland.

NESC (2006a). *Managing Migration in Ireland: A Social and Economic Analysis*. Dublin: National Economic and Social Council.

NESC (2006b). *Migration Policy*. Dublin: National Economic and Social Council.

Niessen, J., T. Huddleston & L. Citron (2007). *Migrant Integration Policy Index*. Brussels: British Council and Migration Policy Group.

Office for Social Inclusion (2006). *National Report for Ireland on Strategies for Social Protection and Social Inclusion*. Dublin: Department for Social and Family Affairs.

Office of the Minister for Integration (2008). *Migration Nation. Statement on Integration Strategy and Diversity Management*. Dublin: Office of the Minister for Integration.

Sheringham, O. (2009). Ethnic Identity and Integration among Brazilians in Gort, Ireland. In: *Irish Migration Studies in Latin America*, no. 7, p. 93-104.

Turner, T., D. D'Art & M. O'Sullivan (2008). Union Availability, Union Membership and Immigrant Workers. In: *Employee Relations*, no. 30, p. 479-493.

9 Measuring integration in a reluctant immigration country: the case of Italy

Corrado Bonifazi, Salvatore Strozza and Mattia Vitiello

9.1 A short overview of foreign immigration in Italy

For almost a century, Italy was one of the leading emigration countries in Europe, and only in the second half of the 1970s did it began to receive immigration flows from the Third World and from Central and Eastern Europe (CEE). There was a lack of legislation governing these early flows, as was typically the case at that time in Southern Europe. This was probably a factor in promoting the start of foreign immigration in this part of the Continent, when traditional European recipient countries closed their borders. During the 1980s, the attitude of Italy towards immigration was basically positive. A large majority approved the first law on immigration in 1986, containing the first regularisation. This law restricted the official immigration channels to meet the requests of the old immigration countries of the EU. The main result was the substantial irregularity of a considerable part of the immigration during this period, something that was destined to become a constant in Italy's immigration history, together with recurrent regularisations. Other regularisation programmes were in fact implemented in 1990, 1995, 1998, 2002, 2006 and 2009 by governments of different political orientation. According to census data, the size of the foreign population remained small, with 211,000 foreign residents recorded in 1981 and 356,000 in 1991.

The climate changed radically after the fall of the Berlin Wall, which set new processes in motion. A new immigration law was approved in 1990 after a harsh parliamentary debate. The immigration problem returned to the centre of attention of politicians and public opinion in a dramatic way in 1991, when several waves of Albanians arrived by boat on Italian shores. In the 1990s Italy suffered a dramatic political crisis that caused the disappearance of many political parties and radical change in others (Ginsborg 1998). This crisis greatly influenced the decision-making process with regard to migration policies. In fact, despite a very obvious need for regulation, there was no new legislation until 1998 when the first comprehensive law on immigration was passed by the centre-left government. During the decade the foreign population almost quadrupled, reaching 1.3 million in 2001.

The tone of the political debate about immigration was becoming steadily harsher, and immigration issues played an important role in the 2001 election campaign. The arrival of the new centre-right government in 2001 had important repercussions for migration policy, leading to the passing of a new law in 2002. In line with the election manifesto of the new government, this law was intended to bring about better management of migration flows and more effective prevention of clandestine immigration (Nascimbene 2003). Although the latter aspect was clearly the most important, the law provided for the regularisation of non-EU irregular workers. This provision led to the regularization of around 650,000 immigrants. This was by far the biggest initiative of its kind in Italy's history and made a decisive contribution to taking the total number of regular immigrants to almost 2.8 million at the start of 2006.

The growth has remained exceptional in the subsequent years. The number foreign residents stood at 4.6 million at the beginning of 2011, accounting for 7.5% of the total population. The total foreign presence in Italy is even larger; it was estimated by ISMU (2011) at 5.3 million as at 1 January 2010, including almost 4.3 million foreign residents, 497,000 regular but non-resident foreigners and 544,000 irregular migrants (figure 9.1). The dramatic increase in the foreign population in Italy in the last twenty years has been driven by the concurrent effects of several structural imbalances in the country (Bonifazi & Marini 2010). They include a prolonged very low fertility rate that has caused a sharp decrease of the native working-age population, the considerable weight of the underground economy, and a Mediterranean welfare system that is largely unable to cope with the effects of the massive ageing process.

Figure 9.1

Foreigners by legal status in Italy, beginning of 2002, 2006 and 2010 (in numbers x 1000)

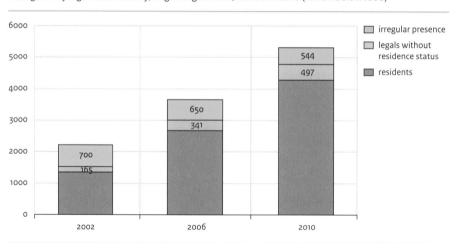

Source: Our elaborations and ISMU estimates (ISMU 2011)

A final point to consider is the marked change in the legal status of foreign immigration driven by EU enlargement. In fact, the share of EU nationals in Italy has risen from less than 6% before the enlargement to almost 30% in 2010. Romania, Albania and Morocco are currently the three main countries of origin of the foreign population in Italy, together accounting for 42% of the total (table 9.1). Other important national groups originate from Eastern Asia, CEE and North Africa, though they are far fewer in number than the three biggest communities.

Table 9.1

Main foreign communities in Italy, beginning of 2010 (resident foreigners in absolute values x 1000 and in percentages)

country of citizenship	absolute values x 1000	%
Romania	887.8	21.0
Albania	466.7	11.0
Morocco	431.5	10.2
China	188.4	4.4
Ukraine	174.1	4.1
Philippines	123.6	2.9
India	105.9	2.5
Poland	105.6	2.5
Moldova	105.6	2.5
Tunisia	103.7	2.4
total	4235.1	100.0

Source: ISTAT data

9.2 Migration policies of a reluctant immigration country

Italy's experience as an immigration country within the European migratory system is fairly well consolidated (Bonifazi et al. 2009). Consequently, it also has well-developed, albeit recent, experience with formulating immigration policies. When Italy first started to witness immigration in the early 1970s, the country was basically open to migration flows because of the lack of any specific rules controlling the entry of foreign workers and the conditions under which they could stay.

Law no. 943/1986 was adopted as a first attempt to regulate migration flows and the foreign presence in Italy. The main aim of the law was to ensure that all non-EC migrants who were legally resident in Italy, as well as their families, would receive equal treatment and equal rights to Italian workers. Another positive aspect of this law was the recognition of the right to family reunion for immigrant workers. Although the legislation was quite advanced, it had little effect on immigration in Italy. The main reason for this failure was the social position of immigrants as perceived by the lawmakers. They thought that the immigrant payroll workers would be the main beneficiaries of the law, but this category only included part of the immigrant population in Italy at that time.

The immigrant population increased in the subsequent years. Part of this increase was linked to an increase in what was referred to as 'clandestine' immigration, entries that were not authorised under the legislation that was in force at the time, and the 'irregular' presence of overstayers. To counter any further increases in clandestine and irregular immigration and to meet the need for better legislation on migration and immigrants' rights, in 1990 a law was passed together with new provisions for regularisation

(Law 39/1990). The main aim of this law was to completely reformulate the rules governing the conditions for the entry, stay and expulsion of immigrants in Italy and, later, to establish strict controls for migration flows. This law was sought to discourage of new flows of immigrants, establishing rigid control mechanisms at the borders with a new visa regime and, within Italy, the creation of a rigid system for expulsions and a series of rules on the renewal of permits to stay (*permesso di soggiorno*). As regards the integration policies, the new law left the previous legislation unchanged. However, it could be said that the years in which Law 39/1990 was in force were characterised by an immigration policy that was made up of circulars and administrative decrees which often contradicted each other (Bolaffi 2001). The most immediate consequence of this migration regime was that immigrants had a rather precarious legal status. This situation necessarily led to the passing of another two regularisation provisions and a new law (Law 48/1998), in an attempt to rectify this situation, to give immigrants greater legal certainty, and to open official and regular channels for immigration into Italy. This law was later included and expanded in the 'Consolidation Act on the Immigration and Status of Foreigners' (Law 286/1998). The main thrust of this law was to try to reduce to a minimum any regulatory ministerial circulars, which had left ample space for discretion and had led to the unequal treatment that was typical under the preceding legislation. Furthermore, in those years, the choice of a system of annual quotas for economic migrants seemed to run counter to European guidelines. In some ways, it would seem that the choices made by Italy were precursors to the EU's later statement of a path beyond the 'zero option', based on recognition of the current and potential role of immigrant labour in the European economies. In this connection, it should be noted that the quota system for admissions did not prove to be an effective way of governing migration flows, mainly because of its structurally ambiguous formulation. Another innovation was the introduction of 'sponsors' which could nominate a foreigner directly. Lastly, it is worth mentioning the considerably more open approach towards the stabilised immigrant population, with an extension of their social rights and guaranteed basic rights for clandestine immigrants, such as the right to healthcare and education.

The Consolidation Act was amended in some ways by Law 189/2002, this time under a centre-right government. The regulatory framework of this law saw the immigration question principally as a problem of public order, in which the basic idea was that foreigners on national territory are first and foremost a national security issue, in the 'true' sense of the protection and defence of public order. Consequently, a series of instruments was devised to provide continuous control of the immigrant population on two fronts. First, there was the need to control the entry flows and the irregular immigrant population more effectively, with stricter policing of regular entry channels and an increase in the number of expulsions. Second, control of regular immigrants already present in Italy was to be increased by creating a new kind of permit to stay, linked to an employment contract, and by tightening up the procedures for the renewal of permits in order to make immigration more temporary in nature and also to discourage stabilisation. In short, the measures contained in this law seemed to constitute a migration regime that reflected what might be termed a 'reluctant' approach (Cornelius et al. 1994).

This is a general attitude that seems to be confirmed by the recent provisions included in the *Pacchetto Sicurezza* (package of 'security' legislation).

9.3   Integration policies

The section of the Consolidation Act governing immigrants' rights and integration policies is mainly concerned with healthcare, the right to education and professional training and, lastly, the right to housing and access to the welfare state. This implies that all regular immigrants in Italy with permits to stay will benefit from social policies. Furthermore, the law also recognises that the right to healthcare and education are fundamental human rights that must be guaranteed regardless of a person's legal status. Consequently, urgent hospital and other medical treatment are also available to foreigners without permits to stay, as is the right to compulsory schooling for foreign minors who are living in Italy.

As regards access to healthcare and social services, the Consolidation Act provides a stable and clear framework. The declared objective is to allow legal immigrants the same access to healthcare services as Italian citizens. In particular, the regulations state that all foreign citizens with a valid permit to stay or who have applied to renew a previous permit can register with the National Health System (SSN) and access healthcare services. Obligatory registration implies rights and duties equal to those of Italian citizens as regards: treatment in Italy, the obligation to contribute and the period of validity. Furthermore, access to healthcare does not stop while the permit to stay is being renewed. Foreigners who are legally present but who have not registered with the SSN have the right to receive immediate urgent treatment.

Foreigners who are living in Italy illegally have the right to urgent treatment (treatment that cannot be postponed without endangering life or health) in public health facilities and in private health facilities contracted by the SSN (Art. 35). They also have the right to essential treatment (treatment for conditions that are not immediately dangerous but which could, over time, cause greater damage to health or death), and to continued treatment (complete treatment and rehabilitation programmes).

Health facilities are forbidden from reporting the presence of irregular immigrants who request treatment to the police authorities, so as not to discourage access to care (Art. 35 para. 5). Another aspect to be considered concerns local arrangements, given the advanced degree of federalism in the organisation of the Italian health system. It should be noted that each Region's regulatory path to providing healthcare for immigrants has led to some striking disparities between different areas, both in terms of access and in terms of which services may be used.

It is important to note that the last measures of the new Berlusconi government, assembled in the package of 'security legislation', do not directly relate to the integration policies. Specifically, they do not prohibit access to health care by clandestine or irregulars immigrants. Nevertheless, with the sanction of illegal immigration as a criminal offence, they could create an obligation for the medical officer to report illegal immigrants who have been provided with care, but without having revoked the rule prohibiting complaint. In such an ambiguous and contradictory legal framework, these rules make access to healthcare much more difficult than previously. A similar argument applies to the compulsory education of the children of illegal immigrants, where the Consolidation Act establishes the extension of compulsory education to all foreign minors on Italian territory (Art. 38).

Access to social integration programmes is restricted to citizens of non-EU countries who can demonstrate that they are abiding by the regulations governing their stay in Italy (Art. 40, para. 1b). Right of access to public housing, on a par with Italian citizens, is only granted to foreigners holding a residence permit for long-term EC residents and to foreigners legally living in Italy who have a permit to stay with a validity of more than two years, with a regular payroll job or who are self-employed.

Furthermore, foreigners with residence cards or permits to stay with a validity of not less than one year, and minors listed on their residence cards or permits to stay, have rights equal to those of Italian citizens with regard to social welfare assistance and benefits (including financial benefits) (Art. 41). The Italian state and local authorities promote the activities undertaken on behalf of foreigners legally residing in Italy (Art. 42). The Act establishes the Counsel for addressing the problems of immigrants and their families, the Commission for immigrant integration policies and the National Fund for migration policies (Art. 45).

Recently, Article 1 paragraph 25 of Law 94/2009 obliged immigrants to sign an Integration Agreement in order to obtain a permit to stay. According to this rule, the immigrant must commit to learn the Italian language and the fundamentals of the Italian Constitution, to respect the principles of the Charter of the values of citizenship and integration (Decree of the Ministry of Interior 04/23/2007). The permit to stay gives a number of credits that can be reduced in the event of criminal convictions or fines for administrative or tax offences. On expiry of Agreement, a certification test is administered to assess whether the immigrant has fulfilled their obligations. If the score exceeds 30 credits, the contract is fulfilled, a score from 1 to 29 leads to an extension, less than 1 implies immediate expulsion.

In the Integration Agreement, the notion of integration does not seem to involve a process of social inclusion of immigrants, but has rather become a juridical and policy mechanism of control to enable the state to better manage who can be included and who cannot. As Besselink (2006) points out, integration measures express the move from social policy measures to immigration measures. According to this point of view, we can state that in Italy there has been a shift away from seeing integration as a basis for positive social measures to mainly repressive ones.

Among the integration policies for immigrants we should also consider the social policies, including both direct and indirect policies, that affect all citizens and, therefore immigrants as well (Hammar 1985). Italian social legislation was reformed by Law 32/2000 on the implementation of the integrated system of interventions and social services. In accordance with this law and the European classification of social protection (ESSPROS), users were classified in seven categories: family and children, disability, addiction, elderly, immigrants, disadvantaged adults, multi-user.

Law 328/2000 established two levels of assistance for immigrants: social welfare assistance, covering national and regional social welfare programmes under central and decentralised social services, and integration support, regulated by immigration legislation. The Law also stipulated that local authorities are responsible for policy decisions and their implementation as regards social welfare assistance for immigrants.

Evaluating the integration policies adopted in Italy on the basis of the inclusion of the immigrant population in quantitative terms (based on the number of foreign immigrants who use the services) and tracking their development as time goes on, we perceive a trend towards steady integration of immigrants into the Italian welfare system. However, this result could be attributable mainly to the increased size of the resident foreign population and the stabilisation of this section of the population, rather than to the creation of new social services for foreign immigrants.

This observation seems to be confirmed by the contradictory trends in the number of social welfare users and in social welfare spending on immigrants. Spending by municipalities on social welfare for immigrants fell in the period 2003-2008, despite a large increase in the number of users. Immigrants have been one of the weakest group in social terms and have suffered a drastic reduction in per capita spending (ISTAT 2011a), which fell from € 67 to € 49.5 between 2003 and 2008, notwithstanding a slight increase in the share of social spending devoted to immigrants (from 2.3% to 2.7%). By and large, the legislative and institutional framework remains basically unchanged, but there has been a striking lack of implementation (Pugliese 2006). The main fact remains the lack of adjustment of the funding to the increased size of the target population.

There is a final point to be made regarding the possibility for immigrants and their children to acquire Italian citizenship, which is regulated by Law 91/1992. This law establishes four main channels for foreign nationals to acquire Italian citizenship: marriage; residence (ten years for non-EU and four for EU citizens); birth (with the proviso of continuous residence in Italy until the age of maturity (18 years)); naturalisation of parents (only for minors). As regards naturalisation for residence, Italian citizenship may be conferred upon a non-EU foreign citizen who has been legally resident in Italy for at least ten years by decree from the President of the Republic, after being heard by the Council of State and following a proposal by the Ministry of Interior (Art. 9, para. 1(f)). Furthermore, proof of income must be supplied, usually for the three-year period immediately prior to the application being made. The children of immigrants who were born in Italy may only apply for citizenship when they reach their eighteenth birthday, and they lose this right permanently if they do not apply within twelve months of that birthday (Art. 4, para. 2). An application for citizenship by children of immigrants also requires proof of uninterrupted legal residency since birth.

9.4   Measuring integration in Italy

9.4.1 First steps and conceptual framework

The need to measure and monitor the integration of immigrants into the various sectors of Italian society has taken on great importance with the increase in the number of foreign immigrants, primarily as they put down roots in the country (Gabrielli et al. 2009). However, interest in this issue is not a recent phenomenon in Italy. In the early 1990s, some scholars began to focus attention on how immigrants were integrating into society, providing a general overview of the situation based on information taken from field surveys conducted in the 1980s in different geographical areas of the country (Birindelli 1991). It should also be noted that among the main aims of the surveys carried out in the early 90s, there was certainly the need to acquire information on foreigners' living conditions, with a focus on two aspects in particular, namely employment and housing (Natale & Strozza 1997).

In the mid-1990s it was already clear that integration could be viewed from several perspectives, that there were different ways of collecting the necessary data and information, and that there were specific methodologies and analysis techniques that could be employed (Strozza et al. 2002). First of all, it is not easy to find a completely unified definition of 'integration', even if everyone agrees on the dynamic and multidimensional nature of the concept. It is possible to attempt to measure the evolution and degree of integration achieved by looking at the degree of immigrant participation in the economic, social and cultural life of the host country, and also at any progression in the position immigrants hold in various sectors such as employment, housing, education and political activity. Viewing integration as a process, it includes all the ways in which immigrants are incorporated into the life of the adopted country. However, the term 'integration' represents a complex concept whose meaning can vary in time and space depending on the country under consideration, the historical and political circumstances and the stage of the migratory process (Golini & Strozza 2006). Integration can take on very different forms and characteristics in a continuum ranging from complete assimilation to multiculturalism (Coleman 1994). As a result, the reference model must be borne in mind in deciding what the relevant dimensions, and consequently the indicators are and how to construct suitable measures. Even deciding which group to investigate can vary over time and place (Bonifazi & Strozza 2003). In Italy and the other new European immigration countries, attention has basically been focused on the first generation of immigrants, and only recently on the education of the second generation now that families are being reunited and there is an increase in births among immigrants (Ambrosini & Molina 2004; Casacchia et al. 2008; Dalla Zuanna et al. 2009).

9.4.2   The work of the Commission for Immigrant Integration Policies

The Commission for Immigrant Integration Policies was established in 1998 to advise the government and prepare an annual report on the state of implementation of immigrant integration policies. This Commission recommended moving towards what it called a 'reasonable' model of integration (Zincone 2000). The planning document on the policy for immigration and foreigners present on Italian territory provided a precise description of the concept of integration as a basis for the legislative action:

> *a process of non-discrimination and of including diversities, and therefore the mixing and ex-perimentation of new forms of relationships and behaviours, in a constant and daily attempt to hold together universal principles and particularisms.*

In this sense, integration should 'prevent situations of marginalisation, fragmentation and segregation that threaten the balance and cohesion of society, and affirm universal principles such as the value of human life, human dignity, recognition of female liberty, the advancement and protection of children, principles which cannot be derogated, including for the sake of the value of diversity'. The Commission considered that reasonable integration implied both the *integrity of the person*, the communities involved in the migration process, and *the positive interaction and peaceful coexistence* between all communities, obviously including the native community (Zincone 2000).

Based on this definition of integration, the Commission identified the various aspects that must be taken into consideration when devising an adequate system for measuring the degree of integration of the foreign communities. It was pointed out that not all the measures proposed could actually work because, in some cases, there was a lack of data, and in others, the data did not correspond to the actual situation being observed (Golini et al. 2001).

In the first place, some general dimensions of integration were determined and then divided into specific areas, for each of which measures and indicators were defined (Golini et al. 2001). The four general dimensions expressed the main aspects that come into play in the integration process:

a   the demographic, social and geographical characteristics that constitute the basic requirements which can generally be ascribed to the immigrants' human and social capital;

b   relationships with origin and host communities, in an attempt to evaluate the propensity to settle and interact with the native population;

c   effective insertion and complete self-fulfilment in the fields of education and employment, given that school and work are fundamental to integration and social mobility;

d   living conditions and active participation in daily life, as evidence of a full and positive process of interaction with the host environment.

These four dimensions were divided into twelve specific aspects, which in turn, gave rise to various indicators (table 9.2).

Particular attention has been paid to the analysis of the actual possibility of creating the proposed indicators, taking into account the availability and capacity of the usable data to adequately capture the phenomenon under study (Golini et al. 2001; Strozza et al. 2002; Golini 2006). A crucial point in the arrangement of the integration indicators is the exact definition of the population groups to which the data refer. At least three target groups have been schematically identified to which different needs and levels of social participation correspond: naturalised persons, legal foreigners (resident and non-resident in Italy) and illegal persons. Based on these groups, the internal structure of the immigrant communities is enormously differentiated, reflecting various migratory phases and models (the most recently formed communities have a higher share of illegal and smaller proportion of naturalised persons than the older immigrant communities), corresponding to differing degrees of propensity to integrate into the recipient society. In reality, however, the data collected and/or available often refer mainly to the legal foreign population. Furthermore, some indicators are difficult to construct because certain information is not available at all, while other data are not reliable when there is a need to distinguish by citizenship and/or by regional or local spatial scale.

Table 9.2
Dimensions, specific areas, measures and indicators of integration of foreign communities

dimensions	specific aspects	measures and indicators
A. demographic, social and geographical characteristics	A.1 demographic structure and reproductive behaviours	A.1.1 total A.1.2 age structure A.1.3 gender structure A.1.4 marital status structure A.1.5 births/fertility rate
	A.2 social structure	A.2.1 level of education
	A.3 geographical structure	A.3.1 spatial distribution of the population
B. relationships with origin and host communities	B.1 relationship with the country of origin	B.1.1 remittances B.1.2 contacts with family members in country of origin
	B.2 relationship with the ethic group of origin and other groups	B.2.1 membership of ethnic associations B.2.2 marriages between partners of the same nationality
	B.3 relationship with the host country	B.3.1 family reunion B.3.2 use of the Italian language B.3.3 mixed marriages B.3.4 naturalisation and acquisition of Italian citizenship
C. educational outcomes and employment insertion	C.1 educational outcomes of first and second generation	C.1.1 school attendance C.1.2 negative outcomes in compulsory education C.1.3 delays and drop-outs
	C.2 employment	C.2.1 activity rates C.2.2 unemployment rate C.2.3 employment sectors and qualifications C.2.4 self-employment C.2.5 use of human capital

Table 9.2 (continued

dimensions	specific aspects	measures and indicators
D. living situation	D.1 housing	D.1.1 geographical concentration and segregation
		D.1.2 type of housing
		D.1.3 percentage of home owners
		D.1.4 percentage of homeless
		D.1.5 overcrowding
	D.2 consumption	D.2.1 percentage of income for non-essential goods
	D.3 health	D.3.1 health status
		D.3.2 abortion rate
		D.3.3 mortality rate
	D.4 deviance	D.4.1 deviant behaviours compared with natives

Source: Golini et al. (2001)

Despite the fact that the Commission was not re-established after the centre-right government took office in 2001, some attempts were made to implement its proposals. In particular, the International and European Forum of Migration Research (FIERI) proposed a critical review at national level of the available data from statistical or administrative sources and an analysis of the degree of integration of foreign communities using the indicators that could actually be calculated (Golini 2006). In a subsequent study, FIERI analysed the integration of foreigners in the Italian regions and in the four largest metropolitan provinces (Rome, Milan, Turin and Naples), paying particular attention to the situation of foreigners living in Piedmont (FIERI 2007).

9.4.3   Measuring integration after the Commission

Another line of research based on available official data was developed by the National Council for Economy and Labour (CNEL) which, together with Caritas Italiana, has been publishing a Report on 'Indices of Integration of Immigrants in Italy' since 2002. This periodic report aims to create a ranking of Italian provinces and regions according to the level of foreign integration. The analytical measures and statistical synthesis procedures have been modified over time, but the approach is basically the following: three dimensions relating to integration have been identified (polarisation, social stability and inclusion in employment), and a synthetic index is calculated for each, starting from a specific set of seven basic indicators. These three synthetic indices make it possible to determine a ranking of Italian provinces and regions for each of these dimensions. Finally a general synthetic index is calculated which allows the various areas to be classified according to immigrants' overall level of integration (CNEL 2004; 2007; 2010).

Generally speaking, two different paths have been followed in measuring migrant integration. One path has focused on national groups, considering the wide range of nationalities living in Italy and their noticeably heterogeneous social and demographic characteristics, migration models, expectations, opportunities and modalities of integration (Rossi, Strozza 2007). The other has focused on the differences between the various Italian areas in the intensity and characteristics of foreign presence, immigrant labour demand, possibilities for stabilisation and opportunities for social integration of newcomers (Bonifazi 2007). According to many scholars, these two coordinates could be used jointly (Birindelli 2003; Zindato et al. 2008).

The main problem was (and to some extent still is) that the available official data, often drawn from administrative datasets, allow us to capture only some aspects of integration, and not always in the best possible way. In order to reduce some of the information gaps, some scholars (Strozza et al. 2002; Golini 2006) have emphasised the need to collect reliable data from national cross-sectional sample surveys on the total population (i.e. both native Italians and foreigners) and/or specific national surveys on the foreign population (or population of foreign/immigrant origin).

Since the early 1990s a question on citizenship and/or country of birth had been inserted into the questionnaire in the most important national sample surveys. However, until a few years ago the variables on citizenship were not checked and processed in the most important national sample surveys because this was considered unreliable. The samples were regularly too small to include a number of aliens that would be sufficient for statistical purposes. Households with at least one foreign member were (and are) more difficult to trace, i.e. the share not found by interviewers was (and is) greater than for all-Italian households. Furthermore, the system that replaced the extracted families did not take account of citizenship and there was no use of specialist interviewers and other solutions to overcome linguistic problems.

It is only since 2005 that data have been published on the subset of foreigners in the continuous labour force survey. This has been possible because the survey has changed from being quarterly to being continuous, and during the transitional phase a careful assessment was made of operational solutions to guarantee the representativeness of the sub-sample of foreign residents (ISTAT 2006). In recent years the traditional indices on participation in the labour market have also been published for the resident foreign population. In 2010 the activity rate of foreign men was 85.1%, compared to 72.3% for native Italians; for women, both figures were lower, standing at 58.7% for immigrants and 50.4% for native Italians. Unemployment rates were higher among foreigners, at 10.5% for men and 13.3% for women compared to 7.4% and 9.4%, respectively, for native Italians.

The survey for the second quarter of 2008 also contained an ad hoc module on integration of migrants and their immediate descendants in the labour market, aimed at foreign citizens and nationals by acquisition, aged between 15 and 74 years (ISTAT 2009). Agreed at European level, this module was finalised to provide information on any assistance received in Italy to find work; the contribution made to inclusion in the labour market by public and private services; recognition of educational qualifications (title of study); the perception of doing a job that was appropriate to the individual's qualifications. Information was also collected for foreign workers on the extent to which the Italian language was used in different contexts (at work, in the family, with friends).

In 2009, ISTAT carried out the first EU-SILC (European Union Statistics on Income and Living Conditions) survey of a sample of 6,000 households with at least one foreigner residing in Italy. This survey was funded by the Italian Ministry of Labour. It used the same methodological tools as the standard EU-SILC survey (questionnaires, sampling techniques, methods of correction, imputation and data integration, etc.), collecting a set of similar socioeconomic data. Consequently, the framework on households with foreigners provided by this survey is comparable to that of households composed only of native Italians. To date, only a note containing the main findings relating to the most relevant characteristics of households with foreigners, housing conditions and some indicators of economic hardship and material deprivation has been published (ISTAT 2011b). Mixed households with native Italian and foreign members accounted for 22.6% of all households with at least one foreign member (just over 2 million). Compared with exclusively Italian households, households with foreigners more frequently live in conditions of severe housing deprivation (13.3% of cases, compared with 4.7% of native Italian households). Moreover, material deprivation affects around one third of households with foreigners (34.5%), as opposed to 13.9% of native households. Mixed households are in an intermediate position between foreign and native households.

The 'Condition and social integration of foreign citizens' survey is currently in progress (data collection period: May-July 2011). This is the first sample survey on this subject designed by ISTAT in the system of multipurpose household surveys. The goal is to provide information on the living conditions of foreign citizens (including naturalised persons) which can support immigration policies. The information required relates to different aspects of the lives of individuals: family, marriages, children, education, religious affiliation and language, migration history, employment history, present working conditions, health status, use of and accessibility to health services, lifestyle, social relationships, social participation, experiences of discrimination, housing conditions, etc.. The survey covers a sample of about 12,000 households with at least one foreign (or foreign origin) member. The sampling design allows the data to be analysed at the level of geographical divisions; however, oversampling is likely in the municipalities of Rome, Milan and Naples to ensure the representativeness of the sample in the three largest Italian cities.

These improvements in national surveys are very important and are providing new and more information on immigrant populations. It should be added, however, that over the last 25 years various field surveys have been carried out in Italy aimed at obtaining statistical information on the living conditions of the immigrant population and their integration process. The most important experience has been gained by the Regional Observatory for Integration and Multi-ethnicity of Lombardy since 2001, with an annual cross-sectional survey on the foreign population in the region realised by the ISMU Foundation. The surveys have been conducted with the centre sampling technique developed in the field survey in the previous decade (Blangiardo et al. 2011). The initial 8,000 interviews with foreigners over 14 years old and coming from less developed countries (LDCs) and CEE have gone up to 9,000 in the last two years. The questionnaire is made up of a fixed part for all years, containing essential information about individual and family structure characteristics and general information on working and living conditions, and a special section devoted to a more in-depth study on a different topic every year.

At national level the most important example is the research financed by the EU, promoted by the Ministry of Labour and Social Policies and organised by the ISMU Foundation with the collaboration of other research institutes, which involved a cross-sectional survey carried out in 2005 based on 30,000 interviews (22,000 in the south of the country and 8,000 in the centre-north) and principally aimed at collecting information on the effects of the 2002 regularisation with particular reference to the south (Blangiardo & Farina 2006). It was also possible to calculate some synthesis indicators on immigrants' general degree of inclusion with specific reference to employment and, at the same time, to determine the role played by the main demographic, social and migratory characteristics (Blangiardo et al. 2006).

Recently, the ISMU Foundation coordinated a national research project on 'Measuring the level and differential characteristics of integration in some areas – Year 2008' which involved 20 local research units. Surveys were carried out by the centre sampling technique on a total sample of 12,000 foreign citizens aged over 18 years coming from LDCs and CEE (including the new EU member states) in 32 different Italian provinces or municipalities. Four thematic indices, relating to cultural, social, economic and political integration, as well as an overall index of integration, were calculated at individual level (for each interviewed foreign national) on the basis of the information collected. It was therefore possible to assess the degree of integration both in overall terms and in relation to a plurality of sub-populations, defined according to demographic, social, economic, geographic and ethno-cultural characteristics (Cesareo & Blangiardo 2009). The survey results point to a positive relationship between degree of integration and length of stay, as well as the importance of area of destination. In addition, women are more integrated than men. Finally, as regards area of origin, persons from Latin America and CEE are more integrated than immigrants of African and Asian origin.

In the past decade the issue of the schooling of the second generation has acquired growing importance. To date, the survey 'Children of immigrants between social inclusion and social exclusion' (ITAGEN2) is the only quantitative survey with statistical relevance at the national level to be carried out on immigrants' children residing in Italy (Dalla Zuanna et al. 2009). The survey is conducted among pupils from 48 Italian provinces enrolled in state lower secondary schools. The survey was carried out during the early months of 2006 and involved a quantitatively significant sample of about 20,700 pre-adolescents (11 to 14 years of age) attending lower secondary school, of whom 10,500 had at least one parent born outside Italy and 10,200 of whom had parents who were both born in Italy. The questionnaire was aimed at investigating the different aspects of the human capital (language skills, academic performance, future educational aspirations), social capital (family and friends), system of values, leisure activities, and socioeconomic status of the family. Among other things it emerged that children of immigrants have less traditional attitudes than their Italian peers, even though they come from countries where family and local community are the cornerstones of society. On the other hand, their educational outcomes are worse than those of their Italian peers and they much more frequently lag behind in their schooling. These problems negatively influence their subsequent educational pathway and could reduce their opportunity for social mobility and positive insertion into Italian society (Dalla Zuanna et al. 2009; Mussino & Strozza 2012).

9.5   Conclusions

An official system for monitoring migrant integration does not exist in Italy. The only attempt to 'translate' political needs into the measurement of integration has been the work of the Commission for immigrant integration policies at the end of the 1990s. The Commission proposed a definition of integration and a set of statistical indicators for measuring this social process. The availability of data did not allow full implementation the Commission's proposal, because at that time some statistical information was not collected or was not reliable. The Commission was not renewed after its first term ended, and the model of integration has not been officially discussed at the political level. In recent years, despite the lack of clear political input, statistical information on integration process has increased and improved. Currently, most of the official statistical surveys collect representative information on the foreign population, which is useful for measuring interesting aspects of integration. The major limitation of these national survey data is the difficulty of using them at the local level, as their representativeness often does not reach even the regional scale. However, the available information have still not been organised into a national continuous monitoring system. Meanwhile, other target groups are emerging in Italy, such as the second generation, the naturalised population and the population with a foreign background. The integration of old and new target groups deserves further investigation and assuredly warrants more attention from policymakers. This is especially true if we take into account recent migration trends in the Mediterranean Basin resulting from the deep political changes taking place in the Arab world.

References

Ambrosini, M. & S. Molina (eds.) (2004). *Seconde generazioni. Un introduzione al futuro dell'immigrazione in Italia.* Turin: Giovanni Agnelli Foundation.

Besselink, L.F.M. (2006). Unequal Citizenship: Integration Measures and Equality. In: Sergio Carrera (ed.), *The Nexus between Immigration, Integration and Citizenship in the EU* (paper presented at the Challenge Conference in Brussels, 25 January 2006).

Birindelli, A.M. (1991). Gli stranieri in Italia: alcuni problemi di integrazione sociale. In: *Polis*, vol. V, no. 2, p. 301-312.

Birindelli, A.M. (2003). Analysis of integration: changes and continuity. In: *Studi Emigrazione*, vol. XL, no. 152, p. 697-716.

Blangiardo, G.C. & P. Farina (eds.) (2006). *Il Mezzogiorno dopo la grande regolarizzazione. Immagini e problematiche dell'immigrazione* (vol. terzo). Milan: Ministero del Lavoro e delle Politiche sociali / Franco Angeli.

Blangiardo, G.C., G. Baio & M. Blangiardo (2011). Centre sampling technique in foreign migration surveys: a methodological note. In: *Journal of Official Statistics*, vol. 27, no. 3, p. 451-465.

Blangiardo, M., S. Strozza & L. Terzera (2006). Indicatori di integrazione degli immigrati in Italia. In: G.C. Blangiardo & P. Farina (eds.), *Il Mezzogiorno dopo la grande regolarizzazione. Immagini e problematiche dell'immigrazione* (vol. terzo, p. 153-189). Milan: Ministero del Lavoro e delle Politiche sociali / Franco Angeli.

Bolaffi, G. (2001). *I confini del patto Il governo dell'immigrazione in Italia*. Turin: Einaudi.

Bonifazi, C. (2007). *L'immigrazione straniera in Italia*. Bologna: il Mulino.

Bonifazi, C., F. Heins, S. Strozza & M. Vitiello (2009). *The Italian transition from emigration to immigration country*. Rome: IRPPS-CNR (WP no. 24).

Bonifazi C. & C. Marini (2010). The irresistible growth of immigration in Italy. In: *Rivista Italiana di Economia, Demografia e Statistica*, vol. LXIV, no. 3, p. 57-78.

Bonifazi C. & S. Strozza (2003). Introduction. In: *Studi Emigrazione*, vol. XL, no. 152, p. 690-696.

Casacchia O., L. Natale, A. Paterno & L. Terzera (eds.) (2008). *Studiare insieme, crescere insieme? Un'indagine sulle seconde generazioni in dieci regioni italiane*. Milan: Franco Angeli / Fondazione ISMU.

Cesareo, V. & G.C. Blangiardo (eds.) (2009). *Indici di integrazione. Un-indagine empirica sulla realtà migratoria italiana*. Milan: Franco Angeli.

CNEL (2004). *Indicatori di inserimento territoriale degli immigrati in Italia. III Rapporto* (doc. no. 44). Rome: Consiglio Nazionale dell'Economia e del Lavoro.

CNEL (2007). *Indici di integrazione degli immigrati in Italia. V Rapporto* (doc. no. 44). Rome: Consiglio Nazionale dell'Economia e del Lavoro.

CNEL (2010), *Indici di integrazione degli immigrati in Italia. Il potenziale di integrazione nei territori italiani. Analisi dell'occupazione e della criminalità per collettività. VII Rapporto*. Rome: Consiglio Nazionale dell'Economia e del Lavoro.

Coleman, D. (1994). *International migration: regional processes and responses* (Economic studies no. 7, p. 41-76). New York / Geneva: UN Economic Commission for Europe, UN Population fund.

Cornelius, W.A., P.L. Martin & J.F. Hollifield (eds.) (1994). *Controlling immigration. A global perspective*. Stanford: Stanford University Press.

Dalla Zuanna, G., P. Farina & S. Strozza (2009). *Nuovi italiani. I giovani immigrati cambieranno il nostro paese?* Bologna: il Mulino.

FIERI (2007). *Integrometro II. Immigrati stranieri: segnali di integrazione*. Turin: CRT Foundation, Alfieri project.

Gabrielli D., S. Strozza & E. Todisco (2009). *Country report Italy*. Report prepared for the PROMINSTAT project.

Ginsborg, P. (1998). *L'Italia del tempo presente: famiglia, società civile, Stato, 1980-1996*. Turin: Einaudi.

Golini, A. (ed.) (2006). *L'immigrazione straniera: indicatori e misure di integrazione*. Bologna: il Mulino.

Golini A., S. Strozza & F. Amato (2001). Un sistema di indicatori di integrazione: primo tentativo di costruzione. In: G. Zincone (ed.). *Secondo rapporto sull'integrazione degli immigrati in Italia* (p. 85-153). Bologna: il Mulino.

Golini, A. & S. Strozza (2006). Misure e indicatori dell'integrazione degli immigrati. In: A. Golini (ed.), *L'immigrazione straniera: indicatori e misure di integrazione*. Bologna: il Mulino.

Hammar, T. (ed.) (1985). *European immigration policy*. Cambridge: Cambridge University press.

ISMU (2011). *Sedicesimo rapporto sulle migrazioni 2010*. Milan: Franco Angeli.

ISTAT (2006). *Gli stranieri nella rilevazione sulle forze di lavoro* (Metodi e Norme n. 27). Rome: Italian National Institute of Statistics (ISTAT).

ISTAT (2009). *L'integrazione nel lavoro degli stranieri e dei naturalizzati italiani*, (Approfondimenti, 14 December). Rome: Italian National Institute of Statistics (ISTAT).

ISTAT (2011a). *Interventi e servizi sociali dei Comuni singoli e associati. Anno 2008*. Rome: Italian National Institute of Statistics (ISTAT).

ISTAT (2011b). *Le famiglie con stranieri: indicatori di disagio economico. Anno 2009* (Statistiche in breve, 28 February). Rome: Italian National Institute of Statistics (ISTAT).

Mussino, E. & S. Strozza (2012). The delayed school progress of the children of immigrants in Lower-Secondary education in Italy. In: *Journal of Ethnic and Migration Studies*, vol. 38, no. 1 (in print).

Nascimbene, B. (2003). Nuove norme in materia di immigrazione. La legge Bossi-Fini: perplessità e critiche. In: *Corriere Giuridico*, no. 4.

Natale, M. & S. Strozza (1997). *Gli immigrati stranieri in Italia. Quanti sono, chi sono, come vivono?* Bari: Cacucci Editore.

Pugliese, E. (2006). *L'Italia tra migrazioni internazionali e migrazioni interne*. Bologna: il Mulino.

Rossi, F. & S. Strozza (2007). Mobilità della popolazione, immigrazione e presenza straniera. In: GCD-SIS, *Rapporto sulla popolazione. L'Italia all'inizio del XXI secolo* (p. 111-137). Bologna: il Mulino.

Strozza, S., M. Natale, E. Todisco & F. Ballacci (2002). *La rilevazione delle migrazioni internazionali e la predisposizione di un sistema informativo sugli stranieri* (Rapporto di Ricerca, no. 02.11, p. 243). Rome: Commissione per la Garanzia dell'Informazione Statistica (COGIS).

Zincone, G. (2000). Introduzione e sintesi. Un modello di integrazione ragionevole. In: G. Zincone (ed.), *Primo rapporto sull'integrazione degli immigrati in Italia* (p. 13-120). Bologna: il Mulino.

Zindato, D., L. Cassata, F. Martire, S. Strozza & M. Vitiello (2008). L'integrazione come processo multi-dimensionale. Condizioni di vita e di lavoro degli immigrati. In: *Studi Emigrazione*, vol. XLV, no. 171, p. 657-698.

10   Monitoring Integration in Latvia

Nils Muiznieks and Juris Rozenvalds

10.1   Introduction

Debates on integration in Latvia differ from those in most European countries. Elsewhere, the focus is generally on two different target groups: recent immigrants[1] and Roma.[2] Most policy debates and efforts to monitor integration in Latvia to date have focused on Russian-speaking settlers who arrived during the period of Soviet rule and their descendants. However, current understandings of integration, at least at the expert level, incorporate both minorities and new immigrants.
In some ways, the Latvian integration debates echo the themes that are prevalent in debates on immigrants' integration elsewhere, which revolve around the desire to inculcate common democratic values, promote proficiency in the national language and regulate access to citizenship. However, post-war settlers in Latvia are quick to point out that they migrated within the borders of a single country, the Soviet Union, and that independence in 1991 marked less a movement of people than a movement of borders. The size of the Russian-speaking population, the circumstances of their arrival in Latvia and the legacy of Soviet rule pose integration challenges of a different nature from those faced by most European countries.[3]

In recent years, partially as a result of Europeanisation, issues pertaining to Roma and immigrant integration in Latvia have begun to enter policy debates as well. Latvia has a Roma community numbering between 8,000 and 15,000 persons whose social situation, according to available data, is as dire as it is in other European countries.[4] The Latvian authorities adopted a Roma integration programme focusing on employment and education, which was implemented from 2007 to 2009.[5] However, in the context of the global economic crisis and budgetary austerity, funding for the programme has been discontinued.

The population of recent immigrants is considerably larger, but is still small by European standards. As can be seen in table 10.1 below, emigration has exceeded immigration by a factor of four over the past twenty years, with the largest outflow taking place in the immediate post-independence years. The vast majority of emigrants in the peak years 1991-1995 consisted of persons linked with the Soviet/Russian military, almost all of whom departed eastwards by August 1994, the deadline set by the interstate treaty governing troop withdrawal.

Since its accession to the EU in 2004, Latvia has seen some labour immigration from neighbouring countries and labour emigration to other EU countries, primarily Ireland and the United Kingdom.[6] In addition to a small community of immigrants, Latvia is also host to a handful of asylum-seekers and refugees. From 1998, when the Geneva Convention entered into force in Latvia, until the end of 2010, Latvia received 367 requests for asylum and granted refugee status to 29 persons.[7]

Table 10.1
Long-term international migration to and from Latvia, 1991-2010 (in absolute numbers)

	immigrated	emigrated	net migration
1991-1995	30,842	168,230	−137,388
1996-2000	12,223	47,064	−34,841
2001-2005	7,786	17,268	−9,482
2006-2010	15,285	33,532	−18,247
total	66,136	266,094	−199,958

Source: Central Statistical Bureau

As can be seen in table 10.2 below, most foreign citizens in Latvia are linked to neighbouring countries, especially Russia, but also Estonia, Lithuania and Belarus. Most of these foreign citizens have been residents of Latvia for many years, with some having arrived during the Soviet era, then adopting foreign citizenship whilst retaining residency status in Latvia after independence. Increasingly, researchers have begun to analyze the integration needs of these foreigners in Latvia.[8]

As can be seen in table 10.2, Latvia has a much larger population of non-citizens (former USSR citizens) than foreigners. It is this group, as well as Latvian citizens of ethnic minority origin, that have been at the centre of integration policy debates. Below, we trace the background to integration policy, outlining the historical circumstances that have given rise to current integration challenges. Then we detail the piecemeal evolution of integration policy after independence, culminating in the adoption of the National Programme for the Integration of Society in Latvia in 2001. After close to a decade of implementation in fits and starts, this policy is now in disarray, as several of the major responsible government agencies have been absorbed into other institutions, budgets have been slashed, and repeated efforts to adopt an updated policy document have stalled due to political disagreements.

Table 10.2

Latvia's inhabitants according to state affiliation as at 1 July 2010 (in absolute numbers)

Latvia	
citizens of Latvia	1,857241
non-citizens of Latvia (former USSR citizens)	335,918
stateless persons of Latvia	172
Other countries, including citizens of:	
Russia	33,683
Lithuania	3720
Ukraine	3116
Belarus	2014
Germany	1109
Estonia	941
Bulgaria	575
USA	518
Poland	493
Sweden	427
United Kingdom	395
Israel	345
Moldova	271
Armenia	266
France	260
Rumania	260
Denmark	248
Italy	237
Finland	231
Georgia	225
other	2752

Source: Citizenship and Migration Affairs Board

Government efforts to measure integration have been sporadic and have consisted primarily of sociological surveys and various ad hoc studies. Academic expertise on integration and measuring it, on the other hand, is quite well developed. However, this expertise finds almost no reflection in policy. At the end of the chapter, we turn to the most recent efforts to monitor integration and the extent to which these include consideration of immigrants and Roma. First, however, some historical background is in order.

10.2   Historical background to integration: the legacy of the Soviet period[9]

Latvia developed historically as an ethnically diverse society, and representatives of around 150 different ethnic groups live in the country. The most far-reaching changes in Latvia's ethnic structure took place during and after World War II. During World War II Latvia lost almost all members of two historical minorities, the Germans and the

Jews. The merciless repression of the 1940s, flight and emigration to a number of Western countries by refugees, as well as post-war deportations, dramatically reduced the number of Latvians living in Latvia; in 1959 there were almost 180,000 fewer Latvians in Latvia than in 1935. On the other hand, the total number of inhabitants in Latvia grew in post-war decades on account of migration from other republics of the USSR. In the post-war Soviet Union, Latvia had the lowest natural rate of population growth of any of the Soviet republics and the largest population growth due to migration.[10]

Table 10.3

Migration to and from Latvia, 1951-1990 (in numbers x 1000)

years	arrived	departed	net migration
1951-1960	639.9	459.9	180.0
1961-1970	476.9	335.9	141.1
1971-1980	548.6	428.2	120.4
1981-1990	506.6	424.0	82.6

Source: Central Statistical Bureau

The total number of inhabitants in 1959 exceeded the 1935 total by 230,000. The majority of this increase was accounted for by Eastern Slavic settlers, whose share in the population grew rapidly.

Table 10.4

Total population and ethnic breakdown of Latvia's population, 1935-2009 (in numbers x 1000 and in percentages)

	1935	1959	1970	1979	1989	2000	2009
total (x 1000)	1950.4	2093.5	2364.1	2502.8	2666.6	2375.3	2261.3
incl. (in %)							
Latvians	75.4	62,0	56.8	53.7	52.0	57.7	59.3
Russians	10.6	26.6	29.8	32.8	34.0	29.6	27.8
Belarussians	1.4	2.9	4.0	4.5	4.5	4.1	3.6
Ukrainians	0.09	1.4	2.3	2.7	3.5	2.7	2.5
Poles	2.5	2.9	2.7	2.5	2.3	2.5	2.4
Lithuanians	1.2	1.5	1.7	1.5	1.3	1.4	1.3
Jews	4.8	1.7	1.6	1.1	0.9	0.4	0.4
Germans	3.2	0.1	0.2	0.1	0.2	0.1	0.2

Source: Central Statistical Bureau of Latvia

In the final decades of Soviet rule, a situation developed in which two numerically similar groups had formed – a Latvian language group and Russian-speakers – which differed in their sources of information, attitudes towards the situation in Latvia, value orientations and – generally speaking – structures of identity.

Language has traditionally played a particular role in the structure of Latvian identity. Soviet language policy granted privileges to speakers of the Russian language and resulted in a situation of asymmetric bilingualism. Thus, according to the 1989 census, 68.7% of Latvians had a command of the Russian language, while only 22.3% of Russians had a command of Latvian.[11] Soviet rule produced a disposition in everyday consciousness which could be termed a 'minority complex'. In Soviet times, Latvians comprised an insignificant minority in the composition of the enormous empire (about 0.5% of the Soviet population). In Latvia itself, the local authorities controlled policy areas touching upon Latvian culture and education, as well as local industry and agriculture (where Latvians predominated). By contrast, Moscow controlled the flow of culture, education and information for new arrivals, as well as the generally Russian management of what were known as 'all-Union enterprises'.

As a result, the aforementioned circumstances created an odd Soviet-era Latvian 'privilege' – concentrating only on one's own problems. Issues of language, culture and ethnicity, in the awareness of broad sections of Latvian society, were linked only to Latvians. The popular motto of the Third Awakening – 'We want to be masters in our native land' – was linked in everyday consciousness with the readiness to stress Latvian rights, without recognising the rights and needs of others in society. Consequently, Latvians were unprepared in the mid-1990s for the idea of a political or civic nation[12] and later reacted with misunderstanding and suspicion towards the ratification of the Framework Convention for the Protection of National Minorities. The truly complex and tragic history of Latvia and Latvians in the 20th century created the conviction in everyday consciousness of the unique character of Latvia's situation. This in turn was linked with the perception that Latvians were a 'chosen people', but in a negative way – that they had suffered more than all other nations in the 20th century.[13] This was thought to impose some special obligations on Western countries towards Latvians and Latvia, while Latvians, for their part, had the right, in the name of overcoming the injustices of the past, to act in ways that were not always in accordance with the accepted standards of civilised political behaviour of the Western world.

In contrast to Latvian identity, during the Soviet period socio-economic affiliations overrode the importance of ethnic origin, language or cultural background in the identity of Latvia's Russian-speakers.[14] In so far as socioeconomic priorities dominated over specifically ethnic considerations in the consciousness of Russians during the period of the 'singing revolution' and the initial years of independence, those priorities did not conflict directly with the efforts of Latvians to achieve the restoration of independence as a decisively important precondition for ensuring the defence of their culture and language. This prevented the emergence of ethnic conflict in the early 1990s and largely ensured the peaceful evolution of events in the revolutionary period of 1988-1991 and the first years after independence. Over the course of the 1990s, as a consequence of the transformation in Latvia, the identity of Latvia's Russians slowly evolved into that of a minority which had to actively stand up for its language and cultural rights. The potential for ethnic mobilisation on the part of Latvia's Russians was illustrated most clearly in the broad protests against educational reform in 2003-04.

With regard to the preconditions for integration policy, it is also important to mention demographic and socio-economic factors which, in certain respects, created a more benign environment for the implementation of integration policy compared with the other Baltic states. Latvia historically has not witnessed the emergence of whole regions (certain parishes in the eastern province of Latgale are the exception) in which minorities live in concentrated settings and in isolation from Latvians. Minorities in Latvia are fairly evenly spread throughout the whole of Latvia's territory, particularly in the cities. Latvia has traditionally had a rather high rate of ethnic inter-marriage. In contrast to Estonia, Latvia has not witnessed the emergence of significant socioeconomic differences between ethnic communities, particularly with regard to income levels. Ethnic origin is not strongly correlated with poverty, which affects Latvians and minorities equally.[15] In these circumstances, the question arises as to how well the Latvian political elite is able to ensure the implementation of policy that is acceptable to the most significant groups in society, and the extent to which it is able to promote rapprochement between these groups. Several basic elements can be distinguished in this regard which characterise integration policy in Latvia in the last two decades.

1   During the entire period Latvian society, and particularly the political elite, has been divided over integration policy goals and means. These divisions have existed not only between Latvians and Russian-speakers, but also among Latvians themselves. The Latvian section of the political elite has shown very little interest in integration issues and does not trust minorities.

2   Integration policy in Latvia has primarily been determined by external pressures, though the sources of these pressures and their vectors have changed over time;

3   Integration policy over the last twenty years has experienced 'ebbs' and 'flows', or periods of intensified activity and passiveness.

4   Even during 'active' periods, integration policy was paternalistic – it did not entail the active involvement of minorities in the preparation or implementation of integration policy. Since the beginning of the 1990s, the notion that only Latvian politicians know what Russians want has dominated the thinking of the Latvian political elite. From this flows the conviction that Russian-speakers should accept unconditionally the rules of the game being offered to them.[16]

During the years of the 'singing revolution', two routes towards independence were actively debated in Latvia's public arena. The first can be called the 'socially realistic' pathway, which was represented by the Popular Front of Latvia (PFL). The first-generation of leaders of the PFL were well aware of the complicated nature of ethnic relations in Latvia and pursued a moderate and realistic policy which took into consideration post-war demographic changes and stressed the consolidation of all inhabitants of Latvia on the road to sovereignty. The other, 'legalistic' pathway to independence was represented by the Citizens' Congress of the Republic of Latvia, which emphasised legal continuity and the illegal nature of the Soviet occupation, and thus viewed all persons who settled in Latvia after 17 June 1940 as illegal immigrants. Clearly, in the context of this approach, the very idea of integrating post-war 'colonists' was unacceptable in principle; the activists in the citizens' movement hoped for the mass emigration of minorities that would bring Latvia back to pre-war demographic proportions.

During the years of the 'singing revolution', the realistic platform of the PFL predominated – to a great extent due to pressure from the central structures of the USSR and imperialistic forces within Latvia. That became the basis for the achievements in terms of integration during the period of the 'singing revolution'. Although even progressive Russian-speakers had serious misgivings about the policy of the PFL, which had at its core liberal nationalism and an emphasis on the primacy of the Latvian nation,[17] sociological surveys demonstrated that in 1990 39% of all minority respondents supported Latvian independence.[18] This was also borne out in the Supreme Soviet elections in March 1990, when pro-independence political groups gained a majority of votes, as well as the referendum on independence on 3 March 1991, when 73.68% of all those voting (64.51% of all eligible voters) opted for independence.

10.3   After independence: stumbling towards an integration policy

It should be acknowledged that the beginnings of integration created during the 'singing revolution' were not developed further. On the contrary, much of what had been achieved was lost in the first years after the restoration of independence, when Latvia did not have a coherent integration policy. It is possible to speak of separate, indirectly connected policies that significantly, but for the most part negatively, influenced spontaneous processes of integration in society. The rapid decrease of external and internal pressure due to the weakness of Latvia's eastern neighbour and the defeat of the pro-imperialistic forces in Latvia became one of the most important factors that furthered the political elite's rapid resort to solutions deriving from the 'legalistic' pathway for attaining independence.

This process could only be accelerated through the intensification of external pressure that would make Latvian politicians more responsive to the recommendations of Western partners. This happened in 1997 and 1998 when crisis situations emerged in several of Latvia's external and internal policy realms. Latvia was not invited to attend European Union membership negotiations, partially because of problems with social In October 1991 the Latvian parliament, in contradiction of the programme of the PFL then in force, adopted a decision to restore citizenship to those inhabitants of Latvia who had held it before 17 June 1940, and to their descendants. Though the decision renewed citizenship regardless of ethnicity, it created the basis for the division of Latvia's inhabitants into 'us' and 'them', in which the latter were almost exclusively post-war non-Latvian settlers. Given the generous promises made in 1990-91, this step had a destructive impact – the action of Latvian politicians in the autumn of 1991 provided a basis for the conviction that is still widespread among many non-Latvians that they had simply been deceived. Those inhabitants of Latvia who lost their civic rights with the 15 October decision had to wait until 1995 for clarification of their status. In the early 1990s, many members of the Latvian political elite nurtured the conviction that the solution to interethnic relations lay in the return migration of many non-Latvians to their places of origin, first and foremost Russia. At the time, this scenario gained some credibility thanks to the active departure of many Soviet/Russian military personnel and their family members from Latvia. In the early to mid-1990s, close to 200,000 people departed from Latvia, with 52,000 leaving in 1992 alone.

There was no scope for the creation of a long-term integration policy in such an atmosphere, especially as citizenship, language and education policy in the early and mid-1990s were all created in line with this spirit. As indicated by Estonian researcher Priit Jarve, one of the additional goals of strict language and citizenship policy in both Estonia and Latvia was to promote the departure of Russian-speakers.[19] In 1994 Parliament supported a citizenship law with a timetable that would allow naturalisation to begin first with the youngest applicants for citizenship, denying this right to the most motivated group of middle-aged persons. Subsequent events demonstrated that the 1994 law was not capable of effectively fulfilling its functions – there was a glaring contradiction between the objective necessity of creating the opportunity for post-war settlers to integrate into political life and the legislators' desire to slow the naturalisation process to a minimum.

The policy towards minorities in the early and mid-1990s embodied the coexistence of overcoming the injustices and interethnic disproportions created by Soviet rule, with the abandonment of the preconditions for social consolidation that were created during the years of the 'singing revolution' Similar trends set the tone in language and education policy at this time. They were marked by efforts to increase pressure on the Russian language and to ensure the functioning of Latvian as the official language. Latvian was in fact enshrined as the official language as early as 6 October 1988, when the Supreme Soviet of the LSSR adopted amendments to the republic's constitution. On 5 May 1989 the Language Law of the LSSR was adopted, granting Russian the status of the language of interethnic communication. The Latvian parliament rescinded this norm on 31 March 1992. In the mid-1990s, a new Official Language Law was drafted which was adopted in 1999. This law placed minority languages on the same level as foreign languages and did not in any way regulate the use of those languages in Latvia. This evoked criticism from both local experts and international organisations, who pointed out that this was contradictory to the Framework Convention for the Protection of National Minorities, which Latvia signed in 1995 but ratified only ten years later. This contradiction has still not been resolved.

Since the beginning of the 1990s, a characteristic trait of the Latvian political elite has been its weakness, which is manifested in the inability to adopt balanced strategic decisions in which interests of state are placed above short-term considerations of political gain. As a consequence, many significant political decisions since the restoration of independence, in particular those affecting relations between Latvia's largest communities, attained their final form not as a result of the conscious decisions of Latvian politicians, but rather as the result of external pressure. All the foregoing hindered the development of a far-sighted and consistent policy. Given the disagreements within the elite and the majority's lack of interest about integration issues, the impetus for formulating integration policy came to Latvia from foreign partners: international organisations and foreign foundations. The main international players in Latvia in the early 1990s were the OSCE Mission to Latvia, the OSCE High Commissioner on National Minorities, the Council of Europe, the United Nations Development Programme (UNDP) office in Latvia, and the Soros Foundation – Latvia. When Latvia was approaching accession to the European Union and NATO, the stance of these organisations became very significant in raising awareness about integration issues and underlining the need for an elaboration of integration policy.

This process could only be accelerated through the intensification of external pressure that would make Latvian politicians more responsive to the recommendations of Western partners. This happened in 1997 and 1998 when crisis situations emerged in several of Latvia's external and internal policy realms. Latvia was not invited to attend European Union membership negotiations, partially because of problems with social integration. Russia accused Latvia of serious human rights violations and urged the international community to intervene to regulate the situation in Latvia, particularly with regard to the situation of Russian-speakers. In this context Latvia's Western partners – both influential countries and international organisations – sought to soften the consequences of Russia's reaction, but also to intensify the pressure on the Latvian political elite by urging it to take real steps towards the consolidation of society. In this situation, the Latvian political elite understood that without a change in policy, Latvia could lose the political support of Western countries. In March 1998 a working group comprising four ministers (Foreign Affairs, Education & Science, Justice and Culture) was created to draft a national programme for the integration of society.

The work of researchers in Latvia also fostered the evolution of public and elite attitudes. An important turning point, and the end of the illusion that the task of integration would be obviated by the mass emigration of minorities from Latvia, was the 'Towards a Civic Society' research programme, organised by the Naturalisation Board with the support of the Soros Foundation – Latvia and the National Human Rights Office.[20] Two very important insights emerged from the research results. First, very few minorities and non-citizens planned to leave Latvia. Second, the research revealed significant differences in the attitudes and values of Latvians and minorities, citizens and non-citizens, which threatened to turn Latvia into a 'binational society' As Elmārs Vēbers notes, 'the thesis that citizenship, education and language policy could be implemented ignoring the presence of non-citizens and minorities lost its socio-political relevance'.[21]

In mid and late 1998 a number of other significant steps linked to integration issues were taken at legislative level. On 22 June 1998 the Latvian parliament adopted amendments to the Citizenship Law, easing the naturalisation conditions, eliminating the 'windows' and permitting non-citizen children born after 1991 to be registered as Latvian citizens. On 3 October 1998 a referendum was held on the amendments to the Citizenship Law together with the parliamentary elections. Though supporters and opponents of the amendments were divided roughly equally (44.98% voted in favour of rescinding the changes, while 52.54% voted against), the amendments stood and entered into force.

The response of the nationalist political forces to this development was the adoption of a new Education Law on the last day of the parliamentary session on 29 October 1998. Article 9 of the law stated that 'in state and local government education establishments education is acquired in the official language',[22] deferring the implementation date for this controversial provision to the seemingly distant date of 1 September 2004. The implementation of this provision nearly six years after its adoption evoked unprecedented protests on the part of Latvia's Russian-speaking population. These protests were directed not so much against the general goal of the education reform – strengthening the position of the Latvian language in society – as against the methods envisioned for achieving this goal and the distinctly paternalistic nature of education policy. On the whole, the education reform led to another result that was unexpected for the nationalists – the strengthening of civic bonds between members of the Russian-speaking population and their transformation from a rather amorphous and politically divided group into a well-organised and increasingly influential political force. The Latvian Language Agency found that Latvian language proficiency increased substantially among minority graduates of schools and interpreted this as a positive outcome of the reform.[23] However, the influence of the education reform on social integration, and particularly on mutual trust between ethnic communities, is ambiguous.

10.4 Official understanding of integration, 2001-2010

While the public debate about integration began in the mid-1990s, the first policy document to specifically enshrine integration was the Framework Document (*koncepcija*) on the Integration of Society in Latvia, adopted by the Cabinet of Ministers on 7 December 1999.[24] Subsequently, on 6 February 2001, the government adopted the National Programme on the Integration of Society in Latvia, which reiterated the basic postulates of the Framework Document and sketched in the main policy directions to be pursued, even mentioning specific projects to be implemented in the short term.[25] Since then, no new policy document redefining integration has been adopted, so that the 1999 and 2001 interpretation retains the force of policy as at the time of writing.
The conceptual basis of the Framework Document and Integration Programme contains certain contradictions and inconsistencies which were determined by the divergent interests of various political forces and their influence in the drafting process. As a result, the documents are political compromises. To make them more acceptable, the most controversial issues related to inter-ethnic relations were combined with issues pertaining to social inclusion and regional integration, even though these were already addressed in other policy documents. A tribute of sorts to the efforts of radical nationalists to prevent the adoption of the programme altogether was the mention of the repatriation of minorities.
According to the Framework Document, 'social integration means mutual understanding and cooperation between individuals and groups within a common state' (p. 4). This initial emphasis on contact and interdependence is supplemented by a strong focus on the normative dimension: 'the goal of integration is to create a democratic, cohesive civil society based on common values' (p. 4). In many ways, the document tries to square

a circle: it posits the two-way nature of integration, then proceeds to stress the primacy of the Latvian language, culture and values and the adaptation required by minorities and non-citizens (new immigrants or refugees are mentioned in one sentence).

> *Thus, the Framework Document notes that:*
>
> *Integration is a multifaceted process – it means not only that minorities [NM: cittautieši – literally, 'other folk' or people of another ethnicity] have acquired the Latvian language and overcome alienation from Latvian cultural values, but also Latvian 'openness' in attitudes to minorities. Until now the view has sometimes prevailed in Latvia that integration is a minority problem. However, in implementing the social integration programme a change in attitudes and understanding must take place in the Latvian environment as well. Social integration in Latvia is a partnership between people belonging to various social strata, Latvians and minorities, citizens and non-citizens, in which all sides involved in integration are active (p. 7).*

Other nods to the two-way element are the mention of 'equal opportunities for all' (p. 18), 'intercultural education' (p. 37) and 'cultural dialogue' (p. 41). Several references are also made to minority rights, which in this conceptualisation include 'ensuring minority rights to cultural autonomy' (p. 5), including 'rights to nurture and maintain their languages and cultures' (p. 26). Considerable attention is devoted to the 'development of minority education programmes' (p. 36) and 'ensuring minority participation' in education policy (p. 39).

However, the Framework Document also specifically highlights the integration 'deficit' of non-citizens:

> *Latvia inherited from the Soviet era more than half a million settlers and their descendants; in the years since many of them have not become a part of the Latvian cultural and linguistic setting and do not feel a connection to the state of Latvia (p. 4).*

The role of the Latvian language and culture as the basis for integration is laid out in no uncertain terms: 'civil society is integrated when minorities have a good command of the Latvian language, have overcome their alienation from Latvian cultural values...' (p. 5). Those who are unwilling to accept the rules of the game offered by Latvia and who want to return to their 'ethnic homelands' should be assisted: 'in cooperation with Western countries, Russia, Ukraine, Belarus and other countries, conditions should be created to assist those persons who want to return to their homelands but who cannot do so for various reasons' (p. 17).

The Framework Document and Integration Programme provide detailed diagnoses of the various divisions in Latvian society, particularly between ethnic Latvians and minorities. However, internal contradictions within the document and the lack of elaboration of many controversial themes or specific mechanisms for overcoming divisions generate serious problems of operationalisation. As Ilona Kunda has written, 'the Integration Programme leaves identifying many solutions and resolving a whole range of contradictions in the hands of the implementing agency'.[26] This vagueness is exacerbated by the fact that neither the Framework Document, nor the Programme contain any explicit progress indicators.

10.5 Evolution of Integration Policy

The Society Integration Foundation

After the integration programme was adopted, international pressure grew to move forward on policy implementation. An important role was played here by the OSCE Mission to Latvia and the OSCE High Commissioner on National Minorities, UNDP Latvia and the European Commission's delegation to Latvia, all of which urged Latvia to create an institutional framework to promote integration.[27] This international pressure, as well as the promise of significant resources to fund integration-related activities, prompted the political elite to adopt legislation establishing an Integration Foundation in July 2001, similar to a Foundation that had already been set up in neighbouring Estonia.

The Society Integration Foundation was to promote integration by supporting projects proposed 'bottom-up' in response to calls open to NGOs, local governments, educational and cultural institutions. The Foundation became a major source of funding for integration-related activities, allocating almost 13 million lats (approx. €18.5 million) for projects from 2001 to 2006 in government and EU funding.[28] In subsequent years, the Foundation disbursed not only EU and government money, but also funding from the Norwegian financial instrument and other sources, branching out to support projects not only in the realm of integration, but also in civil-society development and other realms. In 2008, the Foundation had a budget of about 10 million lats (€14.28 million).[29]

Remarkably, the Foundation has never carried out any broader monitoring of integration or sought to measure the impact of the projects it has supported. Any analysis that does take place is conducted on an ad hoc basis by Foundation staff, or informally by the unwieldy governing council, which includes five ministers, five NGO representatives, five representatives of local governments and a representative of the President. Until recently, no external researcher had ever sought to conduct any sort of analysis of the Foundation's work. A recent initiative led by Ilona Kunda analysed the extent to which projects supported by the Foundation from 2001 to 2006 involved intercultural contact. Kunda and her team found signs of sustained contact in only about 20% of all projects supported, casting doubt on the integrative impact of some of the Foundation's work.[30]

The Integration Minister and Secretariat

While the Society Integration Foundation has operated continuously since 2001, another institution – the Secretariat of the Special Assignments Minister for Social Integration Affairs – functioned in parallel from November 2002 until its closure at the end of 2008. Special Assignments Ministers are fully-fledged Cabinet Ministers with supporting structures called 'secretariats'. Secretariats differ from full ministries in that they are more compact and their tasks (and thus their existence) are intended to be short-lived.

The functions of the minister and the integration secretariat included coordinating social integration policy, addressing the rights of national minorities, promoting civil-society development, combating racial and ethnic discrimination, supporting Latvia's indigenous people, the Livs, supporting the Latvian diaspora, and in the end, promoting immigrant integration policy. Five different individuals held the ministerial post, each with differing priorities. The first minister, who served for two years, focused on minority issues, lobbying for greater support for minority NGOs, seeking to promote the registration of non-citizen children, managing the unrest surrounding minority education reform, and promoting tolerance and intercultural dialogue.[31] Subsequent ministers focused more on issues such as supporting rural NGOs, seeking to ascertain the reasons for the large out-migration of labour in the mid-2000s, adopting and implementing a Roma integration programme and planning immigrant integration policy.[32] The integration secretariat did conduct integration monitoring by commissioning surveys and other studies, creating an integration project database and seeking to reach inter-ministerial agreement on progress indicators (see below). Most often, the monitoring consisted of regular sociological surveys, though ad hoc research was also commissioned in various sectors. In the end, no inter-ministerial agreement was ever reached on progress indicators or priorities, reflecting the disagreement between the elites and the lack of interest in integration issues more broadly.

Current institutional arrangements at the national level

The onset of the 2008 economic crisis in Latvia was accompanied by a broader debate about streamlining government and reducing the size of the public sector. Against this backdrop, the integration secretariat was the first to fall victim to budget cuts. At the end of 2008, the government adopted a decision to absorb the functions of the integration secretariat into the Ministry of Children and Families, to create a Ministry for Children, Families and Social Integration Affairs from 1 January 2009. However, this was a short-lived, politically motivated solution (the Minister for Children and Families came from the same political party as the integration minister); on 28 April 2009, following a change in the governing coalition, the government adopted a decision to do away with this ministry as well.[33]

Primary responsibility for integration policy fell briefly to the Ministry of Justice in 2009, then to the Ministry of Culture in 2010, which created a department of social integration affairs. The small size of this department (six staff), coupled with deep budget cuts pose serious obstacles to the effectiveness of the department's work. At the same time, the Society Integration Foundation continues to operate, though its work is not specifically focused on integration-related issues. In 2009, for example, it announced eight grant competitions. Two (for a total of approx. € 1,308,235) were for state and local government agencies to build local government capacity to implement EU programmes and improve public services. Five (for a total of approx. € 3,691,050) were intended to support NGO capacity-building in general, and only one (approx. € 688,236) was to enable NGOS 'to promote understanding and cooperation between people of different ethnic origin living in Latvia'.[34]

10.6 City integration programmes

Significant integration work and some monitoring have also taken place at the local level. Monitoring at the local level has been sporadic and unsystematic, however, relying in the best case on a local sociological survey, but often merely on information compiled by the various sectoral units (education, social issues, culture) of the city government. Following the start of discussions surrounding the need for an integration programme from 1998 to 2001, a number of local governments began to act. In April 2000, the city of Ventspils adopted its own integration programme and created a non-citizens' advisory council. The Liepāja city government also established an 'integration promotion working group' in 2000 that prepared a draft city integration programme and appointed an integration project coordinator.[35] Over the next few years, there was a virtual explosion of integration activity at the local level, probably prompted by policy movement at the national level.

By the end of 2003, 25 municipal authorities had their own social integration programmes and another 29 had sectoral programmes that were directly linked to social integration (the glaring exception being Riga).[36] In the mid-2000s, 20 different local governments claimed to have a unit (usually a working group, council or commission) with responsibility for social integration issues.[37] The interpretation of integration at the local level differed slightly from the national level. Where issues pertaining to citizenship, language and common values predominated at the national level, at the local level the most common issues addressed in integration policy documents were education, social issues (e.g. the disabled, health), culture and NGOs.[38]

By the end of the decade, much of the integration-related activity at the local level had dissipated or been channelled in other directions. Ventspils, the leading local government on integration work, updated its integration programme in 2004 for the years 2005 to 2007, but not thereafter.[39] Liepāja, for its part, increasingly focused its integration work on cooperation with NGOs, eventually eschewing the word 'integration' in local policy documents, but adopting a 'Liepāja City Civil Society Development Strategy 2009-2014'.[40] After the local elections in 2009, the integration commissions that had worked in the city governments in Rezekne and Daugavpils were quietly discontinued, ostensibly to conserve resources.[41]

Several local governments have continued their integration work, however. On 24 April 2008, the Jelgava city government adopted an updated Jelgava Social Integration Programme for the period 2008 – 2013 focusing on the preservation of minority cultures, social issues and youth.[42] The Jelgava city government has also commissioned research on ethnic integration in the city, apparently focussing on ethnic relations, as well as the situation and needs of minority communities in the city.[43] Having adopted an integration programme in 2003, in late 2009 the Jūrmala city government announced that in 2010 it planned to 'analyze the programme's implementation' and to update it.[44] The Riga City Council, which had no integration policy throughout the 2000s, belatedly created a unit devoted to integration and project work on 10 March 2010, as well as an advisory council on integration issues.[45]

10.7 Measurement of integration

Neither the national government nor any local government has sought to measure integration in any systematic way. However, there is a huge amount of reliable data available for researchers, as well as a number of high-quality thematic studies on integration-related issues. Since Latvia's accession to the European Union in 2004, the availability and comparability of data has improved. Latvia's Central Statistical Bureau now cooperates intensively with Eurostat, Latvia also regularly participates in the Eurobarometer surveys, the European Social Survey and other more specific thematic studies.[46]

At national level, the basic source of information is the national census, which has only been carried out once (in 2000) since the restoration of independence. The next census is scheduled for 2011.[47] From the perspective of measuring integration, the most interesting census data include population by (self-reported) ethnicity at the national and local levels, mixed marriages, (self-reported) command of Latvian and other languages, and international long-term migration by country of origin.

A second national database is the Population Register, which is maintained by the Office of Citizenship and Migration Affairs of the Ministry of Interior.[48] The methodology used for this database is different from that used in the census; here, data on ethnicity are based on the ethnicity entry in passports, which was obligatory until 2002. This ethnicity entry was a Soviet-era control mechanism by which persons inherited the passport ethnicity of their parents (regardless of their self-identification), and in the case of children of mixed parenthood, chose one of the parent's ethnicities upon reaching the age of 16. A person's official ethnicity could only be changed with great difficulty. Data available from the Population Register that are of interest for measuring integration include data on the population by ethnicity, citizenship, and year of birth at national and local levels. When the ethnicity entry became voluntary after 2002, a new category – 'undecided' – appeared in the database.

The only specific long-term systematic monitoring of an integration-related issue has been carried out in the area of language. The National Agency (formerly Programme) for Latvian Language Training commissioned thirteen representative sociological surveys from 1996 to 2008 covering all aspects of language, including self-reported level of Latvian language proficiency (by age, gender, ethnicity), attitudes towards language use, reported language use and habits in various contexts, desire and motivation to improve Latvian language proficiency, as well as Russian language proficiency among Latvians.[49] The surveys were conducted by the reputable Baltic Institute of Social Sciences, which is one of the major sources of reliable survey data on integration issues.[50]

The primary means of seeking to monitor integration more broadly has been through wider-ranging sociological surveys. The baseline reference points in many subsequent studies have been two surveys, one conducted in 1997/1998 and the other in 2000/2001, called 'Towards a Civic Society'.[51] The surveys, which were commissioned by a consortium of state, non-governmental and international organisations,[52] polled citizens and non-citizens on a wide range of issues: attitudes towards the state, democracy, citizenship and naturalisation, language policy, various state institutions, political participation, migration, perceptions of ethnic distance and more. In later years, the integration secretariat commissioned similar surveys on a more or less regular basis.[53] From 2002 to 2004, the integration secretariat convened a series of inter-ministerial meetings with the aim of developing generally agreed integration indicators. However, no consensus was reached; the integration secretariat accordingly abandoned this effort and embarked on its own quest to measure integration in various ways. It not only commissioned a series of surveys, but also commissioned studies (discourse and content analysis) of the role of the media in integration.[54] It commissioned several studies of national minorities, including one focusing on their organisations, another on their history in Latvia more broadly, and a third on their stance towards the Council of Europe Framework Convention on the Protection of National Minorities.[55] In 2004, the integration secretariat commissioned the one systematic study on integration activities at municipal level.[56] That same year, in the context of the controversial reform of minority education, it commissioned a broad sociological overview of civic values in Latvian and minority schools.[57] Finally, as policy at the national level began to falter and official interest in integration began to fade, the integration secretariat commissioned a historical/sociological policy study of opposition to integration.[58]

Several other important efforts to measure integration have been conducted by researchers on their own initiative. In addition to the aforementioned studies on discourse analysis, several other efforts have been made to measure the role of the political elite in promoting or hindering integration. One study of parliamentary discourse found that, over time, the most radical representatives of the government and opposition increasingly took the floor.[59] Another study, in 2007, monitored both parliamentary debate and the media to ascertain the incidence of rhetoric seeking to 'shrink citizenship' by proposing arbitrary limitations to the public visibility and participation rights of 'suspect' groups such as non-citizens, new immigrants, LGBT, and NGO activists. The study found that editors and journalists are the most common source of intolerant media content, and that exclusionary rhetoric among parliamentarians decreased over the course of 2007.[60]

A 2006 study by the Baltic Institute of Social Sciences entitled *Integration Practice and Perspectives* was until recently the most comprehensive effort to measure integration. The study combined quantitative and qualitative methods, including an analysis of the role of the press in constructing collective identities, longitudinal survey data on support for political parties by ethnicity, an analysis of party documents, analysis of the NGO sector's role in integration, interviews with elites and focus group sessions. Interestingly, the study also includes a survey-based analysis of different strategies of acculturation – separation, assimilation, integration, marginalisation and fusion. The study finds that, despite the destructive role of most of the political elite and the media, most inhabitants of Latvia prefer strategies of integration over the alternatives.[61]

Finally, a large, comprehensive study seeking to measure integration in Latvia was recently published, developing a set of conceptually based integration indicators.[62] The study sees integration as a process of unifying society by promoting participation, non-discrimination and intercultural contact. The study contains the first attempt to analyze the incidence of intercultural contact in projects supported by the Society Integration Foundation, but also analyzes participation, inequalities and contact in various domains of life – politics, the labour market, the social sphere, the education system, the media and the cultural arena. The authors observe progress in terms of promoting Latvian language knowledge and moving towards a unified school system, but the crisis has undermined integration in the labour market and the social sphere. However, patterns of exclusion and separation in politics and the media remain persistent and deeply rooted.

It seems that the next steps in measuring integration might combine analyses of sociological survey and other data with the study of discourse and legislation. Future studies might also include an investigation of the position of new immigrants. While immigration has not yet been addressed at policy level in any coherent way, researchers have already produced a number of studies on the issue in Latvia.[63] However, it is unlikely that such research will be undertaken in the near future, given the current lack of political interest and the associated funding for integration.

10.8 Conclusion: recent policy developments

In recent years, there have been three unsuccessful attempts to draft and adopt new integration policy guidelines. The first was undertaken in 2007 and shelved after vigorous protests by the Minister of Culture, who objected to the inclusion of ideas of multiculturalism in the draft document.[64] Two subsequent efforts to adopt guidelines for policy for 2010-2019 and for 2010-2016 both faltered as well due to a lack of political consensus. All three of these recent efforts addressed not only Russian-speakers and other minorities, but immigrants as well. What is more, all three contained progress indicators. The most recent initiative contained 25 different indicators on aspects such as the development of intercultural dialogue, Latvian language proficiency, awareness and knowledge about citizenship issues, levels of civic education, levels of awareness about discrimination and tolerance issues, and the development of immigrant integration policy.[65] When and if the political elite does seek to turn again to integration policy development and measurement, they will find that much of the data, analysis and conceptual equipment is already in place.

Notes

1   See the relevant section of the European Commission's website on immigrant integration at http://
ec.europa.eu/justice_home/fsj/immigration/integration/fsj_immigration_integration_en.htm.
2   See e.g. the homepage of the Decade of Roma inclusion at www.romadecade.org.
3   Estonia is the most prominent exception and is similar to Latvia in many ways. For a detailed overview of integration policy in Latvia, see: Nils Muižnieks (ed.) (2010). *How Integrated is Latvian Society? An
Audit of Achievements, Failures and Challenges*. Riga: University of Latvia Press.
4   For the best analysis to date, see: Latvian Centre for Human Rights and Ethnic Studies (2003). *The Situation of the Roma in Latvia*. Riga: Latvian Centre for Human Rights and Ethnic Studies.
5   See *The National Programme 'Roma in Latvia' 2007-2009* adopted by the Cabinet of Ministers on 18 October
2006.
6   For details see: Mihails Hazans & Kaia Philips (2010). The Post-Enlargement Migration Experience in
the Baltic Labor Markets. In: Martin Kahanec & Klaus F. Zimmermann (eds.), *EU Labor Markets After Post-
Enlargement Migration* (p. 255-304). Berlin-Heidelberg, Germany / London, UK / New York, US: Springer.
7   Data from the Citizenship and Migration Affairs Board, available at http://www.pmlp.gov.lv/lv/statis-
tika/patveruma.html;jsessionid= 9.
8   See e.g. Centre for Public Policy PROVIDUS (2008). *Learning to Welcome: The Integration of Immigrants in
Latvia and Poland*. Riga: Providus; Advanced Social and Political Research Institute (2009). *Immigrant
Integration in Latvia*. Riga: ASPRI (Working Paper No. 1) consulted at: http://www.szf.lu.lv/files/pet-
nieciba/publikacijas/working_paper/immig%20integ%20final%20draft.pdf; and Brigita Zepa & Inese
Šupule (eds.) (2009). *Imigranti Latvijā: Iekļaušanās iespējas un nosacījumi*. Riga: BISS.
9   This and the next section draw heavily on Juris Rozenvalds (2010). The Soviet Heritage and Integration Policy Development Since the Restoration of Independence. In: Muižnieks (ed.), *How Integrated is
Latvian Society?* (see note 3), p. 33-60.
10   Daina Bleiere, Ilgvars Butulis, Inesis Feldmanis, Aivars Stranga & Antonijs Zunda (2005). *Latvijas
vēsture. 20. gadsimts* (p. 364). Riga: Jumava.
11   Latvijas Republikas Valsts statistikas komiteja (1992). *1989.gada tautas skaitīšanas rezultāti Latvijā: statistikas datu krājums* (p. 41-42). Riga: Central Statistical Bureau.
12   Elmārs Vēbers (2007). Vai teiksim ardievas sabiedrības integrācijai? In: Leo Dribins & Aleksejs
Šnitnikovs (eds.), *Pretestība sabiedrības integrācijai: cēloņi un sekas* (p. 119). Riga: University of Latvia Agency – academic institute (LU FSI).
13   For a recent discussion of Latvian history and social memory stressing the 1990s focus on suffering,
see Vita Zelče (2010). History – Responsibility – Memory: Latvia's Case. In: Juris Rozenvalds & Ivars
Ijabs (eds.), *Latvia Human Development Report 2008/2009: Accountability and Responsibility* (p. 44-57). Riga:
University of Latvia Press.
14   Vladislavs Volkovs (1996). *Krievi Latvijā* (p. 67). Riga: University of Latvia Agency – academic institute
(LU FSI).
15   See Mihails Hazans (2010). Ethnic Minorities in the Latvian Labour Market ,1997-2009: Outcomes,
Integration Drivers and Barriers; and Felician Rajevska (2010). Social Policy and Integration. Both in:
Muižnieks (ed.), *How Integrated is Latvian Society?*(see note 3) p. 125-158 and p. 159-188, respectively.
16   Juris Rozenvalds (2002). *Monologu kultūras krīze*. Consulted on 3 January 2002 at http://www.politika.lv/
temas/sabiedribas_integracija/3852/.

17 Nils Muižnieks (1993). Latvia: Origins, Evolution and Triumph. In: Ian Bremmer & Ray Taras (eds.), *Nations and Politics in the Soviet Successor States* (p. 196). Cambridge: Cambridge University Press.

18 Brigita Zepa (1992). Sabiedriskā dome pārējas periodā Latvijā: latviešu un cittautiešu uzskatu dinamika (1989-1992). In: *Latvijas Zinātņu akadēmijas vēstis*. A daļa, vol. 543, no. 10, p. 22.

19 Priit Jarve (2003). Language Battles in the Baltic States: from 1989-2002. In: Farimah Daftary & Francois Grin (eds.), *Nation-Building, Ethnicity and Language Politics in Transition Countries* (p. 82). Budapest: LGI.

20 Baltic Data House (1998). *Pētījumu un rīcības programma 'Ceļā uz pilsonisku sabiedrību'. Atskaite. 1. un 2. posma rezultāti*. Riga: Baltic Data House. Consulted at http://www.biss.soc.lv/downloads/resources/pilsoniskaSabiedriba/pilsoniskaSabiedriba1997.pdf.

21 Vēbers, Vai teiksim ardievas sabiedrības integrācijai? (see note 12), p. 120.

22 See http://www.likumi.lv/doc.php?id=50759.

23 See State Language Agency (n.d.), *Latviešu valodas prasmes un lietojums augstākās izglītības iestādēs. Izglītības reformas rezultāti* (p. 1). Consulted at http://www.valoda.lv/lv/petijumi/veiktiepetijumi.

24 Consulted at http://www.politika.lv/temas/sabiedribas_integracija/4104/.

25 Consulted at http://www.politika.lv/temas/sabiedribas_integracija/4106/.

26 Ilona Kunda (2010). The Society Integration Foundation and 'Ethnic Integration'. In: Muižnieks (ed.), *How Integrated is Latvian Society?* (see note 3), p. 64.

27 On the role of international organisations in influencing minority policy in Latvia, see Nils Muižnieks & Māra Sīmane (eds.) (2005). *UNDP Latvia 1992-2005: Easing the Transition*. Riga: UNDP; Nils Muižnieks & Ilze Brands Kehris (2003). The European Union, democratisation, and minorities in Latvia. In: Paul J. Kubicek (ed.), *The European Union and Democratization* (p. 30-55). London: Routledge; and Jekaterina Dorodnova (2003). *Challenging Ethnic Democracy: Implementation of the Recommendations of the OSCE High Commissioner on National Minorities to Latvia, 1993-2001*. Hamburg: Centre for OSCE Research (CORE Working Paper 10).

28 Ilona Kunda (2010). The Society Integration Foundation and 'Ethnic Integration'. In: Muižnieks (ed.), *How Integrated is Latvian Society?* (see note 3), p. 61.

29 Dita Arāja (2007). *Kam tiks SIF naudas lāde?* Consulted on 26 June 2007 at http://www.politika.lv/index.php?id=14296. For an overview of the Foundation's current activities, see its home page at www.lsif.lv.

30 Kunda (2010). The Society Integration Foundation and 'Ethnic Integration' (see note 26), p. 83.

31 For a personal memoir of the first minister on his activities, see Nils Muižnieks (2009). A Political Scientist's Experience in the Real World of Politics. In: *European Political Science (EPS)*, no. 8, p. 68-78. For a more analytical overview, see Nils Muižnieks & David J. Galbreath (2008). Latvia: managing post-imperial minorities. In: Bernd Rechel (ed.), *Minority Rights in Central and Eastern Europe* (p. 135-150). London: Routledge.

32 On the Roma integration programme, see Īpašu uzdevumu ministra sabiedrīas integrācijas lietās sekretariāts (2007). *Informatīvais ziņojums par valsts programmas 'Čigāni (romi) Latvijā' 2007.-2009. gadam īstenošanu*. Riga: ĪUMSILS. [Special Assignment Minister for Social Integration Affairs Secretariat (2007). *Information Report on the Implementation of the State Programme 'Gypsies (Roma) in Latvia' 2007-2009*. Riga: SAMSIAS.]

33 For a broad overview of the rise and decline of integration policy, see Juris Rozenvalds (2010). The Soviet Heritage and Integration Policy Development Since the Restoration of Independence. In: Muižnieks (ed.), *How Integrated is Latvian Society?* (see note 3), p. 33-60.

34 See the overview of calls in 2009 on the English language interface of web page of the integration foundation at http://www.lsif.lv/en/calls-proposals#_ftn1.

35 See Latvian Centre for Human Rights and Ethnic Studies (2001). *Human Rights in Latvia in 2000* (p. 41-42). Riga: LCRES.

36 Baltijas Sociālo zinātņu institūts (2004). *Pašvaldību loma sabiedrības integrācijas procesā* (p. 7). Riga: BSZI.

37 Ibid, p. 10.

38 Ibid, p. 11.

39 Ventspils pilsētas dome (2004). *Ventspils pilsētas sabiedrības integrācijas programma 2005-2007*. Vetspils, adopted by the Vestpils City Council on 21 February 2005, decision no. 70.

40 Liepājas Pilsētas Pašvaldība (2009). *Liepājas pilsētas pilsoniskās sabiedrības attīstības stratēģija 2009.-2014. gadam*. Liepāja: Liepājas Pilsētas Pašvaldība.

41 E-mail communication from Inese Andiņa, head of the Daugavpils City Council Public Relations division, 15 March 2010. The discontinuation of the Rezeknes city council's Social Integration Promotion Commission was announced on 20 February 2009 in the context of 'economising on budget resources'. See the news item in the Rezekne city council's web page at http:// www.rezekne.lv/.

42 See Jelgavas Dome (2009). *Jelgavas Pašvaldības 2008. gada Publiskais Pārskats* (p. 68-69). Jelgava: Jelgavas Dome.

43 See the relevant section of the Jelgava city government's home page at http://www.jelgava.lv/pilseta/ sabiedriba/integracija/.

44 See the information on the home page of the Jūrmala City Council 'Jūrmalas Pašvaldības iedzīvotāju integrācijas komisija pieņem darba plānu 2010. gadam'. Consulted on 28 October 2009 at http:// www.jurmala.lv/page/1027&news_id=98&comment=news&mode=print.

45 See the interview with Eiženija Aldermane, head of the committee on education in the Riga City Council, in *Vesti segodnya*, 12 March 2010.

46 For the home page of the Central Statistical Bureau of Latvia, see http://www.csb.gov.lv; for standard Eurobarometer reports, see http://ec.europa.eu/public_opinion/standard_en.htm; for European Social Survey results, see http://www.europeansocialsurvey.org/; for the results of a specialized European Union Minorities and Discrimination Survey, see http://fra.europa.eu/fraWebsite/eu-midis/ eumidis_main_results_report_en.htm.

47 For basic information on the census, see http://www.csb.gov.lv/csp/content/?cat=339&cc_ cat=339&mode=arh&period=.

48 For basic information on the Population Register, see http://www.pmlp.gov.lv/en/pakalpojumi/izce-losana.html.

49 For the results of the 2007 survey in English, see http://www.lvava.gov.lv/bildes/dokumenti/Valo-da_2007_ENG.pdf; for the results of the 2008 survey in English, see http://www.lvava.gov.lv/bildes/ dokumenti/VALODA_2008_ENG.pdf.

50 See its homepage at http://www.biss.soc.lv.

51 For the SPSS data files and results of the 1997/1998 survey, see http://www.biss.soc.lv/?lang=en&c ategory=resurss&id=pilsoniskaSabiedriba1997; for the SPSS data files and results of the 2000/2001 survey, see http://www.biss.soc.lv/?lang=en&category=resurss&id=pilsoniskaSabiedriba2000.

52 The first study was funded by the Soros Foundation – Latvia and the National Human Rights Office, together with the United Nations Development Programme (UNDP). The working group that commissioned the survey included representatives of these organisations, as well as the Naturalisation Board, the National Programme for Latvian Language Training, the Citizenship and Immigration Department, and the implementing agency, the Baltic Data House.

53 See SKDS (2006). *Sabiedrības integrācijas aktuālākie aspekti*. Riga: SKDS; SKDS (2007). *Sabiedrības integrācijas aktuālākie aspekti*. Riga: SKDS; SIA 'AC Konsultācijas' (2008). *Kvantitatīvs un kvalitatīvs pētījums par sabiedrības integrācijas unpilsonības aktuālajiem aspektiem*. Riga: AC Konsultācijas.

54 See Sergejs Kruks & Ilze Šulmane (2002). *Pilsoniskās sabiedrības attīstība un sabiedrības integrācija*. Riga: Komunikācijas studiju nodaļa; Ilze Šulmane & Sergejs Kruks (2006). *Neiecietības izpausmes un iecietības veicināšana Latvijā*. Riga: ĪUMSILS.

55 On minorities, see Rīgas Stradiņa universitāte (2004). *Latvijas mazākumtautību sabiedrisko organizāciju dibināšanas mērķi*. Riga: RSU; LU FSI & ĪUMSILS (2007). *Mazākumtautības Latvijā. Vēsture un tagadne*. Riga: LU FSI; Nils Muižnieks (ed.) (2007). *Nacionālo minoritāšu konvencija – diskriminācijas novēršana un identitātes saglabāšana Latvijā*. Riga: LU SPPI.

56 Baltic Institute of Social Sciences (2004). *The Role of Municipality in Society Integration*. Riga: BISS. Consulted at http://www.biss.soc.lv/downloads/resources/pasvaldibas/Pasvaldibas_Engl.pdf.

57 Rīgas Stradiņa universitāte (2004). *Pilsoniskās vērtības latviešu un mazākumtautību izglītības programmās: salīdzinājums*. Riga: RSU.

58 Dribins & Šnitņikovs (ed.) (2007). *Pretestība sabiedrības integrācijai* (see note 12).

59 See Ilze Šulmane (2007). Neiecietības diskurss Saeimas politiķu runās. In: Juris Rozenvalds (ed.), *Parlamentārais diskurss Latvijā: Saeimas plenārsēžu stenogrammu datorizētā analīze* (p. 69-91). Riga: LU Akadēmiskais apgāds.

60 Maria Golubeva & Iveta Kažoka (2007). *Shrinking Citizenship: Analytical Report on the Monitoring of Printed Media, Parliamentary Debates and Legislative Initiative concerning Civic Participation in Latvia*. Riga: Providus. Consulted at http://www.providus.lv/upload_file/Dokumenti_feb07/Tolerance/Shrink_Citi_Eng.doc. For a larger study by the same authors, available only in Latvian, see Marija Golubeva & Iveta Kažoka (2009). *Saeima un pilsoniskā līdzdalība. LR Saeimas plenārsēžu un likumdošanas iniciatīvu monitoringa rezultāti 2007.-2009*. Riga: Providus.

61 Brigita Zepa (ed.) (2006). *Integration Practice and Perspectives*. Riga: Baltic Institute of Social Sciences. Consulted at http://www.bszi.lv/downloads/resources/integracijas_prakse/brosura_EN.pdf.

62 See Muižnieks (ed.) (2010). *How Integrated is Latvian Society?* (see note 3)

63 See Dace Akule (ed.) (2008). *Learning to welcome: The integration of immigrants in Latvia and Poland*. Riga: Providus; Nils Muižnieks (ed.) (2009). *Immigrant Integration in Latvia*. Riga: ASPRI (ASPRI Working Paper No. 1); Brigita Zepa (ed.) (2009). *Imigranti Latvijā: iekļaušanās iespējas un nosacījumi*. Riga: BISS.

64 On the controversy, see Rozenvalds (2010). The Soviet Heritage and Integration Policy Development Since the Restoration of Independence. In: Muižnieks (ed.) *How Integrated is Latvian Society?* (see note 3), p. 57-58.

65 See Ministry of Justice (2009). *Sabiedrības integrācijas politikas pamatnostādnes 2010.-2016. gadam* (p. 35-36). Riga: unpublished draft document. For public criticism of this (the most recent draft document), see Ināra Mūrniece, Integrācijas pamatnostādnes – krēsls ar trim kājām. In: *Latvijas Avīze*, 2 March 2010, p. 5.

11 Monitoring systems for the integration of ethnic minorities and immigrants in Lithuania

Vida Beresnevičiūtė and Karolis Žibas

11.1 Introduction

After restoring independence in 1991, Lithuania experienced significant political and socioeconomic changes. This led to specific patterns of international migration. After 1991, large-scale emigration[1] of Lithuanian citizens to the western regions of the EU brought demographic challenges and led to structural changes in the Lithuanian labour market. After Lithuania joined the EU in 2004, economic emigration became more visible. Together with a growing trend of economic emigration that has prevailed in Lithuania for many years, new migration patterns were identified, as the demographic shortfall combined with labour force shortages triggered immigration from geographically close (Belarus, Russia, Ukraine) and distant (China, Turkey) countries as well as encouraged the initiation of political responses to these processes.

Immigration flows (especially labour-related) to Lithuania began to increase from 2000, reaching a peak after EU enlargement in 2004 and Lithuania's integration into the Schengen Area in late 2007. Consequently, labour immigration became significant, while flows of asylum-seekers remained stable. However, current global economic changes have altered the trends in labour-related immigration: statistics from the Lithuanian Labour Exchange show that the number of work permits issued to foreigners in 2009 was a third of the figure in 2008. The number of immigrants granted refugee status and subsidiary protection also decreased (see figure 11.1).

Despite the relatively low numbers of foreigners residing in Lithuania[2] and arriving in the country annually, labour-related immigration became visible in the public space. It has triggered debates on the need for new regulations covering economic migration and measures to foster migrant integration.

In the light of the new challenges raised by contemporary migration processes, the Economic Migration Regulation Strategy[3] was adopted by the Lithuanian government in April 2007; this could be seen as a backdrop to or the first step towards the establishment of a long-term migration strategy.

Figure 11.1

Immigration in Lithuania 1997-2010[a] (in absolute numbers)

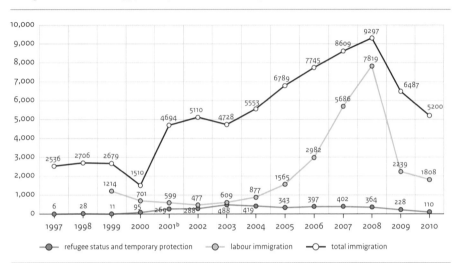

a   About 70% of immigrants are Lithuanian returnees. Therefore, real annual immigration volumes
    of foreigners are small.
b   Since 2001 foreigners who come to Lithuania for one year or longer are regarded as immigrants.

Source: Lithuanian Labour Exchange under the Ministry of Social Security and Labour; Department
of Statistics under the Government of the Republic of Lithuania; Migration Department under the
Ministry of the Interior.

In the Economic Migration Regulation Strategy, implementation of migrant integration
measures is identified as a political priority. However, summarising the content of the
strategy, the proportion of measures relating to different aspects of migration policy
should be emphasised: in 2007, eight out of 35 migration policy implementation measures, and in 2008 four out of 22 were designed for regulation of immigration and only
one for integration policy, which was related to the European Fund for the Integration of
Third-country Nationals. Neither plan, nor any measures, were approved for 2009-2010.
The limited application of these measures renders evaluation of the Strategy in terms of
integration irrelevant.

Summarising the political approach towards integration, we should stress that more
attention is devoted to return migration and regulation of immigration from 'third
countries' than to migrant integration.

It is worth mentioning that the Economic Migration Regulation Strategy was formulated
under conditions of rapid economic growth. However, many objectives that were valid in
the Strategy are no longer as relevant as they were in the current global economic situation.

Until the Strategy was published, Lithuanian migration policy could be defined as
based on migratory patterns in society, in other words an ad hoc approach. Although

regulation of the various migratory processes was adopted in political documents,[4] until 2007 Lithuania did not apply a consistent and long-term immigration policy and migrant integration measures. However, even with the initiative that have been developed, the policy remains fragmented and short-term in nature.

The general approach to migration issues in Lithuania is related to the situation that has characterised many Eastern European countries: huge emigration flows, high unemployment and international migration trends meant that Lithuania did not become an immigration country, while immigration and migrant integration processes were given low priority on the policy agenda.

The lack of a systematic approach to immigration and integration policy means that Lithuania has not developed a set of indicators for monitoring migrant integration. Only a few attempts to establish migrant integration monitoring systems can be identified.[5] Finally, it should be stressed that when analysing the migrant integration monitoring system in Lithuania, only comparative tools (or indicators) that are available in all countries of the EU can be used (e.g. MIPEX 2007, 2010); more elaborate monitoring tools are inconsistent.

11.2   Integration policy

In Lithuania, specific policy documents or national programmes aimed at integration mainly target ethnic minorities, Roma and foreigners granted asylum or subsidiary protection.

Lithuanian legislation does not contain a definition of the term 'national minority'; nor does it list specific minorities. However, in its report on the implementation of the Framework Convention for the Protection of National Minorities (FCNM), Lithuania draws a distinction between nine national minorities, or 'nationalities, most of which have had a historical presence in the country', and 'other national minorities' (Romanians, Georgians, Armenians, Estonians, etc.) which immigrated during the Soviet or post-Soviet period and which are in fact relatively small. It is worth mentioning that on 1 January 2010, the Law on Ethnic Minorities, adopted by the Supreme Soviet of the Lithuanian Soviet Socialist Republic on 23 November 1989, was repealed, and there is currently no national law in Lithuania regulating the rights of ethnic minorities.[6]

The Law on the Legal Status of Aliens[7] establishes the procedures for entry and exit, temporary or permanent residence, granting of asylum, integration and naturalisation and other issues relating to the legal status of aliens in the Republic of Lithuania. Art. 107 of that law, dealing with the integration of aliens, stipulates that the Republic of Lithuania shall provide conditions for aliens holding a residence permit to integrate into the political, social, economic and cultural life of the State in accordance with the procedure established by law, and regulates the allocation of funds for the implementation of Lithuania's national policy in the area of alien integration.

This law targets all immigrants coming to Lithuania, including all grounds for immigration (labour immigration, family reunion, legal activities, asylum, etc.). However, the integration of aliens is specified only with regard to foreigners who have been granted refugee status or subsidiary protection in Lithuania.[8] There are no integration measures for other types of immigrants in Lithuania. The Economic Migration Regulation Strategy describes integration measures for the migrants concerned, but these measures are not applied in practice.

Integration of foreigners granted asylum or subsidiary protection is targeted by the *Social Integration Programme*, implemented by the Ministry of Social Security and Labour and its institutions since 1998. Since August 2005, the task of implementing this Programme has been assigned to the Refugee Reception Center. During participation in the Programme, support is provided for Lithuanian language courses, education, employment, temporary housing, social security, health insurance and public information for foreigners granted asylum in Lithuania. The support for foreigners granted refugee status and foreigners granted subsidiary protection is initially provided by the Refugee Reception Center and is financed from the resources assigned to the Center (governmental institutions and NGOs receive financial support mainly from the European Refugee Fund). Support for integration in municipalities is also financed from the state budget. Support for foreigners granted subsidiary protection is provided only in the Refugee Reception Center. Support for integration in municipalities is provided for up to twelve months after leaving the Refugee Reception Centre, but not after expiry of the permission to stay in the Republic of Lithuania or departure from the country.

The asylum system in Lithuania has operated since 1997 under the regulations and general principles of the EU and other related documents, while the policy on economic migration is currently being developed and is regulated mainly by the Law on the Legal Status of Aliens and The Economic Migration Regulation Strategy (the latter document is less relevant for implementing policy in practice).

The Law on the Legal Status of Aliens provides brief definitions in relation to acceptance, legal stay and departure of foreigners; there is no conceptualised definition of integration. This absence of a definition of integration is reflected in other policy documents and programmes which include the migrant integration process as a political priority. Even where programmes refer to the concept of integration in their names or content, they do not provide an explicit definition of integration, nor do they provide for an assessment of the achievements in terms of integration.

Statistics Lithuania collects statistical data on immigration. Although information on immigration is specified according to the grounds for arrival (labour immigration, family reunion, education, legal activities, asylum, etc.), country of birth, age groups and sex, only a few definitions are specified in policy documents. While data on immigration to Lithuania are collected according to above aspects and are available to all interested institutions, there is no evidence that the data concerned are used for monitoring the integration process. Moreover, the absence of evaluation measures means that the database of immigration statistics (with all its advantages and disadvantages) is underutilised.

More detailed data[9] are also available that could be used to implement local integration programmes as well as for monitoring tools. However, use of those data is not free, and they are hardly relevant for policy development (e.g. there are no integration pro-grammes at municipal level).

The main piece of legislation in relation to migration and integration policy, the Law on the Legal Status of Aliens, provides definitions of the terms *alien* (any person other than a citizen of Lithuania, irrespective of whether he or she is a foreign citizen or a state-less person) and *refugee* (a foreigner who has been granted refugee status in Lithuania). Statistics Lithuania[10] gives a definition of an *immigrant* (a person who arrives in the country for a period of not less than twelve months). The Resolution on Confirmation of Landmarks of Lithuanian Migration Policy gives a definition of *migrant worker* (a person who arrives in Lithuania for economic reasons).

Since the majority of foreigners coming to Lithuania are non-EU nationals (referred to in EU documents as *third-country nationals*), this definition is important as well. However, a definition of *third-country national* is not given in Lithuanian policy documents (there are some clarifications of the definition on the website of the European Social Fund Agency, which is the coordinating institution for the European Fund for the Integration of Third-country Nationals).

The above definitions are used to collect data on immigration to Lithuania. However, there is no evidence that definitions related to migration could be used as indicators for implementing integration programmes (or measures) along with the monitoring tools. Also, there are no clarifications on the subdivision of the definition of *immigrant*. In other words, it is not clear when a foreigner is considered under the definition of *immigrant* and when under they are placed under the definition of *ethnic minority*.

11.3 National policy documents and measures as an instrument for the development of an integration infrastructure

The main governmental actors dealing with issues relating to migrant integration are the Ministry of Foreign Affairs, the Ministry of the Interior, the Ministry of Cul-ture, the Ministry of Social Security and Labour, and the Office of Equal Opportunities Ombudsperson. The non-governmental actors include organisations such as the Chil-dren's Fund, the Human Rights Monitoring Institute, the Lithuanian Red Cross Society and Caritas. The intergovernmental International Organization for Migration also plays an important role in migration processes.

The institutions involved in the integration process could also be seen as part of the monitoring mechanism. Unlike the other Baltic States, which have specific institutions for implementing migration and integration policy, Lithuania has initiated an institu-tional reorganisation in relation to the implementation of migration and integration policy. The Department of National Minorities and Lithuanians Living Abroad (one of the main funding sources for the integration of national minorities) was reorganised with effect from 1 January 2010. All the functions of this Department are now dispersed among the Ministry of Foreign Affairs, the Ministry of Education and Science, and the Ministry of Culture. Also, on 16 November 2009 the Migration Policy Department under the Ministry of the Interior (which was responsible for implementing migration policy) was dissolved. And although a Division of Migration Affairs was established in the Public Security Policy Department under the Ministry of the Interior, the human and financial resources were reduced significantly.

As integration policy is not a political issue in Lithuania, measures identified in the national programmes and other policy documents could also be considered as monitoring tools, at least for identifying the significance of integration policy in the future.
A relevant initiative in this regard is the Programme for the Integration of Ethnic Minorities into Lithuanian Society 2005-2010, which was adopted by the government in 2004 and implemented by the Department of National Minorities and Lithuanians Living Abroad. It was reorganised at the beginning of 2010, with a separate department for national minorities at the Ministry of Culture. The measures in the Programme tend to focus on cultural perspectives and activities, such as nurturing ethnic identity, support for ethnic NGOs, development of cultural centres and Sunday schools. Issues related to employment and other aspects of social inclusion are not even mentioned. The Department publishes annual reports on the use of funds allocated from the state budget. However, assessment of its financial efficiency is not obligatory.

In 2007, the government adopted the Programme for Roma Integration into Lithuanian Society 2008-2010. This Programme had been waiting in the wings since the end of 2004, when the earlier Programme covering the period 2000-2004 ended. It was implemented by the Department of National Minorities and Lithuanians Living Abroad. The main objectives of the Programme are to resolve the problems facing the Roma community in Lithuania through social policy; to secure the rights of Roma and combat discrimination; to improve secondary education standards and foster lifelong learning in the Roma community; and to nurture Roma ethnic identity. The Programme is intended to be implemented in close collaboration between the Ministry of Education and Science, municipalities, labour market institutions governed by the Ministry of Social Security and Labour, the police, the Roma Community Centre and other relevant institutions.

The Ministry of Social Security and Labour is responsible for developing strategic policy documents in the area of social protection and for implementing social integration policy. However, there is no clear definition of the content of social integration, nor of any indicators or benchmarks. The approach to social integration is based on the principles of equal rights, equal opportunities, prevention of discrimination, full participation, self-sufficiency and freedom of choice, accessibility, decentralisation, destigmatisation, continuity and flexibility of service provision, and responsiveness to different needs. Issues relating to the social integration of migrants and ethnic minorities in the framework of the social protection and social inclusion strategies represent specific developments of the national policy. However, experts[11] point out that the measures in the above programmes appear to lack a systematic approach and that, even where they are relevant, they are somewhat isolated or disconnected, rendering them both inadequate and inefficient in improving the situation of the groups targeted. Most social inclusion and social policy measures target just one dimension of social integration and ignore the multi-dimensional issues of poverty, social exclusion and discrimination (e.g. the National Report on Strategies of Lithuania for Social Protection and Social Inclusion 2006-2008 (NRSSPSI)). The ethnic dimension is no exception here.

The following vulnerable residential groups were listed in the National Action Plan on poverty and social exclusion *(NAP/inclusion) 2004-2006*: problem families, orphans and children deprived of parental care, ethnic minorities, asylum-seekers, victims of (sexual) violence, victims of human trafficking, prostitutes and other persons at social risk. The Roma minority, victims of human trafficking, drug addicts, etc., who were targeted in the NAP/inclusion 2004-2006 were no longer mentioned in the NRSSPSI. The Annex to the NRSSPSI and the document Tasks and Measures in Reducing Poverty and Social Exclusion each specifically mentioned 'immigrants' and 'aliens granted asylum' only once. While seeking to increase employment, measure no. 1.2.3. states the following aim:

> *Enhance integration into the labour market and society of immigrants and persons addicted to psychotropic substances, as well as individuals from social risk groups or persons suffering from social exclusion, by providing opportunities and social guidance to help them join the labour market and thus combating their discrimination on the labour market.*

However, the expected outcomes no longer included immigrants: 'Support will be provided for the integration into the labour market of individuals addicted to drugs or other psychotropic substances and victims of human trafficking.' (p. 79). Measure no. 2.2.7. aimed to 'Implement the provision of state assistance for the integration of aliens granted asylum in the Republic of Lithuania', which had to be provided by the Lithuanian Red Cross Society (p. 92-93). Roma or other ethnic groups are not mentioned in the document Tasks and Measures in Reducing Poverty and Social Exclusion.

Annex 4 to the *The National Report of Lithuania on Social Protection and Social Inclusion Strategies 2008-2010* (NR-SPSIS) reviews the measures and results described in the 2006-2008 National Report. The term 'ethnicity' is mentioned only a few times, such as when referring to the implementation of the National Anti-discrimination Programme (p. 40) and to the objectives in relation to fostering participation by all the population, regardless of social status, age, income or nationality, in cultural, sports, community and self-educational activities by providing support to regional and ethnic cultural projects (p. 17-18). Immigrants are also mentioned only a few times. For the first time, reference is made to the increased participation in the labour market. However, the text refers in general terms to the number of members of social risk groups who are employed and/or included in active labour market policy measures, but the number of migrants is not identified (Ibid, p. 5).

Migrants are also mentioned with regard to the implementation of the National Programme for the Prevention and Control of HIV/AIDS (measure no. 2.53), which is aimed at educating and consulting disabled migrants, and preparing and publishing material on HIV/AIDS and related infections in foreign languages for illegal migrants. The Foreigners' Registration Centre has prepared and published 200 leaflets in English and Russian on HIV/AIDS and related infections (Ibid, p. 21).

The NR-SPSIS recognises the importance of the integration of immigrants, while at the same time stating that 'immigration in Lithuania is a rather new phenomenon; however, it will demand increasing attention in the future and suitable conditions will have to be created for the social integration of immigrants' (p. 8), including future challenges in relation to the integration of immigrants' children (p. 29). This, however, leads to the postponement of the main policy documents and instruments in anticipation of future developments.

In the section on the other objectives of the state policy and implementation of horizontal principles (section 2.2.4, p. 34), overcoming discrimination and improving the integration of ethnic minorities and immigrants is defined as another important objective. The objective 'will be implemented according to each of the priorities of the plan', through five essential activity pathways[12]. The purpose of this strategy is to apply measures designed for specific target groups and geared to their situation and the reasons for their social risk, to avoid unjustified segmentation of the government policy measures and apply a common policy for all groups, to avoid stigmatisation of individual groups as a result of the application of policy measures designed for those specific groups, thus setting them apart from others, and to protect the rights of vulnerable groups. However, the horizontal approach chosen should be treated with caution. Research on the Roma community, for example, suggests that Roma have to date not been explicitly mentioned in social policy documents, despite the need for targeted measures in view of their social exclusion; they are left outside the scope of the specific labour market policies and the envisaged synergy between different actions or improvements is not achieved. According to the conclusions of the researchers of the Institute for Ethnic Studies, the present social support and labour market measures produce a certain hierarchy of socially vulnerable groups. Age groups (the young and those aged over 50) and people with disabilities are eligible for the most available measures; gender equality in the labour market is also publicly debated. It helps the aforementioned groups to be visible in society and in social policy, while the Roma (and, potentially, other vulnerable ethnic groups and migrants) still remain beyond the scope of social policy.

The National Anti-discrimination Programme 2006-2008 was the first government programme targeting discrimination. The Programme aims included ensuring implementation of the legislative norms regulating the principles of anti-discrimination and equal opportunities; raising tolerance in society; providing information on equality and non-discrimination. The main activities specified in the Programme included in-depth investigation of cases of discrimination on various grounds (age, gender, sexual orientation, disability, race or ethnic origin, religious belief) in different social spheres; raising public tolerance through education; provision of better information on equal rights and opportunities; principles of non-discrimination; providing legislative protection against discrimination. The Programme was coordinated by the Ministry of Social Affairs and Labour in close collaboration with the Department of National Minorities and Lithuanians Living Abroad and the Office of Equal Opportunities Ombudsperson. With regard to migrants, the measures of the National Anti-discrimination Programme 2009-

2011 include a sociological survey on reasons for immigration to Lithuania, immigrants' adaptation and integration opportunities and the organisation of state-sponsored language courses for immigrants (to be implemented in 2010/2011).

11.4 Institutional infrastructure for establishing integration policy and monitoring tools

Projects and studies relating to integration processes that have been carried out recently in Lithuania can be considered as the main – and in fact only – systematic source of information on immigration and integration processes. These projects collect and summarise statistical data, create databases in relation to particular problems regarding integration (discrimination, ethnic intolerance, integration in the labour market), and also seek to identify indicators for measuring integration processes.

The programmes administered by the European Social Fund in Lithuania (e.g. EQUAL, ESF programmes) provide support in promoting access to the labour market for migrants and minorities. In the period 2004-2006, eleven projects were supported that involved specific actions for national minorities, plus one further project focusing on the Roma community; for the period 2007-2013, by contrast, there is only one project focusing on the Roma community and no national minority projects at all. National minorities receive limited financial support for cultural and leisure activities through the Department of National Minorities, which was reorganised at the end of 2009 and is now part of the Ministry of Culture. The preference for a limited focus on specific groups in the ESF measures can be explained by the function of the other funds, e.g. people with a refugee or recent migrant background are supported through the European Refugee Fund and the European Fund for the Integration of Third-country Nationals.
As regards migrant integration policy in Lithuania, additional resources can only be identified for the implementation of integration measures, such as the European Refugee Fund and the European Fund for the Integration of Third-country Nationals. As a result, projects that are financed from these funds are currently considered to form the background to the migrant integration infrastructure along with the monitoring tools. An overview of the various projects shows that there are at least three areas of activity addressed by these projects: describing the immigration process and the life of immigrants in Lithuanian society; creating services specifically geared to immigrants; and carrying studies of various aspects of integration. However, this is a long way from the kind of unified activities that could lead to a specific integration strategy. Consequently, the absence of a common strategy in relation to integration, the fragmented and project-based character of migrant integration processes, without any progress from a political perspective, bear witness to the absence of a systematic mechanism for monitoring integration processes.

The European Fund for the Integration of Third-country Nationals was launched in 2007. In a case such as Lithuania this Fund could be seen as a first step towards providing an instrument for developing certain integration measures (or at least, an instrument for project development). However, it does not ensure the sustainability of the infrastructure or of integration measures for 'newly arrived' immigrants.

The Fund could provide a background for monitoring immigration and integration processes. Currently, the projects that are financed by the Fund are not coordinated in such a way as to provide an adequate response to the challenges of the integration process and are not unified in a way that would enable them to address the current situation in relation to immigration in Lithuania.

The financial support from different funding sources is closely related to NGO activities in the area of migrant integration. The number of NGOs working with migrants (particularly refugees) is considered to be part of the integration infrastructure in Lithuania. For example, the Lithuanian Red Cross Society is an important partner which is implementing a social integration assistance programme in close collaboration with state institutions by helping refugees to find accommodation, employment, learn the Lithuanian language and establish new social contacts.

On the one hand, NGOs (e.g. the Lithuanian Red Cross Society, Caritas) which receive financial support from the European Refugee Fund are working in a reasonably coordinated way towards a common integration strategy, as the number of refugees in Lithuania is small and the integration infrastructure is already in place. Also, an attempt has been made to evaluate the social integration programme for refugees living in Lithuania[13] and to carry out other types of research[14] that could be considered as tools for monitoring particular aspects of the refugee integration process: social resources, societal attitudes (of the host society and of migrants themselves), the needs of refugees, etc. On the other hand, NGOs and other institutions that receive financial support from the European Fund for the Integration of Third-country Nationals are dealing with the integration of immigrants from non-EU and EFTA countries, excluding refugees. In this case it is more complicated to achieve a comprehensive outcome because the number of these immigrants is much bigger[15] (though is still small when compared to Western European countries). The needs of specific immigrant groups differ because of their different legal status and the obstacles to integration faced by immigrants in Lithuania. However, the list of projects that received financial support from the European Fund for the Integration of Third-country Nationals shows that in 2009 a number of studies were carried out on monitoring integration processes.[16]

11.5 Evaluation of integration policy

Indicators for the assessment of migration and integration policy can be used in different ways. While elementary use is possible in any country with reliable statistics, benchmarking requires a political agreement on strategic goals. In a situation where these goals are not clearly defined and are therefore subject to *ad hoc* changes, it is almost impossible to measure 'progress' using indicators. Also, in some cases indicators could be used by referring to policy documents of a more general character, such as national action plans for social inclusion. This is certainly helpful in building up a powerful

argument, though it is important to realise that the actual significance of such plans is limited if they are perceived to be not much more than a paper exercise.[17]
Given the level of political awareness with regard to migration and integration policy in Lithuania, therefore, the possibilities for using indicators such as statistics and bench-marking are limited. Moreover, the fragmented nature of the monitoring tools means those tools (even assuming they are available and actually applied in practice) cannot be regarded as representing a systematic approach towards the creation of a monitoring system for migrant integration in Lithuania.

Measuring the performance of state institutions is another way of using indicators to measure integration. Theoretically, institutions should have at least some monitoring systems in place (e.g. evaluation of activities or implemented strategies). However, in terms of integration policy implementation, there is only one case where an evaluation has been completed and published: *Evaluation of the Effectiveness of the Economic Migration Regulation Strategy and Preparation of Recommendations for the Action Plan 2009-2012*. This assess-ment should have formed the basis for the development of the action plan for 2009-2012. In the event, however, the action plan was not in place until 2010.

11.6   Public attitudes towards immigration and the media response

Public attitudes towards different ethnic groups (including immigrants) are an impor-tant indicator of the integration monitoring process, since they give an impression of the migrant integration potential and can contribute to a favourable environment in the host society.
According to data from public opinion polls, societal attitudes towards minorities and various groups of migrants (refugees, labour migrants) in Lithuania are more negative than positive. Since 2005, the Institute for Ethnic Studies (IES) at the Lithuanian Social Research Centre has carried out an annual public opinion poll on attitudes towards vari-ous social and ethnic groups (including immigrants). The time series (2005-2010) analysis shows that the list of the most disliked groups (such as mentally disabled persons, Roma, ex-prisoners, homosexuals, Jehovah's witnesses, Chechens, refugees, Muslims and oth-ers) tends to remain stable over time. However, the degree of social distance and the prevalence of negative attitudes have been decreasing in recent years.

In 2008, the IES carried out a special survey of public attitudes towards labour immi-grants that indicated undefined and unspecified opinions on the part of the general public towards labour immigration. According to the survey data, the majority (over 80%) of the Lithuanian population are in favour of equal rights for foreigners and citi-zens of Lithuania in labour relations. However, cautious attitudes dominated: more than 60% believed that migrant workers could trigger social disorder, and almost 47% felt there were enough foreign workers in Lithuania and that no more were needed.
Public opinion research carried out among Lithuanian residents in 2009 showed that on the one hand, immigrants were perceived as a threat (both symbolic and real), while on the other, direct social contacts between immigrants and the majority population

were rare. The Lithuanian population took a more positive view of immigrants from 'culturally similar' countries such as Belarus or Ukraine than of immigrants originating from Africa, Pakistan, Turkey or China. About half the respondents agreed with the statement that the state did not do enough control immigration.[18]

Data from the above surveys show that there is a lack of information in Lithuania about immigration: the majority of people are not aware of the structure of and motives for immigration, whether labour migrants complement or replace the internal labour force, or what status labour migrants have in Lithuania (or are not able to distinguish between the status of labour immigrants and foreigners with refugee status or subsidiary protection), and other important issues. Thus, there is a social gap between the native and immigrant populations (Leončikas & Žibas 2010).

Media response

Media coverage of immigration in Lithuania depends on various circumstances: social actors seeking to shape the course of migration policy (e.g. the business sector), real or symbolic social challenges caused by immigration, societal attitudes, and of course the media itself. Media coverage of immigration has an impact on public opinion: according to several surveys, TV, radio, newspapers and the Internet are the main channels for obtaining information on the life of immigrants in Lithuania.

While considering media coverage of immigration, a distinction could be made between the information that was available before the global economic changes in 2008 and information that was published later (from late 2008/2009 onwards).

According to Leončikas and Žibas (2010), media reports appeared in response to particular events. Most articles were triggered by developments related to immigration:
1 laws, projects, and policies;
2 debates on immigration and its consequences;
3 discrimination and racism issues;
4 migrants' integration; and
5 issues relating to labour immigration.
There were no significant differences between media channels in terms of the subjects handled.

Until the global economical shifts in 2008, when labour immigration to Lithuania was growing, the focus of the media shifted towards labour migrants and issues related to labour immigration and the needs of the labour market. The attitudes of representatives of government institutions, the corporate sector and experts dominated these discussions.[19] Reporting on immigration issues was often driven by perceived threats and problems, and in some cases the media emphasised threats articulated by representatives of government institutions and experts, with the most controversial statements receiving more attention and adversarial rhetoric being used in headlines.

The global economic changes and concomitant decline in immigration flows led to a marked reduction in the general media attention for immigration. The same tendencies did still tend to come to surface, albeit to a much lesser degree. There was for example a considerable amount of negative media coverage of Chinese immigrants (in particular those coming to Lithuania to pursue legal activities), with terms such as 'occupation', 'illegal work', 'Chinatowns', etc., being used frequently. Such media reports were limited to descriptive content, merely presenting a broad overview of basic facts and a few brief comments.[20]

Summarising, it may be concluded that on the one hand, despite the small scale of immigration to Lithuania, media coverage is negative and one-sided, while on the other it can be seen as the main source of information for the majority of Lithuanian society.

11.7   Examples of monitoring

One example of the monitoring system could be provided by the Institute for Ethnic Studies at the Lithuanian Social Research Centre. The Institute has developed a set of indices to monitor the situation of ethnic groups, minorities and immigrants. Resources and instruments used include collection of statistical data, survey and research data, analysis and review of immigration/integration policies, results of public opinion polls, media monitoring and interviews with experts in the field concerned. The monitoring is based on project or research-based activities.

The main products of the monitoring include research projects, articles, studies and reports. The statistical data on minority groups and immigrants are drawn from a variety of sources, such as Statistics Lithuania, the Migration Department, the Lithuanian Labour Exchange and the Residents' Register Service under the Ministry of the Interior. Every institution has specific data; for example, the Residents' Register Service collects precise data on current residents (on request, it can also provide information on the distribution of foreigners across municipalities by gender, citizenship and type of residence permit).

The monitoring of immigration/integration policies is based on analysis of legislation, national action plans, strategies and other documents that regulate or address immigration and integration processes, including infrastructure developments.

The Institute for Ethnic Studies at the Lithuanian Social Research Centre carries out longitudinal public opinion research on the social distance between the native population and different ethnic and social groups, attitudes towards different issues related to migration, minority integration and public preferences. The database from 2005 illustrates both the dynamic and variety of public issues.

Since 2004, the Institute for Ethnic Studies has carried out a media monitoring exercise focusing on ethnic issues, with the aim of ascertaining the main topics on the agenda, identifying perceptions of ethnic groups and related issues. The biggest newspapers and most popular news websites are monitored. The data from this media monitoring are analysed from different perspectives, e.g. identifying manifestations of ethnic intolerance in the Lithuanian press.[21] The data collected are supplemented by qualitative research or expert knowledge.

11.8 Conclusions

This chapter on issues relating to the integration of ethnic minorities and immigrants in Lithuania reviews the main immigration trends, analyses important political and policy documents and identifies the main characteristics of the policy towards integration. Based on the material reviewed, the following conclusions and generalisations can be drawn with respect to Lithuania's response to the new challenges it faces.

Huge emigration flows, high unemployment and international migration trends meant that Lithuania did not become an immigration country, while immigration and migrant integration were given low priority on the policy agenda.

Lack of experience in immigration regulation and migrant integration in Lithuania has resulted in the absence of a systematic policy approach. The policy measures concerned are fragmented and short term in nature, and tend to focus more on return migration and regulation of immigration rather than on migrant integration.

Although migration and integration are recognised as important issues, they are treated more as future challenges than as current objectives.

A late political response to immigration and integration and the absence of early policy contributions or interventions are among the main characteristics of Lithuanian immigration and integration policy. These policies could be described as being a response to migratory patterns in society, or in other words, based on the *ad hoc* principle.

The absence of a common strategy on integration, the fragmented and exclusively project-based approach to migrant integration, with no contribution from a political perspective, illustrate the absence of a systematic mechanism for monitoring integration processes. Only a few attempts to establish monitoring tools for migrant integration have been identified. Moreover, those monitoring tools are inconsistent.

On the one hand, recent studies and research indicate social inequalities among different ethnic groups (ethnic minorities, Roma, refugees and other categories of immigrants), such as in access to employment, health care and housing. On the other hand, the integration of foreigners in Lithuania is a specific objective only for foreigners who have been granted refugee status or subsidiary protection in Lithuania. There are no integration measures for other types of immigrants in Lithuania. Moreover, specific policy documents or national programmes aimed at integration mainly target ethnic minorities and Roma.

The activities undertaken and the programmes and projects implemented mainly represent descriptive approaches (e.g. focus on questions such as numbers of immigrants and their activities). This is closely related to the general lack of data on the content of migration and the ethnic structure of Lithuanian society. Nonetheless, the shift towards a focus on immigrants' adaptation to the host society, social networking and the main problems encountered by communities is very recent and fragmented, and is carried out largely by the public and academic institutions. Some developments could be regarded as progressive, such as the preparation in 2009 by the Office of Equal Opportunities Ombudsperson of a document entitled *Basics of Equality Statistics. National Action Plan for the*

Development of Equality Statistics[22], which could be seen as a step towards the systematic collection of data and their application in policy.

Recent projects and research focusing on minority and migrant integration in Lithuania could be regarded as the sole source of systematic information on immigration and integration processes, since they collect and summarise statistical data, create databases in relation to particular problems concerning integration (experiences of discrimination, level and targets of ethnic intolerance, measures aimed at integration in the labour market) and also seek to identify indicators for measuring integration processes.

Measuring the performance of state institutions is another way of using indicators to measure integration. Given the level of political awareness with regard to migration and integration policy in Lithuania, however, the scope for using such indicators as evaluation tools for policy or activities and for benchmarking the performance of institutions is limited. Moreover, the fragmented nature of the available monitoring tools means they cannot be seen as a systematic approach to monitoring integration processes.

As regards assessing the implementation of migrant integration policy, only one assessment of the Economic Migration Regulation Strategy has been carried out. The results of this evaluation were not put into practice, as the related action plan was not adopted. This illustrates that self-evaluation is not an indicator that is used in Lithuania. At the moment, no migrant integration strategy is in operation. Neither a plan nor any measures were approved for 2009-2010. Moreover, the use of integration measures is limited in practice, making it impracticable to evaluate the integration policy.

The policy measures to promote equal opportunities and integration remain scattered among different institutional agents and represent a fairly narrow scope. The main focus of social interventions is on promoting access to the labour market and cultural activities, with a lack of focus on social issues (e.g. social services, housing, community development, etc.). Even where the programmes include the concept of integration in their names or content, they do not provide an explicit definition of integration, nor do the results provide for assessment of the achievements in terms of integration.

Notes

1   Since Lithuania gained its independence net migration has been negative.
2   Data from the Migration Department under the Ministry of the Interior show that in 2009 foreigners living in Lithuania made up 0.98% of the total Lithuanian population.
3   Economic Migration Regulation Strategy. No. 416. Amended on 9 December 2009. Consulted at: http://www3.lrs.lt/pls/inter3/dokpaieska.showdoc_l?p_id=362754
4   Lithuanian migration policy is regulated by the Law on the Legal Status of Aliens (2004) and the Law on Citizenship (2002). The guidelines of migration policy were indirectly adopted in the country's long-term strategies (Long-term Development Strategy, Strategy of National Demographic Population Policy) and in the Economic Migration Regulation Strategy (2007), along with related documents (Resolution on Confirmation of Landmarks of Lithuanian Immigration Policy).
5   For example, in 2009 the Lithuanian Social Research Centre implemented the project Third Country Nationals in Lithuania: Assessment and Indexes of Integration Policy. For more information, see: *Ethnicity Studies 2009/2* (p. 17-39).

6   Although several new draft laws on ethnic minorities have been prepared since 1996, none of them was adopted. The documents relating to the adoption of the new law were consulted on 20 April 2010 at: http://www3.lrs.lt/pls/inter3/dokpaieska.susije_l?p_id=363451.

7   Law on the Legal Status of Aliens (IX-2206), 29 April 2004, amended on 22 July 2009. Consulted at: http://www3.lrs.lt/pls/inter3/dokpaieska.showdoc_l?p_id=356478

8   The main integration measures for those who have been granted refugee status or temporary protection are Lithuanian language courses, education, employment, provision of accommodation, social protection, health care, public information on the processes of integration. Art 110, Law on the Legal Status of Aliens (IX-2206), 29 April 2004, amended on 22 July 2009.

9   For example, showing the distribution of foreigners living in Lithuanian municipalities by type of residence permits, age, sex, citizenship, etc.

10 Statistics Lithuania. *Demographic Yearbook 2007.* Consulted at: http://www.stat.gov.lt/en/

11 Poviliūnas & Beresnevičiūtė (2006).

12 The following priorities are defined in the NR-SPSIS: to encourage participation in the labour market; to improve access to good-quality services; to eradicate child poverty and increase support for families; to reduce the shortcomings in education and teaching; and to reduce regional differences and improve regional management (Section 2).

13 Institute for Social Research, Lithuanian Centre for Adult Education and Information (2007).

14 In 2009, the Lithuanian Consumer Institute carried out the project *Let's Get to Know One Another*: http://www.vartotojai.lt/emien/5. In 2008 the Institute for Social Research and the Lithuanian Centre for Adult Education and Information carried out the study *Perceptions of Refugees in Lithuanian Society*: http://www.rppc.lt/news_read,920,lt.html

15 At the beginning of 2009 more than 25,000 immigrants from non-EU and EFTA countries were living in Lithuania.

16 http://www.ces.lt/en/wp-content/uploads/2010/03/Etniskumo_studijos_2009_2maketas+.pdf

17 http://www.ces.lt/en/wp-content/uploads/2010/03/Etniskumo_studijos_2009_2maketas+.pdf

18 http://www.ces.lt/en/wp-content/uploads/2010/03/Etniskumo_studijos_2009_2maketas+.pdf

19 Until the increase in labour immigration, media reports were dominated by the potential challenges raised by immigration based on examples of problematic experiences in Western European countries.

20 Given the absolute numbers of immigrants from China, it should be emphasised that they account for only a small part of total immigration in Lithuania.

21 Fréjutė-Rakauskienė (2009).

22 Okunevičiūtė Neverauskienė & Gruževskis (2009).

References

Annual Policy Report: Migration and Asylum in Lithuania in 2009 (2010). Vilnius: European Migration Network. Consulted at: http://www.emn.lt/uploads/documents/lt_policy_report_2009_final.pdf

Ethnicity Studies 2009/2. Migrant Integration: Third Country Nationals in Lithuania (2009) (p. 17-39). Vilnius: Institute for Social Research / Eugrimas.

Fréjutė-Rakauskienė, M (2009). *Ethnicity Studies 2009/1. Ethnic Intolerance in Lithuanian Press.* Vilnius: Institute for Social Research / Eugrimas.

Institute for Ethnic Studies at the Lithuanian Social Research Centre (2008). *Visuomenės nuomonės* apklausos rezultatai *[Results of public opinion poll]*. Vilnius: Institute for Ethnic Studies. Consulted at: http://www.ces.lt/2008/04/etniniu-tyrimu-centro-uzsakymu-uab-%E2%80%9Erait%E2%80%9C-atliktos-visuomenes-nuomones-apklausos-rezultatai/

Institute for Ethnic Studies at the Lithuanian Social Research Centre (2010). *Visuomenės nuomonės apklausos* rezultatai *[Results of public opinion poll]*. Vilnius: Institute for Ethnic Studies. Consulted at: http://www.ces.lt/wp-content/uploads/2010/09/LSTC_ETI_2010_LT-gyvent_apklausa_socdinstanc1.pdf

Institute for Social Research (2007). *Romų bendruomenės socialinės integracijos galimybių tyrimas [Opportunities for the social integration of the Roma Community]* (research report). Vilnius: Institute for Social Research. Consulted at: http://www.lygybe.lt/assets//Rom%C5%B3%20bendruomen%C4%97s%20socialin%C4%97s%20integracijos%20galimybi%C5%B3%20tyrimas.pdf

Institute for Social Research, Lithuanian Centre for Adult Education and Information (2007). *Pabėgėlių* integracijos procesų tyrimas. Valstybės paramos teikimo užsieniečių, gavusių prieglobstį Lietuvos Respublikoje, integracijai efektyvumo įvertinimas *[Assessment of the Social Integration Programme for Foreigners Been Granted Refugee Status or Temporary Protection in the Republic of Lithuania]*. Vilnius: Institute for Social Research. Consulted at: http://www.sppd.lt/lt/informacija/Leidiniai/

Leončikas, T. & K. Žibas (2010). Situation of new immigrants in Lithuania. In: *New immigrants in Estonia, Latvia and Lithuania.* Tallinn, Estonia: Legal Information Centre for Human Rights. Consulted at: http://www.lichr.ee/main/assets/epim-lichr.pdf

Migrant Integration Policy Index (2007). Brussels: British Council and Migration Policy Group. Consulted at: http://www.integrationindex.eu/

National Action Plan against poverty and social exclusion (NAP/inclusion) of Republic of Lithuania 2004-2006 (p. 19-22). Vilnius: Ministry of Social Security and Labour. Consulted on 20 April 2010 at: http://www.socmin.lt/index.php?-311688494

National Report of Lithuania on Social Protection and Social Inclusion Strategies 2008-2010. Vilnius: Ministry of Social Security and Labour. Consulted at: http://www.socmin.lt/index.php?-311688494

National Report on Strategies for Social Protection and Social Inclusion 2006-2008 with the Annex Tasks and Measures in Reducing Poverty and Social Exclusion (NRSSPSI) (2006). Brussels/Luxembourg: European Commission. Consulted at: http://ec.europa.eu/employment_social/social_inclusion/docs/2006/nap/lithuania_en.pdf

Okunevičiūtė Neverauskienė, L. & B. Gruževskis (2009). *Lygybės* statistikos pagrindai. Nacionalinis lygybės statistikos rengimo veiksmų planas. Vilnius: Lithuanian Social Research Centre / Eugrimas. Consulted (in Lithuanian) at: http://www.lygybe.lt/assets/Lygybes_statistika_maketas.pdf

Poviliūnas, A. & V. Beresnevičiūtė (2006). *'Feeding in' and 'Feeding out', and Integrating Immigrants and Ethnic Minorities. Lithuania. A Study of National Policies.* Consulted at: http://www.peer-review-social-inclusion.net/policy-assessment-activities/reports/second-semester-2006/second-semester-reports-2006/lithuania_2_06

Public Policy and Management Institute (2009). *Evaluation of the Effectiveness of the Economic Migration Regulation Strategy and Preparation of Recommendations for the Action Plan for 2009-2012.* Vilnius: Public Policy and Management Institute. Consulted at: http://www.vpvi.lt/en/evaluation-of-the-effectiveness-of-economic-migration-regulation-strategy-and-preparation-of-recommendations-for-the-action-plan-for-2009-201/?start=0

Laws

Law on Social Integration of the Disabled (I-2044). Amended on 1 July 2010. Consulted at: http://www3.lrs.lt/
pls/inter2/dokpaieska.showdoc_l?p_id=373285

Law on the Legal Status of Aliens (1x-2206). Amended on 22 July 2009. Consulted at: http://www3.lrs.lt/pls/
inter3/dokpaieska.showdoc_l?p_id=356478

Law on Citizenship (1x-1078). Amended on 19 March 2009 – No. x1-205. Consulted at: http://www3.lrs.lt/
pls/inter3/dokpaieska.showdoc_l?p_id=347706

Programmes and strategies

Nacionalinė antidiskriminacinė 2006-2008 metų programa [National Antidiscrimination Programme 2006-2008].
No. 907, 19 September 2009.2006, Government of the Republic of Lithuania.

Nacionalinė antidiskriminacinė 2009-2011 metų programa [National Antidiscrimination Programme 2009-2011].
No. 317, 15 April 2009, Government of the Republic of Lithuania.

National Action Plan against poverty and social exclusion (nap/inclusion) of Republic of Lithuania 2004-2006.
Consulted at: http://www.socmin.lt/index.php?-311688494

*Nutarimas dėl ekonominės migracijos reguliavimo strategijos ir jos įgyvendinimo priemonių 2007-2008 metų plano
patvirtinimo [Economic Migration Regulation Strategy].* No. 416. Amended on 9 December 2009. Consulted
at: http://www3.lrs.lt/pls/inter3/dokpaieska.showdoc_l?p_id=362754

*Nutarimas dėl Lietuvos imigracijos politikos gairių patvirtinimo [Resolution on Confirmation of Landmarks of
Lithuanian Migration Policy].* 3 December 2008, No. 1317. Consulted at: http://www.lrv.lt/bylos/Teises_
aktai/2008/12/11884.doc

*Romų integracijos į Lietuvos visuomenę 2008-2010 metų programa [Programme for Roma Integration into Lithuanian
Society 2008-2010].* No. 309, 26 March 2008, Government of the Republic of Lithuania. Consulted
at: http://www3.lrs.lt/pls/inter3/dokpaieska.showdoc_l?p_id=317530&p_query=Rom%F8%20
integracijos%20i%20Lietuvos%20visuomen%E6%202008-2010%20programa&p_tr2=2

*Romų integracijos į Lietuvos visuomenę 2000-2004 metų programa [Programme for Roma Integration into Lithuanian
Society 2000-2004].* No. 759, 1 July 2000, Government of the Republic of Lithuania.

*Tautinių mažumų integracijos į Lietuvos visuomenę 2005-2010 metų programa [Programme for the Integration of
Ethnic Minorities into Lithuanian Society 2005-2010].* No. 703, 8 June 2004. Government of the Republic of
Lithuania.

Institutions

Department of Statistics of the Government of the Republic of Lithuania. *Demographic Yearbook 2007,*
Vilnius. Consulted at: http://www.stat.gov.lt/en/

Ministry of Social Security and Labour: http://www.socmin.lt/index.php?-717884322

Lithuanian Consumer Institute: http://www.vartotojai.lt/emien/5

Migration Department of the Ministry of the Interior: http://www.migracija.lt/

12   Monitoring integration in the Netherlands

Arjen Verweij and Rob Bijl

12.1   Introduction

Brief historical overview of migration in the Netherlands

It was only in the second half of the 20th century that the Netherlands became familiar
with a substantial influx of migrants. In the 1950s, when the former Dutch colony of the
Dutch East Indies became an independent state – Indonesia – a group of 'repatriates'
arrived in the Netherlands. They were followed in the 1960s by migrant labourers (guest
workers) from the Mediterranean. Smaller contingents also began arriving from Italy,
Greece, Spain and Portugal, later followed by more substantial contingents from Turkey
and Morocco. In the 1970s, when the Dutch colony of Surinam gained independence, a
large proportion of the Surinamese population left their home country and moved to
the Netherlands.

Apart from the groups mentioned above, the Netherlands has a substantial group of
migrants within its borders originating from the Netherlands Antilles and, more recently, guest workers from Central and East European countries such as Poland, Bulgaria,
Estonia, etc. The last category of importance are political refugees; they are a varied
group originating from countries such as Iraq, Iran, Somalia, Afghanistan, etc.

Figure 12.1

Population of the Netherlands by ethnic origin[a], 1950-2010 (in numbers)

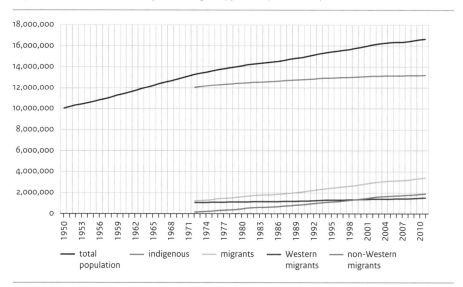

a   Based on country of birth and country of birth of (at least one of) the parents.

Source: Statistics Netherlands

At the moment just over 11% of the Dutch population belong to 'non-Western minorities', while a further 9% are of (non-Dutch) Western descent.

The non-Western population are not evenly distributed across the Netherlands, but are
heavily concentrated in the major cities in the west of the country, and within these
cities in specific – deprived – neighbourhoods. This results in locally high (and rising)
proportions of non-Western migrants living in specific areas. In the three major cities
Amsterdam, Rotterdam and The Hague, non-Western minorities make up over a third
of the population (see figure 12.2). The percentages are even higher in specific neighbourhoods within these cities: The Hague has neighbourhoods were over 90% of the
population is of non-Western descent.

Figure 12.2

Percentage of non-Western immigrants in the four largest cities in the Netherlands, 1 January 2010

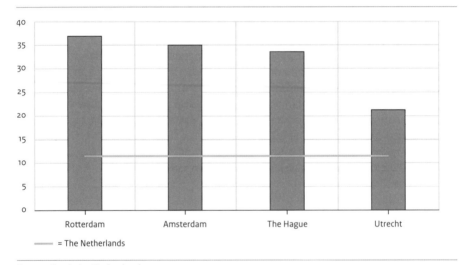

—— = The Netherlands

Source: Statistics Netherlands

12.2 Overview of Dutch policy

The period of non-intervention (from the 1950s to the 1970s)

While first and second-generation immigrants in the Netherlands currently make up a
fifth of the total population of the Netherlands, it took some time before the Dutch government developed an active integration policy.

The first group of immigrants integrated into Dutch society without problems and without active government involvement. The majority of the migrants from the Dutch East
Indies spoke the Dutch language well, were relatively well educated, were familiar with
the Dutch culture and came to the Netherlands with the intention of a permanent stay.
This group integrated fairly smoothly into Dutch society. The exception was a specific

ethnic group from the Indonesian archipelago: the Moluccans came to the Netherlands with a view to staying temporarily until they had established their own independent republic (the Republik Maluko Selatan) in the former Dutch East Indies. As a result, they lived segregated from Dutch society (at first in 'camps', later in specifically Moluccan neighbourhoods) for several decades, with the objective of strengthening their internal bonds and making ready to return to the Indonesian archipelago as soon as their own republic had been founded. This idea of an independent homeland gradually faded during the last decades of the 20th century and was finally abolished in the first decade of the new millennium.

In neither case did the Dutch government see a need for an integration policy: the majority of the Indonesian Dutch integrated without problems, while the Moluccans were staying 'only temporarily' in the Netherlands.

This view did not change substantially when labour migrants began to arrive in the early 1960s. The idea – held by the labour migrants themselves as well as by the Dutch government – was that labour migration was a temporary phenomenon. For the early migrants, from Spain, Italy, Greece and Portugal, this assumption proved to be correct: the majority returned to their homeland within a few years. For the Turks and Moroccans who arrived later, however, this assumption increasingly proved erroneous. Initially, some did return to their homeland within a few years, but over time the intended short stay took on more and more permanent features for an increasing proportion of the immigrant groups . This was due partly to the increasing numbers of (Turkish and Moroccan) immigrants who came to the Netherlands for reasons of family reunification and family formation.

The labour migration of the 1970s was followed by a substantial influx of Surinamese people who migrated to the Netherlands in anticipation of the imminent independence of the former Dutch colony.

Nevertheless, the notion that the Netherlands had in reality developed into a nation with a substantial and more or less permanent immigrant population only became apparent after the publication of an advisory report to the Dutch government by the leading scientific advisory body in the Netherlands – the Scientific Council for Government Policy (WRR) – in 1979 (WRR 1979). The Council concluded that a substantial proportion of the immigrants in the Netherlands would not return to their country of origin *and* that the Dutch government therefore needed to develop a policy to reduce the social and cultural deprivation of immigrants in the Netherlands. In response to this report the Dutch government launched an integration policy in the mid-1980s.

The period of an active integration policy (the 1980s onwards)
In September 1983 the Christian Democratic/Liberal coalition government under prime minister Ruud Lubbers (Lubbers I) published a policy memorandum (the *Minderhedennota*, 1983) in which the government described the newly developed policy on (ethnic) minorities.

Briefly, the aim of the policy was the creation of a society in which minorities, both as a group and individually, had equal opportunities and an equal social position to indigenous Dutch citizens. This main objective was broken down into three subsidiary objectives:

a   fostering emancipation of minorities;
b   reducing social and economic deprivation of minorities;
c   suppression of discrimination and improving the legal position of minorities.

In this newly developed integration policy, the notion of *proportionality* formed both the central idea *and* the central touchstone for monitoring whether or not and to what extent the policy was successful. The long-term objective of the Dutch integration policy was (and remains) that ethnic minorities should participate in proportion to their share in the total Dutch population in key central institutions such as labour market, education and housing. This overall goal was broken down into several specific objectives. For example: the factual overrepresentation of minorities in the unemployment figures (illustrated by unemployment rates) should be reduced until it is in proportion to their share in the labour force; the factual underrepresentation in higher forms of education should be rectified by increasing their participation in proportion to their share in the population of compulsory school age; the overrepresentation in drop-out rates in secondary education should be reduced to the average for the population as a whole; their overrepresentation in social rented housing should be reduced to a proportionate percentage, and so on.

Of course, the Dutch government realized that these kinds of long-term objectives could not be achieved as long as the socioeconomic position of minority groups was inferior to that of the indigenous Dutch. It is after all very unrealistic to expect ethnic minorities to have equal unemployment rates to indigenous Dutch citizens as long as the average education of minorities lags behind that of the native population, or to expect that the overrepresentation in social rented housing will fall as long as the average education of minorities is lower than that of the native Dutch, resulting in lower employment and income levels.[1]
Therefore the relative position of ethnic minorities to *comparable* indigenous categories is used to define the short-term or intermediate goals. This means for example that comparisons are made within education levels (unemployment rates of low-skilled minorities are compared to the unemployment rate of low-skilled Dutch citizens), or in more general terms, it means that the analysis will be controlled for background variables that help determine the outcome. In general this comparison leads to the conclusion that a part of the deprivation can be accounted for by socioeconomic background variables, but that a residual effect remains which can *not* be explained by socioeconomic differences between minority groups and the indigenous Dutch reference group.

The standard method used by the Dutch government to establish its objectives has two different dimensions. The first dimension is the afore mentioned policy of reducing social deprivation (*achterstand*) by increasing social, economic and cultural capital. Education is seen as the key variable for improving the social position of individuals and (ethnic) groups in the meritocratic Western society. Dutch language proficiency is seen as a crucial factor here.

The second approach is to eliminate discrimination (*achterstelling*). This approach targets forms of direct discrimination as well as indirect or institutional discrimination.

Target groups

This brings us to the question of which ethnic groups are the targets of the Dutch integration policy. When the integration policy was first launched, in the 1980s, the target group was defined using three separate criteria. The formal target group existed of
a) ethnic categories, which b) on average occupied a low position in the socioeconomic stratification of Dutch society, and c) whose settlement and residence in the Netherlands had such a direct historical or economic relationship with Dutch society that the Dutch government felt a moral obligation to look after these categories.

In practice this implied that groups originating from (former) Dutch colonies (Moluccans, Surinamese and Antilleans); countries where the Dutch actively recruited labour migrants (Cape Verde, Greece, Italy, (former) Yugoslavia, Morocco, Portugal, Spain, Tunisia, Turkey); and two internationally recognised groups (refugees and gypsies) formed the target groups of the integration policy. Later the definition of 'target group' was broadened to include

a (all) *non-Western* immigrants[2] and their descendants to the second generation; and
b refugees.

In practice, policy and media attention focuses on the so-called 'traditional' immigrant groups (people of Turkish, Moroccan, Surinamese and Antillean origin), the newly arrived refugee groups (Iranians, Iraqis, Somalis, Afghans) and, more recently, (labour) migrants from the new Central and Eastern European member states of the European Union (Poles, Slovaks, Bulgarians).

At present, non-Western immigrants make up 11.2% of the Dutch population, while Western migrants account for a further 9,1%. In other words: more than one in every five inhabitants of the Netherlands has an immigrant background (see table 12.1).

Table 12.1

Population of the Netherlands by ethnic group, 1 January 2010 (in numbers x 1,000 and in percentages)

		total	%
total		16,575	100.0
indigenous Dutch		13,215	79.7
non-Western immigrants		1,858	11.2
of which:	*traditional groups*		
	Turkey	384	2.3
	Morocco	349	2.1
	Suriname	342	2.1
	Netherlands Antilles	138	0.8
	new groups		
	Afghanistan	32	0.2
	Iraq	52	0.3
	Iran	39	0.2
	Somalia	27	0.2
Western immigrants		1,501	9.1

Source: Statistics Netherlands

Integration: the concept

In Dutch integration policy and the monitoring of that policy, integration is seen as a multi-dimensional concept. The two major dimensions are socioeconomic (or structural) integration and ethno-cultural (or cultural) integration. The former dimension covers themes such as education, labour market position, income and housing; the latter covers topics such as attitudes and beliefs in relation to interethnic contacts, interethnic friendships and/or marriages of children (especially daughters), the position of women within the household (the 'modernity of beliefs'), and so on.

In the first period of the Dutch integration policy (the 1980s and 90s) multiculturalism was the dominant paradigm: 'integration whilst retaining one's own culture' was the central motto of the Dutch policy, and integration was characterized as a two-way process. In the late 1990s the focus shifted towards a more assimilatory approach: multiculturalism was seen as too 'soft' and as hampering integration, and the general feeling was that society had a right to demand that 'newcomers' adapt their lifestyles to Dutch mainstream values and beliefs.

This also led to a stricter immigration policy: a 'civic integration' requirement introduced for new and old immigrants. Under this new system, immigrants were required to follow a citizenship course leading to an exam and a contract. Key subjects were proficiency in the Dutch language and knowledge of Dutch society. Since 2006 foreign nationals (non-EU residents) wanting to settle in the Netherlands for a prolonged period have been obliged to take (and pass) the civic integration examination in their country of origin in order to obtain a residence permit. They have to meet certain minimum standards in terms of civic integration as well as linguistic competences before they are allowed to enter the country.

Finally, at the start of the policy in the 1980s there was a consensus that the aim should be to achieve integration using *general* instruments. Specific instruments should be confined to a minimum. Responsibility for the policy was assigned to a coordinating minister, not always from the same ministry (Ministry of the Interior, Ministry of Justice, Ministry of Housing, Communities and Integration, and since 2010 the Ministry of the Interior once again).

The coalition of liberals, Christian Democrats and populist parties which took office in 2010 to some extent fits in with this tradition and at the same time pushes it to its extremes: the policy objective is to eliminate autonomous integration policy as such within the next five years. The integration goals should from that point on be achieved through the general policy instruments: unemployment among minorities will be part of the general labour market policy, reducing drop-out rates in secondary education will be a responsibility of the Minister of Education, and so on. Whether there will still be a coordinating minister is unclear at present.

Summary

Looking back over the past few decades, we can conclude that Dutch integration policy has developed from one of de facto non-interference into a policy where immigrants have to comply with fairly strict requirements. At the same time, Dutch integration policies are also characterized by a number of stable features; for example, the conceptual framework of a structural and cultural dimension is still intact.

12.3   Monitoring integration in the Netherlands

Monitoring of the integration process in the Netherlands started in the mid-1980s. The first report (Roelandt & Veenman 1986) of the 'Accessibility and Proportionality Reporting System' (*Rapportagesysteem Toegankelijkheid en Evenredigheid*) was published in 1986, which was in fact the monitoring system (before the term existed) put in place by the Dutch government to provide policymakers with adequate information. In the early years the system consisted of a descriptive part which was compiled by Statistics Netherlands (CBS) in collaboration with Erasmus University Rotterdam and an analytical part compiled by Erasmus University Rotterdam. This structure is still intact today, although the partners have changed: the Netherlands Institute for Social Research | SCP and Statistics Netherlands are currently the partners responsible for gathering and publishing the information.

In the early years operationalizing a meaningful set of indicators and systematizing and building up sources was one of the major challenges of the project. At the start of the project researchers simply had to do the best they could using the available data. They had to draw largely on data from general registers and surveys, for example national labour market surveys. A major problem was that these kinds of sources and surveys had several shortcomings for use as a basis for monitoring the socioeconomic and ethno-cultural position of minority groups in the Netherlands. To begin with, the sample sizes were often too small to generate reliable results for small (ethnic) categories, stratified sampling methods were not common, questionnaires were only in Dutch, and so on. However, the biggest obstacle was the lack of solid (and standardized) ethnic identification.

Ethnic identification

One of the most common ethnic identifiers in de mid 1980s was *nationality*: this identifier was available in most registers and surveys. In the Dutch context, however, nationality had (and still has) major shortcomings, since a high proportion of ethnic minorities in the Netherlands came from former Dutch colonies and overseas territories (Netherlands Antilles) and therefore held Dutch nationality. Identification of ethnic groups on the basis of nationality consequently resulted in a vast underestimation of the size of the ethnic minority population in the Netherlands.

Following extensive research to determine the most reliable and valid method for establishing ethnicity (Roelandt & Veenman 1991; Verweij & Roelandt 1991; Verweij 1992), the Dutch government decided in 1992 to introduce a standard identification method in which ethnic origin (or background) was based upon a combination of three objective indicators:
a   country of birth;
b   mother's country of birth; and
c   father's country of birth.
Using this method it was possible to identify immigrants (the first generation) and their children (the second generation), who at that time formed the majority of the immigrant population in the Netherlands. People with at least one foreign-born parent are defined as second-generation immigrants. The possibility of using subjective (self-)identification as an extra indicator was rejected on grounds of privacy considerations (Ministry of Internal Affairs 1992). Apart from this consideration, however, self-identification has another shortcoming; research (Verweij & Roelandt 1991) showed that better integrated[3] migrants tended to identify themselves more often as indigenous Dutch rather than belonging to their country of origin than less well-integrated migrants. In combination with a policy aimed at proportional participation, this meant that self-identification was not a suitable means of identifying ethnic groups. After all, selectivity in identification would make it impossible to attain the goals of the integration policy.

As a consequence of the decision to use the (objective) country of birth of the person themselves and of their parents as identifiers, third-generation migrants (and beyond) are identified in the Dutch system as indigenous Dutch. This also applies for specific ethnic groups (such as Moluccans and Roma) who cannot be pinned down to a specific country of origin, and thus (to the extent that they were born in the Netherlands) are identified as indigenous Dutch.
After Statistics Netherlands and, after the publication of a detailed protocol by order of the government in 1993 (Den Heeten & Verweij 1993), municipalities also adopted this

method, thus bringing the de facto establishment of a uniform identification system in registers and national surveys.

Sources

The central and regional/local Population Registers (Registers of Births, Marriages and Deaths) in the Netherlands contain information on country of birth and country of birth of both parents. In addition, by combining and analyzing the register information of the parents (data fusion), it is possible to generate insight in the land of birth of the great-parents of each inhabitant legally residing in the Netherlands and by doing so in the actual size and geographical location of the third generation.[4]

This register occupies a central position within the information structure on integration of ethnic minorities in the Netherlands. It provides up-to-date, precise and detailed information on the size, growth, decline and composition of ethnic groups at all geo-graphical levels. Information is available not only on total numbers of ethnic groups, but also on the composition of the groups. For example, the breakdown by gender, age, generation (first or second) is available for the Netherlands as a whole, but also for regions, cities and neighbourhoods. By combining the indexes of family members infor-mation can be obtained at both individual and household level.

Another important function is as a survey sampling frame. The Population Register ena-bles stratified sampling designs to be designed (with desired strata/representation of different ethnic groups), facilitates the performance of nonresponse analyses and pro-vides a strong basis for weighting data sets.

All in all, the Population Register plays a crucial role within the information structure for monitoring the integration of ethnic minority groups in the Netherlands.

Since the early 1990s most general surveys, like the Labour Force Survey by Statistics Netherlands, contain questions on the country of birth of respondents and their parents (as stated above) and in principle are therefore suitable sources of information on the – in this example: labour market – position of ethnic minorities. Nevertheless, in practice the possibilities offered by general surveys are limited. They suffer from the limitation of different survey sample methods and sizes. For example, the numbers of minorities in the response to general surveys could be too small to provide reliable information, especially when information is needed on sub-categories (such as 'older women', 'un-employed youngsters', 'men aged between 40 and 45 years', etc.). Another limitation of general surveys can be selectivity in response due to language problems (Dutch questionnaires or Dutch interviewers), ethnic bias and weaknesses in the recruitment strategy, or the use of specific survey methods (telephone interviews tend to produce relatively high nonresponse rates for minority groups, as telephone penetration – or at least *known* telephone numbers – is lower among minority groups than for the indig-enous Dutch population).

To resolve these problems, since 1988 a specific survey (Survey of Integration of Minor-ity Groups, SIM) has been held every four years among the four largest – 'traditional' – minority groups (people of Turkish, Moroccan, Surinamese and Antillean origin) and an indigenous Dutch reference group. In addition, since 2005 an equivalent survey has been in operation for the 'new groups' (Survey of Integration of New Groups, SING). These surveys are specifically designed to provide information for the development, adjustment and evaluation of integration policy in the Netherlands. This implies that the SIM and SING questionnaires contain questions on socioeconomic topics as well as on ethno-cultural aspects. The samples in these surveys are large enough to generate reliable insight at the national and regional level into the position of the various ethnic groups as well as socioeconomic subgroups (such as gender, age, education, etc.).

These specific surveys have traditionally focused on a wide variety of dimensions of participation and social status. The questionnaires cover topics such as education, employment and income (including remittances to the country of origin), Dutch language skills, social contacts and spare time activities, cultural integration, media and mass communication, interethnic contacts and perceptions, perceived acceptance, religion and political participation. The data collected play a central role in monitoring the integration of ethnic groups in Dutch society in both the socioeconomic and ethno-cultural dimension. For example, the time series generate an insight into the rise in education levels between and within the different minority groups: distinguishing first and second-generation migrants makes it possible to observe intergenerational mobility.

The availability of a native Dutch reference group also makes it possible to draw direct conclusions as to whether the proportionality that is the central objective of Dutch integration policy is being achieved. This applies both for long-term proportionality, measured by overall group averages, and for short-term proportionality in relation to indigenous categories.

Recent developments

Essentially, the SIM and SING surveys provided information on topics where the general sources were unable to provide adequate insights, and thus played a crucial role in the policy information structure in the Netherlands. However, during the last decade a new development came into vogue: linking microdata using Personal Identification Numbers (PIN) made new information available. Statistics Netherlands was able to use this method to build a new virtual census,[5] whereas the last official census in the Netherlands dates from 1971 when, following strong protests and resistance during the fieldwork for that edition, the census was abolished.

By combining information from different sources (register and survey data) at microlevel Statistics Netherlands actually creates new information. Using this structure it is possible, for example, to present information on unemployment benefits by ethnic group, while the social security registers themselves contain no information on ethnic origin at all. They do however contain PINs. Within the legal constraints concerning privacy, Statistics Netherlands is able to combine these data with the information held in the Population Register on ethnic origin to produce anonymized statistics, thereby adding new information to the existing data stock.

This procedure makes even clearer the importance of the ethnic identification variables in and the central role of the Population Register in providing information on ethnic minorities in the Netherlands.

This development subsequently triggered another process. A deliberate choice has been made to focus as far as possible in the future on register data to obtain information on objective demographic and socioeconomic information, and to use surveys solely as a source of subjective information such as attitudes, opinions and perceptions. Data fusion – the combination of register data and survey at micro-level using PIN – is expected to provide a very rich information structure.

The benefits of this procedure are that the advantages of register data – a complete and integral image with no ambiguities and no confidence intervals; virtually no time lag; cheap – are combined with the possibilities offered by survey data. This process has only just started, but the expectations are high.

Indicator set

All in all, the monitoring system in the Netherlands is comprehensive. It consists of a large number of sources, covers a vast array of topics and comprises a multitude of indicators. And although at the start of the integration policy a system of core indicators was defined (Ministry of Internal Affairs 1992), this format was gradually abandoned. As a consequence, there is currently no formal selection of core indicators or central indicators. This does not however alter the fact that in practice education and labour market position are perceived as very (or possibly: the most) important aspects for integration.

Instead of a limited number of core indicators, the Dutch monitoring system could best be characterized as an information structure which consists of a wide variety of sources, variables and indicators. Since the system goes back to the mid-1980s, it not only enables the socio-economic and ethno-cultural position of minority groups to be analyzed, but because the system has been consistent over time, it also permits analysis of developments in these fields over an extended period.

Information is available not only on the socioeconomic topics mentioned above, such as labour market position (e.g. labour participation, unemployment rates, occupation and occupational levels, self employment), income (income source, net earnings, benefit dependency, etc.) and education (education levels, drop-out rates in higher education, Dutch language proficiency, etc.), but also in relation to demographics (household composition, birth and fertility rates), ethno-cultural features (e.g. modernity of beliefs, interethnic contacts), objective and perceived health, crime rates and housing situation. Moreover, these features can be crossed with gender, age and generation, enabling the integration of subcategories to be monitored and the absolute and comparative position to be compared between and within ethnic categories. The education levels of second-generation migrants are traditionally compared to the education levels of the first generation and to the average education level of natives of the same age, i.e. both intergenerational and intragenerational comparisons.

Of course, while monitoring the integration of ethnic groups is a key objective, gaining a better insight into processes and causal connections is every bit as important as the monitoring itself, since it provides a necessary basis for an effective policy. For example, it is not enough to know that non-Western pupils have higher drop-out rates in secondary education; for an effective approach to reducing drop-out rates it is essential to know *why* they are disproportional high; only then do policymakers have the tools to develop effective interventions.

The two sides mentioned here (descriptive and explanatory research), are still reflected in the policy information structure. By turns, Statistics Netherlands and the Netherlands Institute for Social Research | scp publish an annual report on integration.[6] These reports reflect the twofold aspirations of the reports and the information structure: both descriptive and as a source of analysis.

These questions are only partially answered by monitoring information: in the Netherlands, as in other countries, universities, advisory councils and other research organizations carry out a wide variety of research projects in this field, quantitative as well as qualitative, cross-sectional as well as longitudinal, ad hoc as well as programmed. Furthermore, local research is carried out periodically by local authorities (e.g. by the research institutes in the major cities or by sectoral ministries such as the Ministry of Social Affairs and Employment (for example by gathering data on discrimination on the labour market) or the Ministry of Education, Culture and Science (e.g. data on drop-out rates in secondary education). And although these projects are of the utmost importance for acquiring scientific as well as applied knowledge, within the scope of this book (the focus of which is after all on monitoring[7]) we will not dwell at length on these forms of research. It is worth noting that most of these initiatives tend to use the standard ethnic identification and definitions, and therefore provide a useful benchmark for comparison with other sources.

As described above, the Netherlands has a fairly stable information structure with regard to integration of ethnic minorities, in which labour market position and education are traditionally considered as key indicators for integration. The attention for other fields varies over time. For example, attention for the housing position of minority groups declined in the 1990s, after studies in the 1980s had concluded that deprivation on the housing market was relatively low in comparison with the situation on the labour market and in education. Over the last decade, the growing interest in the scale and effects of spatial segregation has triggered a revival of attention for the position of minorities on the housing market.

Another area that has received varying amounts of attention over time are differences in health status between ethnic groups. A fairly new topic, directly related to the transformation from multiculturalism to a more assimilationist approach, is the attention for civic integration.

Information on these new subjects is gathered in surveys as well as by (linking) registers.

12.4 Concluding remarks

The monitoring of integration in the Netherlands goes back to the mid-1980s. After a few years the Dutch government decided in the early 1990s to introduce a standard identification method and a uniform definition of the target groups of integration policy.

The identification method, based on three objective criteria (country of birth, country of mother's birth and country of father's birth), formed the backbone of the Dutch monitoring system in the early period. It made it possible to combine information from a wide range of sources to form a coherent picture. This gave a strong impulse to the development of a more mature and useful monitoring system.

A subsequent and perhaps even more important incentive for the further development of the monitoring system was the introduction of the linking of different sources at micro-level based on Personal Identification Numbers (PIN). This method provides reliable data, within a flexible structure and in a cost-effective way. Since the information involved is very sensitive, a precondition is that this kind of information should be compiled under the strictest precautions. Privacy must be respected at all times, so only anonymized results are published; combination of original data files is only permitted if it is done in an encrypted and depersonalized way, and access to the files is restricted to a minimal number of professionals under the strictest security measures. Although the organization of the process demands ample and careful attention, it will pay off in the end.

Monitoring information plays a major role within the Dutch integration policy, at national as well as local level. Whether or not policy goals are (ultimately) achieved, or whether or not (monitored) developments are in line with policy objectives, are standard topics of debate in Parliament and city councils.

In the coming period, the continued exploration of the possibilities offered by data fusion could lead to a reduction of the importance of surveys as a source of information through enrichment of the survey content with register data. This method could lead to a reduction in questionnaire-based surveys and time spent conducting interviews, thereby saving costs of field research without loss of information or quality.

Notes

1   A proportion of the ethnic minorities in the Netherlands – the 'guest workers' from the 1960s – were recruited deliberately because of their low skill levels!
2   With the exception of Japanese persons and persons born in the former Dutch Indies.
3   Higher income groups.
4   Recent research by Statistics Netherlands shows that third-generation non-Western immigrants are virtually non-existent: only 55,000 non-Westerners belong to the third generation (Goedhuys et al. 2010).
5   See: Schulte Nordholt et al. (2004).
6   For an example see: Gijsberts & Dagevos (2009).
7   Monitoring: the systematic and periodic measurement of relevant characteristics.

References

Gijsberts, M. & J. Dagevos (eds.) (2009). *At home in the Netherlands? Trends in integration of non-Western migrants, Annual Report on Integration 2009*. The Hague: Netherlands Institute for Social Research | scp.

Goedhuys, M., T. König & K. Geertjes (2010). *Verkenning niet-westerse derde generatie*. Voorburg/Heerlen: Statistics Netherlands.

Den Heeten, J. & A.O. Verweij (1993). *Identificatie en registratie van etnische herkomst. Een handleiding voor registratie en beleid*. The Hague: vng uitgeverij.

Ministry of Internal Affairs (1983). *Minderhedennota*. Tweede Kamer (Chamber of Representatives) 1982-1983, 16102, nos. 20-21, The Hague.

Ministry of Internal Affairs (1992). *Minderhedenbeleid 1992. Registratie en rapportage minderhedenbeleid*. Tweede Kamer (Chamber of Representatives) 1991-1992, 22 314, no. 11.

Roelandt, Th. & J. Veenman (1986). *Minderheden: sociale positie en voorzieningengebruik. Achtergrondstudie 1986 van het rapportagesysteem Toegankelijkheid en Evenredigheid*. Rotterdam: Erasmus University, Institute for Sociological and Economic Research (iseo).

Roelandt, Th. & J.Veenman (1991). *Beter meten 3. Identificatie en classificatie van allochtone personen in registraties en onderzoeken*. Rotterdam: Erasmus University, Institute for Sociological and Economic Research (iseo).

Schulte Nordholt, E., M. Hartgers & R. Gircour (2004). *The Dutch Virtual Census of 2001. Analysis and Methodology*. Voorburg/Heerlen: Statistics Netherlands.

Verweij, A.O. & Th. Roelandt (1991). *Identificatie van Allochtonen. Een haalbaarheidsanalyse*. Rotterdam: Erasmus University, Institute for Sociological and Economic Research (iseo).

Verweij, A.O. (1992). *Koppelen of ontsporen? Lokale registraties en de bruikbaarheid voor het minderhedenbeleid*. Rotterdam: Erasmus University, Institute for Sociological and Economic Research (iseo).

wrr (1979). *Etnische Minderheden*. The Hague: Scientific Council for Government Policy (wrr).

13 Monitoring integration in Norway[1]

Marcus Langberg Smestad

13.1 Introduction

13.1.1 Overview

The following text gives an overview of the Norwegian system for gauging the effects of integration policy measures. The focus is on describing what is unique about the Norwegian system, in that the Government's goals for social inclusion are measured using good-quality register data.

The first section (13.1) gives a general overview of integration policy in Norway today. The terms used are also explained and an overview is given of the current situation of the immigrant population. Measuring the effects of various policy measures requires good-quality register data as well as regular monitoring. These data are mainly analysed and published by Statistics Norway, and to some extent by the Directorate of Integration and Diversity (IMDi). The second section (13.2) provides a basic insight into what is being done in this field. The third section (13.3) focuses on the Norwegian government's 'goals for social inclusion' which provide a tool for ensuring coordinated policy implementation and a system for monitoring the effects of policy measures on the immigrant population. In addition, the use of register data is illustrated. This section also describes the process by which the goals were developed and the specific system of mainstreaming and sector responsibility of the various ministries. Lastly, two examples of specific goals are presented together with their respective indicators. Section 13.4 presents a brief summary and highlights key areas in the Norwegian system for monitoring integration.

13.1.2 Brief description of integration policy in Norway

The aim of Norwegian integration policy is to foster the development of an inclusive and diverse society. In accordance with the principles of the Norwegian welfare state, all persons living in Norway have the same rights, obligations and opportunities, regardless of their ethnic background, gender, religion, sexual orientation or functional ability. Equal rights, equal opportunities, solidarity, fairness and equitable wealth distribution are fundamental values which underpin the government's integration policy.

An important goal for the government is to ensure that every person living in Norway has an equal opportunity to participate in society. The integration policy aims to enable immigrants to make use of their resources in working life and general society as quickly as possible.

In addition, the current policy seeks to prevent the development of a class-divided society where persons from migrant backgrounds have poorer living conditions and a lower rate of social participation than the population in general.

The following four areas are perceived as central in integrating the immigrant population:

- Employment is of major importance for each individual's living conditions and financial situation. Ensuring employment for everyone is one of the biggest factors in reducing social differences. The workplace is an important arena for interpersonal contact and thus one of the main meeting places for immigrants and the native population. The government encourages and supports a more inclusive working environment that includes all types of people, where the expectation is that each and every person participates to the best of their abilities. The first task for newly arrived immigrants is to learn the Norwegian language and become familiar with Norwegian society. Guaranteeing the right and obligation to participate in instruction in the Norwegian language and an introductory programme for refugees are two important measures that help speed up the process of enabling immigrants and refugees to rapidly enter the labour market and become self-reliant.
- A current policy goal is that all children and young people should have the same rights and opportunities to develop, regardless of their parents' financial situation, migrant background, skin colour, education or geographical background. Ensuring that children and young people with migrant backgrounds have a good basis for contributing to and participating in society is considered key.
- An inclusive society requires equal rights and opportunities between the genders. It is an expressed policy intention to achieve gender equality for everyone in Norway, including the immigrant population. Double discrimination is a genuine problem for women with migrant backgrounds, who may find themselves subjected to discrimination as both women and immigrants.
- All inhabitants of Norway must have equal opportunities to participate in political and voluntary organisations, in neighbourhood activities and the local community. Every person has an independent responsibility to use these meeting places and to become involved in their own local community, in their children's leisure activities and in the political and civilian communities. Absence of racism and discrimination is a requirement for participation on equal terms.

13.1.3   Definition of integration

It is generally recognised that the concept of integration covers a very complex process of constant change in an evolving society.
In the Norwegian context, integration should be seen as a two-way process which involves and places duties and obligations on both the immigrant and the host society in order to create and foster an inclusive environment. This understanding serves as a starting point for the development of all policy measures. Recognising this implies that immigrants must adapt to the demands of Norwegian society, but without necessarily

abandoning their own cultural identity. Conversely, it also implies that Norwegian society accepts a wider diversity of lifestyles, as long as these do not come into conflict with
the laws of the country.

The term integration is mainly used to describe the process of facilitating the introduction and establishment of newly arrived immigrants into Norwegian society. In a broader context, integration policy can be seen as a set of policies that are concerned with
ensuring that all people living in Norway have the same opportunities and the same
obligations to contribute to and participate in the community.

Immigrants are defined as persons who were born abroad with two foreign-born parents.
Those born in Norway with two immigrant parents are defined as *Norwegian-born with
immigrant parents*. For the sake of convenience, in this text the term *descendants* is used for
this group. In general terms, the concept 'persons with a migrant background' is used to
designate both persons who have themselves migrated to Norway, as well as their children born in Norway (descendants).

The term non-Western is used in this text, although this term is no longer used for statistical purposes. The term denotes immigrants from Africa, Asia, Latin America and the
former Eastern Bloc.[2]

Given the historical relationship between the Nordic countries, it is still relevant in some
contexts to distinguish Nordic citizens as a separate category. It is also worth mentioning that since Norway is not a member of the European Union, there is no clear distinction between EU and non-EU citizens (third-country nationals) for statistical purposes.
This is also reflected in the terms and definitions used in the statistical data.

Different terms may be used in the political and statistical contexts. In addition, the
same terms may have different definitions depending on the context in which they are
used.

13.1.4 The situation in Norway

The immigrant population in Norway has increased more than eightfold since 1970, and
has almost doubled since 2000. More than 10% of Norway's population has a migrant
background, and this immigrant population is a large and diverse group.

Immigrants come to Norway for various reasons. Many are refugees, but most immigrants who arrive in Norway from other European countries come for work. Government
policy and measures are designed to ensure that immigrants use their resources to contribute to the labour force and to society as a whole as early as possible after their arrival
in the country. Examples of such actions are the introductory programme for refugees
and their families and the previously mentioned right and obligation to attend Norwegian language courses for most groups of newly arrived immigrants.

At the beginning of January 2011, Norway's immigrant population comprised people
from 215 different countries and autonomous regions. According to data from Statistics
Norway, there were around 500,000 immigrants and around 100,000 Norwegian-born

persons with immigrant parents living in Norway at that time. Together, these two groups represent 12.2% of Norway's population. Immigrants and Norwegian-born persons with immigrant parents were represented in all 430 Norwegian municipalities. The highest proportion was in Oslo, with 28.4% of the population, or around 170,000 persons.
Between 1990 and 2008, a total of 377,000 non-Nordic citizens migrated to Norway and were granted residence status. Of these, 24% came as refugees, 24% were labour migrants and 11% were granted residence status in order to undertake education. 23% came to Norway due to family reunification with someone already living in Norway, and 17% were granted residence status because they had established a family. 57% of all Norwegian-born persons with immigrant parents have parents with an Asian background. At the beginning of 2010, Norway had almost 260,000 immigrants and descendants with a European background, of whom 64,000 had a background from a country outside the EU/EEA. A total of nearly 200,000 persons had a background from Asia, 67,000 from Africa, 18,000 from Latin America and 11,000 from North America and Oceania. A high proportion of immigrants come from Poland, Sweden, Germany and Iraq. Four out of ten immigrants have lived in Norway for more than twenty years, while four in ten have lived there for four years or less. 35% of immigrants and 78% of descendants held Norwegian citizenship in January 2010.

Norway's migration policies are partly aligned with those of the EU through its membership of the European Economic Area, the Schengen Agreement on free movement and the Dublin Convention on asylum. Non-EU migrants tend to arrive as family members of migrant workers, skilled workers and asylum-seekers/refugees. Recent legislation has focused on comprehensive introduction programmes, curbing forced marriages, reforming nationality laws and bolstering antidiscrimination and equality laws.

Figure 13.1
Immigrants in Norway, January 2010 (shares, in numbers)

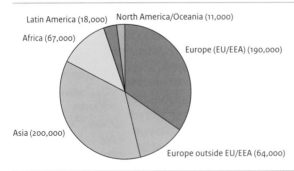

Latin America (18,000)   North America/Oceania (11,000)
Africa (67,000)
Europe (EU/EEA) (190,000)
Asia (200,000)
Europe outside EU/EEA (64,000)

Source: Statistics Norway

According to Statistics Norway, the majority of immigrants participate in society on an equal basis with others in the population.[3] Most speak Norwegian, are employed

and manage well. Many young persons with a migrant background enter higher education and obtain the jobs for which they are qualified. In cultural life, we see a diversity
of actors. Many persons with migrant backgrounds play an active part in politics and
NGOs. At the same time, there is a tendency that reveals systematic differences at the
macro-level between the immigrant population and the rest of the population. The immigrant population as a whole generally have poorer living conditions than the general
population. This is related to several factors, but most importantly it is a result of the fact
that unemployment among immigrants as a group is more than three times higher than
among the general population. In addition, immigrants are overrepresented in households with a persistently low income, at 26% compared to 8.2% for the population as a
whole.[4]

The process of integrating into society takes longer for some groups than others. When
comparing different immigrant groups, varying periods of residence can explain some
of the differences between the groups, with regard to both demography and living conditions. In the 1970s and 80s, persons with a refugee background from Vietnam were
relatively new to Norway, and many of them had problems entering the labour market,
as do immigrants from Somalia today. Persons with a Vietnamese background now have
a higher employment rate than the average for Asian immigrants.[5] Despite the differences between the refugee groups, time appears to be a vital factor in the integration
process.
The employment rate among immigrants increases with the duration of their residence.
The employment rate among immigrants who have lived in Norway for five years or more
is higher than the average for immigrants, and increases to almost 65% among those
with a period of residence of between ten and fifteen years.[6]
There are however considerable differences between the various groups of immigrants
and the rest of the population. The employment rate among immigrants from African
countries is only 30% after less than four years of living in Norway, but rises to 45%
among those who have lived in Norway for longer than four years. The same trend can be
seen among other immigrant groups, but there are almost no groups where the employment rate reaches the national average.

Period of residence does not however fully explain why the employment rate is also
much lower in some groups with a long period of residence. As an example, the female
employment rate is low in some of the groups with the longest period of residence, especially among women with a Pakistani background.[7]

Those who are Norwegian-born with immigrant parents are currently a very young
group; the oldest are in their early thirties, but the vast majority are much younger.
The labour force participation of this group is however higher than among their peers
who migrated to Norway themselves. The unemployment rate among descendants aged
15-29 years stood at 5.1% at the end of 2009. This was 2.4 percentage points lower than
the rate among immigrants in the same age group, which was 7.5%.[8]

13.2   Indicators and monitoring systems – current use and future development

A central element in the Norwegian system for monitoring integration is access to reliable and valid data, as well as the systematic use of those data. In relation to the theme being discussed here, data collection and analysis are mainly performed by Statistics Norway and the Directorate of Integration and Diversity (IMDi).

Statistics Norway is the central body responsible for meeting the need for statistics on Norwegian society. The Act of 16 June 1989 concerning official statistics and Statistics Norway stipulates that Statistics Norway has a national responsibility for Norwegian official statistics. The Act further states that Statistics Norway is a professionally autonomous institution but is subject to the guidelines and financial frameworks as determined by the Norwegian government and parliament. The Statistics Act permits Statistics Norway to make use of national administrative registers. Since the registers use national identity numbers, company registration numbers or addresses, they enable Statistics Norway to combine information from them easily into statistics that portray the interrelationships between various aspects of Norwegian society.

IMDi functions under the auspices of the Ministry for Children, Equality and Social Inclusion, with a mandate to implement the government's policy. IMDi's objective is to contribute to equality in living conditions, equal opportunities and diversity through employment and participation in society. This objective requires the development of core indicators and monitoring systems as a complement to the evaluation of results of integration policies. A key task for IMDi in this context is to evaluate progress on integration, initiate relevant surveys or monitors and produce relevant documentation to aid the government in adjusting policy.

13.2.1   Registers – the basis for national statistical data in Norway[9]

The Central Population Register (CPR)

The main source for Norwegian migration statistics, both on stocks and flows, is information from the Central Population Register, the CPR. All population statistics produced by Statistics Norway are based on the CPR, subordinated to the Norwegian Tax Administration. Statistics Norway is responsible for the production of population statistics based on events reported to CPR, and for all kinds of linkages between the CPR and other registers, but only for statistical and analytical purposes.

Following the introduction of the Population Registers Act 1946, each municipality had to establish a population register covering all residents of the municipality. This information was centralised in 1964 with the establishment of the CPR, based on the 1960 Population Census and these local registers. All persons resident in Norway at the time of the census were included.

One of the main reasons for establishing the CPR was to create a register for taxation, and to serve other administrative needs. In addition the CPR forms the basis for all electoral rolls. The use of the data for population statistics is an added bonus, as the register was established primarily for administrative, not statistical purposes. The registration of individual information is becoming increasingly important for the implementation of a series of legal individual rights. The importance of having correct information and the frequent use of the different variables in all administrative registers is the main guarantee for the quality of this system.

Each person in the register is assigned a unique eleven-digit Personal Identification Number, a PIN-code. This PIN-code is essential in linking the persons registered in the CPR to information held in other administrative registers for the purpose of statistical descriptions and analysis.

Statistics Norway receives electronic copies of the CPR every day. These data are used to update a separate population database held at Statistics Norway for statistical purposes. All vital events (births, deaths, marriages, national and international migration, etc.) and demographic characteristics such as age, marital status, citizenship, number of children, place of birth, national background (including parental country of birth), and year of first immigration are registered in the CPR. Furthermore, all population movements are recorded. In total, there are around 75 variables. In addition to this, Statistics Norway generates a number of variables for statistical use, so that in total there are around 400 variables. The CPR also includes all foreigners with a valid permit to be in Norway and with the intention of staying in the country for at least six months. Foreigners meeting these criteria are assigned a PIN-code. The PIN-code is needed to enable the person concerned to register that they are living in Norway, to go to school, to open a bank account, to obtain a tax card for work, to become a member of the national health insurance scheme and for a long list of other purposes. In short, it is an integral part of being a resident in Norway.

From the information in the CPR it is possible to reconstruct individual demographic biographies for the period over which the register has existed. When someone dies or emigrate, their PIN-code is never reassigned, and all relevant information is kept in the historical archives. Thus, a person is never removed from the CPR. Once registered, their personal file is kept forever.

Migrants in the CPR

For most migrants, the length and validity of the permit determines whether or not they are registered. This information in the CPR is often based on information from the Aliens Register. Similarly, registration as an emigrant requires that the person emigrating must intend to reside abroad for at least six months.

All first time immigrants with non-Nordic citizenship who migrated to Norway after 1989 have been placed in one of the main immigrant categories Refugee, Family, Labour, Education or Other. Most of them are registered with a more specified reason for immigration, for instance who the reference person for a family migrant is. These categories are based on the variable 'reason for (migration) decision' in the Aliens Register, which is owned and operated by the Norwegian Directorate of Immigration.

Nordic citizens do not need a permit when migrating to Norway, and notification of their migration goes directly to the CPR, in the same way as internal migration. There is also a system within the Nordic countries for joint recording of decisions on migration between the local population registers. Migrants from non-Nordic countries must have a residence permit. The immigration authorities are also responsible for providing individual data on these migrants to the CPR. Immigrants without the necessary permits are not included in the register.

Coordination and linking

Pursuant to the Statistics Act of 1989, Statistics Norway is granted access to all official registers in Norway. Not only does the Statistics Act give Statistics Norway the right to use these registers for statistical purposes, but also stipulates that Statistics Norway must be informed in advance of proposals to establish new registers and modify existing registers and has the right to express preferences with regard to all aspects of such registers.

With the consent of the Data Inspectorate, the information in the CPR can be linked for statistical and analytical purposes to all these other administrative registers. The CPR is at the heart of this, and by using the PIN-code Statistics Norway can link population data with the different registers. It is however prohibited to provide information about identifiable individuals.
Based on linkages between different records, statistics on employment and education, etc. are published annually and the immigrant perspective is covered in more or less every publication.
With the informed consent of the respondent, Statistics Norway can also link register information with survey responses, in order to simplify questionnaires and improve data quality. The register used as a sampling frame makes it possible to estimate the representativeness of the respondents, and occasionally to correct for non-response.

In general, the rich variety and availability of administrative data opens the way for detailed monitoring of how immigrants integrate into Norwegian society. Using this system of integrating and linking data from the CPR with administrative sources enables accurate and detailed statistics to be generated on how immigrants perform in different social arenas compared with the population as a whole. The system is also ideal for longitudinal studies, measuring trends in integration over time at the individual level. Based on CPR information, data on integration can be analysed according to all relevant background information, such as gender, year of arrival (arrival cohorts), country background, etc.

Accessibility of data

Microdata[10] may be provided for research and public planning purposes either by Statistics Norway or by the Norwegian Social Science Data Archive[11] (NSD). NSD receives survey data that are available for research from Statistics Norway and supplies them to the research community free of charge. Non-sensitive, anonymised microdata for research and for planning purposes may under specific conditions be distributed with a notification to the Data Inspectorate. Sensitive data are only released if the researchers have received a concession from the Data Inspectorate, and on condition that the data are rendered unidentifiable. Register data are mostly available through Statistics Norway for research purposes. It is normally easier to commission Statistics Norway, for a fee that covers their expenses, to perform tabulations and estimations, than to have access to microdata files. It is also easier for users in Norway to access microdata than users abroad, due to the Privacy Act.[12]

13.2.2 Existing and planned monitors of inclusion and integration

Monitors based on register data

Due to the Norwegian system of register data and the good data quality, Statistics Norway is able to monitor even small subgroups in the immigrant population and their integration. This work is largely commissioned and financed by the Department of Integration and Diversity[13] at the Ministry of Children, Equality and Social Inclusion. Statistics Norway monitors the integration of immigrants in Norway in a series of regular reports. Of particular interest are immigrants with a refugee background. This group is arguably the main target of governmental initiatives compared to other immigrant groups.

Monitoring integration efforts for newcomers

The Introductory Act confers rights and obligations in respect of targeted qualification measures for newly arrived immigrants.[14] Statistics Norway's 'Introduction Programme Monitor' describes the participation in the labour market and education system of persons who have completed the Programme.

The National Introduction Register (NIR) provides a supplementary knowledge base on the attendance, absenteeism, content, progress and outcomes of participants in introductory programmes and in language and social studies. The NIR provides a performance management tool and monitor for the achievement of goals at the national and local level.

In addition to the overall purpose of monitoring, the NIR gives municipalities information about target groups and test results, as well as helping local caseworkers to administrate the somewhat complex legal framework. National authorities use relevant information on participation and test results when channelling subsidies to municipalities and for granting applicants permanent residency and citizenship.

Monitoring geographical mobility

The migration patterns of refugees within and out of Norway are described through the 'Secondary Migration Monitor'. This Monitor covers the extent to which refugees move and where they move to. For example, the Monitor provides a basis for analysing the impact of the obligatory introduction programme on newly arrived refugees' mobility and migration patterns, as participants lose benefits under this programme if they move before completing the programme. Also of interest is the question of whether employment has any impact on mobility.

In addition to the areas mentioned above, having an insight into refugees' migratory patterns within Norway is valuable in evaluating the settlement policy.

Employment and education

The annual report 'Employment and education of young immigrants and Norwegian-born children of immigrants' describes the labour market participation and education status of these two groups compared to the Norwegian majority population in the same age group (16-34 years). The effect of family situation (marriage, children) and of the immigrants' age at the time of immigration is analysed.

Another report, 'Refugees and the labour market', describes the labour market situation of all those with a refugee background (including families reunified with refugees) who arrived in Norway after 1986. The figures for refugees are compared to the immigrant group as a whole and to the entire Norwegian population.

Living conditions

The annual report 'Economy and living conditions for various low-income groups' monitors the situation of various vulnerable groups that are known to be overrepresented at the bottom of the income distribution. This applies for example to social assistance benefit recipients, single parents and beneficiaries of various social security benefits, in addition to immigrants. Various indicators that seek to illustrate economic difficulties for the immigrant population measure the living conditions of these groups.

New monitors

In addition to the monitors described above, Statistics Norway is continually working on developing new monitors. One such monitor, first published in 2011, describes the integration of unaccompanied minor asylum-seekers and their integration into the education system and labour market. Family immigration and marriage patterns among immigrants and children of immigrants will also be described more systematically in an annual monitor, which will probably also highlight different family immigrants' integration into the labour market.

These monitors are part of a continuous activity aimed at describing the inclusion of immigrants in different arenas of Norwegian society. Developments in a large numbers of variables are described, such as fertility, mortality, household structure, education, labour force participation, income, participation in elections, disability and many more. The main purpose is to develop indicators that are free of compositional effects, as the migrant population of Norway is changing continuously. The reports that stem from this work will serve as a backdrop to the other monitors and as a basis for selecting new topics for closer scrutiny in special monitors and identifying missing statistical data needed for monitoring purposes.

13.2.3 Monitors based on surveys

Monitoring the immigrant population

In addition to the monitors based on register data, IMDi and Statistics Norway have taken the initiative to conduct a range of qualitative surveys. These surveys are relevant to policymakers and partners at the local and national level. They monitor outcomes, attitudes and experiences that are linked to the immigrant population's integration via employment, education, social inclusion or active citizenship. These are the same policy areas that it is considered important to monitor in most, if not all member states of the EU.

Statistics Norway has on three occasions surveyed a sample of immigrants on issues concerning their living conditions that are not covered by the registers. Examples of such issues are discrimination, religion, contacts with and background in country of origin, housing. The most recent survey dates from 2005/06, in which a representative sample of 3,053 immigrants and persons born in Norway to two immigrant parents from the ten main non-Western immigrant groups in Norway were interviewed. The results are compared with findings for the population as a whole from the regular surveys of living conditions and a number of other surveys. Where relevant, the results are also compared with findings from the survey 'Living conditions of immigrants 1996'.

The IMDi survey 'Integrated but discriminated' takes immigrants from Africa, Asia, the former Eastern Bloc and South and Central America with more than five years of residency as a frame of reference. The survey was conducted in June 2007, with a sample of around 1,000 persons. The intention of the survey was to improve the knowledge of how immigrants perceive living in Norway and how they relate to Norwegian society.

Monitoring the host population

Attitudes towards immigrants and immigration are surveyed annually by both Statistics Norway and IMDi. A representative sample of the population in Norway are asked by Statistics Norway about their opinions concerning refugees' access to Norway, their contact with and relationship to immigrants, their opinions on immigrants' contribution to Norwegian society, etc. The annual report 'Attitudes towards immigrants and immigration' also analyses whether the attitudes towards immigrants vary with demographic characteristics, human capital, geography, etc.

Also monitored through sample data is the participation in national and local elections by immigrants and Norwegian-born persons with immigrant parents. It was only in the latest national election in 2009 that there were enough Norwegian-born persons in the sample to compare their participation with that of immigrants.

In 2005, 2006, 2008, 2009 and 2010 IMDi conducted a survey which functions as a 'barometer', measuring attitudes towards immigration and integration policies, immigrants and identified vulnerable groups. The survey is based on subjective data drawn from a sample of the general population on aspects such as willingness to take part in voluntary integration work and combating discrimination, as well as the degree of contact with the immigrant population and experience of discrimination. The survey contains up to 150 questions. Essential questions overlap some of the questions and top-ics in Statistics Norway's annual survey on living conditions. The Directorate is therefore currently evaluating the concept of the barometer and discussing the development of alternative survey-based approaches and methods.

Several annual surveys initiated by IMDi, with smaller samples, target employers. These surveys mainly monitor recruitment and diversity at the workplace, e.g.:
– representativeness of employed immigrants;
– initiatives to boost recruitment;
– activities accommodating a diverse workforce;
– attitudes towards diversity at the workplace.

Some questions and topics vary from year to year, such as questions relating to the recent economic downturn and the resettlement of refugees. The surveys monitor developments and attitudes among managers of private companies, political and admin-istrative leaders in municipalities and wholly state-owned companies.

13.3   Goals for social inclusion of the immigrant population

In 2005 the Norwegian government introduced a set of goals with corresponding progress indicators as a means of actively monitoring and steering its integration poli-cies. Such a measure was only possible given the data collection system described in the previous section.

13.3.1   Establishing the goals

The process of establishing the current goals began with a report to Parliament on diver-sity in the 2003-2004 session. The report highlighted the need to gauge the impact of overall government policies and measures on the integration of immigrants and their children.
The implementation of Norwegian integration policy is based on the principles of sec-tor responsibility and mainstreaming. Sector responsibility implies that each sectoral authority is responsible for maintaining immigrant perspectives in all policymaking. In some respects, mainstreaming goes beyond this, and entails an evaluation of the implications for the immigrant population of all planned programmes, actions, laws and regulations in all areas and at all levels. Hence the situation and special needs of the immigrant population are integrated dimensions in forming, implementing, monitor-ing and evaluating policy and actions in all political, economic and social domains. In some areas there may still be a need for special actions directed specifically towards the immigrant population.
The advantage of the sector responsibility system is that the ministry responsible for each sector also has the responsibility of performing the actions and determining what the best tools are for obtaining good results. The role of the coordinating ministry is to assist the sector ministries in mainstreaming the focus on immigrants into its core

activities. The Department of Integration and Diversity, which currently falls under the Ministry of Children, Equality and Social Inclusion is responsible for the overarching policy regarding the social inclusion of immigrants, and as such for coordinating the government's efforts to achieve the goals.

During the development of the monitoring system, it was regarded as crucial that the mainstreaming principle should be strengthened. The approach was to establish concrete and clear goals that specified what the different sector ministries should achieve in their own areas of responsibility, with accompanying indicators to determine whether government policy, measures and resource allocation are working effectively. In order to follow developments and identify the results of the policy, the sector ministries must report annually on the achievement of the goals in accordance with the sector responsibility principle. Until now, these reports have been amalgamated into a single report by the coordinating ministry in the yearly budget proposal presented to Parliament. Determining the goals presented several challenges. Firstly, if the goals were to cover all the most important areas of social inclusion, there would simply be too many or they would be too general. Access to reliable and renewable data was a prerequisite for determining the goals. In addition, it was important to measure results rather than activities or money spent. It is therefore important to bear in mind that the set of goals finally decided upon does not necessarily cover all the key areas of social inclusion. They do, however, contribute to a broader picture of the trends.

An internal working group in the ministry responsible for coordinating policy on inclusion and integration was established to initiate the process of developing the goals. The working group identified the most important sectors and areas. Available data covering the proposed goals were identified in close dialogue with Statistics Norway. The goals and indicators were subsequently approved by the cabinet and responsibility for implementation was handed to the responsible ministries.

The initial fifteen goals for the social inclusion of immigrants and their children were presented in the national budget for 2006 (two additional goals were included in 2007). To monitor progress in achieving the goals and identify measures that need to be taken to ensure that the goals are realised, regular reports ensure that developments are heading in the right direction. In formulating the goals, importance was thus also attached to creating result indicators for each goal to show the development in the field in question. The situation in Norway when the goals were introduced is used as a baseline in measuring the progress of social inclusion of the immigrant population.

13.3.2 An overview of the goals

As mentioned above, there are 17 goals for social inclusion, with a total of eight ministries being responsible for achieving them. Each goal has one or more indicators intended to measure long-term progress. The goals express what the government specifically wishes to achieve through its policy on inclusion of the immigrant population. The indicators are sensitive to shocks from sudden immigration flows and from the composition of the immigrant population. It is also important to obtain a broader information base on how immigrants and their descendants find their place in society and how they experience their life situation and position in Norway. The indicators will help determine whether government measures and resource allocations are working effectively. A clear indication of success measured through the indicators relies on understandable and measurable goals.

All the goals are presented below. The indicators linked to the goals are not listed here. The different phrasing of the goals is the result of an attempt to match the existing goals of each ministry. A fuller presentation of two of the goals, their respective indicators, as well as the current status, is given in section 13.3.3.

- The ministry must strive to strengthen the ties of immigrants and their descendants to the labour market, controlled for conditions in the labour market.
- The proportion of immigrants with persistently low incomes will be reduced towards the level of the general population.
  (Ministry of Labour)
- Contribute to increasing the proportion of employees with immigrant backgrounds in child welfare services.
- To function in society, adult immigrants must acquire an adequate command of Norwegian during the five first years of their residence in Norway.
  (Ministry of Children, Equality and Social Inclusion)
- Health differentials between ethnic groups must be reduced.
  (Ministry of Health and Care Services)
- To reflect the diversity of the population, efforts will be made to increase the proportion of employees with immigrant backgrounds in the police force, the public prosecution service and the correctional services.
- Efforts will be made to increase the proportion of lay judges with immigrant backgrounds.
  (Ministry of Justice and the Police)
- The proportion of persons with immigrant backgrounds and the right to vote at and participate in municipal, regional and parliamentary elections must be the same as in the election turnout of the electorate as a whole.
- Immigrants must be assured of having a place to live and must not be excluded from the housing market.
  (Ministry of Local Government and Regional Development)
- The proportion of persons with immigrant backgrounds who are employed by the State must be increased.
  (Ministry of Government Administration, Reform and Church Affairs and the Ministry of Labour)
- Increased participation and increased proportion of active performers with immigrant backgrounds in the culture and media sector.
  (Ministry of Culture)
- Children and young people with immigrant backgrounds must master the Norwegian language as early as possible in their schooling to ensure that they derive good learning benefit.

- The proportion of descendants completing upper secondary education will correspond to the proportion in the general population.
- The proportion of immigrants who arrive in Norway while of lower secondary school or upper secondary school age and who complete upper secondary education must be increased.
- The proportion of employees in primary and lower secondary school and upper secondary education with immigrant backgrounds will be increased.
- To facilitate optimum language development by preschool children, efforts will be made to increase the number of children with immigrant backgrounds in daycare centres.
- Contribute to increasing the number of preschool teachers with immigrant backgrounds.
  (Ministry of Education and Research)

13.3.3 A detailed example of selected goals and corresponding indicators

In order to gain a better understanding of the system of monitoring the goals over time, a more detailed presentation of two goals, with their corresponding indicators and the current status, is presented here. These examples have been selected because they represent different dimensions of measuring the status of integration; at the individual level and at the level of society as a whole.

Goal:
- The proportion of descendants completing upper secondary education will correspond to the proportion of the general population.

Indicators:
- The proportion of descendants progressing directly from primary and lower secondary school to upper secondary education, compared with the total number of pupils in that year.
- The proportion of descendants attaining vocational competence or qualifying for higher education within five years after completing primary and lower secondary school compared to the total number of pupils in that year.

This goal falls under the responsibility of the Ministry of Education and Research. The latest data available (2009) show that the proportion of descendants progressing directly from lower to upper secondary school is 96%, about equal to the proportion in the general population (97%). At the same time, we see that the proportion of descendants who complete upper secondary education is almost equal to that in the general population, at 66% and 67%, respectively.[15]
These proportions have been stable since the goals were established, and it may be concluded that this goal has been largely achieved. However, it is still important to continue focusing on maintaining this relatively high proportion.[16]

Goal:
- The proportion of immigrants with persistently low incomes will be reduced towards the level of the general population.

Indicators:
- The proportion of immigrants with persistently low incomes compared to the population as a whole.
- The proportion of children under 18 years of age with immigrant backgrounds living in households with persistently low incomes compared to all children.

The Ministry of Labour is responsible for taking actions aimed at achieving this goal. The proportion of immigrants with persistently low incomes is rather high compared to the general population: in the period 2006-2008 the proportion of immigrants and descendants with persistently low incomes was 26%,[17] Compared with 8.2% in the population at large over the same period.[18]
The proportion of children under the age of 18 with a migrant background living in households with persistently low incomes was 36.4% in the period 2006-2008; the figure among children aged under 18 in the general population was 7.6% over the same period.[19]
The proportion of immigrants with persistently low incomes has varied somewhat over the years, but has nonetheless been relatively stable. The same can be said of the situation for the general population. In the period 2002-2004, the proportion of immigrants with persistently low incomes was 29%, while in the population as a whole it was 8.5%. In the same period, around three out of ten children under the age of 18 with a migrant background were living in households with persistently low incomes; this compares with 5.6% of all children aged under 18. This shows that there has been almost no improvement in the situation since the goals were established, and that we are a long way from achieving the goal.[20]

13.3.4 Assessing the goals

The goals for social inclusion have recently been reviewed. The review was part of an ongoing process to further improve the goals and their corresponding indicators, and to improve the mainstreaming of policies on immigrants and their children. The review was performed by the Agency for Public Management and eGovernment (Difi)[21].
One of the findings of the review was that the goals may have served too many objectives, and that those objectives have not been communicated well enough. As a result, the goals have not been functioning optimally and there is room for improvement. Difi further concluded that monitoring the outcome of government policy has thus far been the primary function of the goals; the Difi recommendation to the ministry is that in the future this should the *sole* function of the goals. This will enable efforts to be directed towards improving the monitoring, and will enhance the usefulness of the goals.

13.4 Summary

Access to and use of reliable and valid register data is a prerequisite for the Norwegian system of monitoring the integration and social inclusion of the immigrant population. The power of the Statistics Act that allows Statistics Norway to collect and link data at the micro-level on key areas of society makes this monitoring system possible. Furthermore, regular monitoring provides additional input for the government in developing policy measures.

The goals for social inclusion were developed on the basis of the existence of a broad base of register data, and although it might be possible to imagine a similar set of goals in a situation without such data, that system would be lacking in several respects. The potential for assessing progress and the ability to ensure the representativeness of the groups in question make register data preferable to basing a monitoring system solely on survey data.

The mainstreaming principle, coupled with a coordinating ministry, is also an important element in monitoring integration in Norway. From the perspective of the government, the goals for social inclusion are an aid in developing policy measures, and help determine whether the measures that have been implemented actually work in the long run. Although the system is designed to gauge the actual status in all the areas of interest, it provides an information base for assessing developments in a selection of key areas. This information can then be used by the government in communicating with both the general public and Parliament. The coordinating ministry has recently initiated a process to develop and improve the system of goals and indicators further.

Several challenges have been identified in connection with monitoring the effect of policy measures on the immigrant population, and the monitoring system is undergoing an evaluation. In certain areas, not enough data are available; this is especially the case for data on health, and to some extent education. There are also problems in relation to determining causalities, i.e. whether a given effect is the result of specific policy measures or of exogenous factors.
Although the current system for monitoring integration of the immigrant population poses certain challenges, it is nonetheless based on a strong statistical fundament. Access to good register data is an essential aspect of this.

Notes

1   I would like to thank Lars Østby and Kristin Henriksen at Statistics Norway and Katarina Heradstveit at The Directorate of Integration and Diversity for their extensive and important contributions. In addition, I would like to thank Pia Buhl Girolami, Julian Yehudi Kramer and Anne Folkvord for their contributions.
2   Former Eastern Europe refers to the Warsaw Pact states outside the former Soviet Union.
3   Henriksen et al. (2010).
4   Using the EU criterion of 60% of median income over three years. Figures are from the period 2006-2008. Source: Statistics Norway.
5   Henriksen et al. (2010).
6   Daugstad (2007).
7   Henriksen et al. (2010).
8   Register data from Statistics Norway, www.ssb.no.
9   For a more comprehensive description, see www.prominstat.org.
10 Microdata is information at the level of individual respondents. The data may cover persons, establishments or enterprises.
11 NSD is one of the largest research data archives of its kind and provides data to researchers and students in Norway and abroad.
12 Access to microdata requires an application if the research unit has not already been approved through national qualification criteria.
13 The Department of Integration and Diversity is responsible for the policy on integration and the social inclusion of the immigrant population. The department has been located under various ministries depending on the political constellation of the government, but currently (since the beginning of 2010) resides under the Ministry of Children, Equality and Social Inclusion.
14 Refugees, persons granted humanitarian status, persons who have collective protection and persons who are family members of these categories have a statutory right and obligation to take part in the introductory programme.
15 Prop. 1 S (2010-2011).
16 Ibid.
17 Here and elsewhere, the EU definition of persistently low income is applied, i.e. 60% of median income over a period of three years.
18 Prop. 1 S (2010-2011).
19 Ibid.
20 Ibid.
21 Vik (2011).

References

Daugstad, G. (ed.) (2007). *Fakta om innvandrere og deres etterkommere 2007. Hva kan tallene fortelle* (Notater 2007/56). Oslo/Kongsvinger: Statistics Norway.
Henriksen, K., L. Østby & D. Ellingsen (eds.) (2010). *Innvandring og innvandrere 2010* (Statistiske analyser 119). Oslo/Kongsvinger: Statistics Norway.

Vik, G. (2011). *Mål for inkludering av innvandrerbefolkningen. En gjennomgang av ordningen* (Difi report 2011:1). Oslo: Difi.

Prop. 1 S (2010-2011) *Budget proposal to Parliament*. Oslo: Ministry of Children, Equality and Social Inclusion.

Websites

The government website www.government.no contains all the budget proposals and other relevant background material. In particular, documents from the Ministry of Children, Equality and Social Inclusion may be of interest. The report to Parliament on diversity can be found here, though only in Norwegian: http://www.regjeringen.no/Rpub/STM/20032004/049/PDFS/ STM200320040049000DDDPDFS.pdf.

Statistics and analyses are available (in English) at www.ssb.no/en. Data for migration in particular are available at www.ssb.no/english/subjects/00/00/10/innvandring_en/. Aggregate data may be obtained from the Statistics Bank www.ssb.no/english/statbank where most of the core tables on the immigrant population and the living conditions of immigrants are published. In addition, tables are published for each topic under the title 'Daily statistics'. More detailed tables or distributions may be obtained upon request.

IMDi's website www.imdi.no/en/Spark/English/ contains some information in English. All the published monitors are available in Norwegian on the website.

14 From (many) datasets to (one) integration monitoring system in Poland?

Agata Górny, Aneta Piekut and Renata Stefańska

14.1 Introduction

In comparison to West European countries, immigration of foreigners is a new and, in terms of numbers, still limited phenomenon in Poland. It was one of many consequences of political and economic transition in Central and Eastern Europe, constituting a novelty in Poland at the beginning of 1990s. Foreigners started to come to Poland from two main directions: west and east. Highly qualified migrants from the west helped in the building up of the Polish market economy, acting as experts or coming to set up branches of their companies in Poland. Migrants from the east – mainly citizens of the former Soviet Union – were pursuing circular migration, engaging in small trade or seasonal work. Thus, the inflows from both directions were temporary in nature, and it could be argued that, at that time, Poland was not perceived as a settlement country by foreigners (Iglicka & Sword 1999). Although some authors argue, mainly in reference to the inflow from the east, that, over time, 'primitive' and temporary forms of mobility were transformed through pendular migration into a permanent phenomenon (Iglicka 2001), it could be argued that the persistent temporariness of the inflows is a characteristic feature of immigration to Poland.

Today, over twenty years later, the volume of migration is still moderate and Polish accession to the European Union did not spark off any substantial growth in immigration. The number of foreigners in Poland does not exceed 100 thousand (Okólski 2010). The main groups of migrants coming to Poland originate from neighbouring countries – mainly Ukraine – initially in the context of temporary circular migration. The irregular character of this mobility is widely recognised though difficult to capture in numbers (Okólski 2010). Two more 'exotic' groups demonstrating a propensity to settle in Poland for good are Vietnamese and Armenian immigrants. In recent years, an increased inflow of Asiatic workers – especially Chinese – has been also observed. Nevertheless, Poland is still a net emigration country and it remains to be seen whether it will undergo a transformation into a net immigration country in the future.

Drafting of the Polish immigration policy started at the beginning of the 1990s. The first phase of its development ended with the adoption of the new Aliens Act in 1997. As argued by various authors, its focus has until now been on regulations on the entry and stay of migrants in Poland (cf. Kępińska & Stola 2004). Given the small numbers of incomers and their low propensity to settle in Poland, the issue of integration of migrants does not figure prominently on the political agenda or in the public discourse. Consequently, the current Polish integration policy, to the extent that it exists, is fragmented and lacking in coordination in terms of an institutional framework and legislative regulations. It is also very selective, being target first and foremost at specific migrant groups and neglects the needs of the majority of foreigners coming to Poland – foreign workers, 'ordinary' settlers, not to mention circular and irregular migrants. At the moment, monitoring of migrant integration is not part of the Polish integration policy, though some plans for its implementation are being drafted. It could be argued that the monitoring tasks have effectively been taken over by NGOs and international institutions in the form of ad hoc studies which are generally qualitative in nature, whether they be analyses of legislation and related practices or studies of the situation of migrants in Poland.

The aim of this chapter, apart from describing the framework of migrant integration monitoring in Poland, is first of all to explore the prospects for developing such a monitoring system in Poland. It is approached as a continuous examination of the integration process, integration policy implementation and its results measured using adequate indicators of migrants' functioning in various spheres of life in the destination country. The indicators that refer to labour market, education, host country language proficiency, housing and health are considered to be 'basic, necessary and realistic' indicators of migrants' integration (cf. MTAS 2006: 54). We focus on the prospects for effective quantitative monitoring whilst also acknowledging a need for its qualitative variant. We argue that, in Poland, we are dealing with a gap between migration reality and its representation in official statistics and policy formation process, which would be difficult to close. In our view, this is an important obstacle to creating an effective monitoring system for migrants' integration. On the one hand, we would stress the need for improved access to data on foreigners in Poland, including information on their presence and performance in various domains of Polish society. On the other hand, we would point out the difficulties in collecting information on foreigners given their small share in the population of Poland (less than 1%) and the predominance of temporary migration which is by definition much more difficult to capture in statistical data. In such a context, qualitative studies can serve as an important supplement to the monitoring process.

Our analysis comprises two main components. First is an investigation of the character of the Polish integration policy and related practices; the second examines the quality and availability of information on migrants in Poland. In analysing these two main topics, we aim to uncover facilitators and obstacles to the development of effective monitoring of migrants' integration in Poland. An overview of data on immigrants in Poland draws on two main sources of data – official statistics and administrative registers. The aim is to demonstrate the availability of information on migrants and the basic characteristics of contemporary inflows into Poland, with an emphasis on recent years.

14.2   Integration policy in Poland – legislation, practice and assessment of results

14.2.1 Institutional and legal framework

The Polish approach to immigrant integration could still be described as a 'policy of non-policy' or, to use an expression coined by Aleksandra Grzymała-Kazłowska and Agnieszka Weinar (2006), a policy of 'assimilation via abandonment'. It should be stressed that Poland does not have an integration policy that can be understood as a comprehensive, cohesive strategy covering all fields of integration and all categories of immigrants. Development of such a strategy is constrained by the limited coordination of activities in this field, whether they be tasks and responsibilities or legislation. In fact, up to the present day, it would be difficult to find a definition of the term 'immigrant integration' in Polish legal or political documents[1]. There is moreover no institution with sole responsibility for the integration of migrants.

Moreover, the list of (semi-)governmental actors involved in the integration of migrants in Poland is relatively long, resulting in dispersion of tasks and responsibilities in the field. They comprise:
– Inter-ministerial Committee for Migration, incorporating the inter-ministerial Working Group on Integration of Foreigners: a consultative and advisory body (recently formed, charged with developing Poland's migration strategy, including the strategy on immigrant integration);
– Ministry of Labour and Social Policy, the Department of Social Assistance and Integration (integration of all categories of immigrants, but so far with the focus mainly on refugees);
– Ministry of the Interior and Administration (coordination of migration policy, including integration policy, anti-discrimination and repatriates integration issues);
– Office for Foreigners (pre-integration of asylum-seekers),
– Human Rights Defender, Commissioner for Children's Rights and Government Plenipotentiary for Equal Treatment,
– *Voivodship*[2] offices (coordination and supervision of individual refugee integration programmes),
– *Powiat* Family Support Centres (implementation of individual integration programmes for refugees and foreigners granted subsidiary protection),
– *Gminas* (communes) (social assistance for foreigners granted protection in Poland and permanent residents; integration support for repatriates).

Moreover, there is no single comprehensive piece of legislation entirely devoted to the issue of immigrant integration in Poland. Regulations touching upon this issue are dispersed throughout numerous legislative instruments, usually focusing on both foreigners and Polish citizens. The most important are the Constitution of the Republic of Poland from 1997[3], the 2003 Act on Granting Protection to Foreigners within the Territory of the Republic of Poland, the 2004 Social Assistance Act[4], the 2000 Repatriation Act[5], the 2004 Act on Promotion of Employment and Labour Market Institutions[6], the 2004 Act on Healthcare Services Financed from Public Sources[7], the 1991 Act on the System of

Education[8], the 2005 Higher Education Act[9], the 1989 Associations Act[10], and the Polish Citizenship Act from 1962[11].

The inadequate coordination in the field of migrant integration has been acknowledged by the governmental actors and a number of initiatives have been pursued aimed at strengthening the integration efforts and formulating a comprehensive Polish integration policy. Among these initiatives, the political document 'Proposals for actions aimed at establishing a comprehensive immigrant integration policy in Poland', published by the Ministry of Social Policy[12] in 2005 deserves attention, though it has so far not been implemented. This document provides a comprehensive overview of the situation of various migrant groups in Poland and the actions taken in by the Ministry of Social Policy to foster their integration. The major strength of this document is its attempt to formulate a catalogue of activities needed for the development of a conceptual framework of an integration policy within four important spheres of integration – political, legal, institutional and substantive. It should be stressed, however, that the document is very general and does not provide any guidelines for the implementation of a proposed solution in the Polish context.

Another political document in which integration of migrants – specifically their social and labour integration – has for the first time been set as one of the priorities is the 'Strategy for social policy for the period 2007-2013'. According to this document, this goal should be accomplished through implementation of a social and labour integration policy involving all institutions active in this field in Poland. Proposed activities include anti-discriminatory measures, training programmes for public administration staff and social partners working with refugees, and the design of a cohesive system of cooperation with refugees.

Apart from deficiencies in coordination, another characteristic feature of Polish integration policy, to the extent that such a thing exists, is its selectivity. Most groups of immigrants, both newcomers and those who have lived in Poland for many years, are not entitled to any integration programmes, either voluntary or compulsory. There are only two specific categories of immigrants who are targeted by State efforts to facilitate their integration in Polish society: repatriates and foreigners benefiting from international protection, i.e. recognised refugees and foreigners granted subsidiary protection. Repatriates (immigrants of Polish origin) are the most privileged, though specific, immigrant group as regards integration opportunities created for them by the Polish state. They acquire Polish citizenship simply by crossing the Polish border with a repatriation visa. In doing so, they acquire all the rights that are assigned to Polish citizens with their first step onto Polish soil, and are thus treated in a completely different way from other categories of foreigners. They are also entitled to a number of benefits, such as a settlement and maintenance grant and free Polish language and adaptation courses. Moreover, repatriates are fully reimbursed for the costs of travel to Poland and the education of minor children in Poland, and receive partial reimbursement for the costs of adapting/renovating a home, as well as receiving a contribution to the costs of their salary (paid direct to their employer). The list of benefits is in fact even longer than this. Furthermore, repatriates who are invited to Poland by Polish communes (*gminas*) (which is the case for the majority of them) obtain extra help in starting their new lives in Poland: priority access to accommodation and a job offer in Poland. Last but not least, would-be repatriates can receive pre-integration aid in the form of a free Polish language course in their country of origin.

The assistance available for foreigners granted international protection in Poland is also relatively wide-ranging. They are entitled to participate in the special Individual Integration Programme (IIP), for example, which offers a number of benefits: a financial contribution towards living costs and Polish language courses; health insurance contributions; help from a social worker; specialist psychological, legal and family guidance; access to information and support in contacts with local communities, institutions and NGOS[13]. The programme lasts up to one calendar year and is not mandatory. Provision of assistance within the IIP depends on fulfilment of certain obligations by the foreigner, such as registration at the local employment office and actively searching for a job; attending a Polish language course; and cooperating with a social worker who acts as programme coordinator.

The legal status of foreigners granted international protection can be regarded as favourable in terms of rights – they enjoy almost the same social and economic rights as Polish citizens[14] (e.g. the right to work or run a business without any permits, the right to free public education). A similar range of rights, with the exception of entitlement to the IIP, is granted only to foreigners holding a permanent residence permit in Poland, which can normally be obtained after five or 10 years' continuous legal residence in Poland. Other groups of foreigners enjoy far fewer rights and entitlements. Temporary migrants are not automatically entitled to work in Poland, and their access to other rights depends to a large degree on their professional and family situation. The narrowest range of rights is granted to illegal migrants, but they are still entitled to urgent medical care and their minor children can attend state schools in Poland for free (not tertiary education).

14.2.2 Monitoring migrant integration as a task of NGOS and international institutions

Poland does not have a well-thought out immigrant integration strategy, so it is not surprising that it also does not have a system for monitoring immigrants' integration and the effects of the implementation of IIPs. The few initiatives that have been taken aimed at creating such a system have to date proved unsuccessful[15]. One partial exception relates to foreigners entitled to IIPs. The Ministry of Labour and Social Policy collects information on the number of IIPs implemented, completed as planned, interrupted prior to the planned completion date, countries of origin of foreigners taking advantage of IIPs, and the number of foreigners (including, separately, children) taking part in IIPs. These data are available from the *powiat*, *voivodship* and at national level. Data on the duration of IIPs, the sex and education level of foreigners taking part in IIPs are gathered in selected *voivodships*.

Other initiatives aiming at tracing outcomes of migrant integration are undertaken by NGOs and international institutions. NGOs concentrate on examination of legal regulations and practices in Polish governmental institutions dealing with migrants. The second aspect, in particular, is subject to heavy criticism pointing to the incompetence (especially lack of adequate language skills) and inappropriate attitudes of Polish civil servants (Klaus & Wencel 2010). NGOs also engage in monitoring of outcomes of integration aid and programmes directed towards 'privileged' groups of migrants. The conclusions of their studies are far from optimistic.

In the case of repatriates, the findings of the studies suggest that the financial help, though relatively wide-ranging, is still insufficient since repatriates struggle with difficulties in finding a job, maintaining themselves in Poland and having a limited knowledge of the Polish language. The adaptation of repatriates' children in Polish schools is also problematic, due in part to issues associated with the curriculum, language and cultural differences, but also to the fact that many Polish schools are not well prepared to deal with culturally different children (Frelak & Hut 2006; Hut 2002). Studies devoted to foreigners granted protection indicate that the effectiveness of IIPs in which they take part is very modest. The programmes – contrary to their name – are not tailored to the individual needs of refugees (low social worker to refugee rate) and are too short for foreigners to acquire the cultural competences (especially learning the Polish language) they need to participate in everyday life and to find work in Poland (Kaźmierczak 2005; Klaus & Chrzanowska 2007; Samoraj 2007). Moreover, putting the relatively wide range of rights accorded to this group into practice encounters many barriers – e.g. difficulties in renting apartments, inflexible procedures for recognition of educational degrees and qualifications (Bieniecki & Kaźmierkiewicz 2008; Gracz 2007; Klaus & Wencel 2010; Kosowicz 2007). Another serious problem is a visible number of refusals of integration assistance to foreigners granted protection. It usually takes place when the application for the assistance is submitted too late and when the applicant has committed an intentional crime (e.g. crossed the Polish border illegally). What deserves attention is the fact that a criminal record of an applicant negatively impacts the decision regarding his/her entire family (Klaus et al. 2011).

Among the monitoring activities carried out by NGOs, examination of discrimination practices in Poland deserves attention. Interestingly enough, as stated in several reports, based on the available statistical data it would be difficult to argue that discrimination against foreigners occurs in Poland (cf. Łotocki 2009; Klaus & Wencel 2010). However, as advocated by the same authors, given the small numbers of migrants involved, and the concomitant difficulty in identifying significant trends in the statistics, it is necessary to look more closely at the outcomes of monitoring based on case studies in order to obtain a reliable picture. Such analyses have revealed a number of 'soft' discriminatory practices in three areas in Poland:
1   inadequately formulated regulations;
2   discriminatory practices – mainly in Polish institutions;
3   discriminatory behaviour – on the part of Polish employers and society (Klaus & Wencel 2010).

A pilot study involving discriminatory tests also demonstrated that Polish employers treat Polish and foreign job applicants unequally. However, these results are formulated with caution due to the small scale of the study (Wysieńska 2010).

Finally, an exercise aimed at the general monitoring of Polish migration and integration policy at EU level within the project financed by the European Commission entitled 'Migrant Integration Policy Index (MIPEX)'[16] should be mentioned. Its purpose is to measure policies to integrate migrants. In 2010 in an overall ranking based on 148 indicators grouped in seven integration policy areas, Poland achieved 24th position out of 31 countries examined. Polish integration policy with respect to immigrants was the most favourable in the domain of 'family reunion' (10th position) and 'long-term residence' (10th position) and least favourable in the fields of 'political participation' (next to last position), 'anti-discrimination'(27th position) and 'education' (21st position) (Huddleston et al. 2011).

14.3   Sources of information on immigrants – in search of monitoring basis

14.3.1 Official statistics relating to immigrants

2002 Census data
The population census is the main statistical dataset which, as in other countries, can be used in international comparisons. The last Polish census was conducted in 2002. Among other things, an important goal of the census drafters was to obtain reliable information on the immigrant population resident in Poland, including long-term and short-term immigrants, both legal and illegal. On the one hand, the results of the census were not entirely satisfactory, since apparently the stock of temporary migrants was substantially underestimated due to the population of illegal migrants being virtually absent from the census data[17]. On the other hand, comparison with other data sources suggests that the information on permanent migrants obtained in the census is fairly close to reality. From the perspective of integration monitoring, a variety of data can be extracted from the 2002 census and used as integration indicators, including economic indicators, such as activity in the labour market, sources of livelihood (e.g. relying upon benefits), type of dwelling (owned or rented), or socio-cultural indicators, e.g. nationality of spouse, language spoken at home.

It should be noted that, unlike in most European countries, the foreign-born population is not an adequate measure of the stock of migrants in Poland. The 2002 census would heavily overestimate the 'foreign' population if it were measured on that basis, because a number of people born on the pre-war Polish territory and currently living in Poland are considered as foreign-born persons (Okólski 2010). Consequently, the foreign population in Poland is distinguished on the basis of non-Polish citizenship.

According to the census results, the foreign population residing permanently in Poland[18], comprised 40,700, of whom 29,700 were born in a foreign country. The main groups of foreign permanent residents identified in the census were Germans (23% of the total foreign permanent population),[19] Ukrainians (15.7%), Russians (9.3%),

Belarusians (4.8%), Vietnamese (4.3%) and Americans from the USA (3.8%). The number of foreigners residing in Poland temporarily (more than two months) as recorded in the census was only 24,000. They were dominated by citizens of the former USSR and Germans: Ukraine (27.8% of the total temporary foreign immigrant population), Russian Federation (8%), Belarus (7.6%), Germany (6.6%) and Armenia (4.7%). After adding the two groups – temporary and permanent migrants – we end up with a stock of some 64,000 foreign citizens living in Poland as of 20 May 2002, thus accounting for less than 1% of the total population of Poland.

Central Statistical Office migration statistics

The Polish Central Statistical Office (CSO) distinguishes several categories of immigrants. International immigrants are defined as people who came from abroad and registered for a permanent stay in Poland. Thus, under Polish statistical legislation, immigration is defined in relation to the residence registration that people are required to make each time they change their place of residence for longer than three months. This 'dead law' is not obeyed by many people in Poland, which means that in reality migration statistics reflect '"artefacts" rather than real migratory phenomena' (Okólski 2010).

Since 2006, CSO has measured the stock of foreigners – persons not possessing Polish citizenship – and the volume of international immigration for permanent residence purposes (by both Poles and foreigners) using data from the PESEL register (the Universal Electronic System of Population Registration) (CSO 2011)[20]. All people resident in Poland, both nationals and foreigners, should be entered in this register have a unique personal PESEL number. The register stores data on things such as citizenship, date of registration for a permanent stay and planned duration of residence above three months for temporary migrants[21]. CSO also compiles data on international immigration for temporary stays on the basis of a statistical survey of the population registered for temporary stays of longer than three months.

According to CSO data, in 2009 17,400 international immigrants for permanent stay arrived in Poland. This figure was six and a half times higher than in 1990 (2,700) and more than twice as high as in 2003 (7,100). Taking into account the countries of migrants' previous residence, however, it is clear that a sizeable proportion of the numbers measured in these years by the CSO data was actually return migration by Poles (15,600 in 2009). Top countries of previous residence include the United Kingdom, Germany, USA and Ireland. Among non-Polish citizens, the highest immigrant flows were recorded for Ukraine (27% of foreign immigrants), Belarus (9%) and Vietnam (7%). As regards arrivals from abroad for temporary stays of longer than three months, CSO publishes data by country of previous residence, as well as by country of citizenship. The inflow reached almost 59,000 in 2009, of whom 54,000 were non-Polish citizens. The majority of these immigrants were citizens of Poland's neighbouring countries (Ukraine, Belarus, Germany and Russian Federation), as well as Asia (Vietnam and China).

CSO also collects data on binational marriages contracted in Poland (almost 4,000 in 2009; data available by gender and citizenship) and on the number of foreigners working in companies employing nine or more workers. The number of employed foreigners (those with and without work permits), measured by sections and sectors in the Polish economy, reached 12,400 in 2009 (as at 31 December) (CSO 2010). Both data sources can be used for monitoring purposes: international marriages indicate social integration, while the number of foreigners working in the Polish labour market is an indicator of their economic integration in different sectors of the economy.

14.3.2 Administrative registers devoted specifically to the foreign population

Office for Foreigners register
The administrative register of foreigners run by the Office for Foreigners (OfF) is potentially a very valuable source of data providing information about various residence permits – long-term and short-term – as well as other types of permits including several status categories that are granted to foreigners seeking international protection. All information regarding the issuing procedure is gathered by OfF in a single, complex database called the *Pobyt* system ('Stay' system)[22].

The *Pobyt* system stores foreigners' personal data and data on the administrative procedure, including the following variables: date of birth, country of birth, citizenship, marital status, date of application and decision, type of decision. All this information can be traced at the level of individual applicants. However, OfF publishes only summary tables containing information about documents types and foreign citizenship of applicants. More detailed information can be obtained only on request and after approval by the OfF director. The procedure is time-consuming and not always successful. The database is not geared to statistical analyses, and at present the *Pobyt* system's primary purpose is to store the personal data of foreigners; more detailed immigration and integration monitoring currently goes beyond its objectives.

Notwithstanding, problems in acquiring detailed data from OfF, the *Pobyt* system is currently the most reliable source of information on the stock of temporary migrants in Poland, even though it does not include information on foreigners without adequate documents in Poland. Table 14.1 presents selected categories of foreigners as recorded in the *Pobyt* system. It makes clear that the biggest groups of foreigners possessing permits for settlement and residence permits for a fixed period are Ukrainians, Belarusians, Chinese, Vietnamese, Russians, Armenians and Indians.

Table 14.1

Foreigners possessing valid residence cards as at 31 December 2010 (in numbers)

country of citizenship	permit for a fixed period	permit to settle	long-term EU resident's residence permit	subsidiary protection	refugee status	permit for tolerated stay	total
total	47,545	37,103	5,747	4,832	988	865	97,080
of which:							
Ukraine	10,998	15,338	2,027	13	–	74	28,450
Russian Federation	1,815	4,901	456	4,561	699	118	12,550
Belarus	2,800	5,732	326	11	97	29	8,995
Vietnam	2,811	4,471	943	2	3	337	8,567
Armenia	1,434	1,821	468	20	4	111	3,858
China	2,331	568	94	12	1	10	3,016
USA	1,205	788	113	–	–	2	2,108
India	1,277	515	292	–	1	9	2,094
Turkey	1,329	490	233	16	12	2	2,082
South Korea	1,310	45	89	–	–	1	1,445
Kazakhstan	280	758	23	3	–	4	1,068
Mongolia	419	406	108	–	–	8	941
Japan	759	166	13	–	–	–	938

Source: OfF (2011)

Foreigners seeking international protection constitute a relatively small fraction of the foreign population in Poland (see table 14.1). The volume of applicants for refugee status has been increasing in recent years, fluctuating around 10,000, but the number of persons granted refugee status has remained stable and relatively low at around 100-300 per year. Among recognised refugees, one national group has definitely been dominant in recent years – Chechens originating from the Russian Federation; they have accounted for about 90% of applications and are the group who have most often been granted refugee status[23]. EU citizens, of whom 8,000 registered their stay in Poland in 2010, form a minority among the foreign population in Poland.

Work permits and declaration registers

The Ministry of Labour and Social Policy (MLSP) administers two registers that cover the foreign labour force in Poland: a register of work permits issued to foreigners and a register of employers' declarations of intent to employ a temporary foreign worker on a rotation basis[24].

The register of work permits – which have been issued since 1989 in Poland – contains data on citizenship, country of previous residence, position, occupation, permit duration, economic activity and size of company employing a foreigner. At the moment, it does not cover the total foreign labour force, excluding EU citizens working in Poland as well as seasonally employed workers from countries neighbouring Poland. The latest data are published online and data from previous years are available on request. The number of work permits granted grew steadily through the 1990s, reaching a peak of 25,000 in 2002. In the following years the number fluctuated around 12,000, but has increased again in recent years, with 29,000 work permits granted in 2009 and no fewer than 37,000 in 2010. This significant increase in the last two years is most likely related to the liberalisation (and concomitant lower costs) of the work permit issuing procedure and also to a new and unprecedented wave of Chinese migrant workers coming to Poland.

For years, the greatest number of work permits were issued to Ukrainian workers. The second major group used to be Vietnamese, but they were outnumbered by Chinese workers in the period 2008-2010. In 2010, work permits were issued to citizens of Ukraine (35% of all work permits issued in that year), China excluding Taiwan (17%), Vietnam (6%), Nepal (6%), Belarus (6%), Turkey (5%) and India (4%) (MLSP, 2011).

Seasonal foreign workers in Poland can be traced using data from the register of employers' declarations of intent to employ a temporary foreign worker on a rotation basis. This register contains very limited information on the characteristics of foreigners: citizenship, sex, age, sector in which they will be employed and period of work that can be obtained on request. In 2010, no fewer than 180,000 employers registered declarations at local employment offices. As in previous years, the majority (94% in 2010) were for Ukrainians, followed by small percentages of Belarusians, Moldavians and Russians, most of them working in the agriculture and construction sectors (MLSP 2011).

However, neither register measures foreigners' integration in the Polish labour market; rather, they reflect the presence of certain migrant groups in different sectors of the Polish labour market. Although they do not adequately describe the foreign labour force in Poland, since many work permits are issued for short periods (up to three months) and are renewed systematically – not to mention foreigners entitled to work in Poland without a work permit and persons working in Poland illegally. Moreover, the data on employers' declarations in the register should be viewed with caution, since trading in employers' declarations in order to obtain a visa to Poland has become a recognised fact and many declarations do not lead to employment of a foreigner (Szczepański 2010).

14.3.3 Population registers in Poland

Polish institutions (independently) collect a lot of data on the total Polish population, including data on foreigners. For example, the Ministry of Labour and Social Policy has developed new monitoring system, the National Labour Market Monitoring System (*Krajowy System Monitorowania Rynku Pracy* – KSMRP), which shows the number of foreigners (from EU and non-EU countries) among the unemployed, and the number of unemployed persons with an entitlement to benefits (Kupiszewska 2009)[25]. In May 2010 there were 2,900 registered unemployed foreigners in Poland (0.2% of the total number of unemployed persons), of whom 234 were entitled to receive unemployment benefit. These numbers can be translated into an unemployment rate – an important integration indicator – only for foreigners who are eligible to work and who register as unemployed in Poland. Consequently, the remaining groups of migrants, especially irregular migrants, cannot be included in such an indicator (MLSP 2010).

Other statistics are gathered by the Ministry of Education (ME) in the 'Educational Information System (*System Informacji Oświatowej*) (Szelewa 2010). The aggregate data include number of pupils by citizenship (approx. 4,000 in the 2005/2006 academic year (ME 2006)), national minority and language classes, number of students attending additional free Polish language classes, native language and cultural classes. Other available data in relation to education includes the number of students at Polish universities (almost 17,000 in the 2009/2010 academic year (CSO 2011)). However, these data are not adequate integration measurement tools; basic statistics that would by contrast reflect the degree of educational integration would for example be drop-out rates among foreign pupils, the share of foreign pupils repeating school years, or educational outcomes by citizenship.

Some fundamental analysis of the social insurance status of foreigners is possible. The Polish Social Insurance Institution maintains a Central Register of Contributors and a Central Register of Insured Persons, which contains data on foreigners for whom employers have paid the social insurance contributions. At the end of 2009, employers had paid contributions for over 56,000 foreigners 4,000 more than in the previous year. Almost a third of the foreign workers concerned were Ukrainian, followed by citizens of Afghanistan (11%), Belarus (7%), Russian Federation (5%), Vietnam (5%) and Germany (3%) (Polakowski 2010).

There are other datasets that include a citizenship variable, but the data are either inaccessible or do not distinguish between native Poles and foreigners. In the planned integration monitoring system, other datasets supervised by the Ministry of Labour and Social Policy could be taken into consideration: the National Social Assistance Monitoring System (*Krajowy System Monitoringu Pomocy Społecznej* – KSMPS), National Family Benefits Monitoring System (*Krajowy System Monitoringu Świadczeń Rodzinnych* – KSMSR), National Maintenance Fund Monitoring System (*Krajowy System Monitoringu Funduszy Alimentacyjnych* – KSMFA)[26] and also the National Health Fund register. In all those databases, the citizenship variable is recorded but information on it has never been published.

14.4 Conclusions

In general, what we are witnessing now in Poland is the lack of a framework for monitoring migrant integration. Monitoring activities are currently in the hands of NGOs and international institutions. The results of their efforts demonstrate that there is a need for a comprehensive integration policy in Poland, together with monitoring of its implementation and results.

We would argue that implementing a continuous integration monitoring system will be a difficult task in Poland in the short term. One crucial obstacle here is the underdevelopment of the Polish integration policy compared to that in Western countries, which usually also incorporates a monitoring system. First of all, the absence of an official definition of 'integration of migrants' makes the creation of an integration monitoring system problematic: setting up a framework for monitoring something that is undefined constitutes a real challenge. Another difficulty is the fragmentation and lack of coordination in the drafting of legislation in Poland. Last but not least, we would draw attention to the fact that the limited array of integration programmes being implemented in Poland is directed to a fairly small number of specific groups of foreigners: repatriates and foreigners who have been granted international protection.

Moreover, notwithstanding policy aspects, a precondition for the implementation of effective and continuous integration monitoring is availability of data. The situation in Poland is far from ideal in this regard. Data relating to the integration process are virtually nonexistent in Poland, with the sole exception of data on the integration of participants in integration programmes. Some of the existing population registers (dedicated to unemployment, education or social insurance) could be used for monitoring purposes, since many of them contain information on people's citizenship. However, an adequate amount of information on the foreign population is essential in order to obtain reliable indicators of migrant integration, and this is problematic in Poland due to both the quality of the available statistics and the nature of immigration.

Although the quality and accessibility of data on the immigration process have improved in recent years, there is a still need for further improvement. Statistical data collected by CSO cover only a small selection of characteristics of immigrants. The last population census, in which a good collection of variables was recorded, proved to be unsuccessful in capturing the population of temporary immigrants. Administrative registers on foreigners can also provide only basic information on migrants. More detailed analysis of their situation in Poland could be conducted using data embedded in the *Pobyt* system, but gaining access to these data presents a real challenge. In order to render data from national registers useful for integration monitoring purposes, the procedures for managing adequate datasets would have to be changed. This in fact reflects a broader problem with Polish population registers, in that very limited flows of data between the different registers means that linking different pieces of information and computing basic indicators (e.g. the unemployment rate among foreign workers) is currently problematic.

In our view, the nature of the inflow of foreigners into Poland also makes measurement of the immigration process highly problematic. Firstly, the small scale of immigration makes this a difficult phenomenon to measure; small numbers of foreigners are simply invisible in general population registers. Consequently, some national studies that could be powerful in assessing the level of migrants' integration are simply useless in Poland. This is the case, for example, for the Labour Force Survey (LFS) or the EU Survey on Income and Living Conditions (EU-SILC). The numbers of foreigners 'caught' in these surveys do not exceed a hundred.[27] Secondly, obtaining a true picture of the contemporary inflow of foreigners to Poland is a difficult task given the prevalence of temporary immigration to the country, a phenomenon exacerbated by circular mobility (cf. Górny et al. 2010). In addition, some vague estimates suggest that there are around 50,000-300,000 undocumented foreign workers in Poland (Frelak & Kaźmierkiewicz 2005).

Nevertheless, although the task is difficult, some efforts have been made to build an integration monitoring system in Poland in the form of a draft policy document entitled 'The Polish Migration Policy: current state of play and further actions' adopted by the inter-ministerial Committee for Migration in July 2011. One chapter of this document is entirely devoted to the issue of foreigners' integration. Apart from envisaging, among other things, voluntary integration programmes for all categories of foreigners, the document also proposes activities aimed at enhancing the knowledge about immigrants' integration in Poland and the setting up of a system for monitoring and evaluating integration policy. Proposed activities would include support for research on the integration needs and the extent of migrants' integration, research on monitoring of national/ ethnic/religious communities, research on barriers to integration, and research on discrimination and racism; developing a set of integration indicators that are relevant to Polish conditions; enhancement of existing the system of gathering statistical data on foreigners in Poland; and monitoring of social attitudes and media information having an impact on immigrant integration (MIA 2011). Though promising, the document formulates only general guidelines whereas its implementation is yet to be drafted in a follow-up document.

To sum up, the strategy set out by the inter-ministerial Committee for Migration marks a promising step on the path to creating an integration monitoring system in Poland. In our view, in order to be successful further steps would require changes and initiatives in several areas: policy, statistics and data management with a focus on data which are currently hidden in population registers and registers of foreigners. We also fully concur with the recommendation set out in the document prepared by the inter-ministerial Committee for Migration in April 2011 that rebuilding all national registers (through data standardisation and harmonisation of definitions in accordance with EU and UN standards) and their unification (especially the *Pobyt* system and the PESEL database) (MIA 2011) are necessary in Poland.

It should also be borne in mind that data on housing conditions and civic or political participation by foreigners in Poland currently do not exist. Creating adequate data sources in these fields is something that needs to be addressed. Moreover, the complexity of the immigration phenomenon and the multiplicity of strategies employed by foreigners in Poland, with the focus on temporariness and the irregular character of mobility, demands specific solutions. We would argue that a monitoring system that makes use of qualitative data and analyses of case studies is indispensable in order to obtain a reliable picture of integration processes in Poland. In other words, a crucial task in the process of building an integration monitoring system for Poland is to seek to narrow the gap between what Vertovec (2009), in describing the concept of diversity, calls 'configurations of diversity' – how diversity appears through structural and demographic conditions – and 'representations of diversity' – how diversity is imagined and represented by ready-made categories in statistics and policy.

Notes

1 A definition of 'immigrant integration' can be derived indirectly from the recent draft document prepared by the inter-ministerial Committee for Migration, entitled 'The Polish Migration Policy: current state of play and further actions'. The document states that integration is a complex and lengthy process which should be stimulated by 'enabling immigrants to be self-dependent with access to labour market, education and health care services, ability to participate in social life and to exercise civil rights, under conditions of respect for their cultural and religious needs' (MIA 2011: 70).

2 The territorial structure of administration in Poland consists of three levels. The highest administrative level is *voivodship* (*województwo* in Polish); this corresponds with NUTS 2 level. There are 16 *voivodships* in Poland. The *powiat* is a lower-level administrative layer than the region; it is equivalent to LAU 1 level. There are around 379 *powiats* in Poland. The lowest administrative level comprises is the *gmina* – commune. There are almost 2,500 *gminas* in Poland. *Gmina* is equivalent to LAU 2 level.

3 Journal of Laws, No. 78, item 483 with amendments.

4 Journal of Laws, No. 64, item 593 with amendments.

5 Journal of Laws, No 53, item 532 with amendments.

6 Journal of Laws, No. 99, item 1001 with amendments.

7 Journal of Laws, No. 210, item 2135 with amendments.

8 Journal of Laws 2004, No. 256, item 2572 with amendments.

9 Journal of Laws, No 164, item 1365 with amendments.

10 Journal of Laws 2001, No. 79, item 855.

11 Journal of Laws 2000, No. 28, item 353 with amendments.

12 The Ministry of Social Policy existed from 4 May 2004 to 30 October 2005. On 31 October 2005 it was converted into the Ministry of Labour and Social Policy.

13 It should be noted that accommodation and job offers are not provided within these programmes.

14 Excluding the right to vote and to membership of political parties, and rights attached to EU nationality.

15 An example is the initiative of the Mazovian Voivodship Office, launched in 2005 and partly financed from the European Refugee Fund; it was devoted to the design of a computer program for the evaluation of individual integration programmes for refugees, but has never been implemented.

16 http://www.integrationindex.eu.

17 It goes beyond the scope of this chapter to discuss the reasons for this. For more details see e.g. Tanajewski (2006).

18 People holding permanent residency in Poland.

19 As more detailed analyses show, a relatively large number of Germans recorded in the census were living abroad at the time of the census (cf. Okólski 2010).

20 Before 2006 registration/deregistration data were calculated on the basis of information provided by communes (local level authorities).

21 Other PESEL system variables include date and place of birth (data not published), sex, address and date of registering permanent residence, previous addresses, marital status and, for foreigners: serial number of residence card. Information about education level is not recorded. See for more details http://www.mswia.gov.pl/portal/pl/381/32/PESEL.html.

22 The *Pobyt* system also includes other datasets covering procedures regarding aspects such as the issuing of provisional identity certificates for aliens; acquisition of Polish citizenship; an obligation to leave the territory of Poland; expulsion from the territory of Poland; refusal of entry into the territory of Poland; persons stopped in the border zone and escorted to the border (cf. Kupiszewska 2009).

23 In 2009 a new group of applicants entered the procedure – almost 40% of applicants originated from Georgia. However, none of these applications culminated in a positive decision.

24 This is a new policy introduced in 2006 in a Regulation from the Minister of Labour and Social Policy allowing aliens to take up employment without the need to obtain a work permit, dated 30 August 2006, Journal of Laws 2006, No. 156, item 1116, with amendments.

25 See the monthly reports for the years 2001-2010: http://www.psz.praca.gov.pl/main.php?do=ShowPage&nPID=867997&pT=details&sP=CONTENT,objectID,867970.

26 They will be integrated with National Labour Market Monitoring System in the future.

27 A trial to analyse the situation of migrants in Poland on the basis of national surveys has been carried out in a pilot international study by Eurostat based on indicators of immigrant integration in selected policy areas, using data from the EU-SILC, European Union Labour Force Survey (EU-LFS), Eurostat's migration statistics and the OECD's Programme for International Student Assessment (PISA) (Kraszewska et al. 2011). However, for Poland, most of the results are considered inaccurate due to the exceptionally small numbers of migrants interviewed in the survey.

References

Bieniecki, M. & P. Kaźmierkiewicz (2008). *Learning to welcome: Selected aspects of integration of migrants in Poland*. Brussels: Migration Policy Group. Consulted at: http://www.migpolgroup.com/public/docs/148.part_3_LearningtoWelcome_20.08.08.pdf.

CSO (2010). *Pracujący w gospodarce narodowej w 2009 r. [Employment in the national economy in 2009]*. Warsaw: Central Statistical Office.

CSO (2011). *Rocznik Demograficzny 2010 [Demographic Yearbook of Poland 2010]*. Warsaw: Central Statistical Office.

Frelak, J. & P. Hut (2006). *Polska i Niemcy wobec rodaków na Wschodzie [Poland and Germany towards compatriots in the East]*. Warsaw: Instytut Spraw Publicznych.

Frelak, J. & P. Kaźmierkiewicz (2005). *Rekomendacje dla ukraińskiej polityki migracyjnej [Recommendations for Ukranian migration policy]*. Warsaw: Instytut Spraw Publicznych.

Górny, A., I. Grabowska-Lusińska, M. Lesińska & M. Okólski (2010). General conclusions. In: A. Górny, I. Grabowska-Lusińska, M. Lesińska & M. Okólski (eds.), *Immigration to Poland: policy, employment, integration* (p. 209-216). Warsaw: Wydawnictwo Naukowe Scholar.

Grzymała-Kazłowska, A. & A. Weinar (2005). The Polish Approach to Integration. In: *Canadian Diversity*, vol. 5, no. 1, p. 72-75.

Huddleston, T., J. Niessen, E.N. Chaoimh & E. White (2011). *Migrant Integration Policy Index III. Polska [Migrant Integration Policy Index III. Poland]*. Brussels: British Council / Migration Policy Group.

Hut, P. (2002). *Warunki życia i proces adaptacji repatriantów w Polsce w latach 1992-2000 [Life situation and the process of adaptation of repatriates in Poland, 1992-2000]*. Warsaw: Oficyna Wydawnicza ASPRA-JR.

Iglicka, K. (2001). Shuttling from the former Soviet Union to Poland: from 'primitive mobility' to migration. In: *Journal of Ethnic and Migration Studies*, vol. 27, no. 3, p. 505-518.

Iglicka, K. & K. Sword (eds.) (1999). *The Challenge of East-West Migration for Poland*. London: Macmillan.

Kaźmierczak, T. (2005). *Ocena przebiegu oraz uzyskanych efektów indywidualnych programów integracji realizowanych na terenie województwa mazowieckiego [Assessment of the course and outcomes of individual integration programmes implemented within the Mazowieckie province]*. Warsaw.

Kępińska, E. (2007). *Recent Trends in International Migration* (The 2007 SOPEMI Report for Poland. CMR Working Papers No 29/(87)). Warsaw: Centre of Migration Research.

Kępińska, E. & D. Stola (2004). Migration Policies and Politics in Poland. In: A. Górny & P. Ruspini (eds.), *Migration in the New Europe: East-West Revisited* (p. 159-176). Basingstoke, Hampshire: Palgrave Macmillan.

Gracz, K. (2007). Społeczne uwarunkowania problemów z funkcjonowaniem przymusowych migrantów na polskim rynku pracy [Social determinants of problems with functioning of forced migrants on the Polish labour market]. In: W. Klaus (ed.) *Migranci na polskim rynku pracy. Rzeczywistość, wyzwania, problemy [Migrants in the Polish labour market: Reality, problems and challenges]*. Warsaw: Stowarzyszenie Interwencji Prawnej. Consulted at: http://www.interwencjaprawna.pl/docs/migranci-na-rynku.pdf

Klaus, W. & A. Chrzanowska (2007). *Integracja i pomoc społeczna wobec uchodźców w Polsce. Wyniki badań aktowych [Integration and social assistance for refugees in Poland. Results of the file research]*. Warsaw: Stowarzyszenie Interwencji Prawnej. Consulted at: http://www.interwencjaprawna.pl/docs/ARE-807-integracja-pomoc-spoleczna.pdf

Klaus, W., K. Makaruk, K. Wencel & J. Frelak (2011). *Refusal to Grant Integration Assistance – Law and Practice*. Warsaw: Stowarzyszenie Interwencji Prawnej. Consulted at: http://www.interwencjaprawna.pl/docs/ipi-refusals.pdf

Klaus, W. & K. Wencel (2010). Dyskryminacja cudzoziemców w Polsce w latach 2008-2010 [Discrimination against foreigners in Poland in 2008-2010]. In: W. Klaus (ed.) *Sąsiedzi czy intruzi. O dyskryminacji cudzoziemców w Polsce [Neighbours or intruders? Discrimination against foreigners in Poland]*. Warsaw: Stowarzyszenie Interwencji Prawnej.

Kosowicz, A. (2007). *Access to Quality Education by Asylum-Seeking and Refugee Children – Poland Country Report*. Izabelin: Polish Migration Forum. Consulted at: http://ec.europa.eu/ewsi/en/resources/detail.cfm?ID_ITEMS=14260

Kraszewska, K., B. Knauth & D. Thorogood. *Indicators of Immigrant Integration. A Pilot Study*. Eurostat Methodologies and Working papers. Consulted at: http://epp.eurostat.ec.europa.eu/cache/ITY_OFFPUB/KS-RA-11-009/EN/KS-RA-11-009-EN.PDF

Kupiszewska, D. (2009). *Country Report Poland*. PROMINSTAT. Consulted on 26 June 2010 at:
http://www.prominstat.eu/drupal/?q=system/files/PROMINSTAT_Poland.pdf

Lesińska, M., M. Duszczyk, M. Szczepański, M. Szulecka & R. Stefańska (2010). Migration policy in Poland
and its impact on the inflows and settlement of migrants. In: A. Górny, I. Grabowska-Lusińska,
M. Lesińska & M. Okólski (eds.), *Immigration to Poland: policy, employment, integration* (p. 54-90). Warsaw:
Wydawnictwo Naukowe Scholar.

Łotocki, Ł. (2009). *Integracja i dyskryminacja – krajobraz 2009 [Integration and discrimination – overview
2009]. Instytut Spraw Publicznych.* Consulted at: http://ec.europa.eu/ewsi/UDRW/images/items/
docl_12716_279167653.pdf

ME (2006). *Uczniowie i nauczyciele cudzoziemcy w szkołach w Polsce [Foreign pupils and teachers in schools in Poland].*
Warsaw: Ministry of Education.

MLSP (2011). *Statystyki [Statistics].* Warsaw: Ministry of Labour and Social Policy. Consulted on 21 May 2011
at: http://www.mpips.gov.pl/index.php?gid=1286.

MLSP (2010). *Statystyki strukturalne maj 2010 [Structural statistics, May 2010].* Warsaw: Ministry of Labour and
Social Policy. Consulted on 26 June 2010 at: http://158.66.1.108/_files_/stat_files/strukt_0510.zip

MIA (2011), *Polityka Migracyjna Polski – stan obecny i postulowane działania [The Polish Migration Policy: current state
of play and further actions].* Warsaw: Ministry of the Interior and Administration. Consulted at: http://
www.bip.mswia.gov.pl/portal/bip/227/19529/Polityka_migracyjna_Polski.html

MSP (2005a). *Propozycje działań w celu stworzenia kompleksowej polityki integracji cudzoziemców w Polsce [Proposals
for actions aiming at establishing a comprehensive immigrant integration policy in Poland].* Warsaw: Ministry of
Social Policy. Consulted at: http://ec.europa.eu/ewsi/UDRW/images/items/docl_14679_887286385.pdf

MSP (2005b). *Strategia polityki społecznej na lata 2007-2013 [Strategy for social policy for the period 2007-2013].*
Warsaw: Ministry of Social Policy. Consulted at: http://www.mpips.gov.pl/gfx/mpips/userfiles/File/
nowe/strategiaps.pdf

MTAS (2006). *Immigrant Integration Indicators. Proposal for contributions to the formulation of a system of common
integration indicators.* Ministerio de Trabajo y Asuntos Sociales. Consulted at: http://www.wodc.nl/
images/1365_fulltext_tcm44-80242.pdf

OfF (2010). *Dane liczbowe dotyczące postępowań prowadzonych wobec cudzoziemców w 2009 r. [Data on the number of
procedures conducted for foreigners in 2009].* Warsaw: Office for Foreigners. Consulted on 26 June 2010 at:
http://www.udsc.gov.pl/files/statystyki/2009.xls

Okólski, M. (2010). General introduction. In: A. Górny, I. Grabowska-Lusińska, M. Lesińska & M. Okólski
(eds.), *Immigration to Poland: policy, employment, integration* (p. 17-53). Warsaw: Wydawnictwo Naukowe
Scholar.

Polakowski, M. (2010). *Imigranci z krajów trzecich a system ubezpieczeń społecznych w Polsce [Third-country nationals
and the national insurance system in Poland]* (Raporty i Analizy – Seria Integracja No. 2). Warsaw: Centre
for International Relations.

Samoraj, B. (2007). Ocena skuteczności Indywidualnych Programów Integracji [Assessment of the
effectiveness of Individual Integration Programmes]. In: J. Frelak, W. Klaus & J. Wiśniewski (eds.),
*Przystanek Polska. Analiza programów integracyjnych dla uchodźców [Station Poland. Analysis of integration
programmes for refugees].* Warsaw: Instytut Spraw Publicznych.

Szczepański, M. (2010). Admission of foreigners to the labour market in Poland. In: A. Górny, I.
Grabowska-Lusińska, M. Lesińska & M. Okólski (eds.), *Immigration to Poland: policy, employment,
integration* (p. 67-72). Warsaw: Wydawnictwo Naukowe Scholar.

Szelewa, D. (2010). *Integracja a Polityka Edukacyjna [Integration and Educational Policy]* (Raporty i Analizy – Seria Integracja No. 6). Warsaw: Centre for International Relations.

Tanajewski, Ł. (2006). Cudzoziemcy przebywający w Polsce na stałe – próba oceny danych spisowych na tle danych Urzędu do Spraw Repatriacji i Cudzoziemców [Foreign permanent residents in Poland – attempt to compare census data against Office for Repatriation and Foreigners data]. In: E. Jaźwińska (ed.), *Imigracja do Polski w świetle wyników Narodowego Spisu Powszechnego 2002* (p. 54-66). Warsaw: Centre of Migration Research (CMR Working Papers, 13/71).

Wysieńska, K. (2010). Nguyen, Serhij, czy Piotr? Pilotażowe badanie audytowe dyskryminacji cudzoziemców w rekrutacji [Nguyen, Serhij, or Peter? Pilot audit study of discrimination of foreigners in the recruitment]. In: W. Klaus (ed.), *Sąsiedzi czy intruzi? O dyskryminacji cudzoziemców w Polsce [Neighbours or intruders? Discrimination against foreigners in Poland]* (p. 337-360). Warsaw: Instytut Spraw Publicznych.

Vertovec, S. (2009). *Conceiving and researching diversity.* Göttingen: Max Planck Institute for the Study of Religious and Ethnic Diversity (Working Paper WP 09-01).

15 Monitoring immigrant integration in Portugal: Managing the gap between available data and implemented policy

Catarina Reis Oliveira

15.1 Introduction

In 1950 Landecker posed a very pertinent and still contemporary question:

> Nowadays it seems less pertinent to ask: What is integration? If this question is asked at all, then it is only in preparation for the fruitful question: How can integration be measured?
> (Landecker 1951: 332)

Although policymakers have changed the way in which integration is operationalised in recent decades, only few create policies that are based on monitoring official data about immigrants. Few countries have data available to accurately measure the need for and progress in immigrant integration or to evaluate whether policies have an impact in this regard.

Portugal is no exception in this respect. There is no formal integration monitoring system, and the available data does not allow consistent analysis of immigrant integration processes over time. The operationalisation of the concept of integration has however been consolidated in the last two decades through a complex matrix of policies which are aimed at meeting immigrants' needs and which have been recognised in recent years as good practices (MIPEX 2007, 2010; IOM 2010; UNDP 2009).

Since the turn of the century, Portuguese governments have acknowledged the importance of evaluating their policies and measures. In 2003 an Immigration Observatory was created with the motto of 'getting to know more so as to act better' with the aim of evaluating integration policies and their impact on immigrants. Since 2007, Portugal has also formulated Action Plans for Immigrant Integration based on implementation evaluation mechanisms, which are assessed by the Consultative Council for Immigration Affairs. These evaluation mechanisms do not however claim to measure policy effects in immigrant integration in a systematic way over time, but mainly chart developments in government policy.

Undoubtedly, the fragilities of the statistical system adversely affect Portugal's ability to define an integration monitoring system. Portugal does not have a permanent statistical data set on immigrant integration or a data system that is able to monitor cohorts of immigrants over time in various domains simultaneously, and this hinders the evaluation of integration as a process. Several problems related to this have been reported and/or recognised by the government and are being incorporated in the second National Action Plan for Immigrant Integration by using a measure to improve the official data on immigrants that is currently dispersed across several ministries.

This chapter endeavours to highlight how a recent immigration country that has (very suddenly) been reported as having the best integration policies has such a fragile system for monitoring integration. It analyses how the concept of integration has been incorporated in policies, underlying an imbalanced relationship between the number of policies developed and the availability of official datasets to accurately measure the impact of those policies on immigrants.

The aim of this chapter is not to present a theoretical discussion of the concept of integration, but rather to analyse how integration has been defined by policymakers in Portugal and reflected in normative developments. It also analyses the characteristics of data sources and the feasibility of developing an effective immigrant integration monitoring system in Portugal, as the implications for the interdependence between policy and practice are of real importance.

15.2   Immigration flows to Portugal

For centuries, Portugal has been a country of *emigration*; mass immigration dates only from the mid-1970s. The end of the Portuguese dictatorship in 1974 and concomitant changes in political, economic and social structures were responsible for the shift in Portuguese migration patterns. Emigration decreased during the 1970s, and the independence of the former African colonies resulted in the arrival of repatriates, asylum-seekers and return migrants (see figure 15.1).

According to census data for the period from 1960 to 1981, the overall population living in Portugal increased by 11%, while the foreign population increased by 269%. In 1960, the foreign population with legal status represented only 0.3% of the total population in Portugal; in 1980 that figure had grown to 0.5%, in 1990 to 1.1%, and in 2000 to 2%. The size of the foreign population doubled from 2000 to 2007 and in 2010 represented around 4.4% of the total population.

Historical links between Portugal and its former colonies conditioned the early immigration flows. Until the end of the 1990s, immigrants from the Portuguese-speaking African countries (PALOP) dominated the immigrant population, who responded to the opportunities generated in some segments of the Portuguese labour market, namely civil construction and the domestic services sector.

In 1986 Portugal entered the European Economic Community, which created a new incentive for immigration. Economic liberalisation also led to an upsurge in immigrant labour recruitment, to new forms of labour relations and to flexibility in the labour market (Baganha et al. 1999: 150). The number of Asian and South American immigrants, although fewer in absolute terms, started to show higher rates of growth than those of African origin. The 1990s also brought several extraordinary regularisation processes – in 1992/93 and 1996 – which increased the number of legal immigration to the country.

Figure 15.1

Foreign population with legal residence status and Portuguese emigration, 1960 -2010

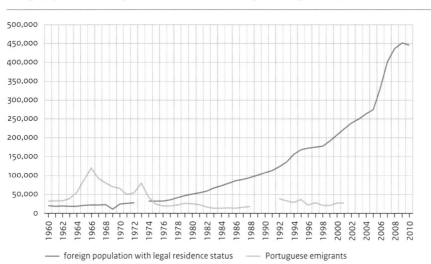

Source: INE and Border Control Police

Later, at the end of the 1990s, new immigration flows came from Eastern Europe. The construction boom linked to several major infrastructure projects and other openings in the labour market created a new geography of immigration, characterised by immigrant dispersion on a national scale. This major shift increased the complexity of contemporary migration flows to Portugal and created new challenges for the integration policies and border control. Since then, there has been an increase in the immigrant population without historical links with Portugal who do not speak Portuguese.
The country had to adapt – and continues to do so – to this new reality, and several changes became identifiable in a normative and institutional framework.

15.3   Integration policies during three decades of a 'new' immigration country

Differences in the interpretation of the concept of integration give rise to integration policies with different objectives (Entzinger et al. 2003: 10), which in turn will determine the areas considered to be a priority. It is therefore relevant to analyse how integration policies started to be implemented in Portugal and how they have changed over the years. Furthermore, as argued by Bijl et al. (2005: 12), keeping in mind that integration processes also occur at institutional level, analysis of policies developed in Portugal in recent decades highlights how opportunities and/or restrictions have been created in relation to the integration of immigrants.

The migratory experience determined the Portuguese options and how integration has been shaped. Political discourses related to immigrant integration (including by the four High Commissioners for Immigration that have held office to date) usually argue that the rights claimed for Portuguese emigrants living abroad are the same as those advocated for immigrants today. A publicity campaign conducted in 2004 to raise awareness about the positive contribution made by immigrants to Portugal was explicitly based on this idea:

> We have been, for many centuries, a country of emigrants. Now it is our turn to welcome, as only we know how, all those immigrants who work together with us to construct a better Portugal.

In the early 1990s several factors contributed to the surfacing of immigration as a relevant issue on the Portuguese national political agenda: the increase in arrivals and the lack of control; the visible inadequacy of the conditions for integrating immigrants (poverty, poor living conditions, underground labour, etc.); the first manifestations of inter-ethnic conflict and racist or xenophobic incidents; the emergence of organised actions directed at promoting the rights of immigrants, in which the role of non-governmental organisations was emphasised for the first time (Fonseca et al. 2002: 46). During the first phase of Portuguese integration policies, developments were based mainly on the fact that the majority of immigrants spoke Portuguese and had strong historical links with the country. The first integration policy was formally developed in the Ministry of Education in 1991 with the creation of Entreculturas[1] Secretariat. Aiming to respond to the new challenges of ethnic and cultural diversity, the Minister of Education created a secretariat for multicultural education programmes with the objective of 'coordinating, fostering and promoting, in the scope of the education system, the programmes and actions that pursue the teaching of the values of coexistence, tolerance, dialogue and solidarity among different peoples, cultures and ethnic origins'. A Council of Ministers Resolution dating from 1993 also strengthened the framework for interventions in the education, employment/vocational training and social welfare sectors, giving the Minister of Employment and Welfare responsibility for ensuring the coordination, development and strengthening of instruments and measures 'aimed at the full social and occupational integration of immigrants and ethnic minorities' (Oliveira et al. 2006:19).

A few years later, in 1996, recognising the importance of clarifying the integration policy, the position of High Commissioner for Immigration and Ethnic Minorities (ACIME) was created based on the argument that the new migratory situation in Portugal demanded new measures.
It is relevant to analyse the rapid evolution of this institution – from a political position, created in 1996, to the present public institute that is the High Commission for Immigration and Intercultural Dialogue (ACIDI). Its legal framework underlines how Portugal has been operationalising the concept of integration in recent years. Since 1996 integration has been politicised as a holistic and transversal issue, linking different ministries and/not merely a matter of labour market or security.

In 1996 the High Commissioner was given the mission of 'promoting the integration of immigrants in an inter-ministerial strategy, keeping in mind that the presence of immigrants enriches Portuguese society.' When ACIME was created, the integration of immigrants was based in five fundamental ideas – first, the positive impact of immigrants on Portuguese society was acknowledged; second, integration was underlined as an inter-ministerial intervention, in other words as a holistic action; third, the promotion of immigrants' integration underlined the consultation and dialogue with entities that represent immigrant communities; fourth, integration meant achieving 'better life conditions in Portugal with respect for the identity and culture of origin of the immigrants'; and, finally, integration of immigrants also implied equal opportunities and combating racial discrimination.

These first legal documents said nothing about the legal status of the target population. Integration was politicised as a general framework for providing better 'life conditions' for immigrants without limiting the goals of those policies for third-country nationals by imposing legal conditions. Reinforcing this political option, access to health care was formalised in 2001 for both legal and illegal immigrants who had resided in Portugal for more than 90 days, based on public health interests.

In 2002, the high commissioner's cabinet was converted into a High Commission, under the direct authority of the Prime-Minister, reinforcing the powers and scope for intervention of ACIME. Portugal hence became one of the few countries to set up a centralised body with responsibility for immigrants' integration. The provision of services to immigrants was subsequently reinforced with the creation of specialised support centres in collaboration with local institutions (the one-stop-shop approach[2]). The concept of integration was changed slightly in 2002 – although the law made clear that immigrants' cultural identity linked to the country of origin should be respected, 'integration' was considered to have been achieved if immigrants 'accept the language, laws and moral and cultural rights of the Portuguese nation'. It was also emphasised that ACIME's mission was 'to seek to ensure that all citizens legally residing in Portugal have equal dignity and opportunities', underlining the granting of rights to those with legal residence status in Portugal. This legal framework further developed the notion of guaranteeing the participation of and collaboration with immigrant associations in policies that directly affected their communities, also defining the competences and the delegates represented in the Consultative Council for Immigration Affairs.

In 2007 ACIME was further reinforced when it became a public institute with administrative autonomy, bringing together several other services working in the integration field and targeting immigrants and culturally diverse groups; it was also renamed the High Commission for Immigration and Intercultural Dialogue (ACIDI), reflecting the priority given by the government to dialogue with all stakeholders. Under this new legal framework, ACIDI's mission became to

> collaborate, define, implement and evaluate both sectorial and crosscutting public policies concerned with the integration of immigrants and ethnic minorities, as well as to promote dialogue between the various cultures, ethnic groups and religions.

It is also relevant to consider that, since 2007, ACIDI's mission is not only to integrate immigrants and ethnic minorities in Portugal, but also to 'host' them. This hosting is intended to highlight the importance not only of integrating immigrants but also making them welcome, creating facilities to accommodate them better in society.

The advocated intercultural model became operational in 2007, and included the formulation and implementation of the first Action Plan for Immigrant Integration, based on a holistic approach. The Plan resulted in a process of broad consultation with immigrant associations and other stakeholders. The measures in the Plan were organised in thematic sections that reflect the priority dimensions in which the concept of integration was operationalised.[3] Immigrants' positive impact on Portugal was further underlined in the first Plan:

> the migratory phenomenon [...] represents an important contribution in dealing with the debilitating demographic situation [...] [and] is a positive factor in terms of economic growth, for sustaining the social security system and for culturally enriching the country.

Two very significant pieces of legislation in relation to immigrants' integration have also been passed in recent years. In 2006 a new Nationality Law was approved by parliament and significantly liberalised the process for acquiring Portuguese nationality; the law was passed with overwhelming support, with not a single vote against from any of the parliamentary parties.

In 2007, after wide public consultation, the immigration law was also changed and passed by majority in the Portuguese parliament, with both the major parties voting in favour. The new legislation simplified procedures and reduced bureaucratic requirements, seeking to promote legal migration, combat illegal migration and facilitate family reunification. The legal regime for temporary migration was also regulated, providing for a temporary stay visa for seasonal work, and a regime for granting visas to immigrant entrepreneurs and highly qualified immigrants.

The rights given to immigrants had not been constant through the years. Whereas until 1998 all immigrants would acquire similar legal status that would confer most rights immediately upon receiving a residence permit, after 1998 (with further diversification of statuses in 2001) and until 2007 different situations were defined according to the status of the resident. Immigrants with a status other than an authorisation of residence (e.g. work permits, student visas, annual permits) would not, for example, have the right to start a business in Portugal, to initiate a family reunification, to accumulate years of residence in order to acquire Portuguese nationality, or the right to family subsidies or social security support for children. Until 2007, those rights were only granted after a certain period of residence (three or five years, depending on the legal status) and under certain conditions.

After 2007 several initiatives and legal changes – e.g. new Immigration Act, new citizenship law, reinforcement of the powers of ACIDI – increased the rights granted to immigrants, and further investments were made in integration programmes and measures, such as those underlined in the first Action Plan for Immigrant Integration. The 2007 Immigration Act emphasised the rights that all immigrants obtained immediately upon receiving a residence permit, namely the right to education, work, training or access to other qualifications, health and justice. It further stated that immigrants have the same rights as native Portuguese in respect of social security, tax benefits, trade unions membership and recognition of qualifications.

Given the way in which the Portuguese policy on immigrant integration has developed since 1996, it is possible to identify intervention areas that accentuate the way in which the concept of integration has been operationalised, namely through education, immigrants' participation, labour, health, religion, social security, anti-discrimination measures, awareness-raising in relation to immigration and cultural diversity, and holistic integration services and measures.

These priorities do not differ much from those proposed to the National Contact Points on Integration of the European Commission (Entzinger & Biezeveld 2003: 47). Hence, in an attempt to contribute to an effective European comparison of the monitoring and evaluation of integration policy, in this chapter Portuguese policy developments are distributed across the integration dimensions that are usually referred to in European Commission documents:

1   socioeconomic integration (including health and housing);
2   cultural integration;
3   legal and political integration; and
4   attitudes of the recipient society.

A fifth dimension will also be included, bearing in mind several other specific features of the Portuguese framework:

5   the holistic dimension of integration.

Table 15.1 shows some of the integration policy directions taken by Portuguese governments in recent decades and/or the dimensions advocated by policymakers as being the priority for immigrants' integration in Portugal.

Table 15.1

Relevant integration policies developed in Portugal since 1991 targeting immigrants, according to integration dimensions

integration dimensions	policy developments	implications
socioeconomic integration	recognition of qualifications and competences obtained outside Portugal	– since 2005 simplification of the equivalences procedures for basic and undergraduate qualifications; – since 2007 clarification of the process of recognition of diplomas or degrees, Masters and PhD programmes (until then administered separately by each university) administered by a national Commission for the Recognition of Foreign Degrees.
	nationals and immigrant workers with equal rights and duties on the labour market (since 1995)	– right to safe working conditions; – right to be represented by a trade union; – right to strike; – right to holidays; – protection by law in the event of discrimination.
	right to become an entrepreneur or start a business in Portugal	– labour law with no restrictions for immigrant entrepreneurs (since 1998) increased the number of immigrant entrepreneurs; – creation of a special permit for immigrant entrepreneurs and highly qualified immigrants (since 2007): simplified procedures for these immigrants.
	right to work in Portugal (with the exception of certain public functions)	– annual report on employment opportunities for foreigners (since 2001) stipulating the number of work permits that Portuguese consulates can issue; – since 2007 the law has defined an exceptional regime for permit acquisition by immigrants who are already in Portugal with an employment contract or a labour relationship.
	family reunification	– Since 2007 family reunification has been a universal right for all immigrants with legal status in Portugal. Before then, only certain legal statuses were eligible for family reunification, and only after one year of residence.
	right to social protection	– People who reside legally in Portugal and pay social security contributions have the right to social protection.
	Intercultural Education Programme (Entreculturas) (since 1991)	Created in 1991, operating mainly in the areas of training, publication of teaching materials and awareness-raising, the main objective is to mobilise Portuguese society to welcome and support the integration of immigrants.
	Choices Programme (created in 2001)	– mainstream programme created in 2001 (now in its fourth generation) for social inclusion of children and young people from the most vulnerable settings, with a special focus on immigrants and descendants and Roma communities.
	universal right to education	– All immigrants (with legal status) have the right to education since 1986. – The right to education even for minors residing illegally was established by law in 2004.

Table 15.1 (continued)

integration dimensions	policy developments	implications
	universal right to health care	– Since 2001 all foreigners who pay social security contributions have the same access to health care as natives and those with illegal status can also access health care by paying health contributions. – Since 2004 no health service (public or private) can refuse access to health care to anyone, whatever their legal status; such refusal is seen by the law as a discriminatory act that violates the principle of equality. – In 2009 a Ministry of Health document further clarified the situations in which immigrants with illegal status can access the health system on equal terms to native Portuguese.
cultural integration	right to religious freedom (since 2001)	– An advisory body to the Parliament and the government was created in 2001 with the official name of Commission for Religious Liberty (Law-Decree no.308/2003). – A unit for the promotion of inter-religious dialogue was created as part of the public administration in 2005.
	support for immigrant associations	– ACIDI recognition process for immigrant associations (since 2000) entitles them to apply for public funding each year to support projects to foster immigrant integration, intercultural dialogue, cultural diversity, and/or empowerment of immigrant associations. – Technical Support Office for Immigrant Associations (as part of the national immigrant support centres) for advice and funding supervision of activities (since 2004).
	Portuguese For All (PPT)	– Programme that aims to develop Portuguese language courses and technical Portuguese courses targeting the immigrant population. Portuguese language courses allow access to a certificate that can be used for acquiring nationality, permanent residence status and/or long-term resident status. Technical Portuguese courses are also certified, permitting better access to and integration into the labour market in the areas of trade, hospitality industry, beauty therapy, civil construction and civil engineering.
legal and political integration	access to Portuguese nationality	– Since 2006 the new Nationality Law has provided a more equitable naturalisation policy, liberalising the process for acquiring nationality. A year after the new law came into force, over 35,000 applications for nationality have been made – more than triple the number of applications in 2005.
	political participation by immigrants	– limited to reciprocity between countries and/or only to local elections; – Brazilians are the only immigrant group who can also vote in national elections.
	immigrants' participation in integration policies	– Consultative Council for Immigration Affairs (COCAI) created in 1998, seeking to ensure the consultation and participation of immigrant communities, social partners and social solidarity associations in the formulation of integration policies; – cultural mediators (immigrants themselves) in public administration service provision (since 2004).
	universal right to legal protection	– All immigrants have the right to legal protection, including those residing illegally whose countries have entered into a reciprocity arrangement and those who are economically vulnerable. – A person who is involved in a legal process and who does not understand Portuguese has the right to an interpreter (at no cost). – People who have been victims of discrimination (including racial discrimination) are protected by the law.

Table 15.1 (continued)

integration dimensions	policy developments	implications
attitudes of recipient society	ACIDI' TV and radio programme about immigrants and intercultural dialogue	– a TV programme broadcast on the public service broadcasting channel (since 2004); – in collaboration with a radio station a weekly programme is broadcast presenting original and current information on immigration issues.
	intercultural trainers network and information campaigns	The ACIDI trainers network (created in 2006) aims to provide public administration (e.g. health professionals, police, teachers) and the private sector free intensive courses on intercultural themes. Ten modules are available: welcoming diversity; intercultural stories; nationality law; immigration law; myths and facts about immigration; intercultural dialogue; inter-religious dialogue; health and immigration; cultural mediation; intercultural education.
	Journalism for Cultural Diversity Prize (since 2003)	– creating awareness in the media about the impact of negative news and/or dissemination of stereotypes about immigrants.
	measures to combat discrimination and racism	– The Portuguese law provides an administrative complaints procedure for cases of racial discrimination, which is dealt with by the Commission for Equality and Against Racial Discrimination (CICDR) created in 2000. The CICDR is a specialist body dealing with racial discrimination. Presided by ACIDI, it includes representatives elected by Parliament, government appointees, employers' associations, trade unions, immigrants associations, NGOs and civil society; – Since 2005 it a Support Unit for Immigrants and Victims of Racial and Ethnic Discrimination has been in operation that provides support free of charge to victims of racial discrimination and to immigrant victims in general.

To sum up, interculturality has been advocated in recent years (especially since 2007) as the reference model for Portuguese integration policies. Further investments have also been made to ensure that integration not only confers rights but also obligations and responsibilities to citizens who are part of Portuguese society, promoting participation by immigrants in the decision-making in relation to the policies and measures that target them.

A comprehensive approach to immigration has been also consensually recognised in Portugal as the most effective way of understanding and fostering integration. Since the integration of immigrants is a holistic process, involving challenges in the economic, political, judicial, health, cultural and social aspects of immigrants' lives, this ensures that immigrants come into contact with different ministries. Thus, according to the principles of 'joined-up government', Portugal has made a political choice to guarantee that different ministries and government agencies will convey a coherent political message on immigrant integration. This has been achieved on the basis of partnership, coordination and common aims between various government ministries. The incoherence of information that is widely reported as a difficulty frequently faced by immigrants in EU member states (Oliveira et al. 2009: 24-26) – and often as a sign of a lack of cooperation between different agencies and ministries, was addressed in Portugal through a holistic approach applied in several integration measures and policies (summarised in table 15.2).

In conclusion, the new century brought a major investment in the development of integration policies and the reinforcement of the integration service provided by the Portuguese public administration. These policy options led to the international recognition of Portugal as one of the countries with the best integration policies (MIPEX 2007, 2010; UNDP 2009; IOM 2010). In 2011 the ACIDI, being the Portuguese public institute for the integration of immigrants, also received first prize in the European Public Sector Award (EPSA 2011) under theme 2 'Opening Up the Public Sector Through Collaborative Governance'.[4]

Having characterised the way policymakers adopted the concept of 'integration' in Portugal, it is important to determine which areas are covered by official data and/or which integration measures have been monitored. Examination of the sources available to each integration policy domain provides an insight into the possibilities open to policymakers and researchers for measuring integration and monitoring policies' impacts.

Table 15.2
Holistic dimension of Portuguese integration policies

policy developments	implications	availability of data
Action Plan for Immigrant Integration: two editions (2007-2009 and 2010-2013)	– 122 measures of integration in the first edition of the Action Plan, with an achievement rate of 81%, and 90 measures in the second edition of the Plan; – mobilisation and coordination of a range of relevant policies and ministries (13 different ministries involved in the first Plan, 14 in the second); – mainstreaming of integration policies in a whole-of-government approach, fostering coherence of information and coordination between different agencies and ministries.	– measures monitoring reports
High Commission for Immigration and Intercultural Dialogue (ACIDI) reporting directly to the Prime-Minister	– inter-ministerial intervention institute that takes into account not only the economic and legal aspects of immigrants' life in Portugal, but also other spheres related to integration; – provision of several integrated and holistic services (the one-stop-shops: all services that immigrants need to contact are centralised in one place, with branches of public administration services and support services managed through protocols between ACIDI and civil-society organisations, including immigrant associations).	– ACIDI activity reports with data of integration services users – IOM external evaluations of the services (2005, 2007, 2010)
Consultative Council for Immigration Affairs (created in 1998)	– representatives from different ministries, immigrant leaders, trade unions and civil-society organisations.	

15.4 Monitoring integration in Portugal: challenges and opportunities ensuing from official data on immigration

To date, integration policies in Portugal have hardly relied on official statistical data sources. Several quantitative and qualitative studies, most of them promoted and published by the Immigration Observatory[5], have taken that role in some cases. Some of those studies not only contributed to evaluating the measures and laws which directly or indirectly affect the lives of immigrants in Portugal, but also led to discussion of those measures and laws and the formulation of new policies (e.g. nationality law, family reunification rights, entrepreneurship facilities, extension of the entitlement to family allowance to include children of all immigrants).

Other evaluation mechanisms have been adopted in specific integration programmes and measures developed in Portugal. ACIDI integration services, for example, has been externally evaluated three times by the International Organization for Migration (IOM 2006, 2008, 2010), and several of its recommendations have been incorporated in the improvement of the services provided. On the other hand, the Action Plans for Immigrant Integration have adopted monitoring and evaluation mechanisms based on process indicators for the adopted measures.

However, these studies and evaluation mechanisms do not provide a permanent statistical description of migration nor a continuous and comprehensive monitor of immigrant integration. Matching the policy options and/or the dimensions underlined in the political operationalisation of the integration concept in Portugal with the official data available is not an easy task, as most of the indicators that could allow coherent monitoring of immigrants' integration are absent or cannot be measured continuously over time.

One frequently used primary data source is the census of the National Institute of Statistics, which provides basic information on household composition and age, nationality and place of birth, labour market participation and employment status, educational attainment and housing characteristics. The obvious advantages of the census data are their nationwide scope, including all residents regardless of their legal status in the country, capturing those who already have Portuguese citizenship but who were born abroad and allowing comparison of the characteristics of immigrants and natives. However, several disadvantages can also be identified in this source for measuring immigrants' integration: the data are only available every ten years, and very quickly become obsolete in terms of integration standards and policy implementation; literacy challenges of the questionnaires for immigrants; religious questions (being optional) attract a higher percentage of non-response; it does not include questions on language skills, health access, discrimination experiences and political participation.

Other problems relating to the feasibility of evaluating statistically immigrant integration in Portugal stem from the fact that official sources refer to foreigners (and not to foreign-borns). In other words, all analyses of data on immigration are based on the nationality of the individuals concerned. Although this seems to be an inconsequential choice, it is important to examine its implications since the notions of 'immigrant' and 'foreign' refer to different groups. An immigrant is defined as an individual who, having been born in a certain territory, migrated to another country where he/she has resided for at least one year. Hence the change of territories itself does not reflect the nationality of an individual. In contrast, the notion of 'foreign' cannot be disassociated from that of nationality, meaning that any individual who has a different nationality to that of the country of residence is foreign. As a consequence, not all foreigners are immigrants. In practice there are individuals with foreign nationality who were born in Portugal and who do not have any migratory experience whatsoever. On the other hand, immigrants who acquire Portuguese nationality disappear from official databases and, as a consequence, can no longer be described and/or measured. It is therefore not possible to statistically monitor either different generations of immigrants or foreign-born citizens who have acquired Portuguese citizenship.

A second set of difficulties relies on the fact that there is no direct source of data collection in Portugal either for monitoring immigrant integration or for assessing the impact of integration policies. Moreover, none of the official statistical sources collect data that consistently allow a characterisation of immigration flows, as most of them tailor their data collection to their particular area of intervention, which is not specifically focused on migration.

However, combining data from several sources enables the description of immigrants in the integration dimensions in question (see table 15.3). It is nevertheless important to acknowledge that most of those sources provide administrative information, which is not collected for statistical purposes. This limits most of the analyses to aggregate sets of data or to specific formatted variables defined by the administrative procedures and objectives of the ministries. Furthermore, the quality of the data is often dependent on the capacity of the entities that collect those data to validate the information for inconsistencies and coding errors. It was concerns of this kind which, for example, were used as justification for the aliens and border control police (SEF) not making available the information relating to the economic activity of foreigners registered since 1998, based on the argument that some changes generally happen that are not recorded in the database and/or the data only reflect the situation of individuals at the moment that they apply for or renew a permit, so that professional mobility would not be captured (Oliveira 2008: 104).

The cooperation between institutions that hold administrative data and/or collect data for statistical purposes about foreigners in Portugal is fairly recent. The directives from the European Commission have been fundamental in both stimulating cooperation between Portuguese institutions and in the harmonisation of methodologies, variables and the coherence of datasets (Fonseca et al. 2009: 9). Nevertheless, while still acknowledging the need for systematic data collection to monitor immigrants' integration in Portugal, the second Action Plan for Immigrant Integration (2010-2013) contained a measure 'to improve official data on the integration of immigrants, broken down by sex, that exist in the various ministries, with the purpose of calculating indicators, without prejudice to the currently available data on the management of migration and border controls.' (measure 4).

The lack of data is not however a weakness that is particular to Portugal. In the past decade the European Commission has several times communicated its concerns about the importance of member states increasing the amount of information available on migration flows and integration of immigrants, improving the comparability of migration statistics, and monitoring and evaluating their immigration policies. Accordingly, the Commission launched a pilot project – in which Portugal was involved – for the evaluation of immigrant integration with a set of common indicators identified in four areas – employment, education, social inclusion and active citizenship – obtained from administrative data sources (Eurostat 2011). The use of the indicators should be complemented by contextual analyses at national and European level.

Although this is a useful publication because it facilitates comparability between member states and therefore provides a perspective on immigrant integration in the various countries of the European Union (EU); there are still several limitations of the data sources analysed which can compromise effective evaluation of immigrants' integration in the EU. The first problem is related to the fact the some of the harmonised sources analysed use small sample sizes which might not be big enough to capture the diversity of characteristics of the people concerned. It is also important to take in consideration that the analyses made (Eurostat 2011) compare immigrant populations as a whole in all countries; this can create problems since different European countries gather data on different immigrant populations (in some cases different nationalities and immigrants with different socioeconomic characteristics) and/or the legal framework may be partially responsible for the patterns observed.

Moreover, it is not clear whether all indicators selected really measure immigrants' integration and/or whether the patterns compared in the various member states translate the same reality. As argued by Lemaitre (2010), international harmonisation of data on integration often produces data which are relatively poorer than those available in a national context alone, due to the 'forcing' of data into common categories and definitions, with loss of national specificities (e.g. differences in governmental and societal institutions, the composition of the immigrant population and the related migratory history and policies). An example of that are the results achieved in Eurostat (2011) on the 'gap of activity rates between foreign-born population and total population' (indicator of employment policy area). This pilot study highlights the very good Portuguese score (contrasting with the majority of EU member states with a zero gap), in which immigrants have much higher activity rates (85%) than natives (79%) and so the gap translates into a positive score (6) for both men (7) and women (6). Does this mean that immigrants are better integrated in the Portuguese labour market than in the other member states? The answer is of course not a straightforward 'yes', since this figure mainly illustrates the fact that immigration is still a very recent phenomenon in Portugal and that the labour market participation of immigrants is attributable to the predominance of labour migration to the country (Peixoto 2008: 27; OECD 2008: 272).

As table 15.3 shows, the socioeconomic, legal and political integration dimensions are areas for which more sources of information are available, thus offering greater scope for identifying the situation of immigrants in Portugal.

By contrast, only limited monitoring is possible of cultural integration and the attitudes of the recipient society towards immigrants. Moreover, the holistic and multidimensional process of integration enshrined in several Portuguese policies is mainly evaluated using process indicators (which essentially measure whether the goals defined for each measure are achieved) and several qualitative evaluations of the integration services. The Action Plans for Immigrant Integration, for example, although a fundamental tool of government policy on immigrant integration, does not contribute to the evaluation of the impact of integration policies, but only provides reports on the progress of measures. Ultimately, the sources available for each integration dimension and the diversity of data, and quality and quantity of information, reflect not only Portuguese statistical traditions, but also the kind of integration models and policies developed over recent years. As the comparison between tables 15.1 and 15.3 shows, the two dimensions with higher diversity of sources are precisely those for which a higher density of policies and measures has been developed in recent years.

Hence, what this chapter analyses is not necessarily the indicators that it would make sense to assess for each integration dimension, but, based on the limited availability of quantitative data, the information that is available and that allows some characterisation of integration aspects related to the policy priorities. Of itself, this places constraints on effective integration monitoring in Portugal because, as also reported in other countries (Bijl et al. 2008: 220), statistical data from national registers will never provide a comprehensive picture of the integration process. In sum, to capture a picture of the immigrant integration process in Portugal more accurately, a wider set of indicators, collected in a consistent way and by a coherent and harmonised source, would be needed.

Table 15.3

Data sources available in Portugal to characterise immigrant integration

dimen-sions of integration	national data collection	characteristics of data source	type of source
socio-economic integration	Housing and Population Census	collected every ten years; describes the foreign population who have been resident in the national territory for at least one year, regardless of their legal status	data for statistical purposes
	Labour Force Survey	quarterly sample survey assessing the relationship of the population to the labour market. Sample not calibrated by nationality / including the 2008 ad hoc module on the labour market position of migrants and their immediate descendants.	data for statistical purposes
	Household Survey	sample survey not calibrated by nationality because the sample size of foreigners is small	data for statistical purposes
	Demographic Statistics	annual publication with detailed information about foreigners with legal status (data from Aliens and Borders Service – SEF)	data for statistical purposes
	Strategy and Planning Office of the Ministry of Labour and Social Solidarity	annual data based on administrative procedures of the Ministry in several areas – register of enterprises and employees, and data on work accidents	administrative data
	Institute of Statistical Information on Social Security	annual data based on administrative social security procedures – beneficiaries of subsidiaries and social security contributions	administrative data
	Working Conditions Authority	annual data based on employment contracts, professional activity of workers and fatal work accidents	administrative data
	Institute for Employment and Professional Training	monthly data on unemployed persons registered with job centres	administrative data
	Office of Planning, Strategy, Evaluation and International Relations	annual data on population enrolled in higher education	administrative data
	Office of Educational Statistics and Planning (Ministry of Education)	annual data on enrolled population in the education system	administrative data

Table 15.3 (continued)

dimensions of integration	national data collection	characteristics of data source	type of source
	NARIC – National Academic Recognition Information Centres (Ministry of Science, Technology and Higher Education)	annual data on recognition of diplomas	administrative data
	Immigration Observatory studies	qualitative data on immigrant integration on several themes (e.g. highly qualified workers, entrepreneurs, work accidents)	surveys and qualitative data
cultural integration	Immigration Observatory studies	qualitative data on immigrant integration on several themes, namely in religious practices, language	surveys and qualitative data
legal and political integration	Aliens and Borders Service statistical reports	annual reports with information on legal residents according to type of residence permit, nationality, age groups, gender, location of residence	administrative data
	General Directorate of Consular Matters	annual information on visas issued by Portuguese consulates	administrative data
	Conservatory of Central Registers (Ministry of Justice)	data on applicants and acquisition of Portuguese nationality	administrative data
	General Directorate of Prison Services	annual data on administrative information on prisoners by nationality	administrative data
	General Directorate of Internal Affairs – Electoral Administration	data on electoral register of persons entitled to vote in national and/or local elections	administrative data
	Immigration Observatory studies	qualitative data on immigrant integration on several themes, namely on the acquisition of Portuguese nationality, immigrant associations and the political participation of immigrants	surveys and qualitative data
attitudes of recipient society	Immigration Observatory studies	two surveys undertaken on attitudes and values in relation to immigration and reciprocal perceptions of immigrants and native Portuguese population (2003 and 2006)	research surveys

Table 15.3 (continued)

dimensions of integration	national data collection	characteristics of data source	type of source
	ACIDI information on the number of discrimination complaints submitted to CICDR	ACIDI annual reports	administrative data
holistic dimension	ACIDI activity reports	annual reports on the users and characteristics of integration services	administrative data
	Integration Plans monitoring reports	six-monthly and annual reports of integration plan monitoring of implemented measures	procedural information
	IOM evaluation reports on ACIDI integration services	three evaluations (2006, 2008 and 2010) with surveys applied to immigrants (service-users) and public servants (service-providers) in relation to integration services	surveys

15.5 Conclusion

Although integration has become a central concept for member states and national policies, it is still a complex issue with no consensus on precisely what it means and how it should be operationalised. As a result, measuring immigrants' integration is still an ambitious and problematic task.

This chapter aimed to highlight how the concept of integration has been understood by Portuguese policymakers and how it has been incorporated in policies and measures. As reported, in the last two decades Portuguese policies have been based on the assumption that integration constitutes a multidimensional connection with Portuguese society. The Portuguese case further shows the imbalanced relationship between policy developments and the availability and analysis of data. Although investments have been made in the development of several evaluation mechanisms for policies and measures, integration monitoring is not yet consolidated in Portugal as an instrument which can also analyse the impact of policy on immigrants. Additional data are needed to provide insights not only into the characteristics of different immigrant groups during certain periods of time, but also about longitudinal changes in immigrants' lives which emphasise integration as a process.

As described in this chapter, legal changes and integration policy developments have often been justified on the basis of the way in which political parties politicise integration and European directives, and not so much of hard statistical facts. Hence, although Portuguese integration policy is proving to be very consistent and is among the best in international comparisons (MIPEX 2011 and UNDP 2009), migration data collection is still very poor and does not allow comprehensive assessment of immigrants' integration or effective monitoring of the impact of the policies developed. Essentially, the available data are based on the census and administrative databases that collect information about foreigners with legal residence status in Portugal using a limited set of variables linked to their particular areas of intervention (normally not focused on migration). Hence, and as acknowledged in the second Action Plan for Immigrant Integration, more needs to be done to harmonise data and increase the coherence of data collection on migration in Portugal. The scope for linking different national registers via the Institute for National Statistics (INE) should also be explored, and cohorts of immigrants could be tracked over time. As stated by Bijl et al. (2005: 87), monitoring integration using longitudinal data gives a more accurate picture of the integration process based on actual behaviours and the actual social positions of individuals.

A national effort to monitor and describe immigrants' integration is not only of interest to enable Portugal to obtain a clearer picture of the real impact of the public investment in policies and measures; but also to gain more precise information on the whys and wherefores of particular integration outcomes for immigrants in the socioeconomic, cultural, political and legal dimensions. The development of a coherent and permanent information system of integration indicators that incorporated different national sources (both administrative and statistical databases) should meet the needs of policymakers and researchers. Additionally, it would allow better comparison with other countries, not only in terms of policy developments, but also (and more importantly) of the real impact of different policy integration options.

Notes

1   'Entreculturas' means 'between cultures' in Portuguese.
2   The National and Local Immigrant Support Centres reinforced the partnership principle of the integration policy – the public administration working for the integration of immigrants with collaboration protocols established with civil-society organizations, namely immigrant associations – and the principle of immigrants participating in the formulation of integration policies and integration service provision, with the presence of cultural mediators (most of them immigrants themselves) to narrow the gap between public administration services and immigrant citizens (Oliveira et al. 2009).
3   The first version of the Plan organised the policy measures in twenty different areas: welcoming; work, employment and professional training; housing; health; education; solidarity and social security; culture and language; justice; the information society; sport; descendants of immigrants; the right to live as a family/family reunification; racism and discrimination; religious freedom; associative activity among immigrants; the media; relations with countries of origin; access to citizenship and political rights; gender equality; and human trafficking. The second edition of the Plan, covering the period 2010-2013, was organised in seventeen thematic areas. Among the new areas were elderly immigrants and the promotion of diversity and intercultural dialogue.
4   Further at www.epsa2011.eu
5   Created in 2003 according to the philosophy 'getting to know more so as to act better', the Observatory has stimulated dialogue between academics and political decision-makers in relation to the proposal, discussion and evaluation of public policies on the integration of immigrants in Portugal. Link: http://www.oi.acidi.gov.pt/

References

Ager, A. & A. Strang (2008). Understanding Integration: A conceptual framework. In: *Journal of Refugee Studies*, vol. 21, no. 2 (April), p.166-191.

Baganha, M. et al. (1999). Os imigrantes e o mercado de trabalho: o caso português. In: *Análise Social*, vol. XXXIV, no. 150, p. 147-173.

Bijl, R.V. et al. (2005). *The integration monitor 2005. The social integration of migrants monitored over time: trend and cohort analyses*. The Hague: WODC (Research and Documentation Centre).

Bijl, R.V. et al. (2008). The integration of migrants in the Netherlands monitored over time: trend and cohorts analyses. In: C. Bonifazi et al. (eds.), *International Migration in Europe: New Trends and New Methods of Analysis*, IMISCOE (p. 199-223). Amsterdam: Amsterdam University Press.

Carrera, S. (2008). *Benchmarking Integration in the EU. Analysing the debate on integration indicators and moving it forward*. Gütersloh: Bertelsmann Foundation.

Entzinger, H. & R. Biezeveld (2003). *Benchmarking in Immigrant Integration*. Rotterdam: Erasmus University (DG JAI-A-2/2002/006).

Eurostat (2011). *Indicators of Immigrant Integration. A Pilot Study*. Luxembourg: Publications Office of the European Union (Eurostat Methodologies and Working Papers).

Fonseca, L. et al. (2002). *Immigrants in Lisbon, Routes of integration*. Lisbon: University of Lisbon, The Centre of Geographical Studies.

Fonseca, L. et al. (2009). PROMINSTAT *Country Report Portugal*. Promoting Comparative Quantitative Research in the Field of Migration and Integration in Europe (PROMINSTAT).

Heckmann, F. et. al. (2010). Qualitative Integration Research in Europe – Data needs and Data Availability. Promoting Comparative Quantitative Research in the Field of Migration and Integration in Europe (PROMINSTAT) (PROMINSTAT Working Paper no. 3, February).

Landecker, W.S. (1951). Types of Integration and Their Measurement. In: *American Journal of Sociology*, vol. 56, no. 4 (January), p. 332-340.

Leal, M. et al. (2007). *Proposals for a European common system of indicators of immigrants integration*. Madrid: Ministerio de Trabajo y Asuntos Sociales.

Lemaitre, G. (2005). The Comparability of International Migration Statistics. Problems and Prospects. In: OECD *Statistics Brief*, no. 9, July 2009.

Lemaitre, G. (2010). *Immigrants' Integration Policies: International Monitoring (and Diagnosis). The added value of international comparisons* (presentation at the International Forum Immigrants Integration, Lisbon, 16-17 December 2010).

Niessen, J. et al. (2009). *Developing and using European Integration Indicators* (background paper prepared for the Swedish Presidency Conference Integration of New Arrivals, Malmo, 14-16 December 2009). Online document consulted at: http://www.migpolgroup.com/public/docs/168. DevelopingandusingEuropeanintegrationindicators_15.12.09.pdf

OECD (2008). The labour market integration of immigrants and their children in Portugal. In: OECD, *Jobs for Immigrants. Labour market integration in Belgium, France, The Netherlands and Portugal* (vol. 2, p. 269-332). Paris: OECD.

Oliveira, C.R. et al. (2006). *First Report – Indicators of Immigrant Integration* (INTI Project 'Immigrants integration indicators'). Lisbon: ACIME.

Oliveira, C.R. (2008). The determinants of immigrant entrepreneurial strategies in Portugal. In: C.R. Oliveira & J. Rath (eds.), *Immigrant Entrepreneurship – Special Issue of Migrações Journal*, vol. 3 (October), p. 101-128.

Oliveira, C.R. et al. (2009). *Handbook on how to implement a One-Stop-Shop for Immigrant Integration*. Lisbon: ACIDI.

Peixoto, J. (2008). Imigração e Mercado de trabalho em Portugal: investigação e tendências recentes. In: J. Peixoto (ed.), *Imigração e Mercado de Trabalho – Special Issue of Migrações Journal*, vol. 2 (April), p. 19-46.

Phalet, Karen & Marc Swyngedouw (2003). Measuring immigrant integration: the case of Belgium. In: *Migration Studies*, vol. XL, no. 152, p. 773-803.

Rosário, E. et al. (2008). *Measuring integration. The Portuguese case. Regional indicators of social and labour market inclusion of third country nationals* (Transnational research project 'Migrants' Integration Territorial Index'). Lisbon: IOM.

SEF (2008). *Annual Report on Migration and International Protection Statistics for Portugal 2008*. Brussels: European Migration Network. Consulted online at: http://emn.intrasoft-intl.com/Downloads/download.do;jsessionid=89BBCCCF70CECF704AE0A9B18727BB7F?fileID=1329

MIPEX (2007). *Migrant Integration Policy Index II*. Brussels: British Council and Migration Policy Group.

MIPEX (2011). *Migrant Integration Policy Index III*. Brussels: British Council and Migration Policy Group.

UNDP (2009). *Human Development Report 2009. Overcoming barriers: human mobility and development*. New York: United Nations Development Programme.

IOM (2010). *World Migration Report 2010 – The Future of Migration: Building Capacities for Change*. Geneva: International Organisation for Migration.

16 Monitoring integration in Sweden

Anna Envall

This chapter presents Sweden's model for monitoring integration at national level. It is divided into three sections. The first section presents a short description of immigration and integration in Sweden' this is followed by a section on Sweden's integration policy. The final section reports on Sweden's work to monitor its integration policy, looking at the argumentation behind the design of the system, data collection and the use of the data.

16.1 Immigration and integration in Sweden

Sweden has had a higher level of immigration than emigration since the end of the Second World War, as can be seen from figure 16.1. The extent of this immigration and the reasons for it have varied over time. During the 1950s, 60s and 70s most immigrants were labour migrants migrating from the Nordic countries as well as countries in Southern and Central Europe. Labour immigration reached a peak in 1970, when a large number of people from Finland came to Sweden as migrant workers. Since the 1980s, the character of immigration has changed, and has been dominated by refugee immigration and the subsequent immigration of close relatives, particularly from the former Yugoslavia, the Middle East and Somalia. Since Sweden's membership of the European Union in 1995, immigration from the rest of the EU and the EEA has also increased significantly.

Figure 16.1
Sweden's immigration and emigration in the period 1851-2009 (in absolute numbers)

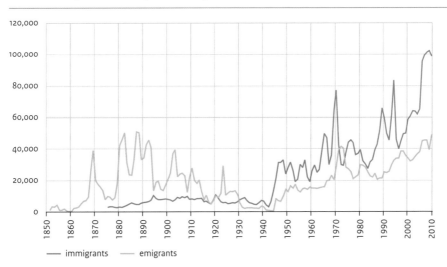

Source: Statistics Sweden

The immigration over recent decades means that more than 14% of Sweden's current population of nine million were born in other countries. People born in Finland are the largest group, followed by people born in Iraq and the former Yugoslavia. The majority of foreign-born persons have lived in Sweden for more than ten years, and some 60% are Swedish citizens. In general, foreign citizens can apply for Swedish citizenship after living in Sweden for five years. A further 5% of Swedes were born in Sweden with two foreign-born parents.

In 2008 a total of 90,021 persons were granted residence permits in Sweden. As can be seen from figure 16.2, the largest proportion of these people, 38%, were granted a residence permit as a relative of a Swedish resident/citizen.

Figure 16.2
Reasons for residence permit in Sweden in 2008 (in percentages)

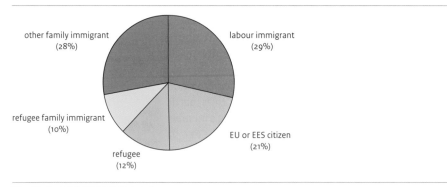

other family immigrant
(28%)

labour immigrant
(29%)

refugee family immigrant
(10%)

EU or EES citizen
(21%)

refugee
(12%)

Source: Swedish Migration Board

Statistics relating to the labour market, education and housing show that the situation of foreign-born persons differs from that of native Swedes. In 2009 the employment rate for people aged between 20-64 years and born in Sweden was 81%, compared with 65% for persons born abroad. Around 60% of foreign-born persons who had studied for two years at tertiary level had a skilled job. The corresponding figure for university-educated persons born in Sweden was 90%.
Similar differences are found among foreign-born and native Swedish children, for example in terms of their results at lower secondary school. The differences are greatest when comparing those who migrated to Sweden before and after school-starting age. In 2009 the proportion of pupils in grade nine who came to Sweden after school-starting age and qualified for entry to upper secondary school was 53%. This compares with 84% of pupils who came to Sweden before school-starting age and 91% of pupils with a Swedish background who left grade nine and qualified for entry to upper secondary school. The situation of foreign-born people and native Swedes also differs in other areas, such as health, housing and turnout at elections. The key determining factors include the time of immigration and the duration of stay in Sweden. The longer immigrants have

lived in Sweden, the greater the probability that their material and social situation will correspond to that of the native Swedish population. The situation for children with parents who are both foreign-born is also affected by how long the parents have been in the country, as well as by their geographic origin; immigrants from Africa and Asia and relatively new arrivals generally have more difficulties gaining a foothold on the labour market.

A number of urban districts, particularly in larger cities, are socio-economically segregated, with a relatively high proportion of foreign-born residents, many of them newly arrived. These urban districts report higher unemployment, a lower average income and a lower level of education than the country as a whole. When the economic situation of the residents improves, e.g. by gaining employment, many of them move to other areas and another newly arrived person settles in their place.

16.2 Swedish integration policy

The overall goal of the Swedish integration policy is 'equal rights, obligations and opportunities for all, regardless of ethnic or cultural background'. The integration policy is based on a vision of a society where individuals with different cultural and ethnic backgrounds can co-exist. However, it is also important that an individual's freedom does not encroach on the fundamental values of society. Swedish integration policy seeks to ensure that 'respect for fundamental values such as human rights, democratic governance and equality between women and men are maintained and strengthened'.

The integration policy covers all areas of social development. This means that the goal of the integration policy is to be achieved mainly through general measures that are designed to benefit the Swedish population as a whole. Special, targeted measures for integration are only carried out as a complement, primarily for new arrivals. Special measures are targeted at this group not because of their immigration per se, but because of their need for things such as language support.

The division of responsibility in integration also has a general basis. All government authorities have a clear responsibility to work to achieve the integration policy objectives of equal rights and obligations. This general basis is in line with the Swedish political model in which the government makes a decision as a collective. The Minister of Integration is responsible for carrying out and developing integration policy, and implementation takes place by incorporating integration policy as a part of all policy areas ('mainstreaming').

In 2008 the government presented a communication, 'Empowerment against exclusion – the Government's strategy for integration', which set out the goal of the integration policy. The strategy identifies seven areas that comprise the focus of the government's integration policy:

1   an effective service for receiving and introducing new arrivals;
2   more people in work, more entrepreneurs;
3   better results and greater equality in schools;

4   better language skills and more adult education opportunities;
5   effective anti-discrimination measures;
6   positive development in urban districts where social exclusion is high;
7   common basic values in a society characterised by increasing diversity.

An overall focus of the government's policies work is to increase the supply and demand of labour, and to create quality and equality in schools. Education and employment are the key areas in the sense that better results in these areas lead to better overall integration.

In Sweden, the term 'immigrant' refers to people who have migrated to Sweden. The term encompasses all immigrants, regardless of their native country. Additionally, the term 'third-country nationals' is also used as this is the legal basis in the Lisbon Treaty and is thus important in the European context.

The term 'second-generation immigrant' is not generally used. Instead, 'person of foreign background' is used, which includes people both of whose parents were born in a foreign country. Subcategories are used when required, the most common being period of stay in Sweden and reasons for granting residence permits.

16.3   Current system for monitoring integration policy

Sweden's current system for monitoring integration policy consists of several different parts. The core of the monitoring system comprises 27 indicators, which were presented for the first time in the budget bill for 2010. Each Ministry also carries out its own monitoring every year within the framework of its particular spheres of responsibility in line with the general nature of the integration policy. In addition, Statistics Sweden has also been commissioned to produce data for a further seventeen integration variables, such as the proportion of income that comes from introduction benefits and the proportion of people who received income support during the year.

The data can be broken down on a regional and municipal level, as well as for the 38 urban districts with widespread exclusion that are covered by local agreements between the government and the municipalities. This means that the monitoring system can be used not only by the government for measuring the trend in integration at national level, but also by regional authorities and municipalities. As a complement to these monitoring data, the Swedish Association of Local Authorities and Regions has initiated the collection and compilation of data relating to the introduction programme for newly arrived immigrants at municipal level. The municipal introduction data focus on results achieved as well as resources spent and activities undertaken to allow comparisons between different municipalities with regard to things such as cost-effectiveness.

In addition to the monitoring activities carried out by the state, regional and local authorities, integration is also monitored by universities and educational organisations. For example, the Institute for Labour Market Policy Evaluation has published several studies focusing on immigrants' entry to the labour market, as well as on segregation in urban areas.

The statistical monitoring provides an overall picture of the situation of foreign-born persons in terms of education, employment, etc. The indicators cannot, however, serve as a basis for conclusions regarding causality. To obtain a picture of what lies behind the situation portrayed by the indicators, other methods are used as a complement, for example qualitative studies or further statistical analysis. Qualitative studies are carried out within specific focus areas, for example examining obstacles to newly arrived women seeking to enter the labour market.

The next section sets out in greater detail Sweden's system for monitoring the 27 indicators. Firstly, the argumentation behind the selection of the indicators is explained. This is followed by two sections describing data and data collection as well as the use of the data. Finally, the plans for future development of the monitoring system are presented.

16.3.1 General basis for the monitoring system

The development of the 27 indicators stemmed from the government's need to track the trends and developments in the area of integration over time. When producing the indicators, experiences from other European countries were taken into consideration, along with lessons learned from an earlier monitoring model. This earlier model, dating from 2006, was very extensive and consisted of 24 targets and 69 indicators. The model was never implemented, mainly because it was overly ambitious, reducing the accuracy, relevance and effectiveness of the indicators.

The 27 indicators were developed to provide a picture of the central aspects of the trend in integration in a clear, current and easy to understand way. The monitoring does not claim to highlight integration from all perspectives or to explain why a certain trend has occurred. The value of limiting and clarifying the purpose of the monitoring system was an important lesson from the previous model. The high number of indicators made it difficult to provide an overview, which resulted in difficulties in using the monitoring results for guiding and developing policy.

The number of indicators in the new model has been limited to ensure that an overview can be produced and to make it easier to interpret the data. The indicators are also comparable over time, as well as between different subgroups of the population. This means, for example, that the employment rate among new arrivals is measured in the same way as the employment rate in general.

The 27 indicators are presented in their entirety in table 16.1.

Table 16.1

Indicators for monitoring the Swedish integration policy

area	indicator
an effective service for receiving and introducing new arrivals	– the number of people employed 2-4 years after national registration (born in the EU/EEA and outside the EU/EEA) – the number of people active 2-4 years after national registration, i.e. in employment or regular education (born in the EU/EEA and outside the EU/EEA)
more people in work, more entrepreneurs	– the proportion who are employed (born in Sweden, the Nordic Region, the EU/EEA and outside the EU/EEA) – the proportion who were employed in the previous year and who are still employed this year (born in Sweden, the Nordic Region, the EU/EEA and outside the EU/EEA) – the proportion (born in Sweden, the Nordic Region, the EU/EEA and outside the EU/EEA) who were unemployed in the previous year, but have gained employment (openly unemployed and in programmes) – the proportion of those educated to a post-secondary level (born in Sweden, the Nordic Region, the EU/EEA and outside the EU/EEA) who have work that requires post-secondary competence – the proportion of entrepreneurs who are employed (born in Sweden, the Nordic Region, the EU/EEA and outside the EU/EEA)
better results and greater equality in schools	– the proportion of pupils (with a Swedish background and a foreign background born in Sweden, the Nordic Region, the EU/EEA and outside the EU/EEA) who have achieved the targets in grade 3 – the proportion of pupils (born in the EU/EEA and outside the EU/EEA) who have qualified for entry to upper secondary school and who were entered in the national registry after the school-starting age, compared with pupils with a Swedish background – the proportion of pupils (with a Swedish background or a foreign background born in the EU/EEA and outside the EU/EEA) who have qualified for entry to upper secondary school and that were entered in the national registry before school-starting age – the proportion of pupils (born in Sweden, the Nordic Region, the EU/EEA and outside the EU/EEA) who have qualified for entry to tertiary education
better language skills and more adult education opportunities	– the proportion of the target group who have passed the national test in Swedish Tuition for Immigrants – the proportion of Swedish Tuition for Immigrants teachers with an educational university degree – the median time from national registration to passing the test in Swedish Tuition for Immigrants

Table 16.1 (continued)

area	indicator
effective anti-discrimination measures	– the number of reports to the Equality Ombudsman concerning ethnic discrimination during the year – the number of cases of ethnic discrimination that the Equality Ombudsman has taken to court during the year and which have led to convictions – the number of settlements in ethnic discrimination cases that the Equality Ombudsman was involved in during the year
positive development in urban districts where social exclusion is high	– the proportion who are employed who live in urban areas with a local development agreement, divided into the population as a whole, and those born in Sweden, the Nordic Region, the EU/EEA and outside the EU/EEA – the proportion furthest away from the labour market (people who have received income support for at least 10 months and have not received any other income-based benefits) in urban areas with a local development agreement, compared with the corresponding proportion in the country as a whole – the proportion of young people between the ages of 20-24 years old who are neither in employment nor studying, compared with young people in urban areas with a local development agreement and the country as a whole – the proportion of pupils in urban areas with a local development agreement who have qualified for entry to upper secondary school compared with the country as a whole – the difference in employment rate between people moving into and out of urban areas with a local development agreement – the proportion who say that they are worried a lot or often about crime, compared with those living in urban areas with a local development agreement and the population in the country as a whole
common basic values in a society characterised by increasing diversity	– the proportion of elected representatives born in Sweden, the Nordic Region, the EU/EEA and outside the EU/EEA – the proportion in a managerial role (born in Sweden, the Nordic Region, the EU/EEA and outside the EU/EEA) – the number of reports of xenophobic hate crimes during the measurement period
citizenship	– the proportion of foreign-born persons who have acquired Swedish citizenship after living in Sweden for six years

Source: Government budget bill 2010, prop. 2009/10:1

A number of guiding principles were used in selecting the indicators. These principles were formulated based on the lessons learnt from the previous monitoring system. In more concrete terms, the ambition was to select indicators that were:
– relevant;
– sustainable over time;
– based on existing data.

The term *relevant* means that the indicators have to say something about the trend in integration with respect to the goals formulated for the integration policy. Sweden's monitoring system is based on the overall objective of equal rights, obligations and opportunities for all, regardless of ethnic or cultural background. The majority of the indicators are therefore relative indicators, which focus on the relationship between different target groups, rather than absolute conditions. This allows the monitoring to provide a picture of whether the integration policy has been successful in evening out the differences between different groups based on their ethnic and cultural backgrounds.

The majority of these relative indicators are broken down by geographic origin (Sweden, the Nordic Region, the EU/EEA and the rest of the world). A number of the indicators for the strategic area 'Better education results and greater equality in schools' are also divided according to time of arrival in Sweden (before or after school-starting age). This division is motivated by the fact that foreign-born pupils who have gone through the whole school system in Sweden show much better results than those who move to Sweden after school-starting age.

The fact that the integration monitoring is based on relative indicators does not mean that absolute indicators describing the actual situation of the target group are not interesting, but they are more imponderable as indicators. For example, a low employment rate among foreign-born nationals is not primarily an integration policy problem if the rate of employment is just as low among native Swedes. Rather, a low general rate of employment is a problem that should be targeted through labour market policy.

The majority of the indicators are linked to the seven strategic areas identified in the government's integration strategy. As with the integration strategy, the indicators primarily focus on the spheres of work and education. A further area, 'citizenship', is also included in the monitoring system. Citizenship is seen as a general indicator of integration. Only Swedish citizens have an absolute right to live and work in Sweden and have the right to vote in parliamentary elections. There are also some professions, including the police, the professional military and some security services, that are only open to Swedish citizens. It is therefore seen as a positive step if people who have received a permanent residence permit become Swedish citizens.

The 27 indicators were chosen to provide a picture of the relevant aspects of integration as set out in the government's integration strategy. In line with the relevance criterion, the monitoring is based on so-called independent indicators of integration. This means that indicators such as participation in cultural and club life have been excluded. Although participation in cultural and club life is certainly interesting from an integration perspective, it is somewhat less of a determinant of integration than participation in the labour market and therefore less relevant for monitoring purposes.

The monitoring system does not contain indicators focusing on socio-cultural aspects, such as values and attitudes. As stated in table 16.1, the proportion of elected representatives as well as the proportion in a managerial role born in Sweden, the Nordic Region, the EU/EEA and outside the EU/EEA are however measured.

In order to secure high relevance, it is also important that the indicators can be easily interpreted. One selection criterion was therefore that there must be a connection between the indicator and increased integration, and that it must be clear what this connection means (i.e. whether an increase in the indicator means that integration has increased or decreased).

The importance of selecting indicators that are easy to interpret was a lesson learned with the previous system of indicators. That system was partly based on activity indicators illustrating the share of the target group who participated in a specific activity, for example labour market programmes. Although it is reasonable to assume that participation in a labour market programme affects the individual's chances of gaining employment, participation in a programme is not the only way for individuals to increase their chances of employment. This fact led to difficulties in interpreting indicators in the previous system, since while a decreased participation share might indicate decreased integration, this was not necessarily the case because the target group's chances of entering the labour market could have been increased in alternative ways. Based on the lessons learned from the previous system, the current indicators therefore focus on the results achieved and the impact of the integration policy, rather than on the activities carried out. This focus on outcomes is an important step towards making interpretation easier, and thus also the use of the data collected.

The focus on results and effect indicators is also linked to the second principle, namely the indicators' *sustainability over time*. While measures (activities) are generally sensitive to change, for example in government, the results that these measures are intended to generate are often more stable. This stability of the indicators over time is important for ensuring that the monitoring can provide a clear picture of the trend in integration and whether the current situation should be seen as an improvement or deterioration. Sustainability is also desirable from a cost perspective, as it requires a lot of resources to develop a new indicator system.

In addition to relevance and sustainability, a third guiding principle when selecting the indicators was that they should be based on *existing data*. Parallel routines for data collection and analysis are not only very time-consuming and inefficient, but also make the system very vulnerable over time. All indicators are therefore built on data that already exist and that have been collected in other contexts.

16.3.2 Description of the data and data collection

The majority of the indicators are based on Sweden's official statistics, which 26 authorities, including the Swedish Public Employment Service, the Swedish Social Insurance Agency and the Swedish Tax Agency, are responsible for providing. Since 2007, Statistics Sweden has been commissioned to compile the integration statistics to improve availability.

Data for all indicators can be broken down to national, regional and municipal level, as well as for the 38 urban areas with widespread exclusion that are covered by local development agreements between the government and the municipalities. The ability to break down the data is desirable mainly from a broad user perspective, as it means that authorities and municipalities can use the data in addition to the government. All variables can also be subdivided into background variables, as set out in table 16.2, in order to provide a more in-depth view of the statistics.

Table 16.2

Background variables for the 27 indicators

background variable	categories
origin	Sweden
	Nordic Region excluding Sweden
	EU/EEA excluding the Nordic Region
	world excluding the EU/EEA
gender	woman
	man
age	age reached by 31/12 of the year in question
educational background	completed lower secondary school
	completed upper secondary education
	post-secondary education
period of stay in Sweden after national registration	less than 2 years
	2-4 years
	4-10 years
	over 10 years
reason for immigration	people in need of protection and their relatives
	other foreign-born immigrants

Source: Statistics Sweden

The monitoring is based primarily on existing registers across the population that have been developed over many years, which means that the data are rich and generally of a very high quality. As the databases cover the whole population, the statistics may be divided into small subgroups, for example foreign-born women aged below 18 years, without losing the representativeness. This in turn means that a very detailed picture can be gained of different groups of native Swedes and foreign-born persons in Sweden. The potential sources of error are relatively small and are mainly linked to the fact that the data cover the registered population, which does not always correspond to the actual population. For example, there are foreign-born people who have left Sweden without deregistration. The statistics would show that these people are outside both the labour market and the welfare system, whereas they actually live in a different country and should therefore be excluded from the national registers.

The timeliness of the data varies between six months and one and a half years. This means that the statistics do not for example give a picture of how many foreign-born entrepreneurs there are now, but the of the situation one year ago. In order to maximise the usefulness of the data, the data are published as they come into Statistics Sweden. As a rule, the variables are monitored on an annual basis. In order to make comparisons possible over time, Statistics Sweden has also published historic data starting from 1997.

At individual level it is possible to link data from different registers, provided the personal identity numbers are available for the people covered by the register. This is the case for around 99% of the registers on which the monitoring of the integration area is based. Linking data at individual level is used, for example, for following up the indicator for the proportion of people educated to post-secondary level who have a job that requires post-secondary competence. However, all the statistics are covered by legislation to protect the individual's integrity, which means that the data cannot be published if the information can be attributed to an individual person. Moreover, all data are rendered anonymous by replacing the personal identity numbers with serial numbers when external users, such as scientists, have access to data at individual level.
As a complement to the register data, there is an existing national survey carried out by the Swedish National Council for Crime Prevention. Data from this survey form the basis for monitoring the indicator for the population's concern about crime in urban areas with widespread exclusion and in Sweden as a whole. The survey is based on a nationally representative, random sample of approximately 20,000 persons aged between 16 and 79 years.

16.3.3 Use of the data collected

The data collected are published on Statistics Sweden's website and are available to people with access to the Internet. A press release and a newsletter from the Ministry of Integration and Gender Equality were published to inform people that the integration statistics were available. The monitoring results are published with a broad target group in mind, which can comprise people from the public sector, as well as researchers and anyone with a general interest. Since publication in November 2009, the interviewed representative from Statistics Sweden believes that the primary users are journalists and civil servants from Sweden's municipalities.

One specific target group for the statistics is the Ministry of Employment. The Ministry has access to the statistics on Statistics Sweden's website. In order to carry out more detailed analyses of the data, the Ministry also has access to the stativ database, which is owned by Statistics Sweden. stativ is a longitudinal database that covers all registered individuals as of 31 December 1997-2007. Some information is also available about the individuals' parents. This database is updated in spring each year with a new annual volume and contains information from different registers from Statistics Sweden, the Swedish Migration Board and the Swedish Public Employment Service.
The Ministry of Employment uses the data on a day-to-day basis and for monitoring the government's integration strategy. Monitoring the integration strategy has a dual purpose. Firstly, monitoring will show how successful the government has been in meeting

its integration policy obligations. The assessment of target achievement is primarily qualitative, as the government has not chosen to formulate quantified, concrete targets (norms) for the individual indicators. This is because there is a fear that quantified targets may be used in the wrong way, prompting organisations to manipulate statistics in order to show a high goal fulfilment.

Secondly, monitoring the integration strategy contributes to policy development and knowledge of the areas that should be in focus in future integration policy work. Monitoring needs to provide a current picture of how integration is proceeding and the areas that are working well and not so well. Special evaluations and studies are used to provide a more in-depth understanding of the reasons behind an existing trend or unexpected deviations. The monitoring and the evaluations and studies complement each other and are all necessary. Monitoring makes the use of in-depth studies more effective, as it provides signals as to which areas would be interesting to study in greater detail. Similarly, evaluations can provide knowledge about the aspects and areas whose development is interesting to monitor continually over time.

Since the statistics were published in November 2009, they have had a relatively high impact in the media. No extensive analysis has been carried out of the role that monitoring has played in social debate, as it is still too early to see the full impact of the monitoring results. However, the representative from Statistics Sweden interviewed for this chapter believes that the media interest has focused primarily on the problem areas that the follow-up work has highlighted. Positive trends, such as the fact that the proportion of people who are neither studying nor in employment, particularly in vulnerable urban districts, has fallen, seem to have received less attention.

16.3.4 Future development of the monitoring system

As Sweden's current system for monitoring integration was launched in 2009 and is therefore relatively new, there are currently no concrete plans in place on how to develop the system in the future. Statistics Sweden is continually trying to improve the reliability and effectiveness of the data collection. As the databases that form the basis for the monitoring have been developed over a period of many years, the collection process can currently only be improved to a marginal extent.

As more monitoring is carried out of the integration policy using the 27 indicators, the Ministry of Employment intends to explore how the statistics can be used and communicated across government as a whole to form the basis for things such as evaluation and studies. In June 2010 the government presented the monitoring work carried out on the integration policy strategy to the Riksdag (Swedish Parliament). Regular evaluations will be carried out to ensure that public measures are effective and reach the population as a whole, irrespective of country of birth or ethnic background.

Sweden is also looking forward to an increase in the international exchange of experiences and collaboration in the area of monitoring, particularly between the member states of the European Union. During the Swedish Presidency of the EU in the autumn of 2009, Sweden worked in a targeted way to develop a basis for producing indicators that are also relevant to other member states.

Notes

1 The chapter was written with contributions from Kajsa Rosén, Ramboll Management Consulting. Thanks to Tor Bengtsson at Statistics Sweden, who has peer reviewed the chapter.
2 Statistics Sweden.
3 Statistics Sweden.
4 Swedish Migration Board. The data include both temporary and permanent residence permits.
5 Statistics Sweden, Labour Force Survey.
6 Statistics Sweden.
7 The Swedish National Agency for Education.
8 Government communication. 2008/09:24 (p. 59).
9 The data can be accessed at http://www.scb.se/Pages/List____223681.aspx
10 From 1 January 2011 the Ministry of Integration and Gender Equality ceased to exist. The Minister for Integration and the staff was absorbed into the Ministry of Employment.

17 Monitoring immigrant integration in Switzerland

Gianni D'Amato and Christian Suter

17.1 Introduction

Switzerland became an immigration country as early as at the beginning of the twentieth century. Since then both the volume of immigration and the profile of nationalities have evolved depending on the economic and political situation. Thus, as a result of the first immigration wave, the proportion of immigrants rose to 16% before the outbreak of World War I. These immigrants mainly came from the neighbouring countries (i.e. Germany, Austria, France and Italy). This first wave paved the way for immigrant legislation at the federal level (i.e. on residence and citizenship). World War I, the global economic crisis of the 1930s and the outbreak of World War II, however, led to a significant reduction in immigration (5% of the total population in the early 1940s; Fibbi & Wanner 2004).

As a consequence of the post-war economic boom, the number of immigrants steadily increased from the early 1950s onwards, reaching a peak in the early 1970s at 17%; predominant countries of origin in this second wave were Italy and Spain. During this period immigrants were actively recruited and brought into Switzerland as so-called 'guest workers'. This policy of recruitment was committed to the principle of rotation: the typical immigrant was young, male, with a low level of educational and professional qualifications, and was employed in the least qualified and least safe jobs (mainly in agriculture, construction and industry); he received a temporary residence permit for a limited period, and had to return to his country of origin after a certain time. After a temporary reduction in immigration in the 1970s (as a result of the economic recession and the introduction of official limits due to pressure from popular initiatives and referenda launched by nationalist and populist parties), immigration increased again from the late 1980s onwards. At present the proportion of foreigners in the total population lies well above 20% and almost reaches 30% if foreign-born Swiss (mostly naturalised foreigners) are also taken into account (Hoffmann-Nowotny 1973; Wicker et al. 2003; Fibbi & Wanner 2004).

Despite this historical experience of immigration, and despite the fact that the proportion of foreign-born residents in Switzerland has been among the highest in Europe for several decades, Switzerland has rather reluctantly, and only very recently, developed an immigrant integration policy. Not considering itself a country of immigration, legal texts in Switzerland never speak of 'immigrants' or 'migrants', but continue to use the terms 'alien' or 'foreigner'. In the mid-1990s there was a switch to the legally less exclusive term 'migrant', which can be found in different governmental reports, indicating a change in the perception by state officials, even if legal definitions are still absent. However, Article 58 of the new Aliens Law which refers to the competences of the new

Federal Commission on Migration still uses the older term Commission for Foreigners under which it was formerly known.[1]

For a long time, the lack of immigrant integration was either not perceived as a major problem (since immigration was assumed to be only temporary, as argued by the rotation approach), or responsibility for integration was left to the immigrants themselves (rather than to the public administration and to policy, as in the assimilation model). In addition, given the low unemployment rate of less than 1% up to the late 1980s, structural integration of immigrants (i.e. integration into the labour market, etc.) was not perceived to be particularly problematic. Only after the protracted economic crisis of the early 1990s was an immigrant integration policy developed. This new policy was first promoted and implemented at the municipal and cantonal levels, with the most important major cities as forerunners.

In what follows we describe the evolution of Swiss integration policy (section 17.2) and its basic theoretical concepts (section 17.3). Since this process, as stated, depended on the federal structure of the Swiss political system, we examine the development of monitoring systems and indicators of immigrant integration on both the national (section 17.4) and local levels (section 17.5). Finally, we conclude by summarising the findings and considering some implications of the Swiss case.

17.2   Swiss integration policy

When the Swiss government dropped its rotation policy in the early 1960s, it recognised that the only alternative was a policy of integration. The belief – both then and now – however, is that in the course of time integration occurs naturally through participation in the labour market and at school, as well as in associations, trade unions, clubs, churches, neighbourhoods, and other informal networks (Niederberger 2004). However, immigrants are expected to dissociate themselves from their former community:

> After several years of residence, [they] should ... no longer be reliant on the community of their fellow countrymen, but start to live as Swiss.
> (Swiss Department of Economy and Work 1964)[2]

Since the 1970s, the Confederation's main integration policy has been aiming to improve the legal status of immigrants, reuniting families more quickly, and granting immigrants more secure status. In order to facilitate the integration of foreigners and to respond to public concerns about foreigners, the government established the Federal Commission for Foreigners (FCF) in 1970 in order to

> study the social problems of foreign workforces ... and to address in particular questions regarding social care, the adaptation to our working and living conditions, assimilation and naturalisation.
> (Swiss Federal Council, Protocols of November 18, 1970, quoted in Niederberger 2004: 81).

After the migratory confusion of the 1980s – the sudden increase in asylum-seekers, a first asylum law, the substitution of the Italian guest workers with workers from Yugoslavia and Portugal – the concept of integration gained acceptance in the 1990s, since the metaphor of assimilation no longer seemed to be adequate but multicultural-ism was not able to gain a foothold. The concept of integration took shape in particular in the context of the political discussions on the revaluation of urban areas. Cities tried to position themselves advantageously in an international competition over geographi-cal locations, but at the same time they were confronted with social difficulties that were identified as strictly related to migration. Since the second half of the 1990s, the debate on integration has been connected with urbanism and urban development; this led to the formulation of official integration guidelines in cities such as Berne, Zurich, and Basel. Integration was the new buzzword, a fresh and powerful idea ready to shape Swiss policies on immigrants. Exempt from the fug of ordinary social policies, and also from any debts to 'old-fashioned' humanitarian beliefs, integration became an unexpectedly creative element for designing future migration policies (D'Amato & Gerber 2005).

This process took several years. A first legislative proposal by the government, supported by all major parties, anticipated the new paradigm, but was refused in 1982 in a popular ballot, when the radical right-wing party National Action mobilised successfully against the expansion of rights for foreigners (Niederberger 2004: 132). At the beginning of the 1990s a government report stated that in the future 'to a larger extent than before, meas-ures should be taken to encourage integration at all levels of the polity' (Swiss Federal Council 1991). The promotion of integration was included as a new target in the legisla-tive planning 1995-1999, and in 1996, the FCF submitted a report broadly delineating the outlines of an integration policy (Riedo 1996).

Therefore, after strong lobbying by the cities during the economic crisis of the 1990s, Swiss immigration policy finally adapted to the new reality, considering the integration of foreigners as a prerequisite for achieving a politically and socially sustainable immi-gration policy. There was however no clear and binding definition of the term: integra-tion was open to both a liberal and a conservative interpretation of future policies. Liberals understood integration as a means to encourage participation in mainstream society. Migrants were supposed to be willing to integrate, but some of them needed particular help or promotion (the German *fördern*). This open interpretation of integra-tion contrasted with the conservative reading, which emphasised the need for manda-tory and coercive measures in order to fight abuse of the right to hospitality accorded by the Swiss administration. This closed interpretation demands a specific set of behav-iours with which immigrants have to comply (the German *fordern*).

Hence, 'integration' stands for the participation of foreigners in economic, social and cultural life. The Integration Article in the old Aliens Law, passed in 1999, paved the way for a more proactive federal integration policy; it also strengthened the FCF's role. Since 2001, the government has spent between 10 and 12 million Swiss francs (€ 6-7 million) per year to support integration projects, including language and integration courses and training for integration leaders. Cantons and larger municipalities also have their own integration and intercultural cooperation committees and offices. In many com-munities, foreigners participate on school boards and, in some cases, in the municipal government. In line with this new spirit, Switzerland recognised itself for the first time as a country of immigration that should actively support immigrant integration, for instance by making it easier for young descendants of immigrants to become naturalised. Thus, the Federal Council proposed to widen access to Swiss citizenship for second-generation immigrants and to introduce *ius solis* principles for the third generation. More than 400,000 second and third-generation immigrants are thought to have benefited from this policy (Wanner and D'Amato 2003).

However, a majority of both the voters and the cantons rejected these measures in September 2004. The right-wing populist parties campaigned aggressively against the government's proposal, arguing that the new naturalisation law would devalue Swiss citizenship and weaken local sovereignty (Kaya 2005). Analysis of the voting pattern shows that a slight majority of the voters in the bigger cities, particularly in the French-speaking part of the country, were in favour of the naturalisation reform, whereas voters living in the suburbs, small towns and rural areas, particularly in the German-speaking cantons, were heavily opposed. Electoral gains by the Swiss People's Party (SVP), a former farmers' party that mutated to a radical right-wing populist contender in the established political system both at the cantonal and, in particular, at the federal level, paved the way for this dramatic shift in immigrant integration policy. Bringing the charismatic SVP chairman Christoph Blocher into service as the new Head of Justice (who is also in charge of the Swiss Federal Office for Migration), the legislation on migration and integration underwent a massive change of direction in 2004-2005.

As a final point, the new immigration law, which passed a popular ballot with a large majority of 68% in 2006 (and came into operation in 2008), prescribes in Article 4 that immigrants have to fulfil certain criteria that are intended to facilitate their integration. Permanent residents and their families are required to integrate on both the professional and social levels (Efionayi-Mäder et al. 2003). Whereas at the federal level the addressed policy goals are quite diffuse (no benchmarks), at cantonal level the expectations may be fairly specific, notably with regard to the minimum required level of language skills and to labour market integration which low-qualified third-country nationals, in particular, have to comply with. The price for migrants may be high if they do not meet these criteria: those who fail can be deported back to their country of origin. The level of education and professional qualifications are seen as helping to improve the integration of foreigners and guarantee their reintegration into the labour market where they are unemployed. Restrictions are aimed at avoiding the errors that were committed in the past, e.g. the granting of temporary work permits to low-qualified seasonal workers. Furthermore, the law explicitly stipulates that it is the immigrant's duty to make every effort necessary to facilitate his or her integration. A widely disseminated government report on immigrant integration (FOM 2007) sought to reflect on the actual situation and to identify fields of action. In fact, several administrative bodies developed proposals for monitoring systems on immigrant integration based on this report (cf. section 17.4).

17.3   Concepts of integration

The aforementioned 2007 immigrant integration report tried to conceptualise integration as equality of opportunity. The Federal Government, however, renounced the idea of defining integration in the immigration law. Formally, the law thus gives no indication of the objectives of the integration policy. Hence, the official integration report helps to understand governmental concepts of immigrant integration. According to the report, immigrant integration can be considered successful if the socioeconomic and structural characteristics of immigrants are comparable to those of Swiss citizens. Inadequate integration thus leads to the risk of foreigners being excluded from societal life because of insufficient economic resources, low levels of schooling and professional qualification, and health and family problems (FOM 2007). Integration is described in the report as a challenge to existing social structures. What is called *structural integration* should allow immigrants to gain access to central social goods (e.g. schooling, professional education, labour market, health and welfare). The federal institutions are to be responsible for coordinating and providing financial support for measures promoting structural integration. *Social and cultural integration*, addressing a common understanding of values, rules and laws, are to be achieved at community, municipal and cantonal levels. In order to guarantee the implementation of integration measures, a comprehensive policy response with coordinated collaboration on all state levels has to be implemented.

Following Esser (1980), four different dimensions of integration can be identified: cognitive, structural, social and identificational integration: *Cognitive integration* refers to the integration of structures on the side of the individual in order to fulfil the conditions for inclusion in social systems. *Structural integration* refers to a more or less successful process of taking over membership roles in organisations, earning of income, occupational and legal position as well as formal education. *Social integration* refers to migrants' social relations such as friendships, marriage, clubs and other associations or social networks. *Identificational integration* finally refers to the claims of belonging and identity made by migrants themselves and to the forms of identity used.

The integration paradigm of the recent Aliens Law and the 2007 immigrant integration report emphasise coercive aspects of cognitive, structural and social integration. They rely on the assumption that EU/EFTA citizens are fully integratable, whereas third-country nationals are supposed to have deficits (if they are not highly qualified). The immigrant integration report thus underlines the various deficits and risks of immigrants (in comparison to Swiss citizens) with regard to education, unemployment, social assistance dependency and criminality. These assumed deficits are located either in the culture, religion or language of immigrants or in the alleged lack of acceptance of their duties towards Swiss society, in particular the lack of respect for laws and constitutional rights. Even if the government does not explicitly define the contents and objectives of its integration concepts, it nevertheless seems clear that the coercive character of integration has been strengthened at the expense of the liberal, emancipative paradigm stressing non-discrimination (e.g. recognition of foreign diplomas, equality of access to occupational positions) and integration incentives (e.g. Wicker 2009). What remains impressive is the semantic shift away from integration as a concept that included emancipation in the 1990s, to a term that now emphasises coercion and repression.

17.4 Monitoring systems, indicators and data on immigrant integration on the national level

The development of indicators focusing on the specific situation of migrants on the national level was recommended twenty years ago by an expert report on social indicators and social reporting in Switzerland, commissioned by the Swiss Federal Statistical Office (Habich et al. 1994). However, the recent detailed stock take of activities in the field of social reporting and monitoring in Switzerland compiled by Suter and Igleasias (2003) shows that, although several comprehensive and group-specific indicator systems and social reports were developed during the 1990s (e.g. on living conditions, social change, sustainable development, health, education, gender equality), no monitoring tool for immigrant integration had been established until then in Switzerland.
It seems that this deplorable situation has not changed much in recent years. Thus, noteworthy new social reporting and monitoring activities in Switzerland focus on topics such as generational relationships, poverty and social assistance and the mapping of spatial change, rather than on immigrant integration. These more recent reports often include nationality and/or immigrant status as explanatory variables, but they do not develop specific migration indicators or monitoring tools. There is, however, an ongoing project by the Swiss Federal Statistical Office to develop a national indicator system for migration and immigrant integration. Before going into details of this new effort, an overview of existing indicators on foreigners and immigrant integration will be provided.

Several institutions and actors, both scientific and official bodies, are engaged in some kind of monitoring and social reporting activities focusing on the topic of immigrant integration. The most important institutions and monitoring instruments are briefly summarised in the following sections.

The Swiss Social Report
The Swiss Social Report, published every four yours since the year 2000 (i.e. 2000, 2004, 2008; the next edition will be 2012) and compiled within the framework of cooperation between the Department of Sociology of the University of Neuchâtel and the Swiss Foundation for Research in Social Sciences at the University of Lausanne, is an instrument for scientifically based regular and comprehensive social reporting on Swiss society (e.g. Suter et al. 2009). The aim of the Swiss Social Report is to provide information about the current social situation and social change in Switzerland on the basis of systematically collected data and indicators. The Social Report aims to act as a window on current research in the social sciences. It contains 75 indicators which are divided into five core areas covering the basic fields or subsystems in human society, namely production

and distribution of social goods, cultural diversity, social integration, political shaping, and environment and society. The Swiss Social Report combines two perspectives: first, a descriptive and indicator-driven view, and second, a problem-specific, detailed and explanatory perspective. In the indicator-based view, fifteen selected indicators are discussed for each of the five domains, with diagrams and a short commentary. The explanatory perspective consists of detailed analytical reviews of the most important trends in each of the five core domains by experts in the respective fields. The detailed reviews often focus on specific subtopics within the domain concerned.

While nationality and migration status are important dimensions of various indicators in each of the five core domains (i.e. as explanatory factors), the report also contains a specific indicator section on migrants and immigrant integration (as part of the core domain of cultural diversity), mainly based on (Swiss and comparative) cross-sectional surveys as well as on Swiss census data. In this context, the following indicators have been established and are regularly updated:

– profile of nationalities, showing the steady increase in the proportion of the foreign population during the post-war era (exceeding 20% from 2000 onwards) and the changing composition of the foreign population regarding the countries of origin, reflecting the different immigration waves;
– duration of stay and naturalisation, demonstrating a relatively high proportion of long-term resident foreigners with a duration of stay of over 25 years and a comparatively low (3%) but rising proportion of naturalisation which confirms the restrictive Swiss practice regarding naturalisation (based almost exclusively on the *ius sanguinis* principle);
– opinions on immigrants (negative and positive), showing a comparatively low level of negative views about the presence of immigrants in Switzerland;
– perception of equal opportunities for the (native) Swiss and the foreign population;
– linguistic integration of foreigners;
– subjective criteria of national affiliation, i.e. the insistence on nativeness (having Swiss ancestry) and/or on cultural adaptation as criteria for being 'truly Swiss'.

In addition to these indicators, each edition of the Swiss Social Report contains detailed reviews focusing on various aspects of immigration, such as the increasing diversity of the cultural landscape in Switzerland as a result of immigration, processes of social disintegration related to rising criminality, migration and citizenship, i.e. the civil, political and social rights of the immigrant population, multilingualism and use of the regional language by immigrants and its role in their integration. The chapter by Fibbi and Wanner (2004), in particular, explicitly analysed the evolution of immigrant integration.

Service for Combating Racism

The Service for Combating Racism (SCRA), part of the Federal Department of Home Affairs, coordinates the activities of federal, cantonal and communal bodies for the prevention of racism, anti-Semitism and xenophobia and supports civil-society institutions, organisations and individuals engaged in fighting racism and protecting human rights.

The Service does not (yet) provide any indicators or statistics on xenophobia, racism or (racial) discrimination, but considers systematic and comprehensive monitoring of racism in Switzerland to be of prime importance. Thus, as a result of the 2007 immigrant integration report of the Swiss Federal Office for Migration (FOM 2007), the Federal Government commissioned the Service to develop a national monitoring system on xenophobic, racist and anti-Semitic tendencies. Based on a pilot survey conducted with 3,000 participants in 2004-2005, a feasibility study suggests bi-annual monitoring based on:

1   xenophobic, misanthropic, racist, anti-Semitic, Islamophobic, right-wing extremist attitudes;
2   attitudes on migration, integration and assimilation, nationalism, patriotism;
3   experiences of discrimination or victimisation (Manzoni 2007, Cattacin et al. 2006).[3]

The Swiss Federal Office for Migration (FOM)

Surprisingly, the Swiss Federal Office for Migration, the principal body of the federal administration responsible for regulating immigration and coordinating federal, cantonal and communal efforts to promote immigrant integration, provides only rather rudimentary statistics and indicators on migration and immigrant integration. Thus, the FOM has established only two small monitoring instruments, with rather specific and narrowly defined objectives, which are based on the traditional concept of indicators on foreigners (rather than on immigrant integration).

– The *Immigration Monitor*, published on a monthly basis, focuses on migration flows. The Immigration Monitor provides monthly figures on the total number in the foreign population, inward and outward migration of foreigners (by country of origin), net migration change, and naturalisations (cf. FOM 2010).
– The *Monitoring of Social Assistance Refusal* provides information on the refusal to grant asylum and on the refusal to grant social assistance to asylum-seekers. This monitoring tool was established in 2004 and further elaborated in 2008 as a result of the tightening up of the asylum law. The aim of this monitoring instrument is to provide the cantons with information on the financial consequences of the new asylum policy (since the cantons have to provide a kind of emergency assistance for asylum-seekers whose applications have been rejected). The monitoring contains the following indicators (cf. FOM 2009): number of asylum decisions, number of people granted emergency assistance, duration and costs of emergency assistance, socio-demographic profile of the recipients of emergency assistance.

Swiss Federal Office of Public Health (FOPH)

Within the framework of the federal strategy 'Migration and Health' (for 2002-2007 and 2008-2013) the Swiss Federal Office of Public Health is proposing a health monitor of the migrant population in Switzerland (GMM – Gesundheitsmonitoring der Schweizerischen Migrationsbevölkerung). One of the reasons for this proposal was the lack of health data on (important) parts of the immigrant population due to limitations of the Swiss health survey (i.e. insufficient representativeness of the data at the level of the different migrant groups, particularly for those with low linguistic competence in the regional language). In a first step, two pilot studies have been commissioned (Bischoff & Wanner 2003; Rommel et al. 2006). In the second study a specific health and migration survey (largely based on the questionnaire for the Swiss health survey) was conducted among 3,000 immigrants and asylum-seekers from different migration backgrounds in 2004. For the first time, this survey provided detailed knowledge of the health situation of immigrants in Switzerland, including subjective perceptions, health (and risk) behaviour, access to and utilisation of health care, and knowledge of health matters and of the Swiss health system. Other dimensions of immigrant integration were also addressed, such as education and training, labour market participation, employment and income, social contacts, language skills, experience of discrimination, migration background and history (Rommel et al. 2006; FOPH 2007; Gabadinho et al. 2007; Gabadinho & Wanner 2008). A follow-up survey with the same sample size is currently being implemented (data collection scheduled for winter 2010; cf. FOPH 2010). Unfortunately, this monitoring instrument is weakly institutionalised and no indicator or monitoring system has so far been developed. However, there seems to be a certain revitalisation of the migration and health monitoring proposition within the larger framework of the SFSO indicator system on immigrant integration (see below).

Swiss Federal Statistical Office (SFSO)

For quite some time the Swiss Federal Statistical Office (as well as several cantonal and communal statistical offices) has provided indicators and statistics on migration in the context of its traditional population statistics, which have been based mainly on data from the federal population census and various administrative registers. These statistics, which have been published among other things in the SFSO Statistical Yearbook but also in more detailed reviews such as the yearly review on Foreigners in Switzerland (e.g. Ausländerinnen und Ausländer in der Schweiz, from 1998 to 2008), were basically indicators about foreigners (i.e. exclusively based on legal criteria) and on migration flows and did not aim to provide a comprehensive portrait of immigrants or of immigrant integration. Only since the late 1990s, as a result of the first Federal Integration Act of 1999/2000, has immigrant integration become a topic in official statistics and social reporting. Despite considerable efforts and conceptual work in the late 1990s (e.g. in the 'Siena Group'; cf. Bühlmann et al. 1998) and early 2000 (e.g. Heiniger 2001), and even some detailed analytical reports with a broader, migration-specific definition of immigrants (e.g. Haug 2003; Rausa-de Luca 2004), no monitoring or indicator-based system could be established. It was only in the late 2000s, as a result of the 2007 immigrant integration report and the Ordinance of 24 October 2007 on the integration of foreigners, that the Swiss Federal Statistical Office resumed its conceptual work to develop a system of immigrant integration indicators (SFSO 2010). This new effort is based on the feasibility study by Wanner (2006, 2007) suggesting the linking of different data sets, particularly the Swiss Labour Force Survey (SLFS) and the Population Register. The future monitoring system will be based on data from the recently established integrated survey system (SHAPE) of the SFSO, which will replace the traditional Federal Population Census from 2010 onwards and include established surveys such as SLFS and SILC. The monitoring system will be organised into five dimensions and various thematic domains.

The five dimensions are largely based on the MONET[4] typology of indicators and include:
1 the general national framework/political and legal context: indicators on population, production, etc.;
2 living conditions and capabilities: indicators on education, health, living conditions, etc.;
3 socioeconomic integration: labour market indicators and indicators on social interaction in different domains;
4 flows: interaction between socioeconomic integration, living conditions and context factors;
5 reactions: impact of political decisions and measures.

The future monitoring system will consider the following ten thematic domains:
1 social assistance and poverty;
2 criminality and security, racism, discrimination;
3 culture, religion and media;
4 education;
5 demography and family;
6 language;
7 housing;
8 labour market;
9 politics;
10 health and sports.

By way of illustration, the indicators with regard to culture and religion refer to aspects such as cultural and religious conditions and practices, multicultural coexistence and societal participation. In autumn 2010 a research group was commissioned to elaborate the indicators and thematic domains further, and notably to:
– specify data and statistical sources;
– operationalise the indicators;
– suggest a useful set of immigrant integration indicators; and
– where the indicators could be calculated, to analyse the selected indicators.
A report presenting the final set of indicators is scheduled for publication in 2012, as are the results of a first series of indicators.

Availability and quality of data on immigrant integration
The above overview of immigrant indicators demonstrates that there were very few data available on immigrant integration before the 2000s. Apart from the decennial federal population census (restricted to the traditional population statistics), there were only a few scattered data from single science-based surveys (e.g. Hoffmann-Nowotny 1973). In particular, there was no continuous population survey on immigrant integration carried out at regular intervals and with representative data at the level of the most important immigrant groups and/or generations. Thus, even the more recent longitudinal and repeated cross-sectional surveys which have been established during the 1990s, notably the Swiss Labour Force Survey (LSFS 1991 onwards), the Swiss Household Panel

(1999 onwards) and the Swiss Health Survey (1993 onwards) hardly improved this situation, mainly due to restricted sample sizes, underreporting of migrants and a lack of information on migrants' origin and migration history. It was only in 2003, due to the implementation of a new migration module as part of the annual Swiss Labour Force Survey, that comprehensive data on immigrant integration in Switzerland became available for the first time. This module, with a sample size of 15,000 immigrants, was repeated in 2008 and contains detailed information on the origin of migrants. This makes it possible to distinguish between first, second and third-generation immigrants and to identify those people of foreign origin who have become naturalised in Switzerland and who normally appear in the statistics as Swiss. Thanks to the recently established (but not yet fully implemented) integrated survey system SHAPE from the Swiss Federal Statistical Office, for the first time linking data from the cantonal and communal population registers with the Swiss Labour Force Survey, the Statistics on Income and Living conditions (SILC) and the Household Budget Survey (HBS), the quality of data on immigrant integration will improve substantially in the near future.

17.5 Local monitoring systems

Switzerland's decentralised federal structure needs to be seen as a central element in the development and implementation of policies on immigrant integration. Measures do and will vary depending on factors such as the urban/rural nature of the canton/municipality, the language composition, and so on. As already mentioned, the cities were forerunners in promoting immigrant integration as a societal and political strategy in order to strengthen what in EU terms would be called 'social cohesion' (D'Amato 2010). Since 1999, the cities of Berne, Zurich and Basel have carried out a local citizens' survey containing questions about aspects of quality of life, perception of social problems as well as about citizens' satisfaction with the city's administration and services. Although these surveys were not established with the objective of monitoring immigrant integration, they provide interesting data on the immigrant population at the local level.

The implementation of municipal immigrant integration policies goes back to the 1990s. In 1999 the Federal Government recognised the efforts of the cities and municipalities to improve integration and published an ordinance that made integration an official federal state objective. It soon became evident that indicators on integration needed to cover various dimensions: age, gender, origin, individual and social resources, as well as the motivation to migrate, had to be taken into consideration (and such indicators were missing at the beginning of 2000). A temporary dimension covering the moment and duration of immigration should not be dismissed, nor should the situation of the 'second' generation compared to that of the 'first' with regard to legal, structural and social indicators (Heiniger 2001). The idea of continuing with this approach emerged at the beginning of the decade with the insertion of an integration article in the old Aliens Law, but the necessity of implementing indicators of this sort was not realised until the end of the decade. Meanwhile, the Tripartite Agglomeration Conference (Tripartite Agglomerationskonferenz TAK), coordinating the federal, cantonal and municipal level on issues such as urban and regional development and integration, decided to enforce and implement a common Swiss integration policy (Tripartite Agglomerationskonferenz 2009). Besides general recommendations on the necessity of integration, the Conference strongly recommended transferring the competence for managing integration to the ordinary administrative structures based in the cantons and municipalities. This responsiveness to local conditions is an important feature of federalism and can help foster greater acceptance of these interventions by the population. Nevertheless, questions have been raised about the variations among the cantons, i.e. the varying degrees to which they have introduced measures to address gaps between foreign-born and native-born citizens.

At local level, two different monitoring and evaluation approaches emerged: the Canton of Basel-Stadt, the City of Basel, tried to develop a comprehensive policy evaluation approach, involving evaluation of the impact of policy measures taken in different branches of the city government on immigrant integration as a whole. The objective of this policy evaluation is to obtain quantitative and qualitative data and knowledge of the actual situation of the immigrant population with regard to their integration in the local community (Wichmann & D'Amato 2010). The Canton of Zurich has opted for a different approach, characterised by the development of a monitoring system based on demographic indicators. The Canton aims at establishing socio-demographic profiles for all municipalities providing an insight into the level of immigrants' structural and social integration into their local communities. These two approaches are described in more detail in the following sections.

Basel

The legal framework for promoting immigrant integration measures in the Canton of Basel-Stadt is provided by the law on the integration of the migrant population (Canton of Basel 2007). It refers to the principle of coexistence between the Swiss and the migrant population based on respect for shared values and the rule of law. Duties are mentioned, particularly those relating to adaptation to local social customs and living conditions, as well as proficiency in the local language. In order to assure horizontal coordination between the different branches of the administration, the 'Interdepartmental Network Integration' (INI) and an operative body have been established, both having the task of coordinating the different programmes.

The Statistical Office of the Canton of Basel-Stadt (www.statistik-bs.ch/kennzahlen/integration) provides statistical data on migration from 1997 (to 2006), particularly on demographics (percentage of foreigners, mean age, proportion of long-term residents and of native-born persons, the naturalisation rate and segregation index), education and occupation (e.g. the proportion of those with a higher education, university graduates, unemployed, employed), income and poverty, delinquent behaviour and well-being. A monitoring system based on statistical and quantitative indicators is not yet available, however.

Very recently, the Canton has commissioned research aimed at providing an overview of the development of the migrant population in the last decade and evaluating the different programmes that have been adopted since the beginning of the integration policies in the late 1990s. The report by Wichmann and D'Amato (2010) demonstrates that the immigrant population in the city of Basel has become more and more diverse, with great variation in both countries of origin and the socioeconomic profile of the migrant population. Recently, there has been an increase in well-educated and well-off immigrants arriving from neighbouring countries (Germany and France), but native-born migrants from the 'second generation', whose parents arrived from Southern Europe, have also experienced modest social mobility. On the other hand, immigrants with a low educational profile and living under harsh social conditions are still arriving in Basel through the family reunification route. This applies particularly for immigrants from the Western Balkans and Turkey.

The Canton of Basel-Stadt pursues a combined policy of promoting and demanding integration. As shown by the aforementioned report, the separation of the migrant population into privileged EU citizens and the rest raises the question of fairness, since several (demanding) measures only apply to third-country nationals. The report also demonstrates the segregational character of the educational system. Thus, although the school system aims to implement an integrative approach, it has not yet been able to overcome the pronounced educational inequalities, particularly the high degree of educational inheritance (i.e. the fact that the second generation attains the same educational level as their parents). This lack of equal opportunities becomes evident when it comes to the transition from school to professional life. The labour force participation rate among the migrant population is nevertheless high, and the comparatively 'young' migrants contribute significantly to economic growth in Basel. By contrast, unemployment statistics show that the share of persons with a migrant background is disproportionately higher. Diversity management does not play a major role, even in public institutions. Although the integration law provides for an active role for employers in promoting the insertion of migrants into different occupations, this approach is often ignored. Since integration policies do not enable immigrants to acquire professional skills, they are an inappropriate way of closing the qualification gap.

Zurich

The legal framework that manages the promotion of integration in the Canton of Zurich stems from its constitution. Article 114 contains provides for the to facilitation of the integration of migrants and accords the right to take specific measures to enforce integration. Larger cities like those of Zurich and Winterthur have so-called integration delegates whose task is to translate the general framework into specific programmes and measures and integrate them into the regular administrative structures. A government report which has evaluated integration policy since 2002 has recommended focusing on groups with integration deficits and strengthening coordination on integration issues (Arbenz 2009).

The Statistical Office of the Canton of Zurich does not offer a specific tool in relation to immigrant integration, but various reports covering the changing composition of the canton's immigrant population have been published (see: www.statistik.zh.ch). The Canton of Zurich is currently introducing a more powerful instrument to monitor the situation of the immigrant population. Data will be available at the level of municipalities, providing them with a profile of their immigrant population and allowing them to find tailored solutions and measures (www.idoc-integration.zh.ch/internet/ji/integr/ idoc/de/home.html). Demographic indicators should provide information on immigrants and their situation with regard to language skills, education, social integration and integration into the workforce. The system includes the theoretical embedding of different variables in order to enable the indicators to be used in an appropriate manner (Carrel et al. 2010). The immigrant integration monitoring includes indicators on the educational system (early child interventions, schooling, post-compulsory education), occupation (labour market participation, unemployment, working conditions), health (health status and access to the health care system), language (first and second language) and religion.

The City of Zurich, using its municipal autonomy, is an independent player and has an avant-garde position in promoting integration, particularly since 1999 when 'Measures for successful coexistence', an immigrant integration report, was published. Changes at the federal level (the integration article of 2001 and the new immigration law of 2008) made the issue of integration one of the most prominent policies. New discourses at the federal and cantonal level had to deal with existing experiences in the city, as well as supporting the work done there, and this also caused some tensions.
The City of Zurich has developed a reporting system based on data from the Statistical Office of the City of Zurich. The system monitors those policy fields that are part of the key legislative focus areas. For the period 2006 to 2010 these are education and language, neighbourhoods, occupation, religion and society, as well as the openness of the administration (cf. City of Zurich 2009). Sporadically the Statistical Office of the City of Zurich also publishes more detailed reports on the situation of immigrants in the city, describing in particular the socio-demographic profile of the resident immigrant population, integration deficits in different domains (e.g. education, language skills, labour market, housing, living standards/poverty, deviant behaviour, religion, etc.) and intervention strategies.

17.6 Concluding remarks

Even though it is planned for the near future (i.e. for 2011), Switzerland is a late runner in establishing an indicator system for monitoring immigrant integration, and an immigrant integration policy has also developed only recently. The government at the federal level has been particularly reluctant, whereas the most important lager cities started to promote and implement immigrant integration policies from the 1990s onwards. The stalemate at the federal level was overcome only very recently. Recent years and months have thus witnessed new efforts to develop a future national monitoring system on immigrant integration. Whether or not these promising new activities, in particular the current sfso project, will manage to become institutionalised remains uncertain, however.

The integration of immigrants in a federal state requires a comprehensive multilevel policy and, while the demand for action came from the cities, regulation of such a comprehensive policy must come from the centre, with implementation then being decentralised. A federal structure allows scope for subnational competencies and autonomy of implementation, but also increases the need to coordinate different experiences in order to trade off variation between subunits and prevent arbitrariness. However, precisely this 'arbitrariness' is a particular feature of federal states, since the learning experience of each unit has to find acceptance in the local population, in addition to coping with national interests. One platform for integrating the coordination vertically is the Tripartite Agglomeration Conference mentioned above. Horizontal coordination, however, has been rather loose so far. Thus, the different federal actors and scientific institutions dealing with integration indicators (e.g. Swiss Social Report, scra, fom, foph, sfso) do not coordinate their efforts, which considerably constrains and retards the development of a common monitoring tool. fom and sfso, for instance, use different definitions and different figures regarding migrants. Cooperation and harmonising concepts and definitions, however, are preconditions for developing an adequate and effective monitoring system for immigrant integration.

For this reason, the Federal Government has installed a working group on integration (Interdepartementale Arbeitsgruppe Migration) to steer and coordinate the measures taken at all levels of the state. Similar steering groups also exist at cantonal and municipal levels in order to facilitate cooperation between different departments. There is also the Conference of Integration Delegates (kid), which intervenes at the operational level. Despite these efforts, there is still no systematic comparison of the myriad of activities aimed at implementing integration programmes. Most of these programmes are directed towards structural integration, and to a lesser degree towards securing equal access to services and markets. But there is no overview of management and monitoring tools on the cantonal level. There is therefore a need to create instruments to capture and interpret such differences between cities and cantons and to help us understand to what degree certain measures and structures have an impact on the implementation of a policy. The utility of such a knowledge-based monitoring approach is demonstrated by the reactions of the government of Basel-Stadt to the public presentation of the aforementioned monitoring report (Wichmann & D'Amato 2010). The canton decided to substantially increase its financial commitment in order to improve immigrant integration (particularly regarding training and labour market integration). In addition, the cantonal authorities and policymakers announced stronger coordination of public-private partnerships in the field of immigrant integration.

Notes

1 A critical reconstruction on the discursive shift from 'foreigner' to migrant' can be found in the introduction of Wicker et al. (2003).
2 English translation by the authors.
3 In this context the yearly monitoring of racist incidents in Switzerland, provided by two civil associations, the Foundation Against Racism and Antisemitism (GRA) and the Society for the Minorities in Switzerland (GMS), is also worth mentioning (cf. the Foundation's website at http://chrono.gra.ch/chron/chron_index.asp).
4 MONET (Monitoring Sustainable Development), established by the SFSO during the 1990s and early 2000s, is a system of indicators aiming at measuring and evaluating the state of sustainable development in Switzerland.

References

Arbenz, Peter (2009). *Zwischenbericht über die Ausländer- und Integrationspolitik des Kantons Zürich*. Zürich: Kanton Zürich.

Bischoff, A. & Philippe Wanner (2003). *Ein Gesundheitsmonitoring von MigrantInnen. Sinnvoll? Machbar? Realistisch? Forschungsbericht*. Neuchâtel: SFM.

Bühlmann, Jacqueline, Paul Röthlisberger & Beat Schmid (eds.) (1998). *Monitoring Multicultural Societies. A Siena Group Report*. Neuchâtel: SFSO.

Canton of Basel (2007). Gesetz über die Integrationsbevölkerung vom 18. April 2007, SG BS 122.500.

Carrel, Noëmi, Nicole Wichmann & Gianni D'Amato (2010). *Integerationsindikatoren – eine Literaturstudie*. Neuchâtel: SFM.

Cattacin, Sandro, Brigitta Gerber, Massimo Sardi & Robert Wegener (2006). *Monitoring misanthropy and rightwing extremist attitudes in Switzerland. An explorative study*. Geneva: University of Geneva (Sociograph 1/2006).

City of Zurich (2009). *Wir leben Zürich. Gemeinsam. Migrantinnen und Migranten in der Stadt Zürich. Migrationsbericht 2009*. Zürich: Stadt Zürich [City of Zurich].

D'Amato, Gianni (2010). Switzerland: a multicultural country without multicultural policies? In: Steven Vertovec & Susanne Wessendorf (eds.), *The Multiculturalism Backlash. European discourses. Policies and practices* (p. 130-151). London: Routledge.

D'Amato, Gianni & Brigitta Gerber (eds.) (2005). *Herausforderung Integration: städtische Migrationspolitik in der Schweiz und in Europa*. Zürich: Seismo.

Efionayi-Mäder, Denise, Sandra Lavenex, Martin Niederberger, Philippe Wanner & Nicole Wichmann (2003). Switzerland. In: Jan Niessen & Yongmi Schibel (eds.), *EU and US approaches to the management of immigration: comparative perspectives* (p. 491-519). Brussels: Migration Policy Group.

Esser, Hartmut (1980). *Aspekte der Wanderungssoziologie*. Neuwied: Luchterhand.

Fibbi, Rosita & Philippe Wanner (2004). La migration entre démographie et démocratie. In: Christian Suter, Isabelle Renschler & Dominique Joye (eds.), *Rapport social 2004* (p. 100-123). Zurich: Seismo.

FOM (2007). *Rapport sur les mesures d'intégration, Rapport à l'intention du Conseil fédéral sur la nécessité d'agir et sur les mesures relatives à l'intégration des étrangers proposées au 30 juin 2007 par les services fédéraux compétents*. Bern: Federal Office for Migration FOM.

FOM (2009). *Rapport de suivi concernant la suppression de l'aide sociale, année 2008* (juin 2009, N° de référence: l271-0167). Bern: Federal Office for Migration FOM. Consulted on 1 April 2010 at: http://www.bfm. admin.ch/etc/medialib/data/migration/asyl_schutz_vor_verfolgung/sozialhilfe/2008.Par.0002.File. tmp/ber-monitoring-2008-f.pdf

FOM (2010). Bulletin Immigration. Evolution et tendances dans les domains de l'immigration et de la nationalité. Situation au 28 février 2010. Bern: Federal Office for Migration FOM. Consulted on 1 April 2010 at: http://www.bfm.admin.ch/etc/medialib/data/migration/statistik/auslaenderstatistik/ monitor.Par.0004.File.tmp/monitor-zuwanderung-2010-02-f.pdf

FOPH (2007). *What about the health of migrant population groups? The most important results of the 'Monitoring on the migrant population's state of health in Switzerland'*. Bern: Federal Office of Public Health FOPH.

FOPH (2010). *Migration and Health*. Bern: Federal Office of Public Health FOPH. Consulted on 28 October 2010 at: http://www.bag.admin.ch/themen/gesundheitspolitik/07685/index.html?lang=en

Gabadinho, Alexis & Philippe Wanner (2008). *La santé des populations migrantes en Suisse: seconde analyse des données du GMM. Le rôle du niveau d'intégration, des discriminations subies, des comportements à risque et de l'isolation sociale.* Genève: Université de Genève, Laboratoire de démographie et d'études familiales.

Gabadinho, Alexis, Philippe Wanner & Janine Dahinden (2007). *La santé des populations migrantes en Suisse: une analyse des données du GMM.* Neuchâtel: SFM (Etudes du SFM 49).

Habich, Roland, Heinz-Herbert Noll & Wolfgang Zapf (1994). *Soziale Indikatoren und Sozialberichterstattung. Internationale Erfahrungen und gegenwärtiger Forschungsstand.* Bern: Swiss Federal Statistical Office.

Haug, Werner (2003). *Recensement fédéral de la population 2000, Structure de la population, langue principale et religion.* Neuchâtel: Swiss Federal Statistical Office.

Heiniger, Marcel (2001). Indicateurs de l'intégration des immigrés en Suisse. In: *Démos – Bulletin d'information démographique*, no. 4. Neuchâtel: Swiss Federal Statistical Office.

Hoffmann-Nowotny, Hans-Joachim (1973). *Soziologie des Fremdarbeiterproblems. Eine theoretische und empirische Analyse am Beispiel der Schweiz.* Stuttgart: Ferdinand Enke.

Kaya, Bülent (2005). Switzerland. In: Jan Niessen, Yongmi Schibel & Cressida Thompson (eds.), *Current immigration debates in Europe: a publication of the European Migration Dialogue* (p. 383-398). Brussels: Migration Policy Group.

Manzoni, Patrick (2007). *Monitoring über Fremdenfeindlichkeit, rechtsextreme Orientierungen und Gewaltbereitschaft in der Schweiz. Machbarkeitsstudie.* Bern: Fachstelle für Rassismusbekämpfung, Generalsekretariat des Eidgenössischen Departementes des Innern.

Niederberger, Josef Martin (2004). *Ausgrenzen, Assimilieren, Integrieren: die Entwicklung einer schweizerischen Integrationspolitik.* Zürich: Seismo.

Rausa-de Luca, Fabienne (2004). Die Bevölkerung mit Migrationshintergrund. In: *Demos – Informationen aus der Demografie*, no. 4. Neuchâtel: Swiss Federal Statistical Office.

Riedo, René (1996). *Umrisse zu einem Integrationskonzept.* Bern: Eidgenössische Ausländerkommission.

Rommel, Alexander, Caren Weilandt & Josef Eckert (2006). *Gesundheitsmonitoring der schweizerischen Migrationsbevölkerung. Endbericht.* Bonn/Bern: Wissenschaftliches Institut der Ärzte Deutschlands (WIAD) / Federal Office of Public Health FOPH.

SFSO (2010). *Entwicklung eines Indikatorensystems zur Integration der Bevölkerung mit Migrationshintergrund. Zusammenfassung des Zwischenberichts, Februar 2010.* Neuchâtel: Swiss Federal Statistical Office.

Suter, Christian & Katia Iglesias (2003). Social reporting in Switzerland. The hidden roots and the present state of the art. In: Isabelle Renschler & Dominique Joye (eds.), *Social Change and Social Measure: Structures and Turbulences* (p. 51-71). Bern: UNESCO.

Suter, Christian, Silvia Perrenoud, René Levy, Ursina Kuhn, Dominique Joye & Pascale Gazareth (2009). *Swiss Social Report 2008: Switzerland Measured and Compared*. Zurich: Seismo.

Swiss Department of Economy and Work (Schweiz. Bundesamt für Wirtschaft und Arbeit) (1964). *Das Problem der ausländischen Arbeitskräfte: Bericht der Studienkommission für das Problem der ausländischen Arbeitskräfte*. Bern: Eidgenössische Drucksachen- und Materialzentrale.

Swiss Federal Council (Schweiz. Schweizerischer Bundesrat) (1991). *Bericht des Bundesrates zur Ausländer- und Flüchtlingspolitik vom 15. Mai 1991*. Bern: EDMZ.

Tripartite Agglomerationskonferenz (2009). *Weiterentwicklung der schweizerischen Integrationspolitik*. Bern: Tripartite Agglomerationskonferenz (TAK).

Wanner, Philippe (2004). *Migration und Integration. Ausländerinnen und Ausländer in der Schweiz. Eidgenössische Volkszählung 2000*. Neuchâtel: Swiss Federal Statistical Office.

Wanner, Philippe (2006). *Recommandations finales. Mandat « Etude de faisabilité d'un système d'indicateurs des processus d'intégration des populations migrantes »*. Neuchâtel: SFM – Swiss Forum for Migration and Population Studies.

Wanner, Philippe (2007). Processus d'intégration des populations étrangères. Une approche fondée sur les registres administratifs. In: *Démos – Bulletin d'information démographique*, no.1. Neuchâtel: Swiss Federal Statistical Office.

Wanner, Philippe & Gianni D'Amato (2003). *Naturalisation en Suisse: le rôle des changements législatifs sur la demande de naturalisation*. Zürich: Avenir Suisse.

Wichmann, Nicole & Gianni D'Amato (2010). *Migration und Integration in Basel-Stadt – Ein „Pionierkanton" unter der Lupe*. Neuchâtel: SFM – Swiss Forum for Migration and Population Studies.

Wicker, Hans-Rudolf (2009). Die neue schweizerische Integrationspolitik. In: Esteban Piñero, Isabelle Bopp & Georg Kreis (eds.), *Fördern und fordern im Fokus. Leerstellen des schweizerischen Integrationsdiskurses* (p. 23-47). Zürich: Seismo.

Wicker, Hans Rudolph, Rosita Fibbi & Werner Haug (eds.) (2003). *Les migrations et la Suisse*. Zürich: Seismo.

18 Monitoring Integration in the UK

Ben Gidley

18.1 Integration in the UK

Britain has a longer history of migration than many European countries, with its connection to the slave trade from the sixteenth century, substantial Huguenot (French Protestant refugee) migration in the seventeenth century and mass migration from its historic colony, Ireland. Britain has traditionally had fairly open borders, although there have been periodic exceptions to this from the expulsion of Jews in 1290 onwards. Systematically tighter immigration (or 'alien') laws began to emerge only in the early twentieth century, a time of mass Jewish migration from Eastern Europe.

In the mid-twentieth century, Britain encouraged mass labour migration from its colonies and former colonies, and the children and grandchildren of these migrants slowly entered the mainstream of British life. Because of these strong links to the Empire and Commonwealth, and Britain's traditional pattern of conferring citizenship by birth in the UK (jus soli), the country's large population of migrant origin has for many decades been understood by policymakers and the public at large as being of 'ethnic minority' status rather than 'migrant' status. The concept of 'second-generation migrant' is not used in the UK, and migrants and especially their descendents often identify as 'black British', 'British Asian' and so on.[1] Consequently, there is no straightforward correlation between ethnicity and migration status in the UK. Analysing the population based on the 2006 Labour Force Survey, Sales and D'Angelo show, for example, that a tenth of UK nationals do not give White British as their ethnicity and around the same percentage of non-nationals do.[2]

However, the emphasis on 'minorities' rather than migrants has had the effect of inhibiting the development of *policies* around *migrant* integration in the UK, as we shall see below. The debate has focused instead on strong borders to keep newcomers out, on the one hand, and the promotion of good 'race relations' and, later, multicultural and equalities policies for the 'minorities' within. The exceptional complexity of the relationship between ethnicity and migration in the UK, as well as the arrested development of a policy debate around migrant integration, has meant that the measurement and monitoring of migrant integration in the UK has not been a policy priority, and is in practice hampered by a striking lack of data.

Integration first appeared in UK government policy in the 1960s, when then Home Secretary Roy Jenkins famously declared: 'I define integration... not as a flattening process of assimilation but as equal opportunity, accompanied by cultural diversity, in an atmosphere of mutual tolerance.'[3] The migration context in which Jenkins was operating was that of the 'Windrush' era, the period of mass labour migration to Britain from its colonies and former colonies in the period after World War II, so known because of the symbolic importance of the Empire Windrush, a passenger ship whose arrival from Kingston, Jamaica, in June 1948 came to symbolise the start of the mass migration of (post)colonial people to the imperial metropolis.[4] Most migrants to Britain in this period, although ethnically distinct from most of the settled population already in the country, were British or Commonwealth citizens, subjects of the Crown, with all or most of the rights of the settled population, speaking English as their first language and with strong cultural links to what many of them considered the 'mother country'.

The 1948 British Nationality Act established the status of *Citizen of the United Kingdom and Colonies* (CUKC), granting citizens of the colonies rights to reside and work in Britain. Successive governments, including Jenkins' own, brought in legislation to limit the immigration rights of the black citizens of Britain's former colonies: the 1962 Commonwealth Immigrants Act, making many subject to immigration control; the 1968 Commonwealth Immigrants Act, which sharpened the distinction between those with 'close ties' to the UK; and the 1971 Immigration Act, which introduced the concept of 'patriality', reducing the right of abode to those with specific family links to British soil. Nonetheless, there remained a strong recognition of the rights of those who had made their home here. This included strong legislation against discrimination, encoded in a series of acts of parliament from 1965. The Race Relations Act 1976 was particularly important, protecting people from discrimination on the basis of national origin. The Race Relations Amendment Act 2000 created a general duty on public authorities to actively promote equality of opportunity and good relations between people of different racial groups. There were also reasonably clear routes for overseas-born residents in the UK to gain citizenship. In Sales and D'Angelo's analysis of the 2006 Labour Force Survey, for example, some 43.5% of non-UK-born residents held UK citizenship, with some long-settled communities having particularly high proportions, such as two-thirds of those born in Bangladesh.[5]

From the late 1960s, academics, anti-racist activists, civil-society and migrant organisations increasingly rejected the concept of integration, seeing it as too close to old-fashioned assimilation. [6] Alternative ideas of anti-racism and then multiculturalism and then diversity and equality became more prominent in the political field, while academics increasingly turned to notions of acculturation and pluralism, and then hybridity and transnationalism. From this period on, public services increasingly saw it as a duty to take account of or even positively value cultural diversity. Some government funding was available for services in the mother tongues of migrants and their children, and schoolchildren were taught about the diverse cultures that co-exist in the UK. This has led to the UK performing fairly well in the MIPEX index of integration policies, which ranked Britain's policies on long-term residence, access to nationality and in particular anti-discrimination measures as fairly close to best practice; on anti-discrimination, the UK scores fourth of 31 countries.[7] And it has led to much of the literature describing Britain as having a 'multiculturalist' model, meaning a model that positively respects and promotes minority cultural identity and difference.

In the first decade of the twenty-first century, the multicultural consensus which had held sway in the previous thirty years began to fall apart, under pressure from two

different directions. In the summer of 2001, a number of mill towns in the post-indus-
trial rustbelt of the North of England saw unrest involving young people of South Asian
descent, in particular British-born young men from Muslim families with backgrounds
in Bangladesh and Pakistan, in violent conflict with both the police and supporters of
the far-right British National Party. Weeks later, the terrorist attacks in New York and
Washington DC further clarified public anxieties around the presence of Islam within
Britain. In the 2000s, evidence suggested that the British public had increasingly negative perceptions of migrants. The 2006 Eurobarometer survey found that Britons were
less open to migrants than other Europeans, with only a minority supporting a migrant
family's right to reunification and only a third supporting migrants' ease of access to
naturalisation.[8]
A growing number of high-profile commentators, from the right but also from the left,
questioned the wisdom of multiculturalism, arguing that it fostered division rather than
solidarity, and suggested that the UK's growing diversity and divisions might endanger
the welfare state and other entitlements derived from Britain's social democratic entitlements. The '7/7' terrorist bombs in London in 2005, perpetrated by British-born Muslims, gave further impetus to this shift in agenda. It was in this context that integration
policy and a parallel agenda around 'community cohesion' developed in the UK.

18.2 Changing immigration patterns in the UK

Meanwhile, from the 1990s the post-war multiculturalist settlement also came under
pressure from the shifting patterns in migration. Although the door was more or less
completely closed to labour migrants from the global South by the end of the 1970s, the
last decades of the twentieth century saw new, intensified global patterns of migration
impacting on the UK. The 'new' migration of the 1980s, with growing numbers of people coming to the UK as refugees or asylum-seekers from sub-Saharan Africa and parts
of Asia as a result of wars and conflicts, was followed by the legal labour migration of
citizens of Central and Eastern Europe after 2004, when the A8 states joined the European Union. This changed the situation, putting migrants and their integration firmly
on the policy agenda. By the end of the 1990s, the flow of asylum-seekers and refugees
was enough to demand a policy response focused on this category of migrants, while
from 2004 there was pressure from local and regional authorities (who bore the costs of
the scale of A8 migration) on central government for resources and policy guidance to
address the issues arising.
By 1981 the privileged status of Commonwealth citizens – citizens of the former British
Empire – had been significantly eroded, and only those descended from British citizens
had the automatic right to acquire citizenship. Other categories of migrant became
increasingly important in UK immigration policy. Refugees and asylum-seekers, receiving much negative attention in the British media but regarded by policymakers as the
most vulnerable of migrants, are the focus of a considerable body of policy, including, as
we will see below, the beginnings of a coherent integration policy.

Family reunification migrants now make up one of the largest categories of migrants, but there has been little or no policy focus on them, and certainly none in terms of integration until recently; the same applies for those who are in the country for purposes of study, another of the numerically largest categories. Labour migrants also feature in policy debates, but again with no emphasis on integration. Instead, debates have focused on how to select the best-quality skilled labour migrants (the points-based system adopted under the last government's 'managed migration' policies) and how to reduce labour migration (the capping policy adopted by the current government in 2010).

Migrants from within Europe, and particularly from the A8 states, became the focus of considerable media attention after 2004, but again there is no national policy relating to their integration. There were, rather, fragmented local and regional responses, and the Improvement and Development Agency, a non-departmental government body, developed a considerable body of guidance for local and regional agencies working on this. Some data are recorded in the UK on the flows of these sorts of migrants, principally in the International Passenger Survey (IPS), a survey of a random sample of passengers entering and leaving the UK by air, sea or the Channel Tunnel. Over a quarter of million face-to-face interviews are carried out each year with passengers entering and leaving the UK. However, little information is kept on the stocks of the different categories.

18.3 UK integration policy since 2000

Migrant integration occupies an anomalous place in the UK's governmental structures, falling between more than one government department. Responsibility for migration in general lies with the UK Border Agency (UKBA) within the Home Office, the government ministry responsible for internal security, policing and community safety. The UKBA's areas of responsibilities include border control, immigration, naturalisation, customs and visa checks, so integration has a slightly anomalous place in its work. It is the UKBA which has led most work on migrant integration, but, apart from the projects funded by the European Integration Fund, in general the focus has been on refugees. The Department for Communities and Local Government (CLG), meanwhile, leads on community cohesion, while the Government Equality Office (the smallest government department) leads on discrimination.

Britain has been one of the slower countries of the EU to respond to the post-2000 European policy initiatives around integration. Although the country is formally signed up to the European Commission's Common Basic Principles on Integration (CPBS), there was no national integration strategy for migrants until 2009. For many categories of migrants (most notably, as with other EU countries, European citizen migrants, particularly numerous after the A8 accessions in 2004) there is no strategy designed to include them in the civic or cultural life of the country or to address their specific social or educational needs.

Integration policy in the UK has always been bound up with immigration policy. Refugees, therefore, have been the focus of most strategic integration policy. In 1996, the Home Office commissioned a five-year research project to inform the development of an integration strategy for refugees. Castles et al.'s report, *Integration: Mapping the Field* (2001) was the result of this, reviewing nearly 50 definitions of integration in order to develop a working definition, focusing on three elements: migrants' *'public outcomes'* (e.g. in the labour market) approximating those of non-migrants, *active relationships* with communities and the state, and *shared notions of citizenship and nationhood.*[9] This study informed the integration strategy sketched in the Home Office paper 'Full and Equal Citizens' (2001). The latter suggested some areas where integration might occur, but offered no definition or description of integration.

Building on this, the Home Office commissioned a study on indicators of integration (this work, done by Alastair Ager and Alison Strang of Queen Margaret University College, Edinburgh, is described fully below). The Home Office also conducted a review of effective interventions, and as part of this hosted the 2004 UK National Integration Conference *What Works Locally?* Which drew together researchers and policymakers to discuss integration best practice, and commissioned a literature review on the evidence on successful approaches to the integration of refugees.[10] This process informed the National Strategy for Refugee Integration, *Integration Matters*, launched in March 2005. This strategy, which was not supported by funding, strongly emphasised economic (and specifically labour market) integration; and it tended to emphasise what was expected of refugees, rather than the idea that integration might be a dynamic two-way process. The following period included interventions under the framework of the strategy, such as the UK-wide refugee integration and employment service (RIES) and expansion of the Gateway Protection Programme for particularly vulnerable categories of refugees, interventions designed to facilitate refugees' incorporation into society, and especially the labour market.

The Department for Work and Pensions (DWP), the government department with specific responsibility for employment support, was charged with the duty of leading on many refugee employment actions; its strategy for refugee employment, *Working to Rebuild Lives: a Refugee Employment Strategy*, was published in 2005, and broadly follows the orientation of *Integration Matters*.

In 2007-2008, government policy shifted towards 'managed migration'. This placed employment, and using migrants to plug labour market shortages at the heart of immigration policy, and in this sense built on the labour market focus of *Integration Matters*. However, the move towards a holistic policy framework (from a period in which integration policy had been framed solely in terms of refugees) suggested the possibility that, on one hand, a wider integration strategy might be developed and, on the other, that refugee integration policy might be able to widen its focus from the labour market: the Minister for Communities and Local Government published *Managing the Impacts of Migration: A cross-government approach* in which it announced that it would be revising *Integration Matters*, and the Corporate Stakeholder Group (CSG) replaced the National Refugee Integration Forum, which had been set up to monitor and develop the DWP's

Refugee Employment Strategy. The new CSG was to cover all forms of migration, not just refugees.[11]

Moving On Together: Government's Recommitment To Supporting Refugees followed in 2009. Again, however, the document focused on the economic (employment) and on what might be expected of refugees (their *responsibility* to share values and learn English), alongside a sense of the specific social *needs* of refugees.[12] In 2009, the government stated explicitly that it would *not* develop a comprehensive national migrant integration strategy. At the time of the preparation of *Moving on Together*, the government declared: 'The Government is not persuaded, however, that at this stage it should be consulting on a wider 'high level' national integration strategy covering every type of migrant group over and above *Moving on together*.' A prescriptive strategy, it felt, would run counter to the locally specific place-based nature of integration.[13]

In the same period as the government was developing a refugee strategy, a second, largely separate agenda was developing around 'community cohesion'. In the wake of the 2001 mill town disturbances, a series of reports – most notably the Cantle report – identified white and non-white communities as living separate and parallel lives, and identified a vaguely defined 'community cohesion' as the solution.[14] These reports drew to some extent on the migrant integration literature, but the focus was not on migrants as such but rather minority ethnic communities, including the second and third generation. The new cohesion literature attacked what it described as a form of de facto apartheid generated by municipal multiculturalist strategies: in the memorable phrase of Trevor Phillips, the head of Britain's Commission for Racial Equality, Britain was accused of 'sleep-walking into segregation'.[15] The new emphasis was on common bonds and on obligations, rather than rights, of groups.

The Commission on Integration and Cohesion was created by the government to develop policy in this area, and took a far broader framework, examining the issues of new migrants *and* established ethnic minorities. It defined its two key terms thus: 'cohesion is principally the process that must happen in all communities to ensure different groups of people get on well together; while integration is principally the process that ensures new residents and existing residents adapt to one another'.[16] It developed a sophisticated typology of communities facing different sorts of pressures in these terms, and a set of principles for moving the debate forward. However, its complex message was not translated into significant policy changes.

The Coalition government elected in May 2010 took some time to make clear policy statements in this area. Its main focus on immigration has been on numbers, with the introduction of a cap on labour migrants. In terms of integration, themes emphasised so far include a concern about de facto segregation, the importance of compelling migrants to share core British values, the need for migrants to earn citizenship, and, in a key prime ministerial speech in February 2011, the insistence that 'state multiculturalism' has failed.[17] Law developed under the previous government making integration a precondition for settlement and citizenship, including a points-based citizenship system, was dropped in November 2010, but the government has indicated that it intends to develop this theme. Most recently, in April 2011, another key prime ministerial speech set out some key ideas on integration: that it is a natural process occurring in communities over long periods of time, at a local level, in real neighbourhoods, through social bonds that develop in spaces of interaction such as the pub or the school gate. The prime minister also spoke of migrants unwilling to integrate and refusing to learn English, continuing the theme of integration as duty developed by the previous government.

18.4 Measurement and monitoring in UK policy

Britain's social policy has been described in terms of an 'audit culture'[18] or 'audit society'.[19] Already by 1994, an 'audit explosion' had been noted in Britain,[20] but the emphasis on audit and measurement increased considerably under the 1997 Labour government. At the same time, the late 1990s and early 2000s saw the consolidation of the equalities legislation which had started to emerge in the 1960s when Roy Jenkins was Home Secretary. Among the landmarks in this was the judicial inquiry into the failed investigation of the racist murder of Stephen Lawrence, a black teenager killed in 1993. This was known as the Stephen Lawrence Inquiry, held under the chair of Sir William Macpherson of Cluny and its report, known as the *Macpherson Report*, was published in 1999. The report identified institutional racism in certain British public institutions, including the police, and recommended a number of areas where quantitative monitoring should take place, including the recording of racist crimes, and ethnic minority recruitment, promotion and retention levels in the police force. At the same time, equalities guidance promoted proactive measurement of similar data in other public services.
The Race Relations Amendment Act 2000 was highly significant in this regard. For the first time, equalities legislation moved beyond a principle of individual redress (whereby individuals who were victims of discrimination could seek redress through the courts on the basis of the legislation) to one of a *statutory duty* on public services to tackle systemic inequalities. Specific duties for most public bodies included workforce ethnic monitoring and equality impact assessments for policies and services. The Equality Act 2006 went a step further, mandating a new body, the Equality and Human Rights Commission (EHRC) to monitor seven major strands of discrimination and inequality (including race and religion, but also disability, gender, and so on) and to promote good relations between and within different groups in society. The Equality Act 2010 further consolidated and deepened this shift, replacing all previous legislation and aligning UK law with the EU's Equal Treatment Directives.

As a result of the developing audit culture and of the emphasis on equalities after 1997, there has been a significant increase in the amount of data collected by public institutions. Monitoring by ethnicity has become a common practice, and many service providers orient towards rigorous targets based on ethnic monitoring. However, it is striking how few of these exercises monitor outcomes for migrants and how inadequate an ethnic monitoring framework is for measuring migrant integration. We can illustrate this by taking one policy area, public health.
There is considerable evidence on health needs and access which feeds into health policy and practice, based on minority ethnic groups some of whom are second or

third-generation UK-born. Thus the government's target to reduce health inequalities is measured by achieving improvements in cross-cutting social determinants of health (such as child poverty, education, housing, smoking prevalence and area deprivation) by *ethnic* differences, but does not identify migrants by including country of birth and date of arrival, apart from mortality statistics where country of birth but not ethnicity is recorded. And while there are concerted moves to improve the collection of ethnicity data in hospital records and to promote such a collection uniformly in GP Practices, there is little emphasis as yet on collecting data on migrants, including on specific health needs of different migrant categories and on barriers to access.

This emphasis on ethnicity and invisibility of migration is particularly striking in the context of the UK's long tradition of immigration, which means that ethnicity bears little relationship to migration, as discussed above. It is significant, for example, that in ethnic monitoring, nationally standard categories explicitly delink ethnicity from migration status: categories take the form of 'Black or Black British', 'Asian or Asian British' and so on. While some local authorities monitor for locally relevant migrant populations (e.g. Somalis), robust comparisons over time and place can only be made using the nationally standard categories set by the UK Census, in which migrants have a low visibility.

18.5   A framework for monitoring integration in the UK

Early in the first decade of the twenty-first century, Britain did however make a serious effort to develop a framework for monitoring and measuring migrant integration, but focusing specifically on *refugees*. As noted above, the Home Office commissioned work to develop a framework for measuring integration. The immediate context of this was a need to evaluate the impact of work being funded through the Home Office, specifically the Challenge Fund and the European Refugee Fund (ERF), which were broadly guided by the Home Office's *Full and Equal Citizens* (2001). Ager and Strang, at Queen Margaret University College, Edinburgh, were commissioned in 2002 to develop a framework, eventually published in 2004 as *Indicators of Integration*. Ager and Strang started with a review of existing proposed indicators, finding nearly 200 which had been proposed. These were initially grouped according to the four categories – economic, social, cultural and political – set out in the Council of Europe's *Measurements and Indicators of Integration*. However, they saw the conceptual weakness of that framework as inadequate.[21] The long list of potential indicators was therefore tested in two fieldsites, an inner-city area in London, where there is a long history of refugee and other migrant self-settlement, and an area of Glasgow with only a very recent history of significant migrant presence, produced by settlement of refugees under the government policy of the time of 'dispersal'. After a social mapping exercise in each fieldsite, to identify key population groups, semi-structured interviews were carried out with refugees and with other local residents or workers, to explore the core domains of integration as the basis for identifying the most appropriate indicators and provide a framework in which to understand them. Meanwhile, MORI, a large private survey company, was commissioned to conduct a parallel national cross-sectional survey of refugees, examining both refugees' experience of particular

services as well as their experiences in a number of domains, such as housing and language learning. From this, an initial framework was built, which was then explored in
consultation with potential users of the framework to check its meaningfulness and
efficacy with such users. Ultimately, Ager and Strang developed a sophisticated and complex framework.

Figure 18.1

The indicators of integration framework

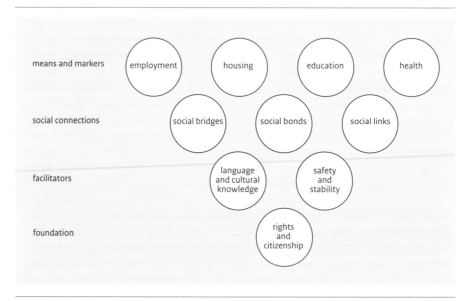

Source: A. Ager & A. Strang (2004). *Indicators of Integration: Final Report* (p. 27), Home Office
Development and Practice Report.

'Means and markers' refer to the core domains which are most widely accepted as indicative of successful integration, broadly understood as social rights which refugees and
other migrants may or may not access. The term 'means and markers', replacing Castles
et al.'s title of 'public outcomes', refers to the fact that these domains are both the most
concrete indicators of successful integration and the most concrete pathways by which
migrants are able to achieve incorporation. 'Foundations' refers to the legal and political
order in which other aspects of integration are or are not made possible, and in particular the set of civil and political rights which migrants have in a specific, usually national,
context.

Between the foundations and the means and markers lie two further levels, conceptualised by Ager and Strang as the processes which 'mediate or provide connective tissue'
between the foundational principles and concrete public outcomes. The first level is
that of 'facilitators', the domains which make the difference between integration being
enabled or constrained. This includes two domains, in their framework: language and

cultural knowledge, and safety and stability. Finally, there is a layer of 'social connections'. This captures the same substance as Castles et al.'s 'active relationships'. Castles et al. had stressed three sets of active relationships: with one's own ethnic community, with the wider host community and with the state and its institutions. These three sets of relationships map on to the three sorts of connections proposed by Ager and Strang: *bonds*, drawing together immediate migrant communities; *bridges*, connecting them to other groups in the wider community; and *links*, connecting them to institutions such as the local state. This language is drawn from the literature on social capital.

The framework is not designed as a tool to measure a general societal level of integration, but as an evaluative tool, 'to help local projects to plan and evaluate their services through the use of the framework, and to measure the progress of their clients towards integration.'[22] Consequently, it included indicators at both policy and practice levels.[23] There has been one significant study testing the relevance of Ager and Strang's framework. Jenny Phillimore and Lisa Goodson of the Institute of Applied Social Studies at the University of Birmingham conducted four studies of the experiences, needs and aspirations of refugees in areas of Birmingham, the UK's second largest city, in 2004, including 1,770 household surveys and 93 in-depth interviews (Phillimore and Goodson 2008). They use this to reflect both on the levels of integration shown using Ager and Strang's indicators, as well as on the availability and quality of data under each indicator. In line with UK policy at the time and with the intentions of the Indicators of Integration Framework, Phillimore and Goodson concentrate on the integration of refugees in particular, rather than migrants in general. They further focus on the four domains of 'functional' integration captured in Ager and Strang's 'means and markers' indictors: employment, housing, health and education.

There is some evidence that the framework designed by Ager and Strang for the UK government has had an impact on policy and practice. Phillimore and Goodson claim that 'Ager and Strang's work was a major influence in the development of the government's integration strategy' (309). Writing in 2008, Ager and Strang found some evidence of it being used to inform policymaking.[24] However, the examples they cite are generally academic studies and consultation papers, rather than actual strategic frameworks. The two examples of the latter they note are regional rather than national in scope.

As well as the uses mentioned by Ager and Strang, the framework was used to organise a major review of the evidence on successful approaches to integration for the Home Office in 2004, which reported on some of the possibilities of measuring integration under each of Ager and Strang's headings (Spencer et al. 2006). Alongside Ager and Strang's own work, this was used to inform *Integration Matters*, the Home Office's refugee integration strategy published in 2005. Focusing specifically on refugees rather than migrants in general, the strategy identified seven indictors under three themes, attempting to simplify and operationalise Ager and Strang's complex and sophisticated framework:

1 achieving full potential;
  - employment rates of refugees;
  - levels of English attainment over time;

2   contributing to the community;
   – the number of refugees involved in voluntary work;
   – the number of refugees in touch with community organizations;
   – the proportion of refugees reporting racial, cultural or religious harassment;
3   accessing services;
   – rates of access to housing services;
   – proportion of parents indicating satisfaction with their children's education.

It is striking that the 'foundations' level of Ager and Strang's model – the domain of legal rights and responsibilities – disappears in this framework. The domains within the 'facilitators' level have been recognised: safety and security as indicated by reporting of harassment, language and cultural knowledge by levels of English attainment. The 'social connections' level has been absorbed by the theme of 'contributing to the community', while the 'means and markers' domains are captured both under 'achieving full potential' (employment rates) and 'accessing services' (access to housing and satisfaction with schooling), but with health outcomes excluded.

Phillimore and Goodson note that the narrow scope of these indicators will limit their usefulness, given the complexity of the process. They also note the omission of the issue of equity between refugees and the receiving population, the stress on assimilation alongside hard outcomes like jobs and the neglect of social bonds and civic participation.[25]

18.6 The practice of monitoring integration in the UK

Despite Ager and Strang's sophisticated framework, and the examples of its take-up, there has been no effort to build from the framework towards the creation of a systematic monitor of migrant integration. Nor, as the MIPEX reports note, does the state set national policy targets to further integration.

There is no agency responsible for monitoring migrant integration in the UK, although there are a number of agencies with responsibility for collating some of the key information. The UKBA has a small unit focusing on integration, which has led some of the research on integration and manages and evaluates all the UK projects funded by European Union's integration and refugee funds. UKBA's Analysis, Research and Knowledge Service (ARK) has the responsibility of collating and disseminating statistics on visa clearances, as well as supporting the UK Border Agency more widely. Hence it has commissioned research on specific integration-related topics (including a longitudinal study of refugee integration), but its primary focus is not on migrant integration. ARK has been working with the Office of National Statistics (ONS) on improving the quality of immigration data, in the wake of an Inter-Departmental Task Force on this in 2006, but again there is no focus on integration outcomes within the improvement programme.

The most useful datasets giving information about integration outcome include the Census, the Labour Force Survey, the Citizenship Survey, the Place Survey and Community Cohesion Indicators in the National Indicator Set, as well as the *How Fair is Britain?* study. Many of these were developed under the 1997-2010 Labour government, and reflected both the audit culture associated with that government, as discussed above, and its particular priorities and understanding of integration, focusing on cohesion. The 2010 Coalition government has shifted away from this audit culture (indeed, the Audit Commission, which had ultimate responsibility for much of much public sector measurement, has now been closed), and consequently the continuation of many of these data sets is under question.

– *The Census* is the most reliable source of information about the migrant population, as it is universal and the data are available at every geographical scale, down to small Super Output Areas of 1,500 residents. Ethnicity is recorded, based on a set of categories which reflect an earlier post-colonial migration period and, as discussed above, are increasingly inadequate for the UK's new diversity. Country of birth is a variable, but not nationality, and socio-economic variables are limited.

– *The Labour Force Survey* (LFS), a representative survey of residents, includes variables for country of birth, year of arrival and reason for coming to the UK, and so enables analysis of other variables for migrants, although actual migrant numbers represented are small. Interestingly, there is also one important variable relating to the domain of identity and belonging: identification with Britain, England, Scotland, Wales, Ireland or other.[26] The lowest geographical level is the region, and the representation of most non-UK nationalities or countries birth is too small to be used rigorously.

– *The Citizenship Survey* is a biennial social survey covering community cohesion, race and faith, volunteering and civil renewal. It has been commissioned every two years since 2001. The survey was originally commissioned by the Home Office, and is hence sometimes referred to as HOCS, the Home Office Citizenship Survey, and sometimes also as the People, Family and Communities Survey. Responsibility for it passed from the Home Office to CLG after the 2005 survey. Approximately 10,000 adults in England and Wales (plus an additional minority ethnic boost sample) are surveyed face to face. Topics covered include influencing decisions, civic engagement, formal and informal volunteering, trust in institutions, cohesion, belonging, satisfaction with the local area, meaningful interaction with people from different backgrounds, racial and religious harassment and discrimination. Published reports from the survey identify different outcomes for ethnic minorities but not for migrants and non-migrants; however, country of birth is recorded and so the raw data can be analysed.

The National Indicator Set (NIS) was announced by CLG in October 2007, following the Government's Comprehensive Spending Review 2007. Since 1 April 2008, the NIS has been the set of indicators on which central government monitors the performance of local government. It covers services delivered by local authorities alone and in partnership with other organisations like health services and the police.[27] The NIS replaced a range of other sets of indicators including the Best Value Performance Indicators and the Performance Assessment Framework. Within this framework, the Labour government created a structure for the measurement and monitoring of *cohesion*. Ten national cohesion indicators were developed in 2003.[28] The government's national Community Cohesion and Race Equality Strategy *Improving Opportunity, Strengthening Diversity* (2005) set out targets in relation to these indicators cohesion, and required all local authorities to develop local community cohesion plans.[29] The NIS included indicators determined by measuring citizens' views and perspectives collected through a Place Survey administered postally by local authorities on behalf of the CLG.[30] The Place Survey was to be a major source of data on civic integration and cohesion at a neighbourhood level, intended to enable longitudinal analysis. Indicators included a number directly relevant, including the percentages of people who believe people from different backgrounds get on well together in their local area, feel that they belong to their neighbourhood, participate civically or volunteer, and feel they can influence decisions in their locality. Data quality for the Place Survey was complicated by the fact that each local authority was responsible for delivering it in their area. This was due to be conducted again in 2010 but was postponed and then cancelled as part of cost-cutting measures by the new Coalition government.[31]

The EHRC has a responsibility for monitoring inequalities between social groups, including migrants. *How Fair is Britain?*, its major new triennial annual review of the evidence on achieving equality (the first report was published in 2010), gives extensive information on different outcomes for different ethnic groups, but no data by place of birth or nationality. Immigrants feature in the report in the section on public attitudes, where it records the high levels of prejudice against migrants[32] Immigration features again in the section on crime, but shows a lack of data on migrants as victims of hate crime. The EHRC has commissioned some other reports focusing specifically on migrants' outcomes, notably *The Equality Implications of Being a Migrant in Britain*.[33] In addition, the non-governmental Equality and Diversity Forum, an umbrella of the main civil-society organisations working on these issues, has also started to work in this area.[34]

As well as these data sources, several administrative data sources are sometimes used to research and measure integration. Most include a variable for nationality but not country of birth.

— *The National Pupil Database* (formerly known as PLASC) includes information on every school pupil in the country, and can be aggregated at fairly local geographical scales. The range of ethnicities used is much greater than in the Census or other standard administrative data (e.g. Asian includes fourteen sub-categories, such as Kashmiri Pakistani and Mirpuri Pakistani), as well as home language.

— *The GP Patient Register* is a database kept on the records of general practitioners. Recent migrants are registered under the category 'flag 4' and include some irregular migrants, so this database is used to gain an insight into migration patterns and is aggregated at fairly local geographical scales; patients retain flag 4 status as long as they are registered with the same practitioner (and thus some long-settled migrants are counted) but lose it on registering at another practice (and thus some recent migrants are not counted), so there are limits to its usefulness. CORE, the record of people living in social housing, includes both nationality and ethnicity but not country of birth, and again can be accessed at very local levels.

— NINO (*National Insurance Number*) data is also useful, as it gives information on those entering the labour force or starting to claim welfare benefits.[35]

Kofman et al. also set out some of the data sources that are useful for measuring socio-economic outcomes, with the migration related variable:
- index of multiple deprivation percentage of migrants living in each area (that is, the likelihood that migrants live in deprived areas);
- long term-illness by country of birth (Source: Census);
- disability rate by nationality (Sources: Census, LFS);
- house overcrowding by country of birth (Source: Census);
- unemployment by country of birth (Sources: Census, LFS);
- economic activity rates by nationality (Source: LFS);
- provision of informal care by country of birth (Source: Census).

18.7 Gaps in knowledge

There remain a number of areas where there are significant gaps in evidence that make monitoring integration in the UK difficult if not impossible. Phillimore and Goodson note that there is a significant lack of data for each indicator. Under *employment*, where Ager and Strang recommend the indicators of employment rates, earnings and under-employment, Phillimore and Goodson note the absence of data due to the lack of a marker for refugees in the key national data sets, the General Household Survey (GHS), Labour Force Survey (LFS) and National Census. However, all of these data sets do include country of birth and nationality, so are of more utility in relation to these indicators for migrants in general. Under *housing*, Ager and Strang suggest measures of the proportion of refugees in secure housing, the proportion in areas targeted for renewal, and housing occupation/overcrowding rates compared to the general population. Again, Phillimore and Goodson note a lack of data for refugees. Although there is a considerable amount of information on ethnicity, housing providers are only just beginning to collect information on refugee status and nationality and do not collect information on country of birth, and the process of collating and making accessible the available data is extremely uneven and underdeveloped. Under *education*, Ager and Strang suggest as main measures the achievements of refugee children and the numbers of refugees obtaining vocational qualifications. Phillimore and Goodson note that 'Interviews with the Local Education Authority (LEA) revealed that data is not collected on the attainment levels of refugee children because schools and the LEA do not use a refugee marker and the ethnicity data collected is very basic.'[36] Neither are any data collected by nationality or country of birth; there is even less data available on the overall numbers of adult migrants accessing vocational education. Finally, under *health*, Ager and Strang recommend mortality and morbidity as key indicators. Again, Phillimore and Goodson note an absence of data on refugee morbidity and mortality, an absence that is equally marked for migrants in general, as noted above.

In general, Phillimore and Goodson conclude that 'The majority of data collected in Birmingham has been accessed on a one off basis through specially commissioned research programmes.'[37] The literature suggests that this situation, and the resulting data gaps, is replicated across the country, at both local and national level. A review of evidence produced for the Home Office and published by COMPAS (Spencer et al. 2006) similarly found a number of areas where gaps existed. First, they noted that there is a need for:

> National education, employment, health, housing and public attitude data not just on the foreign-born but on new migrants, where necessary disaggregated by age, gender, country of origin and crucially, date of entry to the UK and immigration status. Date of entry and immigration status have not traditionally been included in mainstream government surveys. (Spencer p.xiv)

The review also noted specific groups where there are particular data gaps: marriage migrants, temporary workers and students. There has been no significant consolidation of the data since then, and there remains a need to incorporate markers for refugee status, place of birth and nationality into mainstream data collection.

EHRC have also noted that migrants are among those for whom data are lacking, especially the most mobile elements of the population, such as migrants, who are also among the most excluded, and argue that improving data collection is therefore a human rights and equality issue.[38] Kofman et al. have suggested that the lack of official statistics on both migrant population and inequality issues requires the use of the available sources as proxies. They recommend an improvement in sources such as the LFS to achieve a more representative picture of the migrant population and the development of ad-hoc surveys on migrant population and issues of inequality and integration (p. 58-9). Spencer notes the tension between this sort of need and the ethical difficulties of providers identifying migration statuses, while Kofman et al. also note concerns around privacy, data protection and surveillance, as well as issues of trust between migrants and the state.

18.8 Conclusion

The landscape in the UK is characterised by the absence of a single agency charged with monitoring and measuring migrant integration and by the absence of much of the data required to monitor and measure integration robustly. This picture is unlikely to change in the immediate future; on the contrary, the spending cuts being introduced by the current government are likely to see the sources of data reduced rather than augmented, as signalled by the decision noted above to cancel the Citizenship Survey, as well as current consideration from the government around the future of a regular whole-population Census. It also remains unclear whether the Coalition government will develop any strategy around migrant integration that would provide a framework for this. On the other hand, the Coalition government has placed much emphasis on localism and devolving powers from central government to local government. Another plank of the Coalition's philosophy is 'the Big Society', the reduction of the state's role and empowerment of civil society to deliver services. This might provide the scope for local government and local civil society to take a more proactive position on migrant integration and develop more local strategies, including local monitoring and benchmarking, although there is no government funding or support for this. If there is a new strategy, the fiscal environment makes it likely that this will not be a strategy that requires substantial resources to deliver it; monitoring and measurement, which are not a government priority, are even less likely to be resourced.

Notes

1   Tariq Modood (2001). British Asian Identities: Something Old, Something Borrowed, Something New. In: David Morley & Kevin Robins, *British Cultural Studies*. Milton Keynes: Open University Press; G. Connor & M. Farrar (2003). Carnival in Leeds and London, UK – Making New Black British Subjectivities. In: M.C. Riggio (ed.), *Carnival in Action*. London/New York: Routledge.

2   R. Sales & A. D'Angelo (2008). *Migrants Integration Territorial Index: United Kingdom National Report* (p. 38, table 11a). London: Middlesex University.

3   Anthony Lester (ed.) (1967). *Essays and Speeches by Roy Jenkins* (p. 267). London: Collins.

4   Paul Gilroy (1987). *There Ain't No Black In the Union Jack*. London: Hutchinson; M. Phillips & T. Phillips (1998). *Windrush: The Irresistible Rise of Multi-Racial Britain*. London: HarperCollins.

5   p.38, table 11a.

6   See discussion in A. Kundnani (2007). *The End of Tolerance: Racism in 21st Century Britain*. London: Pluto.

7   *Migration Policy Index III* (2011). Brussels: Migration Policy Group. Consulted at: http://www.mipex.eu/

8   Eurobarometer (2006). Consulted at: http://ec.europa.eu/public_opinion/archives/eb/eb66/eb66_en.pdf

9   Stephen Castles et al. (2001). *Integration: Mapping the Field*. Oxford: COMPAS.

10 Sarah Spencer (ed.) (2005). *Refugees and new migrants: A review of the evidence on successful approaches to integration*. Oxford: COMPAS.

11 Mary Carter & Jacob Lagnado (2008). *ICAR Briefing: Employment issues for refugees and asylum seekers in the UK* (p. 3-4). London: Information Centre about Asylum and Refugees (ICAR).

12 Meg Hillier MP (2009). Foreword. In: *Moving On Together: Government's Recommitment To Supporting Refugees*. UK Border Agency.

13 CLG (2009). *Managing the impacts of migration: Improvements and innovations* (p. 50). London: Department for Communities and Local Government.

14 Ted Cantle (2001). *Community Cohesion: A Report of the Independent Review Team*. London: Home Office; Herman Ouseley (2000). *Community Pride not prejudice*. Bradford: Bradford Vision; David Ritchie (2001). *The Oldham Independent Review Panel Report*. Oldham: Oldham Independent Review; John Denham (2002). *Building Cohesive Communities: A Report of the Ministerial Group on Public Order and Community Cohesion*. London: Home Office.

15 Britain 'sleep-walking to segregation'. In: *The Guardian*, 19 September 2005. Consulted at: http://www.guardian.co.uk/world/2005/sep/19/race.socialexclusion.

16 CIC (2007). *Our Shared Future* (p.9). Wetherby, West Yorkshire: Commission on Integration & Cohesion.

17 David Cameron, speech at Munich Security Conference, 5 February 2011. Consulted at: http://www.number10.gov.uk/news/speeches-and-transcripts/2011/02/pms-speech-at-munich-security-conference-60293

18 C. Shore & S. Wright (1999). Audit Culture and Anthropology: Neo-Liberalism in British Higher Education. In: *The Journal of the Royal Anthropological Institute*, vol. 5, no. 4, p. 557-575; M. Strathern (2000). *Audit Cultures: Anthropological Studies in Accountability, Ethics and the Academy*. London: Routledge.

19 Michael Power (1997). *The audit society: rituals of verification*. Oxford: Oxford University Press.

20 Michael Power (1994). *The Audit Explosion*. London: Demos.

21 A. Ager & A. Strang (2004). *Indicators of Integration: Final Report* (p. 9). Home Office Development and Practice Report.

22 Ibid., p. 1.

23 Ibid., p. 5.

24 1998: 185.

25 2008: 312.

26 See the analysis of migrants' sense of national identity based on the LFS in: Alan Manning & Sanchari Roy (2010). Culture Clash or culture club? National Identity in Britain. In: *The Economic Journal*, vol. 120, no. 542, p. F72-F100.

27 http://www.audit-commission.gov.uk/localgov/audit/nis/Pages/niguidancesearch.aspx

28 Home Office (2003). *Building a Picture of Community Cohesion*. London: Home Office.

29 Home Office (2005). *Improving Opportunity, Strengthening Society. The Government's strategy to increase race equality and community cohesion*. London: Home Office.

30 http://www.audit-commission.gov.uk/localgov/audit/nis/pages/placesurvey.aspx

31 http://www.audit-commission.gov.uk/SiteCollectionDocuments/MethodologyAndTools/ PerformanceIndicatorInfo/2010-08-10GSLettertoLAsonCancellingPlaceSurvey.pdf

32 EHRC (2010). *How Fair is Britain?* (p. 33). Manchester/London/Glasgow/Cardiff: Equality and Human Rights Commission.

33 Eleonore Kofman, Sue Lukes, Alessio D'Angelo & Nicola Montagna (2009). *The equality implications of being a migrant in Britain*. Manchester/London/Glasgow/Cardiff: Equality and Human Rights Commission.

34 Ibid., p. 159.

35 See Kofman et al. (2009: 53) on using NINO to explore migrants' take-up of welfare.

36 p. 317.

37 p. 320.

38 p. 633.

About the authors

Gianni D'Amato is a professor at the University of Neuchâtel and Director of the Swiss Forum of Migration and Population Studies (SFM). His research interests are focused on citizenship, transnationalism, populism and the history of migration. He is Coordinator of the DG FP7 Research on Support and Opposition to Migration (www.som-project.eu).

Vida Beresnevičiūtė is a sociologist and senior researcher at the Institute for Ethnic Studies at the Lithuanian Social Research Centre. Her research interests include analysis of the ethnic structure of society, social integration of ethnic groups and migrant groups, issues of discrimination, and development of monitoring indicators on migrant groups in Lithuania. She is a member of the Lithuanian Sociological Association.

Rob Bijl is a sociologist and a director of the Netherlands Institute for Social Research | SCP in The Hague (www.scp.nl). He has published on monitoring the processes of immigrant integration and social participation, on quality of life and on integration policy evaluation. He has been involved in various international networks and studies on migration and integration. He is currently a member of the board of the ISA Research Committee on Social Indicators.

Corrado Bonifazi is a demographer and is director of research at the Italian National Research Council (CNR). He chairs the Population Trends, Migration Studies and Spatial Mobility research unit at the CNR Institute of Research on Population and Social Policies (http://www.irpps.cnr.it/en). He has numerous publications to his name in the fields of migration and demography.

Didier Boone holds a Master's degree in Educational Sciences (Ghent University). He works as a policy officer at the Belgian Centre for Equal Opportunities (www.diversiteit.be). He is the Belgian National Contact Point on Integration to the European Commission. He has built expertise in Integration Policy Development (advice and recommendations) and in Integration Monitoring (indicators and evaluation).

Lisa Brandt is a junior researcher at the Expert Council of German Foundations on Integration and Migration (SVR), a Berlin-based think tank. She holds a Master's degree in Migration Studies from the University of Sussex.

Gunilla Fincke is Director of the Expert Council of German Foundations on Integration and Migration (SVR), a Berlin-based think tank. Her areas of expertise are migration regimes and the integration of the second generation. She holds a PhD from Freie Universität Berlin. From 2003 to 2005 she was a McCloy Fellow at the Harvard Kennedy School.

Ben Gidley is a senior researcher at the Centre on Migration, Policy and Society (COMPAS) at the University of Oxford (www.compas.ox.ac.uk). He works on issues of multiculturalism, integration and diversity, especially in cities.

Agata Górny is an economist and sociologist. She is based at the University of Warsaw, where she is Head of the Integration and Ethnic Relations Team at the Centre of Migration Research (www.migracje.uw.edu.pl) and Head of the Demography Chair at the Faculty of Economic Sciences (www.wne.uw.edu.pl). She has published on immigration to Poland, social and economic aspects of migrant integration and methods of migration research.

Kristina Kallas is a policy analyst focusing on issues of integration, social cohesion, immigration, asylum and minority rights. She has participated in the development of an Estonian national integration strategy and carried out several analyses of Estonian integration policy. She is a member of the board of the independent think tank Institute of Baltic Studies (www.ibs.ee).

Albert Kraler is a political scientist and a research officer at the International Centre for Migration Policy Development (ICMPD, http://research.icmpd.org) in Vienna. Apart from his work at ICMPD, he also teaches at the University of Vienna and the Vienna University of Technology. His areas of research include migration statistics, migration policy and dynamics of migration, with a focus on irregular and family-related migration in the EU, and has published extensively on these topics.

Elin Landell is an economist and director at the Swedish Ministry of Employment. She was head of the Division for Integration and Urban Development from 2008 to 2011 and is currently heading a public inquiry on labour market participation among migrant women as well as a public inquiry on labour market measures for the inclusion of people with disabilities.

Steven Loyal is Senior Lecturer in Sociology working at University College Dublin (www.ucd.ie). His research interests include sociological theory, migration and the sociology of knowledge.

Selma Muhič Dizdarevič holds a PhD in Public and Social Policy. She currently chairs the Department of Civil Society Studies in the Faculty of Humanities at Charles University in Prague (www.fhs.cuni.cz). Her main research interests include immigration, asylum and integration policies in the Czech Republic and the EU, social exclusion, theories of multiculturalism and questions of civil society and minority rights.

Marcus Langberg Smestad is an economist and adviser at the Norwegian Ministry of Children, Equality and Social Inclusion, Department of Integration and Diversity (www.regjeringen.no/en/dep/bld). He works on integration policy in general and on goals for social inclusion of the migrant population in particular. He has also worked on issues of experimental economics and fairness in distributional policies.

Line Møller Hansen is an economist and special consultant at the Ministry for Social and Integration Affairs in Denmark. She has worked for many years on measuring and monitoring integration, including in international projects.

Nils Muiznieks is a political scientist and director of the Advanced Social and Political Research Institute at the University of Latvia (www.szf.lu.lv/eng/petnieciba/sppi-instituts/). He has published on social integration and minorities in Latvia, Latvian-Russian relations and other topics. Since 2010 he has also served as chairman of the Council of Europe's independent anti-racism monitoring body, the European Commission against Racism and Intolerance (ECRI).

Aneta Piekut is a sociologist, currently working as a Postdoctoral Research Fellow at the School of Geography, University of Leeds. She is also a member of the Centre of Migration Research at the University of Warsaw. Her research interests include integration of ethnic minorities, socio-spatial segregation, urban sociology and highly skilled migration.

Catarina Reis Oliveira is Head of the Research and International Relations Unit at ACIDI (www.acidi.gov.pt) and Editorial Coordinator of Migrações Journal (www.oi.acidi.gov. pt). She is a sociologist who has published on integration and immigrant entrepreneurship. She has been involved in various international projects and networks, was the European coordinator of the INTI project One-Stop-Shop: a new answer for immigrants' integration. In 2000 she was distinguished with an academic award in Multiculturalism and Ethnicity in Contemporary society by the Gulbenkian Foundation.

David Reichel is a sociologist and an Associate Research Officer at the International Centre for Migration Policy Development (ICMPD, http://research.icmpd.org), Vienna. In addition, he teaches at the University of Vienna as an external lecturer. He has been involved in various research projects and has published several articles and papers on migration policy, irregular migration, non-discrimination and citizenship.

Juris Rozenvalds is Professor of Political Theory and Dean of the Faculty of Social Sciences at the University of Latvia (www.szf.lu.lv). He has published on democracy, accountability and the role of intellectuals in politics.

Nanette Schuppers is a PhD student at the School of Sociology at University College Dublin (www.ucd.ie). Her research investigates integration processes, particularly of Polish and Indian migrants, and the role that human and social capital, society and the government play in these processes. The impact of language abilities on social and economic integration and the differences created by governments between EEA and non-EEA nationals are at the core of her research.

Renata Stefańska is a political scientist. She has been attached to the Centre of Migration Research at the University of Warsaw since 2004. Her main research interests focus on migration policy, including integration policy aimed at migrants and naturalisation policy.

Salvatore Strozza is a Professor of Demography in the Department of Theories and Methods of Human and Social Sciences at the University of Naples Federico II (http://www.teomesus.unina.it/). He is section editor of Genus and a member of the editorial board of Studi Emigrazione/Migration Studies. His main area of research is international migration, and in particular foreign immigration in Italy, with special attention for the analysis of demographic behaviours, labour market insertion and integration processes.

Christian Suter is Professor of Sociology at the University of Neuchâtel, Switzerland (http://www2.unine.ch/socio/cms/op/edit/lang/fr/pid/3243). He is editor of the Swiss Social Report and has published on social indicators and social reporting in Switzerland, on social inequality, poverty and social policy, global debt crises, globalisation and world society, as well as on Latin America. He is a member of the Editorial Board of Social Indicators Research and secretary of the ISA Research Committee on Social Indicators.

Arjen Verweij is an economic sociologist. For almost fifteen years he was a researcher at the Department of Economics at Erasmus University Rotterdam, and has published on identification and classification of ethnic minorities, their integration in the Netherlands, on quality of place and on the methodology of applied social research (monitoring). Currently he is a research advisor at the Dutch Ministry of the Interior and Kingdom Relations on issues relating to housing, integration, neighbourhoods and communities.

Mattia Vitiello is a sociologist and researcher at the Italian Institute of Research on Population and Social Policies IRPPS-CNR (http://www.irpps.cnr.it/en). His main research interests concern migration policies and the incorporation processes of immigrants, in particular labour market insertion.

Karolis Žibas is a political scientist, junior researcher and PhD student in Sociology in the Institute for Ethnic Studies at the Lithuanian Social Research Centre. He is a fellow of the ERSTE foundation Social Research Fellowship 'Generations in Dialogue: Migration and its Effects on Demographic and Economic Development in CEE'. His scientific interests lie in the area of new patterns of migration in CEE after EU enlargement, immigration and integration policies and measures, labour migration and integration of migrant workers, and development of monitoring indicators.

Publications of the Netherlands Institute for Social Research | scp in English

Sport in the Netherlands (2007). Annet Tiessen-Raaphorst, Koen Breedveld.
ISBN 978 90 377 0302 3

Market Place Europe. Fifty years of public opinion and market integration in the European Union. European Outlook 5 (2007). Paul Dekker, Albert van der Horst, Henk Kox, Arjan Lejour, Bas Straathof, Peter Tammes, Charlotte Wennekers. ISBN 978 90 377 0306 1

Explaining Social Exclusion. A theoretical model tested in the Netherlands (2007). Gerda Jehoel-Gijsbers, Cok Vrooman. ISBN 978 90 377 0325 2

Out in the Netherlands. Acceptance of homosexuality in the Netherlands (2007). Saskia Keuzenkamp, David Bos. ISBN 978 90 377 0324 5

Comparing Care. The care of the elderly in ten EU-countries (2007). Evert Pommer, Isolde Woittiez, John Stevens.ISBN 978 90 377 0303 0

Beyond the breadline (2008). Arjan Soede, Cok Vrooman. ISBN 978 90 377 0371 9

Facts and Figures of the Netherlands. Social and Cultural Trends 1995-2006 (2008). Theo Roes (ed.). ISBN 978 90 377 0211 8

Self-selection bias versus nonresponse bias in the Perceptions of Mobility survey. A comparison using multiple imputation (2008). Daniel Oberski. ISBN 978 90 377 0343 6

The future of the Dutch public library: ten years on (2008). Frank Huysmans, Carlien Hillebrink. ISBN 978 90 377 0380 1

Europe's Neighbours. European neighbourhood policy and public opinion on the European Union. European Outlook 6 (2008). Paul Dekker, Albert van der Horst, Suzanne Kok, Lonneke van Noije, Charlotte Wennekers. ISBN 978 90 377 0386 3

Values on a grey scale. Elderly Policy Monitor 2008 (2008). Cretien van Campen (ed.). ISBN 978 90 377 0392 4

The Netherlands Institute for Social Research | scp at a glance. Summaries of 16 scp-research projects in 2008 (2009). ISBN 978 90 377 0413 6

Sport in the Netherlands (2009). Annet Tiessen-Raaphorst, Koen Breedveld. ISBN 978 90 377 0428 0

Strategic Europe. Markets and power in 2030 and public opinion on the European Union (2009). Paul Dekker, Albert van der Horst, Paul Koutstaal, Henk Kox, Tom van der Meer, Charlotte Wennekers, Teunis Brosens, Bas Verschoor. ISBN 978 90 377 0440 2

Building Inclusion. Housing and Integration of Ethnic Minorities in the Netherlands (2009).
Jeanet Kullberg, Isik Kulu-Glasgow. ISBN 978 90 377 0442 6

Making up the Gap, Migrant Education in the Netherlands (2009). Lex Herweijer.
ISBN 978 90 377 0433 4

Rules of Relief. Institutions of social security, and their impact (2009). J.C. Vrooman.
ISBN 978 90 377 0218 7

Integration in ten trends (2010). Jaco Dagevos and Mérove Gijsberts. ISBN 78 90 377 0472 3

Monitoring acceptance of homosexuality in the Netherlands (2010). Saskia Keuzenkamp.
ISBN 978 90 377 484 6

The minimum agreed upon. Consensual budget standards for the Netherlands (2010). Stella Hoff, Arjan
Soede, Cok Vrooman, Corinne van Gaalen, Albert Luten, Sanne Lamers.
ISBN 978 90 377 0472 3

The Social State of the Netherlands 2009 (2010). Rob Bijl, Jeroen Boelhouwer, Evert Pommer,
Peggy Schyns (eds.). ISBN 978 90 377 0466 2

*At home in the Netherlands. Trends in integration of non-Western migrants. Annual report on Integration
2009* (2010). Mérove Gijsberts and Jaco Dagevos. ISBN 978 90 377 0487 7

In the spotlight: informal care in the Netherlands (2010). Debbie Oudijk, Alice de Boer, Isolde Woittiez, Joost Timmermans, Mirjam de Klerk. ISBN 978 90 377 0497 6

Wellbeing in the Netherlands. The SCP life situation index since 1974 (2010). Jeroen Boelhouwer.
ISBN 978 90 377 0345 0

Just different, that's all. Acceptance of homosexuality in the Netherlands (2010). Saskia Keuzenkamp et
al. (ed.) ISBN 978 90 377 0502 7

*Acceptance of homosexuality in the Netherlands 2011. International comparison, trends and current
situation* (2011). Saskia Keuzenkamp. ISBN 978 90 377 0580 5

*Living together apart. Ethnic concentration in the neighbourhood and ethnic minorities' social contacts and
language practices* (2011). Miranda Vervoort. ISBN 978 377 0552 2

Frail older persons in the Netherlands. Summary (2011). Cretien van Campen (ed.)
ISBN 978 90 377 0563 8

Frail older persons in the Netherlands (2011). Cretien van Campen (ed.) ISBN 978 90 377 0553 9

Measuring and monitoring immigrant integration in Europe (2012). Rob Bijl and Arjen Verweij (eds.)
ISBN 978 90 377 0569 0

The Social State of the Netherlands 2011. Summary (2012). Rob Bijl, Jeroen Boelhouwer, Mariëlle
Cloïn, Evert Pommer (eds.) ISBN 978 90 377 0605 5